D0554519

FOOD FOR 50

Fifth Edition

FOOD FOR 50

COMPILED BY

Sina Faye Fowler

*Formerly
Restaurant Dietitian,
Quality Control Section
Western Electric Company
Chicago, Illinois*

Bessie Brooks West

*Professor Emeritus of
Institutional Management
Formerly
Head of Department
Kansas State University*

Grace Severance Shugart

*Head of Institutional
Management Department
Kansas State University*

John Wiley & Sons, Inc.   *New York   London   Sydney   Toronto*

PREFACE

The first edition of *Food for Fifty*, published in 1937, was planned to supplement the textbook *Food Service in Institutions* that was created for college instruction in the field of institutional services and their management. This remains one of the major objectives of this edition of *Food for Fifty*.

The intervening years have brought significant changes in institution feeding and a subsequent broadening of the original objectives of *Food for Fifty*. The present edition has been revised to meet the demands of persons responsible for buying and serving food to various sizes and types of groups. One major change has been the clarification of directions in recipe preparation through more detailed instructions. New recipes have been added, and the general information section has been brought up-to-date and reorganized. These changes have greatly expanded the usefulness of this book.

We acknowledge the assistance of Kansas State University staff members, former students, and other co-workers in the institution field who have given generously of their knowledge and experience to aid in this revision of *Food for Fifty*. We hope that the fifth edition will be of value to former users and to those who use the book for the first time.

Sina Faye Fowler
Bessie Brooks West
Grace Severance Shugart

Shortly after completing work on the manuscript for this edition, Sina Faye Fowler died following a short illness. Her contributions through the years have made possible the esteem in which *Food for Fifty* has been held.

CONTENTS

FOOD FOR 50

PART ONE
GENERAL
INFORMATION

GENERAL
INFORMATION

Amounts of Food as Purchased to Serve 50

The table that follows is presented as a guide for the manager of a food service who is responsible for preparing three meals a day for approximately 50 persons, such as in a small hospital; or for those persons who need to order food for one meal only, such as for a school lunch or an occasional banquet. It may serve also as a basis for determining amounts to buy for larger groups.

The quantity of any item ordered or prepared must be adjusted to the particular requirements of the group to be served. Rarely is 50 the exact number to be served, nor do all groups require the same amount of food for a given number. The amounts given in this table are based on average servings with knowledge that there will need to be an adjustment to fit each situation. For example, 2 2-lb. loaves of bread would provide not more than 56 slices of bread. The order must be increased to 4 loaves if 2 slices per portion are desired. Inexperienced employees may find it difficult to obtain the exact number of portions indicated for a given quantity, so a small increase in allowance for these items may be desirable. Odd amounts, as 4¼ dozen rolls, would need to be adjusted to the next whole unit. If the number to be served is a few less or more than 50, the order would be for 4 or 5 dozen.

The weight of ingredients in a package, or the number of slices of bread in a loaf, may vary with different suppliers. The count of peaches or other fruit and the weight of berries in a can varies with the pack. Information usually may be obtained from the purveyer as to the count or weight of foods in a container.

Amounts of Food as Purchased to Serve 50

(*Amounts are approximate*)

Food	Weight or Measure	Serving Portion	Amount to Serve 50	Miscellaneous Information
BAKERY PRODUCTS				
Biscuits, to bake	8-oz. can	1 biscuit	5–7 cans	8–10 biscuits per can
Bread, loaf				
Small	1 lb.	1–2 slices	3–4 loaves	16 slices per loaf
Sandwich	1½ lb.	1–2 slices	3 loaves	24 thin slices per loaf
Pullman	2 lb.	1 slice	1½ loaves	36 slices per loaf
Cake				
Angel food	10 in. round	12–14 cups per cake	3–4 cakes	
Fruit	Varies	2½ oz.	8–10 lb.	
Cup cakes	doz.	1	4½ doz.	
Layer	2 layer, 9 in.	14–16 cuts per cake	3–4 cakes	
Sheet	12 × 20 in.	1¾ oz.	1 pan	Cut 6 × 8
Cookies				
Cream filled	19 per lb.	2 cookies	3 lb.	
Vanilla wafers	113 per lb.	2 wafers	1 lb.	
Crackers				
Graham	60–65 per lb.	2 crackers	1¾–2 lb.	
Soda	82 per lb.	2 crackers	1½–2 lb.	
Saltines	112 per lb.	4 crackers	1¾ lb.	
Pies	8 in.	6 cuts per pie	8–9 pies	
Rolls				
Dinner	doz.	1½–2	6–8½ doz.	
Hard	doz.	1–1½	4½–6½ doz.	
Buns	doz.	1	4½ doz.	
Sweet	doz.	1	4½ doz.	
BEVERAGES				
Cider	gal.	½ c.	1½ gal.	
Cocoa				
Unsweetened	1-lb. pkg.	6-oz. cup	½ lb.	Makes 2½ gal.
Instant	2-lb. pkg.	6-oz. cup	2–2½ lb.	
Coffee				
Urn grind	1 lb.	6-oz. cup	1–1½ lb.	
Instant	10-oz. jar	6-oz. cup	3 oz.	2 oz. freeze dried
Juices, canned	46-oz. can	6 oz.	7 cans	
Lemons for lemonade	doz.	8 oz.	3 doz.	Size 195
Lemonade, frozen conc.	32-oz. can	8 oz.	4 cans	
Orange juice				
Frozen	12-oz. can	4 oz.	5 cans	
Frozen	32-oz. can	4 oz.	2 cans	
Fresh	qt.	4 oz.	6¼ qt.	

Amounts of Food as Purchased to Serve 50 (Continued)

Food	Weight or Measure	Serving Portion	Amount to Serve 50	Miscellaneous Information
Oranges, for juice	doz.	4 oz.	16–18 doz.	Size 113
Tea, hot, bulk	lb.	6-oz. cup	2 oz.	Amount will vary with quality of tea
Iced	1-oz. bag	12-oz. glass	6 bags	6 bags will make 3 gal. tea
Instant, iced	2-oz. jar	12-oz. glass	1–1½ oz.	

CEREALS AND CEREAL PRODUCTS

Food	Weight or Measure	Serving Portion	Amount to Serve 50	Miscellaneous Information
Barley, for soup	lb.		14 oz.	3 gal.
Cornmeal	lb.	⅔ c.	2 lb.	
Cream of wheat	lb.	⅔ c.	2 lb.	
Hominy grits	lb.	⅔ c.	2 lb.	
Macaroni	lb.	½–¾ c.	3–4 lb.	Yield varies with quality of macaroni
Noodles, medium	lb.	½–¾ c.	3–4 lb.	
Pettijohns	lb.	⅔ c.	3 lb.	
Rice	lb.	½ c.	3–4 lb.	Yield varies with type of rice
Rolled oats	lb.	⅔ c.	2 lb.	
Spaghetti	lb.	½–¾ c.	3–4 lb.	Yield varies with quality
Cereal, ready to eat				
All Bran	lb. pkg.	½ c.	3 pkg.	16 serv. per lb.
Cornflakes	lb. pkg.	¾ c.	2¾ pkg.	18 serv. per lb.
Puffed Rice	½-lb. pkg.	¾ c.	4 pkg.	12 serv. per pkg.
Rice Krispies	9½-oz. pkg.	⅔ c.	4 pkg.	20 serv. per lb.
Shredded Wheat	12-oz. pkg.	1 large or 2 small	6¾ pkg.	10 serv. per lb.
Wheaties	12-oz. pkg.	¾ c.	4 pkg.	16 serv. per lb.

CONVENIENCE FOODS

Food	Weight or Measure	Serving Portion	Amount to Serve 50	Miscellaneous Information
Bread Mixes				
Biscuits	5-lb. bag	1–1¼ oz.	2½ lb.	
Muffins, plain	5-lb. bag	1–1½ oz.	3½ lb.	
Rolls	5-lb. bag	1–1¼ oz.	2⅔ lb.	
Pancakes	5-lb. bag	2 pancakes	6 lb.	
Cake Mixes				
Angel food	1-lb. box	12–14 cuts per cake	4 boxes	Wt. of box will vary with brand

Amounts of Food as Purchased to Serve 50 (Continued)

Food	Weight or Measure	Serving Portion	Amount to Serve 50	Miscellaneous Information
Chocolate, yellow, white	1 lb. 2½ oz.	2-in. pieces	5 boxes	Wt. of box will vary with brand
	5-lb. pkg.	16 cuts per 9 in. layer	1 pkg.	3½ 2-layer cakes
Soup bases, beef, chicken, paste	1-lb. jar		8 oz.	3 gal. soup
Dehydrated	1 lb.		1½ lb.	3 gal. soup
Soup, concentrated	No. 10 can		2 cans	3 gal. soup
Pudding				
Chocolate	lb.	4 oz. (½ c.)	3½ lb.	
Vanilla	lb.	4 oz. (½ c.)	3 lb.	

DAIRY PRODUCTS AND EGGS

Food	Weight or Measure	Serving Portion	Amount to Serve 50	Miscellaneous Information
Butter or margarine				
For sandwiches	lb.		1 lb.	Spread 100 slices —50 sandwiches
For table	lb.	1–2 pats	1–1½ lb.	72 pats per lb. (may be purchased in other sizes)
For vegetables	lb.	1 t.	½ lb.	
Cheddar cheese	lb.	1¼–1½ oz.	4–5 lb.	For sandwich or with cold cuts
Cottage cheese	1-lb. carton	No. 20 dipper	6½ lb.	For salad or side dish
Cream, coffee	qt.		1–1½ qt.	
Whipping	pt.	1 T.	1½ pt.	For garnish
Cream cheese	2 lb.	½ oz.	2 lb.	For sandwich or salad garnish
Eggs, in shell	doz.	1–2 eggs	4½–8½ doz.	
Ice cream, brick	qt.	8 slices per brick	6½ bricks	
Bulk	gal.	No. 12 dipper	2 gal.	Dish of ice cream
Bulk	gal.	No. 16 dipper	1½ gal.	For sundaes
Bulk	gal.	No. 20 dipper	1¼ gal.	For à la mode
Carton	12 portions	3 oz. each	4½–5 cartons	
Milk, fluid	gal.	7–8 oz. glass	2½–3 gal.	For dispenser
Instant nonfat	1 lb.	8 oz.	3 lb.	3.2 oz. dry per qt.
Sherbet	gal.	No. 20 dipper	1¼ gal.	Meal accompaniment

FRUITS

Food	Weight or Measure	Serving Portion	Amount to Serve 50	Miscellaneous Information
Canned	No. 10 can	Varies	2–3 cans	See table, page 31
Dried				
Apricots	lb.	3 oz.	4½ lb.	

Amounts of Food as Purchased to Serve 50 (Continued)

Food	Weight or Measure	Serving Portion	Amount to Serve 50	Miscellaneous Information
Dates, pitted	lb.	5–6 ea.	3–4 lb.	
Prunes, with pits	lb.	4–5 prunes	6 lb.	
Raisins, seedless	lb.	2½ oz. or ⅓ c.	4 lb.	
Fresh				
Avocado	lb. (2 med.)	8–9 per avocado	3 lb.	For salad combinations
Apples, baking	box	1 apple	½ box	Size 113
For pie	lb.	6–7 cuts per pie	12–15 lb.	8 8-in. pies
For sauce	lb.	3–4 oz.	12–15 lb.	
Bananas	lb., small	1 each	16 lb.	
For pie	lb.	6–7 cuts per pie	5 lb.	8 8-in. pies
For salad	lb.	2½–3 oz.	8–10 lb.	
Blackberries, for pie	qt.	6–7 cuts per pie	6–8 qt.	8 8-in. pies
Cherries, red, for pie	qt.	6–7 cuts per pie	8–10 qt.	8 8-in. pies
Cranberries	lb.	¼ c. sauce	4 lb.	
Grapes, seedless	lb.	¼ c.	15 lb.	
Lemons	Size 165	1/6 lemon	8–10 lemons	For tea or fish
Melon, sliced	lb.	8-oz. slice	30 lb.	
Pineapple	2 lb. ea.	½ c. diced	5 pineapples	
Strawberries, for shortcake or sundaes	qt.	½–⅔ c.	6–7 qt.	
Frozen				
Apricots, apples	40-oz. pkg.	3 oz.	4 pkg.	
Cherries, peaches	40-oz. pkg.	3 oz.	4 pkg.	
Rhubarb, cut	40-oz. pkg.	2¼ oz.	3 pkg.	
Fruit for topping	40-oz. pkg.	1½ oz.	2 pkg.	
MEATS				
Beef		*Cooked Weight**		
Chuck, boneless pot roast	lb.	3 oz.	18–20 lb.	1 lb. A.P. = 0.67 lb. cooked meat†

* As Purchased weights given in the table are estimated amounts to yield 50 portions of cooked weights as given in this column. When calculating amounts for roasts or other meats to be sliced after cooking, a 10% slicing loss should be allowed.

† Yields of cooked meat from Food Buying Guide for Type A School Lunches, U.S.D.A. PA-270, revised Jan. 1964.

Amounts of Food as Purchased to Serve 50 (Continued)

Food	Weight or Measure	Serving Portion	Amount to Serve 50	Miscellaneous Information
Corned beef	lb.	3 oz.	25–30 lb.	Yield varies with extent of trimming
Rib roast, standing	lb.	6 oz.	45–50 lb.	Bone-in, oven prepared
Rib roast, rolled	lb.	3 oz.	20–22 lb.	Oven ready
Round, boneless	lb.	3 oz.	15–18 lb.	1 lb. A.P. = 0.73 cooked meat
Rump roast, boneless	lb.	3 oz.	18–20 lb.	1 lb. A.P. = 0.73 cooked meat
Sirloin, boneless roast, trimmed	lb.	3 oz.	15–18 lb.	
Steaks				
Round, boneless, cut 3/lb.	lb.	3½ oz.	16–18 lb.	1 lb. A.P. = 0.73 cooked meat
Cubed, cut 4/lb.	lb.	3 oz.	13 lb.	
Flank, cut 4/lb.	lb.	3 oz.	13 lb.	1 lb. A.P. = 0.67 cooked meat
Loin, strip	lb.	8 oz. A.P.	25 lb.	Short cut, bone in
Sirloin, boneless	lb.	3½ oz.	15–17 lb.	
Tenderloin, trimmed	lb.	4 oz.	17 lb.	
T-bone	lb.	8 oz. A.P.	25 lb.	
Short ribs, trimmed	lb.	3 oz.	35–40 lb.	1 lb. A.P. = 0.25 lb. cooked meat
1 in. cubes for stew	lb.	3 oz.	12–15 lb	1 lb. A.P. = 0.66 lb. cooked meat
Ground	lb.	3 oz.	13–15 lb.	1 lb. A.P. = 0.60 lb. cooked meat
Veal				
Chops, loin or rib	lb.	4 oz.	17 lb.	Cut 3/lb.

Amounts of Food as Purchased to Serve 50 (Continued)

Food	Weight or Measure	Serving Portion	Amount to Serve 50	Miscellaneous Information
Cutlets, leg, boneless, cut 3/lb. or 4/lb.	lb.	3–3½ oz.	12½–15 lb.	1 lb. A.P. = 0.75 lb. cooked meat
Ground	lb.	3–4 oz.	15 lb.	1 lb. A.P. = 0.64 lb. cooked meat
Roast, leg, bone in, rump and shank off	lb.	3 oz.	20 lb.	1 lb. A.P. = 0.69 lb. cooked meat
Pork, fresh				
Roast loin, boneless	lb.	3 oz.	16–20 lb.	1 lb. A.P. = 0.68 lb.cooked meat
Roast ham, boneless	lb.	3 oz.	16–20 lb.	1 lb. A.P. = 0.68 lb. cooked meat
Whole with bone	lb.	3 oz.	25 lb.	1 lb. A.P. = 0.54 lb. cooked meat
Roast, tenderloin, trimmed	lb.	3 oz.	12½–15 lb.	
Pork cutlets, cut 3/lb. or 4/lb.	lb.	3–3½ lb.	12½–15 lb.	1 lb. A.P. = 0.75 lb. cooked meat
Pork chops, loin, cut 3/lb.	lb.	1 chop	17 lb.	
Cut 4/lb.	lb.	1 chop	12½–13 lb.	
Pork sausage, bulk	lb.	2-oz. cake	12½–15 lb.	1 lb. A.P. = 0.48 lb. cooked meat
Links	lb.	2 links	8–10 lb.	
Spareribs	lb.	6 oz.	25–30 lb.	1 lb. A.P. = 0.26 lb. cooked meat

Amounts of Food as Purchased to Serve 50 (Continued)

Food	Weight or Measure	Serving Portion	Amount to Serve 50	Miscellaneous Information
Pork, smoked				
Bacon, sliced, hotel pack	lb.	2 slices	4–4½ lb.	24 slices per lb.
Sliced	lb.	1 slice	2½ lb.	17–20 slices per lb.
Canadian bacon	lb.	2 oz.	10 lb.	
Ham, with bone	lb.	3 oz.	20 lb.	1 lb. A.P. = 0.56 lb. cooked slices; 0.67 lb. cooked slices and pieces
Boneless	lb.	3 oz.	15 lb.	1 lb. A.P. = 0.64 lb. cooked slices; 0.77 lb. cooked slices and pieces
Slices	lb.	2 oz.	17 lb.	Served with eggs
Steak	lb.	5 oz.	19 lb.	Dinner meat
Pullman, canned	6–6½-lb. can	3 oz.	2 cans	
Lamb				
Chops, rib, cut 4/lb.	lb.	2 ea.	25 lb.	1 lb. A.P. = 0.54 lb. cooked meat
Leg, roast, bone in	lb.	3 oz.	18–20 lb.	1 lb. A.P. = 0.54 lb. cooked meat
Boneless	lb.	3 oz.	15 lb.	1 lb. A.P. = 0.7 lb. cooked meat
Variety and Luncheon Meats				
Bologna	lb.	3 oz.	10 lb.	
Frankfurters				
8/lb.	lb.	2 franks	12½ lb.	
10/lb.	lb.	1 frank	5 lb.	
Heart	lb.	3 oz.	20–24 lb.	1 lb. A.P. = 0.39 lb. cooked heart
Liver	lb.	3 oz.	12–13 lb.	1 lb. A.P. = 0.69 lb. cooked liver
Liverwurst	lb.	2 oz.	6½ lb.	

Amounts of Food as Purchased to Serve 50 (Continued)

Food	Weight or Measure	Serving Portion	Amount to Serve 50	Miscellaneous Information
Salami, cooked	lb.	2 oz.	6½ lb.	
Spiced ham	lb.	2 oz.	6½ lb.	
Tongue	lb.	3 oz.	18–20 lb.	1 lb. A.P. = 0.51 lb. cooked tongue
Fish				
Fish fillets	lb.	3 oz.	14–16 lb.	1 lb. A.P. = 0.64 lb. cooked fish
Whole, dressed	lb.	3 oz.	35–40 lb.	1 lb. A.P. = 0.27 lb. cooked fish
Oysters	gal.	3 oz.	1½–2 gal.	Amount will vary with method of preparation
Scallops, to fry	lb.	3 oz.	10–12 lb.	
Shrimp, raw, in shell	lb.	2 oz.	12½ lb.	1 lb. A.P. = 0.5 lb. cooked shrimp
		3 oz.	18–20 lb.	
Raw, peeled	lb.	3 oz.	16 lb.	1 lb. peeled = 9 oz. cooked shrimp
Cooked, peeled and cleaned	lb.	2 oz.	6–6½ lb.	1 lb. A.P. = 1.00 lb. cooked shrimp
		3 oz.	10 lb.	
Poultry				
Chicken, to fry	2½–2¾ lb.	½ breast, 1 drumstick with wing or back; 1 thigh with wing or back	8–9 fryers	
To barbecue	2–2½ lb.	¼ chicken	13 fryers	
To broil	1½–2½ lb.	½ broiler	25 broilers	
To bake	5–6 lb.	3 oz.	40 lb.	
To stew	lb.	2 oz. cooked meat	20 lb.	1 lb. A.P. = 0.34 lb. cooked chicken exclusive of neck or giblets. Yield will vary with size

Amounts of Food as Purchased to Serve 50 (Continued)

Food	Weight or Measure	Serving Portion	Amount to Serve 50	Miscellaneous Information
Turkey, ready to cook	lb.	3 oz.	35–40 lb.	1 lb. A.P. = 0.44 lb. cooked turkey meat exclusive of neck, giblets and skin. For slicing use larger amount
Roll	8–9 lb.	3–4 oz.	12–15 lb.	
VEGETABLES				
Canned	No. 10 can	2½–3 oz.	2–3 cans	
Dried				
Beans, kidney, lima, or navy	lb.	4 oz.	4–5 lb.	
Potatoes, sliced, dehydrated	lb.	3–4 oz.	2 lb.	
Instant for mashing	lb.	4 oz.	2–2½ lb.	
*Fresh**				
Asparagus	lb.	3–4 oz.	18–20 lb.	
Beans, green	lb.	3 oz.	10–12 lb.	
Beans, lima	lb.	3 oz.	18–20 lb.	
Beets, topped	lb.	3 oz.	12–14 lb.	
Broccoli	lb.	3 oz.	16–20 lb.	
Brussels sprouts	lb.	2½–3 oz.	12–15 lb.	
Cabbage, wedges	lb.	2½–3 oz.	11–12 lb.	
shredded for salad	lb.	1–2 oz.	5–8 lb.	
Carrots, topped	lb.	3 oz.	12½ lb.	
Carrot strips	lb.	3 strips 4 × ½ in.	2½ lb.	
Cauliflower, cello	lb.	3 oz.	18–20 lb.	
Celery, for relishes	lb.	4 strips 4 × ½ in.	4 lb.	
Corn on cob	doz.	1 ear	5 doz.	
Cucumber	lb.	1½–2 oz.	5–6 lb.	

* As Purchased amounts given should yield 50 portions cooked vegetables. To convert to ready-to-cook weight, see page 29.

Amounts of Food as Purchased to Serve 50 (Continued)

Food	Weight or Measure	Serving Portion	Amount to Serve 50	Miscellaneous Information
Eggplant	lb.	3 oz.	12–15 lb.	
Lettuce, for wedges	Head	cut 6 per head	8–10 heads	
Head, garnish	Head		4–5 heads	
Leaf, garnish	lb.	leaf	3–4 lb.	
Mushrooms, for sauce	lb.	2 oz.	3–4 lb.	
Onions, whole, to bake	lb.	1 med.	12–15 lb.	
Parsnips	lb.	3–3½ oz.	10–12 lb.	
Peas, green	lb.	3 oz.	20–25 lb.	
Potatoes, to bake	lb.	1 potato	17–25 lb.	2 or 3 per lb.
To mash	lb.	4 oz.	12–14 lb.	
To brown	lb.	4 oz.	15–20 lb.	
To cream or scallop	lb.	5 oz.	10 lb.	
Potato chips	lb.	1 oz.	3 lb.	
Potato, sweet, to bake	lb.	4½–5 oz.	20–25 lb.	
Radishes with tops	Bunch	2 ea.	10–12 bunches	
Spinach, cello bag, to cook	lb.	3 oz.	10 lb.	
For salad	lb.	1 oz.	4–5 lb.	
Squash, to mash	lb.	3 oz.	18–20 lb.	
To bake	lb.	4 oz.	20–25 lb.	
Zucchini	lb.	3 oz.	8–10 lb.	
Tomato, to slice	lb.	3 slices	10–12 lb.	
Wedges	lb.	3 oz.	10 lb.	
Turnips, to dice or mash	lb.	3 oz.	15 lb.	Without tops
Frozen				
Asparagus, lima beans, Brussels sprouts, broccoli, cauliflower or spinach	40-oz. pkg.	3 oz.	4 pkg. (10 lb.)	

* As Purchased amounts given should yield 50 portions cooked vegetables. To convert to ready-to-cook weight, see page 29.

Amounts of Food as Purchased to Serve 50 *(Continued)*

Food	Weight or Measure	Serving Portion	Amount to Serve 50	Miscellaneous Information
Green beans, corn, peas	40-oz. pkg.	2½ oz.	3 pkg. (7½ lb.)	
Onions	12-oz. pkg.			Contains approximately 3 c. chopped onions
Potatoes, for french fries	40-oz. pkg.	4 oz.	5 pkg.	
MISCELLANEOUS				
Gelatin, flavored	24-oz. pkg.	⅓ c.	1 pkg.	1 pkg. makes 1 pan 12 × 20 × 2 in. using 1 gal. liquid
Marshmallows	lb.	3 (1¼ in.)	2 lb.	
Nuts, mixed, for cups	lb.	1½ T.	1–1½ lb.	
Nondairy creamer	oz.	1 t.	3 oz.	3 oz. = 1½ c.
Olives, green	qt.	3–4	2 qt.	88–90 per qt.
Olives, ripe	No. 1 tall	3	3 cans	1½ qt. (120– 150 per qt.)
Pecans, salted, for tea table	lb.	1¼ T.	1–1¼ lb.	
Pickles, dill	qt.	1 pickle	2½ qt.	
Sweet, sliced	qt.	1 oz.	2¼ qt.	
Pickle relish	qt.	1 oz.	2 qt.	
Sweets				
Candies, small	lb.	2	1 lb.	
Honey	lb.	2 T.	5 lb.	
Jam	lb.	1 T.	2¼ lb.	
Jelly	lb.	1–1½ T.	2–3 lb.	
Sirup	qt.	¼ c.	3 qt.	
Sugar, cubes	1-lb. pkg.	1–2 cubes	1½ lb.	
Granulated	lb.	1½ t.	¾ lb.	
Toppings for dessert	qt.	2 T.	1½ qt.	
Ice, for water glasses	lb.	3–4 oz.	10–12 lb.	
For punch bowl	lb.		10 lb.	

Amounts of Prepared Foods to Serve 50

The following table gives amounts of *prepared* food needed to serve 50 people, for example, the number of quarts, gallons, or pounds of a finished product needed for 50 portions.

This table can be used in conjunction with the table on "Amounts of Food *as Purchased* to Serve 50" (p. 4) in determining amounts to buy and to prepare. For example, the following table suggests 6¼ qt. mashed potatoes for 50 people. The preceding table indicates that 12 lb. potatoes should be purchased.

Amounts of Prepared Foods to Serve 50
(Amounts are Approximate)

Food	Serving Unit	Quantity
BEVERAGES		
Cocoa, coffee, hot tea	6-oz. teacup	2½ gal.
Lemonade	8-oz. glass	2½–3 gal.
Iced tea	12-oz. glass	3 gal.
Punch	3-, 4-, or 5-oz. punch cup	1½–2½ gal.
(1 gal. yields 30–35 4-oz. (½ c.) servings. 2½ gal. would provide 50 servings plus 30 refills.)		
BREADS		
Bread, thin, for sandwiches	2 oz. (2 slices)	7 lb. bread
Quick, loaf (brown, nut, orange)	2–3 slices	5 loaves 4 × 9 in.
Rolls, breakfast	3 oz. (1 roll)	4⅓–4½ doz.
Raised yeast	1½–2 rolls	6–9 doz.
Coffee cake	2 oz. (1 piece 2 × 2½ in.)	1 pan 12 × 20 in.
Corn bread	1 piece 2 × 2½ in.	1 pan 12 × 20 in.
Muffins	2 oz. (2 muffins)	9 doz.
Biscuits	2–3 oz. (2–3 biscuits)	9–12½ doz.
Griddle cakes	3½ oz. (2 cakes)	6½ qt. batter
Waffles	3 oz. (1 waffle)	6½ qt. batter
Doughnuts, cake type	1½ oz. (2 doughnuts)	9 doz.
Yeast type	1½ oz. (2 doughnuts)	9 doz.
Toast, French	4 oz. (2 slices)	7 lb. bread
Buttered or cinnamon	2 oz. (2 slices)	7 lb. bread

Amounts of Prepared Foods to Serve 50 (Continued)

Food	Serving Unit	Quantity
CEREAL PRODUCTS, COOKED		
Farina, Cream of Wheat, hominy grits, macaroni, spaghetti, rolled oats, noodles, pettijohns, rice for cereal	5 oz. (⅔ c.)	2 gal.
Rice, as vegetable	4 oz. (½ c.)	6¼ qt.
Corn meal	6 oz. (⅔ c.)	2 gal.
Bread stuffing	1–1½ oz.	7¼ qt.
DESSERTS		
Cake		
Layer, 2 (10 in.)	2½ oz.	3 cakes
Pound or loaf	3 oz.	4 loaves
Sheet cake	2½ oz.	1 pan 12 × 20 in. (40–48 portions) 1 bun pan 18 × 26 in. (60 portions)
Fruit cake	2½ oz.	8 lb. (2 cakes)
Cup cakes	1½ oz.	4½ doz.
Angel food cake, plain	1 oz.	3–4 10-in. cakes
Cake frosting		
Layer cake, 2 (10 in.)	3 cakes	2¼–2½ qt.
Sheet cake	1 cake	1–1½ qt.
Angel food	3 cakes	2–2½ qt.
Cookies for tea	2–3	10–12 doz.
Fruit cup, fresh	3 oz. (½ c.)	6 qt.
Pies (8 in.)	6 cuts per pie	8 pies
Filling for pies		
Fruit	2½–3 c. per pie	5–6 qt.
Cream	3 c. per pie	6 qt.
Custard or pumpkin	3 c. per pie	6 qt.
Pastry for pies		
For 2-crust pie	9 oz. per pie	4 lb. 8 oz.
For 1-crust pie	5 oz. per pie	2 lb. 8 oz.
Meringue for pies	3 oz. per pie	1½ lb.
Puddings		
Cornstarch or tapioca	½ c. (No. 10 dipper)	6¼ qt.
Gelatin dessert	½ c.	6¼ qt.
Whips, fruit	½ c.	6¼ qt.
Steamed pudding	2½ oz. (No. 16 dipper)	4½ qt.
Baked pudding	3 oz.	1 pan 12 × 20 in.
MEATS, COOKED		
Chicken, cubed	1½–2 oz.	5–6 lb. (3¾–4½ qt.)
Chicken or ham, creamed	½–⅔ c.	6½–8½ qt.
Ham, boiled, sliced	3 oz.	9½ lb.
Meat loaf	4 oz.	5 loaves (4 × 9 in.)
Beef stew	⅔ c.	3 gal.
Roast beef, boneless	3 oz.	9 lb.

Amounts of Prepared Foods to Serve 50 (Continued)

Food	Serving Unit	Quantity
LUNCHEON DISHES		
Baked	½ c.	2 pans 12 × 20 × 2 in.
Creamed	½ c.	6½ qt.
Chili	1 c.	3¼ gal.
SALADS AND SALAD DRESSINGS		
Salads		
Bulky vegetable	½–⅔ c.	2 gal.
Fish or meat	⅔ c.	2 gal.
Fruit	⅓ c.	4¼ qt.
Gelatin, liquid	½ c.	6¼ qt.
Potato	½ c.	6¼ qt.
Dressings mixed in salad		
French, thin	2 t.	1–1½ pt.
Mayonnaise	1 T.	1 qt.
Dressings for self service		
French, thin	2 t.	1 qt.
Mayonnaise	1 T.	1 qt.
Thousand Island or		
Roquefort	1 T.	1–1¼ qt.
SAUCES		
Gravy	3–4 T.	3–4 qt.
Sauce, meat accompaniment	2 T.	2 qt.
Pudding sauce	2–3 T.	2–3 qt.
Vegetable sauce	2–3 T.	2–3 qt.
Frozen strawberries for		
sundaes	½–⅔ c.	15 lb.
Fresh strawberries for		
sundaes or shortcake	½–⅔ c.	6–7 qt.
SOUPS		
Soup, first course	⅔ c.	2 gal.
Soup, main course	1 c.	3¼ gal.
VEGETABLES		
Buttered	½ c.	6 qt.
Creamed, diced	½ c.	6 qt.
Kidney and other dry beans	½–¾ c.	6¼–9½ qt.
Potatoes, mashed	½ c.	6¼ qt.
Creamed	½ c.	6¼ qt.
Chips	¾–1 oz.	2½–3 lb.
French fried		12–15 lb.

Tables of Weights and Measures

Weights, Measures, and Their Abbreviations

Abbreviations	Equivalent
f. g. few grains	
t. teaspoon	5 ml. = 1 t.
T. tablespoon	3 t. = 1 T.
c. cup	16 T. = 1 c. = 8 fluid oz.
pt. pint	2 c. = 1 pt. = 16 fluid oz.
qt. quart	2 pt. = 1 qt. = 32 fluid oz.
gal. gallon	4 qt. = 1 gal. = 128 fluid oz.
oz. ounce	28.35 g. = 1 oz. (2 T. fluid)
lb. pound	16 oz. = 1 lb. or 453.6 g.
pk. peck	8 qt. = 1 pk.
bu. bushel	4 pk. = 1 bu.
ml. milliliter	
l. liter	1 l. = 1000 ml. or 1.06 qt.
g. gram	
kg. kilogram	2.2 lb. = 1 kg.

Food Weights and Approximate Equivalents in Measure

Food	Weight	Approximate Measure
Allspice	1 oz.	4½ T.
Almonds, blanched	1 lb.	3 c.
Apples, A.P.*	1 lb.	3–4 medium
Apples, A.P.	1½ lb.	1 qt. sliced
Apples, diced, ½-inch cubes, peeled	1 lb.	4½ c.
Applesauce	1 lb.	2 c.
Apples, canned, pie pack	1½ lb.	1 qt.
Apricots, dried, A.P.	1 lb.	3 c.
Apricots, dried, cooked, no juice	1 lb.	4½–5 c.
Apricots, fresh	1 lb.	5–8 apricots
Apricots, canned, halves, without juice	1 lb.	2 c. or 12–20 halves
Apricots, pie pack	1 lb.	1¾ c.
Asparagus, fresh	1 lb.	16–20 stalks
Asparagus, canned tips, drained	1 lb.	17–19 stalks
Asparagus, canned, cuts, drained	1 lb.	2½ c.
Avocado	1 lb.	2 medium
Bacon, raw	1 lb.	15–25 slices
Bacon, cooked	1 lb.	85–95 slices
Baking powder	1 oz.	2 T.
Baking powder	1 lb.	2 c.
Bananas, A.P.	1 lb.	3 medium
Bananas, diced	1 lb.	2–2½ c.
Barley, pearl	1 lb.	2 c.
Beans, baked	1 lb.	2 c.
Beans, dried, Lima, A.P.	1 lb.	2½ c.
Beans, dried, Lima, 1 lb. A.P., after cooking	2 lb. 9 oz.	6 c.
Beans, Lima, fresh or canned	1 lb.	2 c.
Beans, kidney, A.P.	1 lb.	2⅔ c.
Beans, kidney, 1 lb., A.P., after cooking	2 lb. 6 oz.	6–7 c.
Beans, navy, A.P.	1 lb.	2⅓ c.
Beans, navy, 1 lb. A.P., after cooking	2 lb. 3 oz.	5½–6 c.

* A.P. denotes "as purchased."

Food Weights and Approximate Equivalents in Measure (*Continued*)

Food	Weight	Approximate Measure
Cornstarch	1 oz.	3½ T.
Cornstarch	1 lb.	3½ c.
Crabmeat, flaked	1 lb.	3½ c.
Crab in shell	2 lb.	1 c. cooked meat
Crackers, graham	1 lb.	58–66 crackers
Crackers, 2⅝ in. sq.	12 oz.	50 crackers
Crackers, 2 × 2 in.	1 lb.	108 crackers
Cracker crumbs, medium fine	1 lb.	5–6 c.
Cranberries, raw	1 lb.	1 qt.
Cranberries, cooked	1 lb.	1 qt.
Cranberries, sauce, jellied	1 lb.	2 c.
Cranberries, dehydrated, sliced	1 lb.	8½ c.
Cream of tartar	1 oz.	3 T.
Cream of Wheat, A.P.	1 lb.	2⅔ c.
Cream, whipping*	1 pt.	1 qt. whipped
Cucumbers, diced, E.P.	1 lb.	3 c.
Currants, dried	1 lb.	3 c.
Curry powder	1 oz.	4 T.
Dates, pitted	1 lb.	2½ c.
Eggplant	1 lb.	8 slices 4 × ½ in.
Eggs, whole, A.P.	1 lb.	8–9 eggs
Eggs, whole,† fresh or frozen	1 lb.	2 c. (9–11 eggs)
Eggs, whites, fresh or frozen	1 lb.	2 c. (17–20 eggs)
Eggs, yolks, fresh or frozen	1 lb.	2 c. (19–22 eggs)
Eggs, hard cooked, chopped	1½ lb.	1 qt.
Eggs, dried	1 lb.	4 c.
Eggs, frozen, whole	1 lb.	2 c. (10 eggs)
Eggs, whites, dried	1 lb.	5 c.
Eggs, yolks, dried	1 lb.	5⅔ c.
Farina, cooked	6 oz.	¾ c.
Farina, A.P.	1 lb.	3 c.
Farina, 1 lb. A.P., after cooking	8 lb.	3¾ qt.
Figs, dry, cut fine	1 lb.	2½ c.
Flour, all-purpose	1 lb.	4 c.

* Volume approximately doubles when whipped.

† One case (30 doz.) eggs weighs approximately 41 to 43 lb. and yields approximately 35 lb. liquid whole eggs.

Food Weights and Approximate Equivalents in Measure (Continued)

Food	Weight	Approximate Measure
Flour, white, bread, unsifted	1 lb.	3½ c. (scant)
Flour, white, bread, sifted	1 lb.	4 c.
Flour, cake, sifted*	1 lb.	4¾ c.
Flour, whole wheat	1 lb.	3¾ c.
Flour, rye	1 lb.	5¾ c.
Flour, soya, low fat	1 lb.	5 c.
Gelatin, granulated	1 oz.	4 T.
Gelatin, granulated	1 lb.	3 c.
Gelatin, prepared, flavored	1 lb.	2⅓ c.
Ginger, ground	1 oz.	5 T.
Ginger, ground	1 lb.	5 c.
Ginger, candied	1 oz.	1 piece 2 × 2 × ⅜ in.
Grapefruit, medium†	1 lb.	1 grapefruit, 10–12 sections
Grapefruit, medium†		⅔ c. juice
Grapefruit sections, size† 36		1 gal., 238 sections
Grapenuts	1 lb.	4 c.
Grapes, cut, seeded, E.P.	1 lb.	2¾ c.
Grapes, on stem	1 lb.	1 qt.
Ham, cooked, diced	1 lb.	3 c. (+)
Ham, cooked, ground	1 lb.	2 c.
Ham, 1 lb. A.P., after cooking	8 oz.	1 c. cooked
Hominy, coarse	1 lb.	2½ c.
Hominy grits, raw	1 lb.	3 c.
Hominy grits, 1 lb. A.P., after cooking	6½ lb.	3¼ qt.
Honey	1 lb.	1⅓ c.
Horseradish	1 oz.	2 T.
Jam	1 lb.	1⅓ c.
Jelly	1 lb.	1½ c.
Krumbles	1 lb.	16 c.
Lard	1 lb.	2 c.
Lemons, size 165	1 lb.	4–5 lemons
Lemons, large†		6 = 1 c. juice
Lemons, large†		1 = 3 T. grated peel

* Or pastry flour.
† *Sunkist Fresh Citrus Quantity Serving Handbook,* Sunkist Growers, Inc.

Food Weights and Approximate Equivalents in Measure (*Continued*)

Food	Weight	Approximate Measure
Lemon juice	1 lb.	2 c. (8–10 lemons)
Lettuce, average head	9 oz.	1
Lettuce, shredded	1 lb.	6–8 c.
Lettuce, leaf	1 lb.	25–30 salad garnishes
Macaroni, 1-inch pieces, A.P.	1 lb.	4 c.
Macaroni, 1 lb., after cooking	4 lb.	2¼ qt.
Macaroni, cooked	1 lb.	2½ c.
Margarine	1 lb.	2 c.
Marshmallows (1¼ in.)	1 lb.	80
Mayonnaise	1 lb.	2 c. (scant)
Meat, chopped, cooked	1 lb.	2 c.
Milk, fluid, whole	1 lb. 1 oz.	2 c.
Milk, sweetened condensed	1 lb.	1½ c.
Milk, evaporated	1 lb.	1¾ c.
Milk, evaporated, tall can	14½ oz.	1⅔ c.
Milk, nonfat, dry	1 lb.	4 c.
Milk, nonfat, dry	1 oz.	4 T.
Mincemeat	1 lb.	2 c.
Molasses	1 lb.	1⅓ c.
Mushrooms, fresh	1 lb.	6¾ c.
Mushrooms, fresh, 1 lb. A.P. after sautéeing		1½ c.
Mushrooms, canned	1 lb.	2 c.
Mustard, ground, dry	1 lb.	4½ c.
Mustard, prepared	1 oz.	4 T.
Mustard seed	1 oz.	2½ T.
Noodles, dry, A.P.	1 lb.	6 c.
Noodles, 1 lb. A.P., after cooking	3 lb.	2¼ qt.
Nutmeats	1 lb.	3½ c.
Nutmeg, ground	1 oz.	3½ T.
Oats, rolled, A.P. (quick)	1 lb.	6 c.
Oats, rolled, 1 lb. A.P. (quick), after cooking	2½ lb.	4 qt.
Oil, vegetable	1 lb.	2–2⅛ c.
Olives, green, small size 180–200, 1 qt.		109–116 olives

Food Weights and Approximate Equivalents in Measure (Continued)

Food	Weight	Approximate Measure
Olives, ripe, small size 120–150, 1 qt.		152 olives
Olives, A.P.	4½ lb.	3 c. chopped
Onions, A.P.	1 lb.	4–5 medium
Onions, chopped	1 lb.	2–3 c.
Onions, dehydrated, chopped	1 lb.	7½ c.
Onions, dehydrated, chopped, 1 lb. A.P., after cooking	4½–5 lb.	7½–11 c.*
Onions, dehydrated, sliced	1 lb.	12 c.
Onions, dehydrated, sliced, 1 lb. A.P., after cooking	4 lb. 6 oz.–5 lb.	12–18 c.*
Onions, dehydrated, 2 No. 10 cans	3½ lb.	50 lb. raw (equivalent)
Oranges, size 72	1 lb.	2
Oranges, diced with juice (size 150)	3 lb.	1 qt.
Oranges, medium†		2–4 = 1 c. juice
		2 = 1 c. bite-size pieces
		1 = 10–11 sections
		1 = 4 T. grated peel
Orange juice, frozen	6 oz.	2¼ c. reconstituted
Orange juice, frozen	32 oz.	3 qt. reconstituted
Oysters, 1 qt.	2 lb.	40 large, 60 small
Paprika	1 oz.	4 T.
Parsley, coarsely chopped	1 oz.	1 c.
Parsnips, A.P.	1 lb.	4
Peanuts, E.P.	1 lb.	3¼ c.
Peanut butter	1 lb.	1¾ c.
Peaches, medium, A.P.	1 lb.	4
Peaches, canned, sliced, drained	1 lb.	2 c.
Peas, A.P. in pod	1 lb.	1 c. shelled
Peas, canned, drained	1¼ lb.	2–2½ c.
Peas, dried, split	1 lb.	2⅓ c.
Peas, 1 lb. dried, after cooking	2½ lb.	5½ c.
Pears, fresh, A.P.	1 lb.	3–4
Pears, canned, drained, diced	1 lb.	2½ c.

* 2-hr. rehydration gives 10% more volume than 30 min.; overnight rehydration, 10% more volume than 2 hr.

† *Sunkist Fresh Citrus Quantity Serving Handbook,* Sunkist Growers, Inc. 1963.

Food Weights and Approximate Equivalents in Measure (Continued)

Food	Weight	Approximate Measure
Pears, halves, large, drained	1 lb. 14 oz.	1 qt. (9 halves)
Pecans	1 lb. E.P.	3¾ c.
Peppers, green	1 lb.	7–9 medium
Peppers, green, chopped	1 lb.	3 c.
Pepper, ground	1 oz.	4 T.
Pepper, ground	1 lb.	4 c.
Pickles, chopped	1 lb.	3 c.
Pickles, halves, 3 in.	1 lb.	3 c. or 36 halves
Pimiento, chopped	1 lb.	2½ c.
Pineapple, canned tidbits	1 lb.	2 c.
Pineapple, fresh	2 lb.	1 pineapple, 2–3 c.
Pineapple, canned, slices, drained	1 lb.	8–12 slices
Poppy seed	5 oz.	1 c.
Potatoes, white, medium, A.P.	1 lb.	3
Potatoes, 2 lb. A.P., after cooking (diced and creamed or mashed)		1 qt.
Potatoes, sweet	1 lb.	3 medium
Potato chips	1 lb.	4–5 qt.
Potato chips	¾–1 oz.	1 serving
Prunes, dried, A.P., size 30 to 40	1 lb.	2½ c.
Prunes, dried, 1 lb. A.P., after cooking	2 lb.	3–4 c.
Prunes, cooked, pitted	1 lb.	3¼ c.
Pumpkin, cooked	1 lb.	2½ c.
Raisins, A.P.	1 lb.	3 c.
Raisins, 1 lb. A.P., after cooking	1 lb. 12 oz.	1 qt.
Raspberries, A.P.	1 lb.	3⅜ c.
Rhubarb, raw, 1-in. pieces	1 lb.	4 c.
Rhubarb, 1 lb. E.P., after cooking		2½ c.
Rice, A.P.	1 lb.	2 c.
Rice, 1 lb. A.P., after cooking	4–4½ lb.	2 qt.
Rice, puffed	1 oz.	1⅔ c.
Rutabagas, raw, cubed, E.P.	1 lb.	3⅓ c.
Sage, finely ground	1 lb.	8 c.

Food Weights and Approximate Equivalents in Measure (*Continued*)

Food	Weight	Approximate Measure
Sage, finely ground	1 oz.	½ c.
Salad dressing, cooked	1 lb.	2 c.
Salmon, canned	1 lb.	2 c.
Salt	1 oz.	1½ T.
Sardines, canned	1 lb.	48, 3 in. long
Sausage, link, small	1 lb.	16–17
Sauerkraut	1 lb.	3 c. packed
Sesame seed	1 oz.	3 T.
Shortening, hydrogenated fats	1 lb.	2¼ c.
Shrimp, small, cleaned	1 lb.	3¼ c.
Soda	1 oz.	2⅓ T.
Soybeans	1 lb.	2¼ c.
Spaghetti, 2-in. pieces	1 lb.	5 c.
Spaghetti, 1 lb. A.P., cooked	4 lb.	2½ qt.
Spinach, raw	1 lb.	5 qt. (lightly packed)
Spinach, 1 lb. raw, E.P., after cooking	13 oz.	2¾ c.
Spinach, canned	1 lb.	2 c.
Squash, summer, A.P.	2 lb.	1 squash, 5-in. diameter
Squash, Hubbard, cooked	1 lb.	2 c.
Starch, waxy maize	1 oz.	3 T.
Strawberries, A.P.	1 lb.	2¼ c.
Suet, ground	1 lb.	3¾ c.
Sugar, brown, light pack	1 lb.	3 c.
Sugar, brown, solid pack	1 lb.	2 c.
Sugar, cubes	1 lb.	96 cubes
Sugar, granulated	1 lb.	2–2⅛ c.
Sugar, powdered, XXXX sifted	1 lb.	3 c.
Sweetbreads, 5 lb. A.P.		1¾ qt. cooked
Tapioca, quick cooking	1 lb.	3 c.
Tapioca, pearl	1 lb.	2¾ c.
Tapioca, 1 lb. after cooking		7½ c.
Tea	1 lb.	6 c.
Tea, instant	1 oz.	½ c.
Tomatoes, canned	1 lb.	2 c.

Food Weights and Approximate Equivalents in Measure (*Continued*)

Food	Weight	Approximate Measure
Tomatoes, fresh	1 lb.	3–4 medium
Tomatoes, fresh, diced	1 lb.	2¼ c.
Tomatoes, dehydrated, flaked	1 lb.	2¾ c.
Tomatoes, dehydrated, flaked, 1 lb. A.P., after reconstituting (1 gal. water)	1 lb.	11 c.
Turkey A.P. dressed weight	14 lb.	11–12 c. diced, cooked meat
Turnips, A.P.	1 lb.	2–3
Tuna	1 lb.	2 c.
Vanilla	½ oz.	1 T.
Vinegar	1 lb.	2 c.
Walnuts, English, 1 lb. E.P.	1 lb.	4 c.
Watercress	1 lb.	5 bunches
Watermelon	1 lb.	1-in. slice, 6-in. diameter
Wheat, puffed	1 lb.	32 c.
Wheat, rolled	1 lb.	4¾ c.
Wheat, shredded	1 lb.	15–16 biscuits
Yeast, compressed	3/5 oz.	1 cake
Yeast, dry	¼ oz.	1 envelope
Yeast, dry		1 oz = 2 oz. compressed yeast
Yeast, dry		1 small package = 1 package compressed yeast

Approximate Yield in the Preparation of Fresh Fruits and Vegetables[1]

Weight of Ready-to-Cook or Ready-to-Serve-Raw Food from 1 lb. as Purchased

	lb.		lb.
Apple	0.76	Kale	0.74
Asparagus	0.56	Lettuce, head	0.74
Avocado	0.75	Lettuce, leaf	0.67
Banana	0.68	Mushrooms	0.97
Beans, green or wax	0.88	Okra	0.78
Beans, lima	0.39	Onions, mature	0.89
Beet greens	0.56	Orange sections	0.56
Blueberries	0.92	Parsnips	0.85
Broccoli	0.61	Peaches	0.76
Brussels sprouts	0.74	Pears	0.78
Cabbage, green	0.79	Peas, green	0.38
Cantaloupe, served without		Peppers, green	0.82
rind	0.50	Pineapple	0.52
Carrots	0.82	Plums	0.94
Cauliflower	0.45	Potatoes	0.81
Celery	0.75	Potatoes, sweet	0.80
Chard	0.77	Rhubarb, partly trimmed	0.86
Cherries, pitted	0.89	Radishes	0.63
Cranberries	0.96	Rutabagas	0.85
Cucumber, unpared	0.95	Spinach, untrimmed	0.74
pared	0.73	partly trimmed	0.92
Eggplant	0.81	Squash, Acorn	0.88
Endive, chicory, escarole	0.74	Squash, Hubbard	0.66
Grapefruit sections	0.47	Squash, Zucchini	0.98
Grapes, seedless	0.94	Strawberries	0.87
Honeydew melon, served		Tomatoes	0.91
without rind	0.60	Turnips	0.80
		Watermelon	0.46

HOW TO USE THIS TABLE

To determine the amount of fruits or vegetables to yield the amount stated in a recipe as E.P. or as ready-to-cook in the Timetable for Boiling or Steaming Fresh Vegetables, p. 406.

Divide the weight of ready-to-cook or E.P. desired by the figure given in this table. For example, the recipe for Mashed Potatoes, p. 409, calls for 12 lb. (E.P.) potatoes. To change the 12 lb. (E.P.) to A.P. divide 12 lb by 0.81, the ready-to-cook weight from 1 lb. A.P.

12 lb. E.P. ÷ 0.81 lb. = 14.8 or 15 lb. to purchase

[1] Adapted from *Food Buying Guide for Type A School Lunches,* U.S. Dept. Agriculture PA-270 Revised Jan. 1964.

Common Container Sizes[1]

Industry Term	Container		Principal Products
	Consumer Description		
	Approximate Net Wt. or Fluid Measure	Approximate Cups	
6 oz.	6 oz.	¾	Frozen concentrated and single strength juices. 5 servings.
8 oz.	8 oz.	1	Fruits, vegetables, specialties* for small families. 2 servings.
Picnic	10½–12 oz.	1¼	Mainly condensed soups. Some fruits, vegetables, meat, fish, specialties.* 2–3 servings.
12 oz.	12 oz.	1½	Frozen fruit juices. 10 servings; vacuum packed corn, 3–4 servings.
No. 300	14–16 oz. (14 oz.–1 lb.)	1¾	Pork and beans, baked beans, meat products, cranberry sauce, blueberries, specialties.* 3–4 servings.
No. 303	16–17 oz. (1 lb.–1 lb. 1 oz.)	2	Principal size for fruits and vegetables. Some meat products, ready-to-serve soups, specialties.* 4 servings.
No. 2	20 oz. (1 lb. 4 oz.) or 18 fl. oz. (1 pt. 2 fl. oz.)	2½	Juices,† ready-to-serve soups, some specialties,* pineapple, apple slices. No longer in popular use for most fruits and vegetables. 5 servings.
No. 2½	27–29 oz. (1 lb. 11 oz.– 1 lb. 13 oz.)	3½	Fruits, some vegetables (pumpkin, sauerkraut, spinach, and other greens, tomatoes). 5–7 servings.
32 oz.	32 oz.	4	Frozen fruit juices. 25 servings.

* Specialties: Usually a food combination such as macaroni, spaghetti, Spanish style rice, Mexican type foods, Chinese foods or tomato aspic.

† Juices are now being packed in a number of can sizes.

[1] Adapted from *Canned Food Tables*, Home Economics—Consumer Services, National Canners Association, Washington, D.C.

Common Container Sizes (Continued)

Industry Term	Container		Principal Products
	Consumer Description		
	Approximate Net Wt. or Fluid Measure	Approximate Cups	
No. 3 cyl. or 46 fl. oz.	51 oz. (3 lb. 3 oz.) or 46 fl. oz. (1 qt. 14 fl. oz.)	5¾	Fruit and vegetable juices,† pork and beans. Institutional size for condensed soups, some vegetables. 10–12 servings.
No. 10	6½ lb–7 lb. 5 oz.	12–13	Institutional size for fruits, vegetables, and some other foods. 25 servings.

Notes:
1. Strained and homogenized foods for infants, and chopped junior foods, come in small jars and cans suitable for the smaller servings used. The weight is given on the label.
2. Meats, poultry, fish, and seafood are almost entirely advertised and sold under weight terminology.

Substituting One Can for Another Size[1]

	Approximate	
1 No. 10 can =	7 No. 303 (1 lb.)	cans
1 No. 10 can =	5 No. 2 (1 lb. 4 oz.)	cans
1 No. 10 can =	4 No. 2½ (1 lb. 13 oz.)	cans
1 No. 10 can =	2 No. 3 Cyl. (46 to 50 oz.)	cans

[1] Adapted from *Canned Food Tables*, Home Economics—Consumer Services, National Canners Association, Washington, D.C.

Aproximate Dipper Equivalents

Dipper No.*	Approximate Equivalent		Suggested Use
	Measure	Weight	
100	scant 2 t.		Tea cookies
70	scant 1 T.	⅜ oz.	Drop cookies
60	1 T.	½ oz.	Small cookies, garnishes
50	1¼ T.	⅝ oz.	Drop cookies
40	1½ T.	¾ oz.	Drop cookies
30	2 T. +	1–1½ oz.	Drop cookies
24	2⅔ T. +	1½–1¾ oz.	Cream puffs
20	3 T. +	1¾–2 oz.	Muffins, cup cakes, sauces
16	4 T. (¼ c.)	2–2¼ oz.	Muffins, desserts, croquettes
12	5 T. + (⅓ c.)	2½–3 oz.	Croquettes, vegetables, muffins, desserts, salads
10	6 T. +	3–4 oz.	Desserts, meat patties, vegetables, hot cereals
8	8 T. (½ c.)	4–5 oz.	Luncheon dishes, creamed meats
6	10 T. +	6 oz.	Luncheon salads

Note:

These measurements are based on level dippers. If a heaping dipper is used, the measure and weight are closer to that of the next larger dipper.

* Portions per quart.

Approximate Ladle Equivalents

Measure	Weight	Suggested Use
⅛ c.	1 oz.	Sauces
¼ c.	2 oz.	Gravies, some sauces
½ c.	4 oz.	Stews, creamed dishes
¾ c.	6 oz.	Stews, creamed dishes
1 c.	8 oz.	Soup

Note:

These measurements are based on level ladles. If a heaping ladle is used, the measure is closer to that of the next larger ladle.

Fractional Equivalents[1]

(The following chart is designed to help change fractional parts of pounds, cups, gallons, etc., to accurate weights or measures. For example, reading from left to right in the second line, the table shows that 7/8 of 1 c. is 1 c. less 2 T., 7/8 of 1 qt. is 3½ c., 7/8 of 1 lb. is 14 oz.)

Fraction	Tablespoon	Cup	Pint	Quart	Gallon	Pound
1	3 t.	16 T.	2 c.	2 pt.	4 qt.	16 oz.
7/8	2½ t.	1 c. less 2 T.	1¾ c.	3½ c.	3 qt. 1 pt.	14 oz.
¾	2¼ t.	12 T.	1½ c.	3 c.	3 qt.	12 oz.
⅔	2 t.	10 T. 2 t.	1⅓ c.	2⅔ c.	2 qt. 2⅔ c.	10⅔ oz.
5/8	2 t. (scant)	10 T.	1¼ c.	2½ c.	2 qt. 1 pt.	10 oz.
½	1½ t.	8 T.	1 c.	2 c.	2 qt.	8 oz.
⅜	1⅛ t.	6 T.	¾ c.	1½ c.	1 qt. 1 pt.	6 oz.
⅓	1 t.	5 T. 1 t.	⅔ c.	1⅓ c.	1 qt. 1⅓ c.	5⅓ oz.
¼	¾ t.	4 T.	½ c.	1 c.	1 qt.	4 oz.
⅛	½ t. (scant)	2 T.	¼ c.	½ c.	1 pt.	2 oz.
1/16	¼ t. (scant)	1 T.	2 T.	¼ c.	1 c.	1 oz.

[1] Adapted from *Quantity Recipes for Type A School Lunches,* U.S. Dept. of Agriculture, PA-631.

Weight (1–16 oz.) and Measure Equivalents for Commonly Used Foods

Food Item	1 oz.	2 oz.	3 oz.	4 oz.	5 oz.	6 oz.	7 oz.	8 oz.
Baking powder	2 T.	¼ c.	⅓ c. + 2 t.	½ c.	½ c. + 2 T.	¾ c.	¾ c. + 2 T.	1 c.
Bread crumbs, dry	¼ c.	½ c.	¾ c.	1 c.	1¼ c.	1½ c.	1¾ c.	2 c.
Butter or margarine	2 T.	¼ c.	⅓ c. + 2 t.	½ c.	½ c. + 2 T.	¾ c.	¾ c. + 2 T.	1 c.
Celery, chopped	¼ c.	½ c.	¾ c.	1 c.	1¼ c.	1½ c	1¾ c.	2 c.
Cornstarch	3½ T.	⅓ c. + 2 T.	⅔ c.	¾ c. + 2 T.	1 c. + 2 T.	1¼ c. + 1 T.	1½ c. + 1 T.	1¾ c.
Eggs, whole, whites or yolks, fresh or frozen	2 T.	¼ c.	⅓ c. + 2 t.	½ c.	½ c. + 2 T.	¾ c.	¾ c. + 2 T.	1 c.
Eggs, dried	¼ c.	½ c.	¾ c.	1 c.	1¼ c.	1½ c.	1¾ c.	2 c.
Flour, all purpose	¼ c.	½ c.	¾ c.	1 c.	1¼ c.	1½ c.	1¾ c.	2 c.
Flour, cake	¼ c. + 1 T.	½ c. + 2 T.	¾ c. + 2 T.	1 c. + 3 T.	1½ c.	1¾ c. + 1 T.	2 c. + 1 T.	2½ c.
Gelatin, granulated	3 T.	⅓ c. + 2 t.	½ c. + 1 T.	¾ c.	¾ c. + 3 T.	1 c. + 2 T.	1¼ c. + 1 T.	1½ c.
Gelatin, flavored	2 T. + 1 t.	¼ c. + 2 t.	⅓ c. + 2 T.	½ c. + 1 T.	⅔ c. + 1 T.	¾ c. + 2 T.	1 c.	1 c. + 3 T.

Onion, chopped	2 T.	¼ c.	⅓ c. + 2 t.	½ c.	½ c. + 2 T.	¾ c.	¾ c. + 2 T.	1 c.
Nutmeats	3½ T.	⅓ c. + 2 T.	⅔ c.	¾ c. + 2 T.	1 c. + 2 T.	1¼ c. + 1 T.	1½ c. + 1 T.	1¾ c.
Pepper, green, chopped	3 T.	⅓ c. + 2 t.	½ c. + 1 T.	¾ c.	¾ c. + 3 T.	1 c. + 2 T.	1¼ c. + 1 T.	1½ c.
Salt	1½ T.	3 T.	¼ c. + 1½ t.	⅓ c. + 2 t.	⅓ c. + 2 T.	½ c. + 1 T.	⅔ c.	¾ c.
Shortening, hydrogenated fat	2 T. + 1 t.	¼ c. + 2 t.	⅓ c. + 2 T.	½ c. + 1 T.	⅔ c. + 1 T.	¾ c. + 2 T.	1 c.	1 c. + 2 T.
Soda	2 T. + 1 t.	¼ c. + 2 t.	⅓ c. + 2 T.	½ c. + 1 T.	⅔ c. + 1 T.	¾ c. + 2 T.	1 c.	1 c. + 3 T.
Sugar, brown, light pack	3 T.	⅓ c. + 2 t.	½ c. + 1 T.	¾ c.	¾ c. + 3 T.	1 c. + 2 T.	1¼ c. + 1 T.	1½ c.
Sugar, granulated	2 T.	¼ c.	⅓ c. + 2 t.	½ c.	½ c. + 2 T.	¾ c.	¾ c. + 2 T.	1 c.
Sugar, powdered, sifted	3 T.	⅓ c. + 2 t.	½ c. + 1 T.	¾ c.	¾ c. + 3 T.	1 c. + 2 T.	1¼ c. + 1 T.	1½ c.
Yeast, dry	¼ c.	½ c.	¾ c.	1 c.	1¼ c.	1½ c.	1¾ c.	2 c.

Weight (1–16 oz.) and Measure Equivalents for Commonly Used Foods (Continued)

Food Item	9 oz.	10 oz.	11 oz.	12 oz.	13 oz.	14 oz.	15 oz.	16 oz.
Baking Powder	1 c. + 2 T.	1¼ c.	1⅓ c. + 1 T.	1½ c.	1½ c. + 2 T.	1¾ c.	1¾ c. + 2 T.	2 c.
Bread crumbs, dry	2¼ c.	2½ c.	2¾ c.	3 c.	3¼ c.	3½ c.	3¾ c.	4 c.
Butter or Margarine	1 c. + 2 T.	1¼ c.	1⅓ c. + 1 T.	1½ c.	1½ c. + 2 T.	1¾ c.	1¾ c. + 2 T.	2 c.
Celery, chopped	2¼ c.	2½ c.	2¾ c.	3 c.	3¼ c.	3½ c.	3¾ c.	4 c.
Cornstarch	2 c.	2 c. + 3 T.	2⅓ c. + 2 T.	2½ c. + 2 T.	2¾ c. + 2 T.	3 c. + 1 T.	3¼ c. + 1½ t.	3½ c.
Eggs, whole, whites or yolks, fresh or frozen	1 c. + 2 T.	1¼ c.	1⅓ c. + 1 T.	1½ c.	1½ c. + 2 T.	1¾ c.	1¾ c. + 2 T.	2 c.
Eggs, dried	2¼ c.	2½ c.	2¾ c.	3 c.	3¼ c.	3½ c.	3¾ c.	4 c.
Flour, all purpose	2¼ c.	2½ c.	2¾ c.	3 c.	3¼ c.	3½ c.	3¾ c.	4 c.
Flour, cake	2¾ c.	3 c.	3¼ c.	3½ c. + 1 T.	3¾ c. + 2 T.	4 c. + 2 T.	4⅓ c. + 2 T.	4¾ c.
Gelatin, granulated	1⅔ c.	1¾ c. + 2 T.	2 c. + 1 T.	2¼ c.	2⅓ c. + 2 T.	2½ c. + 2 T.	2¾ c.	3 c.
Gelatin, flavored	1¼ c. + 1 T.	1⅓ c. + 2 T.	1½ c. + 2 T.	1¾ c.	1¾ c. + 2 T.	2 c. + 1 T.	2 c. + 3 T.	2⅓ c.

Onion, chopped	1 c. + 2 T.	1¼ c.	1⅓ c. + 1 T.	1½ c.	1½ c. + 2 T.	1¾ c.	1¾ c. + 2 T.	2 c.
Nutmeats	2 c.	2 c. + 3 T.	2⅓ c. + 2 T.	2½ c. + 2 T.	2¾ c. + 2 T.	3 c. + 1 T.	3¼ c. + 1½ t.	3½ c.
Pepper, green, chopped	1⅔ c.	1¾ c. + 2 T.	2 c. + 1 T.	2¼ c.	2⅓ c. + 2 T.	2½ c. + 2 T.	2¾ c.	3 c.
Salt	¾ c. + 2 T.	¾ c. + 3 T.	1 c. + 1 T.	1 c. + 2 T.	1¼ c.	1¼ c. + 1 T.	1⅓ c. + 1 T.	1½ c.
Shortening, hydrogenated fat	1¼ c.	1⅓ c. + 1 T.	1½ c. + 1 T.	1⅔ c.	1¾ c. + 1 T.	2 c.	2 c. + 2 T.	2¼ c.
Soda	1¼ c. + 1 T.	1⅓ c. + 2 T.	1½ c. + 2 T.	1¾ c.	1¾ c. + 2 T.	2 c. + 2 t.	2 c. + 3 T.	2⅓ c.
Sugar, brown, light pack	1⅔ c.	1¾ c. + 2 T.	2 c. + 1 T.	2¼ c.	2⅓ c. + 2 T.	2½ c. + 2 T.	2¾ c. + 1 T.	3 c.
Sugar, granulated	1 c. + 2 T.	1¼ c.	1⅓ c. + 1 T.	1½ c.	1½ c. + 2 T.	1¾ c.	1¾ c. + 2 T.	2 c.
Sugar, powdered, sifted	1⅔ c.	1¾ c. + 2 T.	2 c. + 1 T.	2¼ c.	2⅓ c. + 2 T.	2½ c. + 2 T.	2¾ c. + 1 T.	3 c.
Yeast, dry	2¼ c.	2½ c.	2¾ c.	3 c.	3¼ c.	3½ c.	3¾ c.	4 c.

Ounces and Decimal Equivalents of a Pound[1]

Ounces	Decimal Part of a Pound	Ounces	Decimal Part of a Pound
¼	0.016	8¼	0.516
½	0.031	8½	0.531
¾	0.047	8¾	0.547
1	0.063	9	0.563
1¼	0.078	9¼	0.578
1½	0.094	9½	0.594
1¾	0.109	9¾	0.609
2	0.125	10	0.625
2¼	0.141	10¼	0.641
2½	0.156	10½	0.656
2¾	0.172	10¾	0.672
3	0.188	11	0.688
3¼	0.203	11¼	0.703
3½	0.219	11½	0.719
3¾	0.234	11¾	0.734
4	0.250	12	0.750
4¼	0.266	12¼	0.766
4½	0.281	12½	0.781
4¾	0.297	12¾	0.797
5	0.313	13	0.813
5¼	0.328	13¼	0.828
5½	0.344	13½	0.844
5¾	0.359	13¾	0.859
6	0.375	14	0.875
6¼	0.391	14¼	0.891
6½	0.406	14½	0.906
6¾	0.422	14¾	0.922
7	0.438	15	0.938
7¼	0.453	15¼	0.953
7½	0.469	15½	0.969
7¾	0.484	15¾	0.984
8	0.500	16	1.000

Note:
When increasing or decreasing recipes, the division or multiplication of pounds and ounces is simplified when decimals are substituted for ounces. For example, when multiplying 1 lb. 7 oz. by 4, convert from ounces to the decimal part of a pound. Thus, 1.438 lb. times 4 is 5.752.

[1] Adapted from *Standardizing Recipes for Institutional Use.* The American Dietetic Association, 1967.

Instructions for Using Table 1 Which Follows[1]

1. Locate column which corresponds to the original yield of the recipe you wish to adjust. For example, let us assume your original recipe for meat loaf yields 100 portions. Locate the 100 column.

2. Run your finger down this column until you come to the amount of the ingredient required (or closest to this figure) in the recipe you wish to adjust. Say that your original recipe for 100 portions of meat loaf requires 21 pounds of ground beef. Run your finger down the column headed 100 until you come to 21 pounds.

3. Next, run your finger across the page, in line with that amount, until you come to the column which is headed to correspond with the yield you desire. Suppose you want to make 75 portions of meat loaf. Starting with your finger under the 21 lb. (in the 100 column), slide it across to the column headed 75 and read the figure. You see you need 15 lb. 12 oz. ground beef to make 75 portions with your recipe.

4. Record this figure as the amount of the ingredient required for the new yield of your recipe. Repeat Steps 1, 2, 3 for each ingredient in your original recipe to obtain the adjusted ingredient weight needed of each for your new yield. You can increase or decrease yield in this manner.

5. If you need to combine two columns to obtain your desired yield, follow the above procedure and add together the amounts given in the two columns to get the amount required for your adjusted yield. For example, to find the amount of ground beef for 225 portions of meat loaf (using the same basic recipe for 100 we used above) locate the figures in columns headed 200 and 25 and add them. In this case they would be: 42 lb. + 5 lb. 4 oz., and the required total would be 47 lb. 4 oz.

6. The figures in Table 1 are given in exact weights including fractional ounces. After you have made yield adjustments for every ingredient, refer to Table 4 for "rounding-off" fractional amounts which are not of sufficient proportion to change product quality. No "rounding-off" is required for amounts needed for adjusted ingredients in the examples we have used here.

TABLE 1 Direct-Reading Table for Adjusting Yield of Recipes with Ingredient Amounts Given in Weights(a).

(This table is primarily for adjusting recipes with original and desired portion yields which can be divided by 25. It may be used along with Table 2 which is similarly constructed for measures.)

ABBREVIATIONS IN TABLE: oz. = ounce # = pound BASIC INFORMATION: 1 pound = 16 ounces

25	50	75	100	200	300	400	500
(*b*)	(*b*)	(*b*)	¼ oz.	½ oz.	¾ oz.	1 oz.	1¼ oz.
(*b*)	(*b*)	(*b*)	½ oz.	1 oz.	1½ oz.	2 oz.	2½ oz.
(*b*)	(*b*)	(*b*)	¾ oz.	1½ oz.	2¼ oz.	3 oz.	3¾ oz.
¼ oz.	½ oz.	¾ oz.	1 oz.	2 oz.	3 oz.	4 oz.	5 oz.
(*b*)	(*b*)	(*b*)	1¼ oz.	2½ oz.	3¾ oz.	5 oz.	6¼ oz.
(*b*)	¾ oz.	(*b*)	1½ oz.	3 oz.	4½ oz.	6 oz.	7½ oz.
(*b*)	(*b*)	(*b*)	1¾ oz.	3½ oz.	5¼ oz.	7 oz.	8¾ oz.
½ oz.	1 oz.	1½ oz.	2 oz.	4 oz.	6 oz.	8 oz.	10 oz.
(*b*)	(*b*)	1¾ oz.	2¼ oz.	4½ oz.	6¾ oz.	9 oz.	11¼ oz.
(*b*)	1¼ oz.	2 oz.	2½ oz.	5 oz.	7½ oz.	10 oz.	12½ oz.
(*b*)	(*b*)	2 oz.	2¾ oz.	5½ oz.	8¼ oz.	11 oz.	13¾ oz.
¾ oz.	1½ oz.	2¼ oz.	3 oz.	6 oz.	9 oz.	12 oz.	15 oz.
(*b*)	(*b*)	2½ oz.	3¼ oz.	6½ oz.	9¾ oz.	13 oz.	1# ¼ oz.
(*b*)	1¾ oz.	2¾ oz.	3½ oz.	7 oz.	10½ oz.	14 oz.	1# 1½ oz.
1 oz.	2 oz.	2¾ oz.	3¾ oz.	7½ oz.	11¼ oz.	15 oz.	1# 2¾ oz.
1 oz.	2 oz.	3 oz.	4 oz.	8 oz.	12 oz.	1#	1# 4 oz.
1 oz.	2¼ oz.	3¼ oz.	4¼ oz.	8½ oz.	12¾ oz.	1# 1 oz.	1# 5¼ oz.
(*b*)	2½ oz.	3½ oz.	4½ oz.	9 oz.	13½ oz.	1# 2 oz.	1# 6½ oz.
(*b*)	2½ oz.	3½ oz.	4¾ oz.	9½ oz.	14¼ oz.	1# 3 oz.	1# 7¾ oz.
1¼ oz.	2½ oz.	3¾ oz.	5 oz.	10 oz.	15 oz.	1# 4 oz.	1# 9 oz.

(*b*)	2¾ oz.	4¼ oz.	5½ oz.	11 oz.	1# ½ oz.	1# 6 oz.	1# 11½ oz.
1½ oz.	3 oz.	4½ oz.	6 oz.	12 oz.	1# 2 oz.	1# 8 oz.	1# 14 oz.
(*b*)	3¼ oz.	4¾ oz.	6½ oz.	13 oz.	1# 3½ oz.	1# 10 oz.	2# ½ oz.
1¾ oz.	3½ oz.	5¼ oz.	7 oz.	14 oz.	1# 5 oz.	1# 12 oz.	2# 3 oz.
2 oz.	3¾ oz.	5¾ oz.	7½ oz.	15 oz.	1# 6½ oz.	1# 14 oz.	2# 5½ oz.
2 oz.	4 oz.	6 oz.	8 oz.	1#	1# 8 oz.	2#	2# 8 oz.
2¼ oz.	4¼ oz.	6½ oz.	8½ oz.	1# 1 oz.	1# 9½ oz.	2# 2 oz.	2# 10½ oz.
2¼ oz.	4½ oz.	6¾ oz.	9 oz.	1# 2 oz.	1# 11 oz.	2# 4 oz.	2# 13 oz.
2½ oz.	4¾ oz.	7¼ oz.	9½ oz.	1# 3 oz.	1# 12½ oz.	2# 6 oz.	2# 15½ oz.
2½ oz.	5 oz.	7½ oz.	10 oz.	1# 4 oz.	1# 14 oz.	2# 8 oz.	3# 2 oz.
2¾ oz.	5½ oz.	8¼ oz.	11 oz.	1# 6 oz.	2# 1 oz.	2# 12 oz.	3# 7 oz.
3 oz.	6 oz.	9 oz.	12 oz.	1# 8 oz.	2# 4 oz.	3#	3# 12 oz.
3¼ oz.	6½ oz.	9¾ oz.	13 oz.	1# 10 oz.	2# 7 oz.	3# 4 oz.	4# 1 oz.
3½ oz.	7 oz.	10½ oz.	14 oz.	1# 12 oz.	2# 10 oz.	3# 8 oz.	4# 6 oz.
3¾ oz.	7½ oz.	11¼ oz.	15 oz.	1# 14 oz.	2# 13 oz.	3# 12 oz.	4# 11 oz.
4 oz.	8 oz.	12 oz.	1#	2#	3#	4#	5#
4½ oz.	9 oz.	13½ oz.	1# 2 oz.	2# 4 oz.	3# 6 oz.	4# 8 oz.	5# 10 oz.
5 oz.	10 oz.	15 oz.	1# 4 oz.	2# 8 oz.	3# 12 oz.	5#	6# 4 oz.
5½ oz.	11 oz.	1# ½ oz.	1# 6 oz.	2# 12 oz.	4# 2 oz.	5# 8 oz.	6# 14 oz.
6 oz.	12 oz.	1# 2 oz.	1# 8 oz.	3#	4# 8 oz.	6#	7# 8 oz.
6½ oz.	13 oz.	1# 3½ oz.	1# 10 oz.	3# 4 oz.	4# 14 oz.	6# 8 oz.	8# 2 oz.
7 oz.	14 oz.	1# 5 oz.	1# 12 oz.	3# 8 oz.	5# 4 oz.	7#	8# 12 oz.
7½ oz.	15 oz.	1# 6½ oz.	1# 14 oz.	3# 12 oz.	5# 10 oz.	7# 8 oz.	9# 6 oz.
8 oz.	1#	1# 8 oz.	2#	4#	6#	8#	10#
8½ oz.	1# 1 oz.	1# 9½ oz.	2# 2 oz.	4# 4 oz.	6# 6 oz.	8# 8 oz.	10# 10 oz.
9 oz.	1# 2 oz.	1# 11 oz.	2# 4 oz.	4# 8 oz.	6# 12 oz.	9#	11# 4 oz.

TABLE 1 *(Continued)*

ABBREVIATIONS IN TABLE: oz. = ounce # = pound BASIC INFORMATION: 1 pound = 16 ounces

25	50	75	100	200	300	400	500
9½ oz.	1# 3 oz.	1# 12½ oz.	2# 6 oz.	4# 12 oz.	7# 2 oz.	9# 8 oz.	11# 14 oz.
10 oz.	1# 4 oz.	1# 14 oz.	2# 8 oz.	5#	7# 8 oz.	10#	12# 8 oz.
11 oz.	1# 6 oz.	2# 1 oz.	2# 12 oz.	5# 8 oz.	8# 4 oz.	11#	13# 12 oz.
12 oz.	1# 8 oz.	2# 4 oz.	3#	6#	9#	12#	15#
13 oz.	1# 10 oz.	2# 7 oz.	3# 4 oz.	6# 8 oz.	9# 12 oz.	13#	16# 4 oz.
14 oz.	1# 12 oz.	2# 10 oz.	3# 8 oz.	7#	10# 8 oz.	14#	17# 8 oz.
15 oz.	1# 14 oz.	2# 13 oz.	3# 12 oz.	7# 8 oz.	11# 4 oz.	15#	18# 12 oz.
1# 1 oz.	2#	3#	4#	8#	12#	16#	20#
1# 2 oz.	2# 2 oz.	3# 3 oz.	4# 4 oz.	8# 8 oz.	12# 12 oz.	17#	21# 4 oz.
1# 3 oz.	2# 4 oz.	3# 6 oz.	4# 8 oz.	9#	13# 8 oz.	18#	22# 8 oz.
1# 4 oz.	2# 6 oz.	3# 9 oz.	4# 12 oz.	9# 8 oz.	14# 4 oz.	19#	23# 12 oz.
1# 5 oz.	2# 8 oz.	3# 12 oz.	5#	10#	15#	20#	25#
1# 6 oz.	2# 10 oz.	3# 15 oz.	5# 4 oz.	10# 8 oz.	15# 12 oz.	21#	26# 4 oz.
1# 7 oz.	2# 12 oz.	4# 2 oz.	5# 8 oz.	11#	16# 8 oz.	22#	27# 8 oz.
1# 8 oz.	2# 14 oz.	4# 5 oz.	5# 12 oz.	11# 8 oz.	17# 4 oz.	23#	28# 12 oz.
1# 10 oz.	3#	4# 8 oz.	6#	12#	18#	24#	30#
1# 12 oz.	3# 4 oz.	4# 14 oz.	6# 8 oz.	13#	19# 8 oz.	26#	32# 8 oz.
1# 14 oz.	3# 8 oz.	5# 4 oz.	7#	14#	21#	28#	35#
2# 2 oz.	3# 12 oz.	5# 10 oz.	7# 8 oz.	15#	22# 8 oz.	30#	37# 8 oz.
2# 4 oz.	4#	6#	8#	16#	24#	32#	40#
	4# 4 oz.	6# 6 oz.	8# 8 oz.	17#	25# 8 oz.	34#	42# 8 oz.
	4# 8 oz.	6# 12 oz.	9#	18#	27#	36#	45#

8 oz.	12 oz.	8 oz.	8 oz.	8 oz.	8 oz.		8 oz.
2# 6 oz.	4# 12 oz.	7# 2 oz.	9# 8 oz.	19#	28# 8 oz.	38#	47# 8 oz.
2# 8 oz.	5#	7# 8 oz.	10#	20#	30#	40#	50#
2# 12 oz.	5# 8 oz.	8# 4 oz.	11#	22#	33#	44#	55#
3#	6#	9#	12#	24#	36#	48#	60#
3# 4 oz.	6# 8 oz.	9# 12 oz.	13#	26#	39#	52#	65#
3# 8 oz.	7#	10# 8 oz.	14#	28#	42#	56#	70#
3# 12 oz.	7# 8 oz.	11# 4 oz.	15#	30#	45#	60#	75#
4#	8#	12#	16#	32#	48#	64#	80#
4# 4 oz.	8# 8 oz.	12# 12 oz.	17#	34#	51#	68#	85#
4# 8 oz.	9#	13# 8 oz.	18#	36#	54#	72#	90#
4# 12 oz.	9# 8 oz.	14# 4 oz.	19#	38#	57#	76#	95#
5#	10#	15#	20#	40#	60#	80#	100#
5# 4 oz.	10# 8 oz.	15# 12 oz.	21#	42#	63#	84#	105#
5# 8 oz.	11#	16# 8 oz.	22#	44#	66#	88#	110#
5# 12 oz.	11# 8 oz.	17# 4 oz.	23#	46#	69#	92#	115#
6#	12#	18#	24#	48#	72#	96#	120#
6# 4 oz.	12# 8 oz.	18# 12 oz.	25#	50#	75#	100#	125#
7# 8 oz.	15#	22# 8 oz.	30#	60#	90#	120#	150#
8# 12 oz.	17# 8 oz.	26# 4 oz.	35#	70#	105#	140#	175#
10#	20#	30#	40#	80#	120#	160#	200#
11# 4 oz.	22# 8 oz.	33# 12 oz.	45#	90#	135#	180#	225#
12# 8 oz.	25#	37# 8 oz.	50#	100#	150#	200#	250#

(a) This table was adapted from conversion charts developed by the Nutrition Services Division of the New York State Department of Mental Hygiene, Albany, New York.

(b) The amounts cannot be weighed accurately without introducing errors. Change to measurement by using conversion table p. 19.

[1] From Standardizing Recipes for Institutional Use. The American Dietetic Association, 1967.

Instructions for Using Table 2 Which Follows

1. Locate column which corresponds to the original yield of the recipe you wish to adjust. For example, let us assume your original sour cream cookie recipe yields 300 cookies. Locate the 300 column.

2. Run your finger down this column until you come to the amount of the ingredient required (or closest to this figure) in the recipe you wish to adjust. Say that your original recipe for 300 cookies required 2¼ c. fat. Run your finger down the column headed 300 until you come to 2¼ c.

3. Next, run your finger across the page, in line with that amount, until you come to the column which is headed to correspond with the yield you desire. Suppose you want to make 75 cookies. Starting with your finger under the 2¼ c. (in the 300 column), slide it across to the column headed 75 and read the figure. You see you need ½ c. + 1 T. fat to make 75 cookies from your recipe.

4. Record this figure as the amount of the ingredient required for the new yield of your recipe. Repeat Steps 1, 2, 3 for each ingredient in your original recipe to obtain the adjusted measure needed of each for your new yield. You can increase or decrease yield in this manner.

5. If you need to combine two columns to obtain your desired yield, follow the above procedure and add together the amounts given in the two columns to get the amount required for your adjusted yield. For example, to find the amount of fat needed to make 550 cookies (using the same basic recipe as above) locate the figures in columns headed 500 and 50 and add them. In this case they would be 3¾ c. + 6 T. and the required total would be 1 qt. + 2 T. fat.

6. The figures in Table 2 are given in measurements which provide absolute accuracy. After you have made yield adjustments for each ingredient, refer to Table 4 for "rounding-off" odd fractions and complicated measurements. You can safely "round-off" to 1 qt. as shown in Table 4, for the amount of fat needed in the recipe for 550 cookies.

TABLE 2 Direct-Reading Table for Adjusting Yield of Recipes with Ingredient Amounts Given in Measurement

(This table is primarily for adjusting recipes with original and desired portion yields which can be divided by 25. It is intended for use along with Table 1 which is similarly constructed for adjusting weights.)

ABBREVIATIONS IN TABLE

BASIC INFORMATION

Equivalents

3 t. = 1 T.
4 T. = ¼ c.
5 T. + 1 t. = ⅓ c.
8 T. = ½ c.
10 T. + 2 t. = ⅔ c.
12 T. = ¾ c.
16 T. = 1 c.
4 c. = 1 qt.
4 qt. = 1 gal.

t. = teaspoon
T. = Tablespoon
c. = cup
qt. = quart
gal. = gallon
(r) = slightly rounded
(s) = scant

Measuring spoons
1 T.
1 t.
½ t.
¼ t.
for ¾ t. combine ½ t. + ¼ t.
for ⅛ t. use half of the ¼ t.

25	50	75	100	200	300	400	500
¼ t.	½ t.	¾ t.	1 t.	2 t.	1 T.	1 T. + 1 t.	1 T. + 2 t.
¼ t. (r)	½ t. (r)	1 t. (s)	1¼ t.	2½ t.	1 T. + ¾ t.	1 T. + 2 t.	2 T. + ¼ t.
¼ t. + ⅛ t.	¾ t.	1 t. + ⅛ t.	1½ t.	1 T.	1½ T.	2 T.	2½ T.
½ t. (s)	¾ t. (r)	1¼ t. (r)	1¾ t.	1 T. + ½ t.	1 T. + 2¼ t.	2 T. + 1 t.	2 T. + 2¾ t.
½ t.	1 t.	1½ t.	2 t.	1 T. + 1 t.	2 T.	2 T. + 2 t.	3 T. + 1 t.
½ t. (r)	1 t. + ⅛ t.	1¾ t. (s)	2¼ t.	1½ T.	2 T. + ¾ t.	3 T.	3 T. + 2¼ t.
½ t. + ⅛ t.	1¼ t.	2 t. (s)	2½ t.	1 T. + 2 t.	2½ T.	3 T. + 1 t.	4 T. + ½ t.
¾ t. (s)	1¼ t. + ⅛ t.	2 t. (r)	2¾ t.	1 T. + 2½ t.	2 T. + 2¼ t.	3 T. + 2 t.	4 T. + 1¾ t.
¾ t.	1½ t.	2¼ t.	1 T.	2 T.	3 T.	¼ c.	5 T.
1 t. + ⅛ t.	2¼ t.	1 T. + ¼ t. + ⅛ t.	1½ T.	3 T.	¼ c. + 1½ t.	⅓ c. + 2 t.	¼ c. + 3½ T.

TABLE 2 Direct-Reading Table for Adjusting Yield of Recipes with Ingredient Amounts Given in Measurement (*Continued*)

25	50	75	100	200	300	400	500
1½ t.	1 T.	1½ T.	2 T.	¼ c.	¼ c. + 2 T.	½ c.	½ c. + 2 T.
1¾ t + ⅛ t.	1 T. + ¾ t.	1 T. + 2½ t. + ⅛ t.	2½ T.	¼ c. + 1 T.	¼ c. + 3½ T.	½ c. + 2 T.	¾ c. + ½ T.
2¼ t.	1½ T.	2 T. + ¾ t.	3 T.	⅓ c. + 2 t.	½ c. + 1 T.	¾ c.	¾ c. + 3 T.
2¼ t. + ⅛ t.	1 T. + 2¼ t.	2 T. + 1½ t. + ⅛ t.	3½ T.	¼ c. + 3 T.	½ c. + 2½ T.	¾ c. + 2 T.	1 c. + 1½ T.
1 T.	2 T.	3 T.	¼ c.	½ c.	¾ c.	1 c.	1¼ c.
1 T. + 1 t.	2 T. + 2 t.	¼ c.	⅓ c.	⅔ c.	1 c.	1⅓ c.	1⅔ c.
2 T.	¼ c.	¼ c. + 2 T.	½ c.	1 c.	1½ c.	2 c.	2½ c.
2 T. + 2 t.	⅓ c.	½ c.	⅔ c.	1⅓ c.	2 c.	2⅔ c.	3⅓ c.
3 T.	6 T.	½ c. + 1 T.	¾ c.	1½ c.	2¼ c.	3 c.	3¾ c.
¼ c.	½ c.	¾ c.	1 c.	2 c.	3 c.	1 qt.	1¼ qt.
¼ c. + 1 T.	½ c. + 2 T.	¾ c. + 3 T.	1¼ c.	2½ c.	3¾ c.	1¼ qt.	1½ qt. + ¼ c.
⅓ c.	⅔ c.	1 c.	1⅓ c.	2⅔ c.	1 qt.	1¼ qt. + ⅓ c.	1½ qt. + ⅔ c.
⅓ c. + 2 t.	¾ c.	1 c. + 2 T.	1½ c.	3 c.	1 qt. + ½ c.	1½ qt.	1¾ qt. + ½ c.
6 T. + 2 t.	¾ c. + 4 t.	1¼ c.	1⅔ c.	3⅓ c.	1¼ qt.	1½ qt. + ⅔ c.	2 qt. + ⅓ c.
¼ c. + 3 T.	¾ c. + 2 T.	1¼ c. + 1 T.	1¾ c.	3½ c.	1¼ qt. + ¼ c.	1¾ qt.	2 qt. + ¾ c.
½ c.	1 c.	1½ c.	2 c.	1 qt.	1½ qt.	2 qt.	2½ qt.
½ c. + 1 T.	1 c. + 2 T.	1½ c. + 3 T.	2¼ c.	1 qt. + ½ c.	1½ qt. + ¾ c.	2¼ qt.	2¾ qt. + ¼ c.
½ c. + 4 t.	1 c. + 2 T. + 2 t.	1¾ c.	2⅓ c.	1 qt. + ⅔ c.	1¾ qt.	2¼ qt. + ⅓ c.	2¾ qt. + ⅔ c.
½ c. + 2 T.	1¼ c.	1¾ c. + 2 T.	2½ c.	1¼ qt.	1¾ qt. + ½ c.	2½ qt.	3 qt. + ½ c.
⅔ c.	1⅓ c.	2 c.	2⅔ c.	1¼ qt. + ⅓ c.	2 qt.	2½ qt. + ⅔ c.	3 qt. + 1⅓ c.
½ c. + 3 T.	1¼ c. + 2 T.	2 c. + 1 T.	2¾ c.	1¼ qt. + ½ c.	2 qt. + ¼ c.	2¾ qt.	3¼ qt. + ¾ c.

¾ c.	1½ c.	2¼ c.	3 c.	1½ qt.	2¼ qt.	3 qt.	3¾ qt.
¾ c. + 1 T.	1½ c. + 2 T.	2¼ c. + 3 T.	3¼ c.	1½ qt. + ½ c.	2¼ qt. + ¾ c.	3¼ qt.	1 gal. + ¼ c.
¾ c. + 4 t.	1⅔ c.	2½ c.	3⅓ c.	1½ qt. + ⅔ c.	2½ qt.	3¼ qt. + ⅓ c.	1 gal. + ⅔ c.
¾ c. + 2 T.	1¾ c.	2½ c. + 2 T.	3½ c.	1¾ qt.	2½ qt. + ½ c.	3½ qt.	1 gal. + 1½ c.
¾ c. + 2 T. +2½ t.	1¾ c. + 4 t.	2¾ c. + ½ t.	3⅔ c.	1¾ qt. + ⅓ c.	2¾ qt.	3½ qt. + ⅔ c.	1 gal. + 1⅔ c.
¾ c. + 3 T.	1¾ c. + 2 T.	2¾ c. + 1 T.	3¾ c.	1¾ qt. + ½ c.	3 qt. + ¼ c.	1 gal.	1 gal. + 3¾ c.
1 c.	2 c.	3 c.	1 qt.	2 qt.	3 qt.	1 gal.	1¼ gal.
1¼ c.	2½ c.	3¾ c.	1¼ qt.	2½ qt.	3¾ qt.	1¼ gal.	1½ gal. + 1 c.
1½ c.	3 c.	1 qt. + ½ c.	1½ qt.	3 qt.	1 gal. + 2 c.	1½ gal.	1¾ gal. + 2 c.
1¾ c.	3½ c.	1¼ qt. + ¼ c.	1¾ qt.	3½ qt.	1¼ gal. + 1 c.	1¾ gal.	2 gal. + 3 c.
2 c.	1 qt.	1½ qt.	2 qt.	1 gal.	1½ gal.	2 gal.	2½ gal.
2¼ c.	1 qt. + ½ c.	1½ qt. + ¾ c.	2¼ qt.	1 gal. + 2 c.	1½ gal. + 3 c.	2¼ gal.	2¾ gal. + 1 c.
2½ c.	1¼ qt.	1¾ qt. + ½ c.	2½ qt.	1¼ gal.	1¾ gal. + 2 c.	2½ gal.	3 gal. + 2 c.
2¾ c.	1¼ qt. + ½ c.	2 qt. + ¼ c.	2¾ qt.	1¼ gal. + 2 c.	2 gal. + 1 c.	2¾ gal.	3¼ gal. + 3 c.
3 c.	1½ qt.	2¼ qt.	3 qt.	1½ gal.	2¼ gal.	3 gal.	3¾ gal.
3¼ c.	1½ qt. + ½ c.	2¼ qt. + ¾ c.	3¼ qt.	1½ gal. + 2 c.	2¼ gal. + 3 c.	3¼ gal.	4 gal. + 1 c.
3½ c.	1¾ qt.	2½ qt. + ½ c.	3½ qt.	1¾ gal.	2½ gal. + 2 c.	3½ gal.	4¼ gal. + 2 c.
3¾ c.	1¾ qt. + ½ c.	2¾ qt. + ¼ c.	3¾ qt.	1¾ gal. + 2 c.	2¾ gal. + 1 c.	3¾ gal.	4½ gal. + 3 c.
1 qt.	2 qt.	3 qt.	1 gal.	2 gal.	3 gal.	4 gal.	5 gal.
1¼ qt.	2½ qt.	3¾ qt.	1¼ gal.	2½ gal.	3¾ gal.	5 gal.	6¼ gal.
1½ qt.	3 qt.	1 gal. + 2 c.	1½ gal.	3 gal.	4½ gal.	6 gal.	7½ gal.
1¾ qt.	3½ qt.	1¼ gal. + 1 c.	1¾ gal.	3½ gal.	5¼ gal.	7 gal.	8¾ gal.

[1] From *Standardizing Recipes for Institutional Use*. The American Dietetic Association, 1967.

TABLE 2 Direct-Reading Table for Adjusting Yield of Recipes with Ingredient Amounts Given in Measurement
(*Continued*)

25	50	75	100	200	300	400	500
2 qt.	1 gal.	1½ gal.	2 gal.	4 gal.	6 gal.	8 gal.	10 gal.
2¼ qt.	1 gal. + 2 c.	1½ gal. + 3 c.	2¼ gal.	4½ gal.	6¾ gal.	9 gal.	11¼ gal.
2½ qt.	1¼ gal.	1¾ gal.	2½ gal.	5 gal.	7½ gal.	10 gal.	12½ gal.
2¾ qt.	1¼ gal. + 2 c.	2 gal. + 1 c.	2¾ gal.	5½ gal.	8¼ gal.	11 gal.	13¾ gal.
3 qt.	1½ gal.	2¼ gal.	3 gal.	6 gal.	9 gal.	12 gal.	15 gal.
3 qt. + 1 c.	1½ gal. + 2 c.	2¼ gal. + 3 c.	3¼ gal.	6½ gal.	9¾ gal.	13 gal.	16¼ gal.
3½ qt.	1¾ gal.	2½ gal.	3½ gal.	7 gal.	10½ gal.	14 gal.	17½ gal.
3½ qt. + 1 c.	1¾ gal. + 2 c.	2¾ gal. + 1 c.	3¾ gal.	7½ gal.	11¼ gal.	15 gal.	18¾ gal.
1 gal.	2 gal.	3 gal.	4 gal.	8 gal.	12 gal.	16 gal.	20 gal.
1 gal. + 1 c.	2 gal. + 2 c.	3 gal. + 3 c.	4¼ gal.	8½ gal.	12¾ gal.	17 gal.	21¼ gal.
1 gal. + 2 c.	2¼ gal.	3¼ gal.	4½ gal.	9 gal.	13½ gal.	18 gal.	22½ gal.
1 gal. + 3 c.	2¼ gal. + 2 c.	3½ gal. + 1 c.	4¾ gal.	9½ gal.	14¼ gal.	19 gal.	23¾ gal.
1¼ gal.	2½ gal.	3¾ gal.	5 gal.	10 gal.	15 gal.	20 gal.	25 gal.
1¼ gal. + 1 c.	2½ gal. + 2 c.	3¾ gal. + 3 c.	5¼ gal.	10½ gal.	15¾ gal.	21 gal.	26¼ gal.
1¼ gal. + 2 c.	2¾ gal.	4 gal. + 2 c.	5½ gal.	11 gal.	16½ gal.	22 gal.	27½ gal.
1¼ gal. + 3 c.	2¾ gal. + 2 c.	4¼ gal. + 1 c.	5¾ gal.	11½ gal.	17¼ gal.	23 gal.	28¾ gal.
1½ gal.	3 gal.	4½ gal.	6 gal.	12 gal.	18 gal.	24 gal.	30 gal.
1½ gal. + 1 c.	3 gal. + 2 c.	4½ gal.	6¼ gal.	12½ gal.	18¾ gal.	25 gal.	31¼ gal.
1½ gal. + 2 c.	3¼ gal.	4¾ gal.	6½ gal.	13 gal.	19½ gal.	26 gal.	32½ gal.
1½ gal. + 3 c.	3¼ gal. + 2 c.	5 gal. + 1 c.	6¾ gal.	13½ gal.	20¼ gal.	27 gal.	33¾ gal.
1¾ gal.	3½ gal.	5¼ gal.	7 gal.	14 gal.	21 gal.	28 gal.	35 gal.

Instructions for Using Table 3 Which Follows[1]

1. Locate column which corresponds to the original yield of the recipe you wish to adjust. For example, let us assume your original custard sauce recipe yields 24 portions. Locate the 24 column.

2. Run your finger down this column until you come to the amount of the ingredient required (or closest to this figure) in the recipe you wish to adjust. Say that your original recipe for 24 portions requires 1½ T. cornstarch and 1¼ qt. milk. Run your finger down the column headed 24 until you come to 1½ T. (for cornstarch) and then 1¼ qt. (for milk), etc.

3. Next, run your finger across the page, in line with that amount, until you come to the column which is headed to correspond with the yield you desire. Suppose you want to make 32 portions. Starting with your finger under the 1½ T. (in the 24 column), slide it across to the column headed 32 and read the figure. You need 2T. cornstarch for 32 portions. Repeat the procedure starting with 1¼ qt. in the 24 column; tracing across to the 32 column, you find you need 1½ qt. + ⅔ c. milk.

4. Record this figure as the amount of the ingredient required

for the new yield of your recipe. Repeat Steps 1, 2, 3 for each ingredient in your original recipe to obtain the adjusted measure needed of each for your new yield. You can increase or decrease yield in this manner.

5. Amounts for 8–48 portions are given on pp. 50–53. This part of the table is helpful when increasing home size recipes to quantities of 24 and 48 portions, logical steps in recipe enlargement. Adjustments between 56 and 96 servings may be made from information on pp. 54–57. However, if increasing from a number of portions in the first pages of the table to one in the last four pages, care should be taken to locate the corresponding lines in the two tables.

6. The figures in Table 3 are given in measurements which provide absolute accuracy. After you have made yield adjustments for all ingredients refer to Table 4 for "rounding-off" awkward fractions and complicated measurements. In our example (increasing from 24 to 32 portions) you can "round" the adjusted amount of milk to 1¾ qt. without upsetting proportions. The total amount of cornstarch in our example need not be "rounded-off" since it can be measured easily (2T).

TABLE 3 Direct-Reading Table for Adjusting Yield of Recipes with Ingredient Amounts Given in Measurement

(This table is primarily for use with recipes with original or desired portion yields which can be divided by 8, yields of 20 and 60 portions are also included.)

ABBREVIATIONS IN TABLE

t. = teaspoon	(*a*) = too small for accurate measure; use caution
T. = tablespoon	
c. = cup	
qt. = quart	
gal. = gallon	
(r) = slightly rounded	
(s) = scant	

BASIC INFORMATION

Measuring Spoons	Equivalents	
1 T.	3 t. = 1 T.	12 T. = ¾ c.
1 t.	4 T. = ¼ c.	16 T. = 1 c.
½ t.	5 T. + 1 t. = ⅓ c.	4 c. = 1 qt.
¼ t.	8 T. = ½ c.	4 qt. = 1 gal.
for ¾ t. combine ½ t. + ¼ t.	10 T. + 2 t. = ⅔ c.	
for ⅛ t. use half of the ¼ t.		

8	16	20	24	32	40	48
(*a*)	(*a*)	⅛ t. (s)	⅛ t.	⅛ t. (r)	¼ t. (s)	¼ t.
(*a*)	⅛ t. (r)	¼ t. (s)	¼ t.	¼ t. (r)	½ t. (s)	½ t.
¼ t. (s)	¼ t. (r)	½ t. (s)	½ t.	¾ t. (s)	¾ t. (r)	1 t.
¼ t.	½ t.	½ t. (r)	¾ t.	1 t.	1¼ t.	1½ t.
¼ t. (r)	¾ t. (s)	¾ t. (r)	1 t.	1¼ t. (r)	1¾ t. (s)	2 t.
½ t. (s)	¾ t. (r)	1 t.	1¼ t.	1¾ t. (s)	2 t.	2½ t.
½ t.	1 t.	1¼ t.	1½ t.	2 t.	2½ t.	1 T.
½ t. (r)	1¼ t. (s)	1½ t.	1¾ t.	2¼ t. (r)	1 T. (s)	1 T. + ½ t.
¾ t. (s)	1¼ t. (r)	1¾ t. (s)	2 t.	2¾ t. (r)	1 T. + ¼ t.	1 T. + 1 t.
¾ t.	1½ t.	1¾ t. (r)	2¼ t.	1 T.	1 T. + ¾ t.	1 T. + 1½ t.
¾ t. (r)	1¾ t. (s)	2 t.	2½ t.	1 T. + ¼ t. (r)	1 T. + 1¼ t.	1 T. + 2 t.
1 t. (s)	1¾ t. (r)	2¼ t. (r)	2¾ t.	1 T. + ¾ t. (s)	1 T + 1½ t.	1 T. + 2½ t.

[1] From *Standardizing Recipes for Institutional Use.* The American Dietetic Association, 1967.

8	16	20	24	32	40	48
1 t.	2 t.	2½ t.	1 T.	1 T. + 1 t.	1 T + 2 t.	2 T.
1½ t.	1 T.	1 T. + ¾ t.	1½ T.	2 T.	2½ T.	3 T.
2 t.	1 T. + 1 t.	1 T. + 2 t.	2 T.	2 T. + 2 t.	3 T. + 1 t.	¼ c.
2½ t.	1 T. + 2 t.	2 T + ¼ t.	2½ T.	3 T + 1 t.	¼ c. + ½ t.	¼ c. + 1 T.
1 T.	2 T.	2½ T.	3 T.	¼ c.	¼ c. + 1 T.	⅓ c. + 2 t.
1 T. + ½ t.	2 T.+ 1 t.	2 T. + 2¾ t.	3½ T.	¼ c. + 2 t.	⅓ c. + ½ T.	¼ c. + 3 T.
1 T. + 1 t.	2 T. + 2 t.	3 T. + 1 t.	¼ c.	⅓ c.	⅓ c. + 4 t.	½ c.
1 T. +2¼ t.	3 T. + 2¾ t.	¼ c. + 1¼ t.	⅓ c.	¼ c. + 3 T.	½ c. + 2½ t.	⅔ c.
2 T. + 2 t.	⅓ c.	⅓ c. + 2 T.	½ c.	⅔ c.	¾ c. + 4 t.	1 c.
3 T. + 1¾ t.	⅓ c. + 5 t.	½ c. + 2¾ t.	⅔ c.	¾ c. + 2 T.	1 c. + 5½ t.	1⅓ c.
¼ c.	½ c.	½ c. + 2 T.	¾ c.	1 c.	1¼ c.	1½ c.
⅓ c.	⅔ c.	¾ c. + 2 t.	1 c.	1⅓ c.	1⅔ c.	2 c.
⅓ c. + 4 t.	¾ c. + 4 t.	1 c. + 2 t.	1¼ c.	1⅔ c.	2 c. + 4 t.	2½ c.
⅓ c. + 5¼ t.	⅔ c. + 3½ T.	1 c. + 5¼ t.	1⅓ c.	1¾ c. + 1¼ t.	2 c. + 3½ T.	2⅔ c.
½ c.	1 c.	1¼ c.	1½ c.	2 c.	2½ c.	3 c.
½ c. + 2¼ t.	1 c. + 5¼ t.	1⅓ c.	1⅔ c.	2 c. + 3½ T.	2⅔ c.	3⅓ c.
½ c. + 4 t.	1 c. + 3 T.	1⅓ c. + 2 T.	1¾ c.	2⅓ c.	2¾ c. + 1½ T.	3½ c.
⅔ c.	1⅓ c.	1⅔ c.	2 c.	2⅔ c.	3⅓ c.	1 qt.
¾ c.	1½ c.	1¾ c. + 2 T.	2¼ c.	3 c.	3¾ c.	1 qt. + ½ c.
¾ c. + 1¼ t.	1½ c. + 2¾ t.	1¾ c. + 3 T.	2⅓ c.	3 c. + 2 T.	3¾ c. + 2 T.	1 qt. + ⅔ c.
¾ c. + 4 t.	1⅔ c.	2 c. + 4 t.	2½ c.	3⅓ c.	1 qt. +2½ T.	1¼ qt.

TABLE 3   Direct-Reading Table for Adjusting Yield of Recipes with Ingredient Amounts Given in Measurement
(Continued)

8	16	20	24	32	40	48
⅔ c. + 3½ T.	1¾ c. + 1¼ t.	2 c. + 3½ T.	2⅔ c.	3½ c. + 1 T.	4¼ c. + 3 T.	1¼ qt. + ⅓ c.
⅔ c. + ¼ c.	1¾ c. + 4 t.	2¼ c. + 2 t.	2¾ c.	3⅔ c.	4½ c. + 4 t.	1¼ qt. + ½ c.
1 c.	2 c.	2½ c.	3 c.	1 qt.	1¼ qt.	1½ qt.
1 c. + 4 t.	2 c. + 2½ T.	2⅔ c. + 2 t.	3¼ c.	1 qt. + ⅓ c.	5⅓ c. + 4 t.	1½ qt. + ½ c.
1 c. + 5¼ t.	2 c. + 3½ T.	2¾ c. + ½ T.	3⅓ c.	4¼ c. + 3 T.	5½ c. + 1 T.	1½ qt. + ⅔ c.
1 c. + 2 T. + 2 t.	2¼ c. + 4 t.	2¾ c. + 2½ T.	3½ c.	1 qt. + ⅔ c.	5¾ c. + 1 T.	1¾ qt.
1 c. + 3½ T.	2¼ c. + 3 T.	3 c. + 1 T.	3⅔ c.	4¾ c. + 2 T.	1½ qt. + 2 T.	1¾ qt. + ⅓ c.
1¼ c.	2½ c.	3 c. + 2 T.	3¾ c.	1¼ qt.	1½ qt. + ¼ c.	1¾ qt. + ½ c.
1⅓ c.	2⅔ c.	3⅓ c.	1 qt.	1¼ qt. + ⅓ c.	1½ qt. + ⅔ c.	2 qt.
1⅔ c.	3⅓ c.	1 qt. + 2½ T.	1¼ qt.	1½ qt. + ⅔ c.	2 qt. + ¼ c. + 1 T.	2½ qt.
2 c.	1 qt.	1¼ qt.	1½ qt.	2 qt.	2½ qt.	3 qt.
2⅓ c.	1 qt. + ⅔ c.	5¾ c. + 1½ T.	1¾ qt.	2¼ qt. + ⅓ c.	2¾ qt. + ⅔ c.	3½ qt.
2⅔ c.	1¼ qt. + ⅓ c.	1½ qt. + ⅔ c.	2 qt.	2½ qt. + ⅔ c.	3¼ qt. + ⅓ c.	1 gal.

8	16	20	24	32	40	48
3 c.	1½ qt.	1¾ qt. + ½ c.	2¼ qt.	3 qt.	3¾ qt.	1 gal. + 2 c.
3⅓ c.	1½ qt. + ⅔ c.	2 qt. + ⅓ c.	2½ qt.	3¼ qt. + ⅓ c.	1 gal. + ⅔ c.	1¼ gal.
3⅔ c.	1¾ qt. + ⅓ c.	2¼ qt. + 2½ T.	2¾ qt.	3½ qt. + ⅔ c.	1 gal. + 2⅓ c.	1¼ gal. + 2 c.
1 qt.	2 qt.	2½ qt.	3 qt.	1 gal.	1¼ gal.	1½ gal.
1 qt. + ⅓ c.	2 qt. + ⅔ c.	2½ qt. + ¾ c. + 1½ T.	3¼ qt.	1 gal. + 1⅓ c.	1¼ gal. + 1⅔ c.	1½ gal. + 2 c.
1 qt. + ⅔ c.	2¼ qt. + ⅓ c.	2¾ qt. + ⅔ c.	3½ qt.	1 gal. + 2⅔ c.	1¼ gal. + 3⅓ c.	1¾ gal.
1¼ qt.	2½ qt.	3 qt. + ½ c.	3¾ qt.	1¼ gal.	1½ gal. + 1 c.	1¾ gal. + 2 c.
1¼ qt. + ⅓ c.	2½ qt. + ⅔ c.	3 qt. + 1⅓ c.	1 gal.	1¼ gal. + 1⅓ c.	1½ gal. + 2⅔ c.	2 gal.
1½ qt. + ⅔ c.	3¼ qt. + ⅓ c.	1 gal. + ⅔ c.	1¼ gal.	1½ gal. + 2⅔ c.	2 gal. + 1⅓ c.	2½ gal.
2 qt.	1 gal.	1¼ gal.	1½ gal.	2 gal.	2½ gal.	3 gal.

TABLE 3 Direct-Reading Table for Adjusting Yield of Recipes with Ingredient Amounts Given in Measurement
(Continued)

56	60	64	72	80	88	96
¼ t.(r)	¼ t.(r)	¼ t.(r)	¼ t. + ⅛ t.	½ t.(s)	½ t.(s)	½ t.
½ t.(r)	½ t.(r)	¾ t.(s)	¾ t.	¾ t.(r)	1 t.(s)	1 t.
1¼ t.(s)	1¼ t.	1¼ t.(r)	1½ t.	1¾ t.(s)	1¾ t.(r)	2 t.
1¾ t.	1¾ t.(r)	2 t.	2¼ t.	2½ t.	2¾ t.	1 T.
2¼ t.(r)	2½ t.	2¾ t.(s)	1 T.	1 T. + ¼ t.	1 T. + ¾ t.	1 T. + 1 t.
1 T.(s)	1 T + ⅛ t.	1 T. + ¼ t.	1 T. + ¾ t.	1 T. + 1¼ t.	1½ T.	1 T. + 2 t.
1 T. + ½ t.	1 T. + ¾ t.	1 T. + 1 t.	1½ T.	1 T. + 2 t.	1 T. + 2½ t.	2 T.
1 T. + 1 t.	1 T. + 1¼ t. + ⅛ t.	1 T. + 1¾ t.	1 T. + 2¼ t.	1 T. + 2¾ t.	2 T. + ½ t.	2 T. + 1 t.
1 T. + 1¾ t.	1 T. + 2 t.	1 T. + 2¼ t.	2 T.	2 T. + ¾ t.	2 T. + ¼ t.	2 T. + 2 t.
1 T. + 2¼ t.	1 T. + 2½ t.	2 T.	2 T. + ¾ t.	2½ T.	2 T. + 2¼ t.	3 T.
1 T. + 2¾ t.(r)	2 T + ¼ t.	2 T. + ¾ t.	2 T. + 1½ t.	2 T. + 2¼ t.	3 T.	3 T. + 1 t.
2 T. + ½ t.	2 T. + ¾ t.	2 T. + 1¼ t.	2 T. + 2¼ t.	3 T.	3 T. + 1 t.	3 T. + 2 t.
2 T. + 1 t.	2½ T.	2 T. + 2 t.	3 T.	3 T. + 1 t.	3 T. + 2 t.	¼ c.
3½ T.	3 T. + 2¼ t.	¼ c.	¼ c. + 1½ t.	¼ c. + 1 T.	⅓ c. + ½ t.	⅓ c. + 2 t.
¼ c. + 2 t.	¼ c. + 1 T.	⅓ c.	⅓ c. + 2 t.	⅓ c. + 4 t.	⅓ c. + 2 T.	½ c.
⅓ c. + ½ T.	⅓ c. + 2¾ t.	⅓ c. + 4 t.	¼ c. + 3½ T.	½ c. + 1 t.	½ c. + 3½ t.	½ c. + 2 T.

56	60	64	72	80	88	96
¼ c. + 3 T.	¼ c. + 3½ T.	½ c.	½ c. + 1 T.	½ c. + 2 T.	½ c. + 3 T.	¾ c.
½ c. + ½ t.	½ c. + 2¼ t.	½ c. + 4 t.	½ c. + 2½ T.	⅔ c. + 1 T.	¾ c. + 2½ t.	¾ c. + 2 T.
½ c. + 4 t.	½ c. + 2 T.	⅔ c.	¾ c.	¾ c. + 4 t.	¾ c. + 2½ T.	1 c.
¾ c. + ½ T.	¾ c. + 4 t.	¾ c. + 2 T.	1 c.	1 c. + 5 t.	1 c. + 3½ T.	1⅓ c.
1 c. + 2½ T.	1¼ c.	1⅓ c.	1½ c.	1⅔ c.	1¾ c. + 4 t.	2 c.
1½ c. + 1 T.	1⅔ c.	1¾ c.	2 c.	2c. + 3½ T.	2¼ c. + 3 T.	2⅔ c.
1¾ c.	1¾ c. + 2 T.	2 c.	2¼ c.	2½ c.	2¾ c.	3 c.
2⅓ c.	2½ c.	2⅔ c.	3 c.	3⅓ c.	3⅔ c.	1 qt.
2¾ c. + 2½ T.	3 c. + 2 T.	3⅓ c.	3¾ c.	1 qt. + 2½ T.	4½ c. + 4 t.	1¼ qt.
3 c. + 2 T.	3⅓ c.	3½ c. + 2½ t.	1 qt.	4¼ c. + 3 T.	4¾ c. + 2 T. + 1 t.	1¼ qt. + ⅓ c.
3½ c.	3¾ c.	1 qt.	1 qt. + ½ c.	1¼ qt.	1¼ qt. + ½ c.	1½ qt.
3¾ c. + 2 T.	1 qt. + 2½ T.	4¼ c. + 3 T.	1¼ qt.	1¼ qt. + ⅓ c.	1½ qt. + 5 t.	1½ qt. + ⅔ c.
1 qt. + 4 t.	1 qt. + ¼ c. + 2 T.	1 qt. + ⅔ c.	1¼ qt. + ¼ c.	5½ c. + 3 T.	1½ qt. + ¼ c. + 2½ T.	1¾ qt.
1 qt. + ⅔ c.	1¼ qt.	1¼ qt. + ⅓ c.	1½ qt.	1½ qt. + ⅔ c.	1¾ qt. + ⅓ c.	2 qt.
1¼ qt. + ¼ c.	1¼ qt. + ⅔ c.	1½ qt.	1½ qt. + ¾ c.	1¾ qt. + ½ c.	2 qt. + ¼ c.	2¼ qt.
5¼ c. + 3 T.	5¾ c. + 1½ T.	1½ qt. + ¼ c.	1¾ qt.	1¾ qt. + ¾ c.	2 qt. + ½ c. + 1 T.	2¼ qt. + ⅓ c.
5¾ c. + 1 T.	1½ qt. + ¼ c.	1½ qt. + ⅔ c.	1¾ qt. + ½ c.	2 qt. + 5 T.	2¼ qt. + 3 T.	2½ qt.

TABLE 3 Direct-Reading Table for Adjusting Yield of Recipes with Ingredient Amounts Given in Measurement (*Continued*)

56	60	64	72	80	88	96
1½ qt. + ¼ c.	1½ qt. + ⅔ c.	1¾ qt. + 2 T.	2 qt.	2 qt. + ¾ c. + 2 T.	2¼ qt. + ¾ c. + ½ T.	2½ qt. + ⅔ c.
1½ qt. + ¼ c. + 3 T.	1½ qt. + ¾ c. + 2 T.	1¾ qt. + ⅓ c.	2 qt. + ¼ c.	2¼ qt. + 2½ T.	2½ qt. + 1½ T.	2¾ qt.
1¾ qt.	1¾ qt. + ½ c.	2 qt.	2¼ qt.	2½ qt.	2¾ qt.	3 qt.
1¾ qt. + ⅓ c. + ¼ c.	2 qt. + 2 T.	2 qt. + ⅔ c.	2¼ qt. + ¾ c.	2½ qt. + ¾ c. + 1½ T.	2¾ qt. + ¾ c. + 3 T.	3¼ qt.
1¾ qt. + ¾ c.	2 qt. + ⅓ c.	2 qt. + ¾ c. + 2 T.	2½ qt.	2¾ qt. + 2 T.	3 qt. + ¼ c.	3¼ qt. + ⅓ c.
2 qt. + 3 T.	2 qt. + ¾ c.	2¼ qt. + ⅓ c.	2½ qt. + ½ c.	2¾ qt. + ½ c. + 2 T.	3 qt. + ¾ c. + 1½ T.	3½ qt.
2 qt. + ½ c. + 1 T.	2¼ qt. + 2½ T.	2¼ qt. + ¾ c.	2¾ qt.	3 qt. + ¼ c.	3¼ qt. + ¼ c. + 3 T.	3 qt. + 2⅔ c.
2 qt. + ¾ c.	2¼ qt. + ¼ c. + 2 T.	2½ qt.	2¾ qt. + ¼ c.	3 qt. + ½ c.	3 qt. + 1¾ c.	3 qt. + 3 c.
2 qt. + 1⅓ c.	2½ qt.	2¾ qt. + ⅓ c.	3 qt.	3 qt. + 1⅓ c.	3 qt. + 2⅔ c.	1 gal.
2¾ qt. + ⅔ c.	3 qt. + ½ c.	3¼ qt. + ⅓ c.	3¾ qt.	1 gal. + ⅔ c.	1 gal. + 2⅓ c.	1¼ gal.
3½ qt.	3¾ qt.	1 gal.	1 gal. + 2 c.	1¼ gal.	1¼ gal. + 2 c.	1½ gal.
1 gal. + ⅓ c.	1 gal. + 1½ c.	1 gal. + 2⅔ c.	1¼ gal. + 1 c.	1¼ gal. + 3⅓ c.	1½ gal. + 1⅔ c.	1¾ gal.
1 gal. + 2⅔ c.	1¼ gal.	1¼ gal. + 1⅓ c.	1½ gal.	1½ gal. + 2⅔ c.	1¾ gal. + 1⅓ c.	2 gal.

56	60	64	72	80	88	96
1¼ gal. + 1 c.	1¼ gal. + 2½ c.	1½ gal.	1½ gal. + 3 c.	1¾ gal. + 2 c.	2 gal. + 1 c.	2¼ gal.
1¼ gal. + 3⅓ c.	1½ gal. + 1 c.	1½ gal. + 2⅔ c.	1¾ gal. + 2 c.	2 gal. + 1⅓ c.	2¼ gal. + ⅔ c.	2½ gal.
1½ gal. + 1⅔ c.	1½ gal. + 3½ c.	1¾ gal. + 1⅓ c.	2 gal. + 1 c.	2¼ gal. + ⅔ c.	2½ gal. + ⅓ c.	2¾ gal.
1¾ gal.	1¾ gal. + 2 c.	2 gal.	2¼ gal.	2½ gal.	2¾ gal.	3 gal.
1¾ gal. + 2⅓ c.	2 gal. + ½ c.	2 gal. + 2⅔ c.	2¼ gal. + 3 c.	2½ gal. + 3⅓ c.	2¾ gal. + 3⅔ c.	3¼ gal.
2 gal. + ⅔ c.	2 gal. + 3 c.	2¼ gal. + 1⅓ c.	2½ gal. + 2 c.	2¾ gal. + 2⅔ c.	3 gal. + 3⅓ c.	3½ gal.
2 gal. + 3 c.	2¼ gal. + 1½ c.	2½ gal.	2¾ gal. + 1 c.	3 gal. + 2 c.	3¼ gal. + 3 c.	3¾ gal.
2¼ gal. + 1⅓ c.	2½ gal.	2½ gal. + 2⅔ c.	3 gal.	3¼ gal. + 1⅓ c.	3½ gal. + 2⅔ c.	4 gal.
2¾ gal. + 2⅔ c.	3 gal. + 2 c.	3¼ gal. + 1⅓ c.	3¾ gal.	4 gal. + 2⅔ c.	4½ gal. + 1⅓ c.	5 gal.
3½ gal.	3¾ gal.	4 gal.	4½ gal.	5 gal.	5½ gal.	6 gal.

TABLE 4   Guide for Rounding off Weights and Measures[1]

Item	If the total amount of an ingredient is	Round it to
	WEIGHTS	
	less than 2 oz.	measure unless wt. is in ¼, ½, ¾ oz. amounts
	2 oz.–10 oz.	closest ¼ oz. or convert to measure
Various miscellaneous ingredients	more than 10 oz. but less than 2 lb. 8 oz.	closest ½ oz.
	2 lb. 8 oz.–5 lb.	closest full oz.
	more than 5 lb.	closest ¼ lb.
	MEASURES	
	less than 1 T.	closest ⅛ t.
Primarily spices,	more than 1 T. but less than 3 T.	closest ¼ t.
seasonings, flavorings,	3 T.–½ c.	closest ½ t. or convert to weight
condiments, leavenings,	more than ½ c. but less than ¾ c.	closest full t. or convert to weight
and similar items	more than ¾ c. but less than 2 c.	closest full T. or convert to weight
	2 c.–2 qt.	nearest ¼ c.
	more than 2 qt. but less than 4 qt.	nearest ½ c.
Primarily milk,	1 gal.–2 gal.	nearest full c. or ¼ qt.
water, eggs, juice, oil,	more than 2 gal. but less than 10 gal.	nearest full qt.
syrup, molasses, etc.	more than 10 gal. but less than 20 gal.	closest ½ gal.
	over 20 gal.	closest full gal.

Note:
These values for rounding have been calculated to be within the limits of error normally introduced in the handling of ingredients in preparing foods. They are intended to aid in "rounding" fractions and complex measurements and weights into amounts that are as simple as possible to weigh or measure while maintaining the accuracy needed for quality control in products.

[1] From *Standardizing Recipes for Institutional Use.* The American Dietetic Association, 1967.

Weighing and Measuring Ingredients

WEIGHING

Weighing ingredients, when possible, is recommended since it is more accurate. Reliable scales are essential. A table model scale, 15 to 20 lb. capacity, with $\frac{1}{4}$ to $\frac{1}{2}$ oz. gradations, is suitable for weighing ingredients for 50 portions.

MEASURING

When measuring, use standard measuring equipment and make measurements level. Use the largest appropriate measure to reduce the possibility of error and to save time. Example: Use a 1-gallon measure once instead of a 1-quart measure four times. (Flour is the exception. Use measure no larger than 1 quart for flour.)

CONVERTING FROM WEIGHT TO MEASURE

If accurate scales are not available or if scales do not have gradations for weighing small amounts, the weights of ingredients may need to be converted to measures. The following tables will be helpful:

Food Weights and Approximate Equivalents in Measure (pp. 19–29)
Weight (1–16 oz.) and Measure Equivalents for Commonly Used Foods (pp. 34–37)
Basic Information on Equivalents in Table 2 (p. 45)
Fractional Equivalents (p. 33)
A Guide for Rounding off Weights and Measures (p. 58)

Example: To convert ingredients in Plain Muffins (p. 100): Turn to Food Weights and Approximate Equivalents in Measure (p. 22). Change 2 lb. 8 oz. ($2\frac{1}{2}$ lb.) flour to measure by multiplying by 4 c. The resulting 10 c. would be equivalent to $2\frac{1}{2}$ qt. (p. 45). By referring to the table on p. 34, the 2 oz. baking powder, 6 oz. sugar, and 8 oz. fat may be quickly converted by finding the amount in the appropriate columns. The same information is included in the longer table (pp. 19–29), but for conversion of small amounts of commonly used foods, the table beginning on p. 34 is useful.

Food Substitutions and Proportions
Approximate Equivalent Substitutions

Ingredient	Approximate Equivalent
Thickening Agents	
1 oz. flour	3½ whole eggs (5½ oz.) 7 egg yolks (5 oz.) 1⅓ oz. quick-cooking tapioca ⅔ oz. cornstarch ½ oz. waxy maize ¾ oz. bread crumbs
1 T. flour	½ T. cornstarch ½ T. waxy maize 2 t. quick-cooking tapioca
Shortening Agents	
1 lb. butter	1 lb. margarine ⅞ lb. hydrogenated shortening plus 1 t. salt ⅞ lb. lard plus 1 t. salt ⅞ lb. oil (1⅜ c.) plus 1 t. salt ⅞ lb. chicken fat plus 1 t. salt
Leavening Agents*	
1 t. baking powder	¼ t. soda plus ⅝ t. cream of tartar ¼ t. soda plus ½ c. sour milk ¼ t. soda plus ½ T. vinegar used with 7½ T. sweet milk ¼ t. soda plus ¼ to ½ c. molasses 2 egg whites
1 small pkg. active dry yeast	1 cake compressed yeast
1 oz. dry yeast	2 oz. compressed yeast
Chocolate and Cocoa	
1 oz. or 1 square chocolate	3 T. cocoa plus 1 T. fat

Approximate Equivalent Substitutions (*Continued*)

Ingredient	Approximate Equivalent
Milk	
1 c. whole milk	¼ c. (approximately) dry whole milk* plus 1 c. water 3 T. instant nonfat dry milk powder* plus 1 c. water and 3 T. butter 6 T. nonfat dry milk crystals plus 1 c. water and 3 T. butter ½ c. evaporated milk plus ½ c. water
1 c. sour milk**	1 c. sweet milk plus 1 T. lemon juice or vinegar
Cream	
1 c. cream, thin (18–20%)	⅞ c. milk plus 3 T. butter
1 c. cream, heavy (36–40%)	¾ c. milk plus ⅓ c. butter
Flour	
1 c. all purpose flour	1 c. plus 2 T. cake flour ⅞ c. corn meal 1 c. graham flour 1 c. rye flour 1¼ c. bran 1½ c. bread crumbs 1 c. rolled oats
Seasoning	
1 medium-size onion	1 T. instant minced onion

* A general guide is to use 3.2 oz., by weight, of instant or regular spray process nonfat dry milk to make 1 qt. of liquid milk; or 4.5 oz. of dry whole milk per qt.

** To substitute sour milk or buttermilk for sweet milk, add ½ t. soda and decrease baking powder by 2 t. per cup of milk. To sour reconstituted dry milk, add 1 c. cultured buttermilk to 1 gal. reconstituted dry milk.

Relative Proportions of Ingredients

Ingredient	Relative Proportion
Thickening Agents	
Eggs	4–6 whole eggs to 1 qt. milk 8–12 egg yolks to 1 qt. milk 8–12 egg whites to 1 qt. milk
Flour°	½ oz. to 1 qt. liquid—very thin sauce (cream soups, starchy vegetables) 1 oz. to 1 qt. liquid—thin sauce (cream soups, nonstarchy vegetables) 2 oz. to 1 qt. liquid—medium sauce (creamed dishes, gravy) 3–4 oz. to 1 qt. liquid—thick sauce (soufflés) 4–5 oz. to 1 qt. liquid—very thick sauce (croquettes) 1 lb. to 1 qt. liquid—pour batter (popovers) 2 lb. to 1 qt. liquid—drop batter (cake muffins) 3 lb. to 1 qt. liquid—soft dough (biscuit, rolls) 4 lb. to 1 qt. liquid—stiff dough (pastry, cookies, noodles)
Gelatin	2 T. to 1 qt. liquid—plain jellies (gelatin and fruit juices) 2 T. to 1 qt. liquid—whips (gelatin and fruit juices whipped) 3 T. to 1 qt. liquid—fruit jellies (gelatin, fruit juices, and chopped fruit) 3 T. to 1 qt. liquid—vegetable jellies (gelatin, liquid, and chopped vegetables) 3 T. to 1 qt. liquid—sponges (gelatin, fruit juices, and beaten egg whites) 4 T. to 1 qt. liquid—Bavarian cream (gelatin, fruit juice, fruit pulp, and whipped cream)

° For thickening equivalents for flour, see p. 60.

Relative Proportions of Ingredients (Continued)

Ingredient	Relative Proportion
Seasonings	
Salt	1–2 t. to 1 lb. flour 1¼ t. to 1 lb. meat 2 t. to 1 qt. water (cereal) 2½ t. to 1 pt. liquid (rolls)
Leavening Agents	
Baking powder, quick acting (tartrate or phosphate)	2–2⅔ T. to 1 lb. flour
Baking powder, slow acting (S.A.S. or combination)	1½–2 T. to 1 lb. flour
Baking soda	2 t. to 1 qt. sour milk or molasses
Yeast	½–1 compressed cake (3/10–3/5 oz.) or ½–1 envelope dry (⅛–¼ oz.) to 1 lb. flour (varies with ingredients and time allowed)

Dry Milk Solids[1]

The substitution of dry milk for fluid milk is becoming increasingly important in institutional food services because of the comparatively low cost of dry milk and its ease in handling and storage. It is available as whole, nonfat, and buttermilk. Nonfat dry milk is pure fresh milk from which only the fat and water have been removed. It has better keeping qualities than dry whole milk, although both should be kept dry and cool. There are on the market different types and kinds of nonfat dry milk of equal nutritional food value. Instant nonfat milk is the type that is readily reconstituted in liquid form. Whatever the type, it may be used in dry form or reconstituted as fluid milk.

When dry milk is used in recipes containing a large proportion of dry ingredients, such as bread, biscuits, and cakes, the only change in method would be to mix the unsifted dry milk with the other dry ingredients and use water in place of fluid milk. For best results, dry milk should be weighed rather than measured. Package directions for reconstituting dry milk solids should be followed. A general guide is to use 3.2 oz., by weight, of instant or regular spray process nonfat dry milk to make one quart of liquid milk; or 4.5 oz. of dry whole milk per quart.

Additional amounts of nonfat dry milk may be added to some foods to supplement their nutritional value. Reconstituted milk may be used immediately for cooking purposes. It should be refrigerated for several hours if it is to be used as a beverage. General rules for the use of instant nonfat dry milk follow:[1]

Ground Meats, Fish, or Chicken. ½ c.–¾ c. instant nonfat dry milk to each pound of ground meat. Mix with meat, fluid, or crumbs.
Cooked Cereal. Mix equal mesasurement of instant nonfat dry milk and cereal before cooking, then cook as directed on cereal package.
Mashed Vegetables. Such as potatoes, squash, sweet potatoes, rutabagas, and turnips. Add ⅓ c. instant nonfat dry milk to each 2 c. of mashed vegetable— use cooking water to give the right consistency. Season with butter, or margarine, salt, and pepper.
Sauces, Gravies, Soups, and Custards. Add 4 T. instant nonfat dry milk to each cup of fluid milk or ½ c. instant nonfat dry milk to each cup of water or broth in recipe.

Instant nonfat dry milk, when used with flour or crumbs for breading the food should be oven fried because the higher temperature of kettle frying causes the product to brown too rapidly.

[1] Adapted from *Instant Nonfat Dry Milk in Family Meals*, Bulletin No. 522, American Dry Milk Institute, Inc., Chicago, Illinois.

Nonfat dry milk is satisfactory in pudding recipes, sauces, and entrée items, but is not recommended for instant puddings of the uncooked variety.

Egg Products[1]

Whole eggs, whites, yolks, and various blends are processed and are available in liquid, frozen, and dried forms. Only those egg products that bear the U.S.D.A. inspection mark should be purchased. This stamp indicates that the products were prepared from wholesome eggs, pasteurized, cooled, and packaged under sanitary conditions in accordance with the U.S.D.A. regulations governing the grading and inspection of egg products.

Thawed frozen eggs and reconstituted dried eggs are highly perishable, and careful handling by the user is essential to prevent contamination. To insure such safety, the guides that follow should be observed.

GUIDES FOR STORING, THAWING, AND RECONSTITUTING

Frozen Eggs. Store in freezer at 0° F. or below. Thaw only the amount needed at one time. Thaw in refrigerator, or to speed thawing place container in cold running water without submerging it. Use thawed eggs immediately, or refrigerate promptly in an airtight container and use within 24 hours.

Dried Eggs. Store unopened packages in cool, dry place where temperature is not more than 50° F., preferably in refrigerator. After opening, refrigerate any unused portion in container with a close-fitting lid. Reconstitute only the amount needed at one time. Reconstitute by blending with water, or combine with other dry ingredients in recipe and add amount of water needed to reconstitute. Use reconstituted eggs immediately, or refrigerate promptly in an airtight container and use within 1 hour.

Purchasing Egg Products. Frozen egg products usually are packed in 10-lb., 30-lb., or 45-lb. containers. Dried whole eggs are packed in 13-oz., 3-lb., or 150-lb. containers. Egg whites or yolks or a blend of the two are packed in 3-lb. containers. Equivalents of egg products as a guide for purchasing:

[1] Adapted from U.S. Department of Agriculture, *Egg Products Inspection*, PA-886, July, 1968.

Product	Whole Eggs per lb.	Egg Yolks per lb.	Egg Whites per lb.
Frozen	10	26	16
Dried	32	54	100

Egg products needed to replace a specific number of whole eggs, egg yolks, or egg whites is shown as follows:

Product	Amount of Product to Use	Shell Egg Equivalent
Frozen (thawed)		
Whole	3 T.	1 egg
Whole	2¼ c.	12 eggs
Yolks	1⅓ T.	1 egg
Yolks	1 c.	12 eggs
Whites	2 T.	1 egg
Whites	1½ c.	12 eggs
Dried (sifted)		
Whole	2½ T. + 2½ T. water	1 egg
Whole	2 c. + 2 c. water	12 eggs
Yolks	2 T. + 2 t. water	1 egg
Yolks	1½ c. + ½ c. water	12 eggs
Whites	2 t. + 2 T. water	1 egg
Whites	½ c. + 1½ c. water	12 eggs

Baking Temperatures

Terms for Oven Temperatures

Term	Temperature	
	Degrees F.	Degrees C.
Very slow	250–275	121–135
Slow	300–325	149–163
Moderate	350–375	177–191
Hot	400–425	205–219
Very hot (quick)	450–475	232–246
Extremely hot	500–525	260–274

Temperatures and Times Used in Baking

Type of Product	Approximate Time Required for Baking* (Minutes)	Oven Temperature Degrees F.	Degrees C.
Bread			
Biscuits	10–15	425–450	218–232
Corn Bread	30–40	400–425	204–218
Cream puffs	40–60	375	191
Muffins	20–25	400–425	204–218
Popovers	60	375	191
Quick loaf bread	60–75	350–375	177–191
Yeast bread	30–40	400	204
Yeast rolls: plain	15–25	400–425	204–218
sweet	20–30	375	191
Cakes, with fat			
Cup	15–25	350–375	177–191
Layer	20–35	350–375	177–191
Loaf	45–60	350	177
Cakes, without fat			
Angel food and sponge	30–45	350–375	177–191
Cookies			
Drop	8–15	350–400	177–204
Rolled	8–10	375	191
Egg, meat, milk, cheese dishes			
Cheese soufflé (baked in pan of hot water)	30–60	350	177
Custard, plain, corn, other (baked in pan of hot water)	30–60	350	177
Macaroni and cheese	25–30	350	177
Meat loaf	60–90	300	149
Meat pie	25–30	400	204
Rice pudding (raw rice)	120–180	300	149
Scalloped potatoes	60	350	177
Pastry			
1-crust pie (custard type)	30–40	400–425	204–218
Meringue on cooked filling in preheated shell	12–15	350	177
	or		
	4–4½	425	218
Shell only	10–12	450	232
2-crust pies and uncooked filling in prebaked shell	45–55	400–425	204–218
2-crust pies with cooked filling	30–45	425–450	218–232

* For convection ovens follow time and temperature recommendations of manufacturer.

Sirups and Candies

Temperatures and Tests for Sirups and Candies

Product	Temperature of Sirup at Sea Level (Indicating Concentration Desired)*		Test	Description of Test
	Degrees F.	Degrees C.		
Sirup	230–234	110–112	Thread	Sirup spins a 2-in. thread when dropped from fork or spoon.
Fondant Fudge Penoche	234–240	112–115	Soft ball	When dropped into very cold water, sirup forms a soft ball which flattens on removal from water.
Caramels	244–248	118–120	Firm ball	When dropped into very cold water, sirup forms a firm ball which does not flatten on removal from water.
Divinity Marshmallows Popcorn balls	250–266	121–130	Hard ball	When dropped into very cold water, sirup forms a ball which is hard enough to hold its shape, yet plastic.
Butterscotch Taffies	270–290	132–143	Soft crack	When dropped into very cold water, sirup separates into threads, which are hard but not brittle.
Brittle Glacé	300–310	149–154	Hard crack	When dropped into very cold water, sirup separates into threads which are hard and brittle.
Barley sugar	320	160	Clear liquid	Sugar liquefies.
Caramel	338	170	Brown liquid	Liquid becomes brown.

* Cook sirup about 1° C. lower than temperature at sea level for each increase of 900 ft. in elevation, or 1° F. lower than temperature at sea level for each increase of 500 ft. in elevation.

SUGAR SIRUPS

Sugar Sirup (Thin) 2 lb. sugar and 1 qt. water, boil together; for a thicker sirup increase sugar to 2½ lb. and add 1 T. corn sirup to prevent crystallization. May be kept on hand for use in beverages or where recipe specifies simple sirup.

Burnt Sugar Sirup or *Caramel Flavoring* 1 lb. sugar and 1 pt. boiling water. Put sugar in a pan and melt slowly, stirring constantly. Cook until light brown (caramelized), being careful not to scorch. Add boiling water. Cook slowly until a sirup is formed.

Deep-Fat Frying

METHODS OF PREPARING FOOD FOR DEEP-FAT FRYING

Light Coating. Dip prepared food in milk. Drain. Dredge with seasoned flour. (Use 1 lb. flour, 2 T. salt, and other seasonings as desired.)

Egg and Crumb. Dip prepared food in flour (may omit), then in a mixture of egg and milk or water. Drain and roll in fine crumbs to cover. (Use 3 eggs to 1 c. milk or water for most products. In some cases 1 egg to 1 c. milk may be satisfactory. For soft mixtures, such as Egg Cutlets, use 6 eggs to 1 c. liquid.) Allow 12 oz. crumbs for 50 servings of most items.

Batter. Dip prepared food in a batter made in the following proportions: 12 oz. flour, 1½ t. salt, 2 t. baking powder, 3 T. melted fat, 2 c. milk, and 6 well-beaten eggs. This quantity is sufficient for 50 servings of most items.

CARE OF FAT AND FRYER

For best results, select a bland-flavored frying fat with a high smoking point. Use the amount of fat recommended for the fryer, which should be enough to cover the food entirely. Clarify the fat regularly at least once a day when fryer is in constant use to remove accumulated sediment. This may be done by straining the fat through cheesecloth or by following instructions provided by the fryer manufacturer. Thoroughly wash, rinse, and dry fryer before replacing strained fat, then add enough fresh fat to bring back the required weight or amount necessary for best use of the deep fat frying equipment.

Proper care will prolong the life of the fat; but when undesirable flavors develop, fat should be discarded.

Deep-Fat Frying Temperatures

Type of Product	Preparation	Temperature Degrees F.	Frying Time* Minutes
Bananas	Skin and scrape. Cut in pieçes 2 in. long. Sprinkle with powdered sugar and lemon juice. Let stand 30 min. Dip in batter.	375	1–3
Cauliflower, precooked	See p. 404	370	3–5
Cheese balls	See p. 295	360	2–3
Chicken, disjointed,			
1½–2 lb. fryers	Light coating or egg and crumb†	325	10–12
2–2½ lb. fryers	Light coating or egg and crumb	325	12–15
Chicken, half			
1½–2 lb. fryers	Light coating or egg and crumb	325	12–15
Croquettes (all previously cooked foods)		360–375	2–5
Cutlets, ½ in. thick	Egg and crumb	325–350	5–8
Doughnuts	See p. 108	360–375	3–5
Eggplant	See p. 404	370	5–7
Fish fillets	Egg and crumb	375	4–6
Fritters	See p. 112	370–380	2–5
Onion rings	Batter	350	3–4
Oysters	Egg and crumb	375	2–4
Potatoes, ½ in.	See p. 404, 412		
Complete fry		365	6–8
Blanching		360	3–5
Browning		375	2–3
Frozen, fat blanched		375	2–3
Sandwiches	See p. 355	350–360	3–4
Scallops	Egg and crumb	360–375	3–4
Shrimp	Batter or egg and crumb	360–375	3–5
Timbale cases	See p. 112	350–365	2–3
Fish sticks	Egg and crumb	375	3–4
French toast	See p. 134	360	3–4

* The exact frying time will vary with the equipment used, size and temperature of the food pieces, and the amount of food placed in the fryer at one time. If the kettle is overloaded, foods may become grease-soaked. If food is frozen, use lower temperatures listed and allow additional cooking time.

† See p. 69 for directions for egg and crumb.

Note:

At high altitudes, the lower boiling point of water in foods requires lowering of temperatures for deep-fat frying.

Spices and Seasonings

Use of Spices and Seasonings in Cooking

Spice	Use
Allspice, whole	Pickling, gravies, consommé, boiled fish and meat, eggplant, tomatoes, baked beans.
Allspice, ground	Baked products, puddings, relishes, some fruit preserves, gravies.
Anise seed, whole or ground	Coffee cakes, sweet rolls, cookies, candies.
Basil, whole or ground	Tomato juice, beef stew, chicken, tomatoes, Lima beans, peas, French dressing.
Bay leaves (laurel)	Pickling, stews, soups, roast beef, beets, tomatoes, kidney beans, string beans, eggplant.
Caraway seed, whole or ground	Rye bread, sprinkled over pork liver, or kidney before cooking.
Cardamom (cardamum)	Pickling, flavoring in coffee cakes, Danish pastry, curries, and soups.
Celery seed, whole or ground	Pickling, salads, fish, salad dressings, cream cheese spread, ham spread, beef stew, meat loaf, croquettes, cabbage, cauliflower, onions, cole slaw.
Cayenne pepper	Lima beans, meats, fish, sauces, Mexican dishes.
Chili powder	Chili con carne, tamales, shell fish and oyster cocktail, sauces, cooked eggs, kidney beans, Spanish rice, meat sauces, gravies.
Cinnamon, ground	Puddings, pastry, rolls.
Cinnamon stick and Cassibuds	Pickling, preserving, stewed fruits.
Cloves, whole	Pickling, hams, fruits, string beans.
Cloves, ground	Baked products, desserts, cranberry juice, tomato soup, Mulligatawny soup, pot roast, boiled beef, beets, onions, sweet potatoes, tomato sauce, tomato aspic.
Coriander, whole or ground	Pickling, curries, baked products.
Cumin (Cumino), whole	Mexican cookery, sausages, stews, soups. (Ingredient of curry and chili powder.)
Curry powder	Mulligatawny soup, lamb, veal stew, chicken, rice dishes, fish.
Dill seed, whole or ground	Pickling, sauerkraut, cabbage, cauliflower, turnips.
Fennel seed	Italian and Swedish cookery.
Ginger, whole	Pickling, beverages.
Ginger, ground	Baked products, barbecue sauce, pear salad.
Horseradish	Sauces, relishes.
Mace, ground	Fish, fish sauces, pickling, preserving, baked products, pastries, tomato juice.

Use of Spices and Seasonings in Cooking (Continued)

Spice	Use
Marjoram, leaf or ground	Soups, stews, sausage, lamb, tomatoes, Swiss chard, spinach, peas, cottage cheese, French dressing.
Mint leaves	Peas, lamb, iced tea, sauces.
Mustard seed, whole	Pickling, salad garnish.
Mustard seed, ground	Salad dressing, sauces, baked beans, sandwich fillings.
Nutmeg, ground	Sauces (dessert), chicken, sweet potatoes, spinach, cauliflower, baked products, puddings, eggnog.
Oregano leaves (Mexican sage)	Pork. (Ingredient of chili powder.)
Paprika	Fish, salad dressing, garnishes, corn, stews.
Peppercorn (white and black)	Pickling, soups, meats.
Pepper, ground (white and black)	Meat, sauces, gravies, vegetables.
Poppy seed	Cake, cookies, topping for breads.
Rosemary leaves	Italian sausages, Italian dishes.
Sage, leaf or ground	Stuffing, sausage, cheese, soup, sauces.
Saffron	Baked products, special dishes.
Savory leaves	Poultry, meat.
Sesame seed	Rolls, breads.
Thyme, leaf or ground	Stews, meat loaf, soups, stuffing.
Tarragon leaves	Vinegar, dressing, pickles, sauces, mustard.
Turmeric, ground	Ingredient of curry powder, coloring for condiments.

Cookery Terms

COOKING PROCESSES AND METHODS

Baking. Cooking by dry heat, usually in an oven but occasionally on heated metals. This term is used interchangeably with **roasting** when applied to meats in uncovered containers.

Barbecuing. Roasting slowly, usually basting with a highly seasoned sauce.

Basting. Moistening meat or other food while cooking to add flavor and to prevent drying of the surface. Melted fat, meat drippings, water, or water and fat may be used for basting.

Beating. A brisk regular motion that lifts a mixture over and over and thereby introduces air or makes the mixture smooth.

Blanching. Preheating in boiling water or steam (1) to remove inactive enzymes and shrink food for canning, freezing, and drying; (2) to aid in the removal of skins from nuts, fruits, and some vegetables.

Blending. Thoroughly mixing two or more ingredients.

Boiling. Cooking in water or a liquid, mostly water, in which the bubbles are breaking on the surface and steam is given off. The boiling temperature of water at sea level is 100° C. (212° F.) but will be approximately 1° C. less for every 1000-foot elevation. The boiling point will be increased by the solution of solids in the water.

Braising. Cooking slowly in a covered utensil in a small amount of liquid. Meat stock, water, milk, or cream may be used for the liquid. (Meat may or may not be browned in a small amount of fat before braising).

Breading. Dipping a food into an egg-milk mixture and then into fine dry crumbs.

Broiling. Cooking by direct heat. This may be done by placing the food under or over a clear flame.

Candying. Cooking in heavy sirup until plump and transparent, then draining and drying.

Caramelizing. Heating sugar, or food containing a high percentage of sugar, until a brown color and a characteristic flavor develops.

Chopping. Cutting food into fairly fine pieces with a knife or other sharp tool.

Creaming. The working of one or more foods until soft and creamy. This term is ordinarily applied to the mixing of fat and sugar.

Crisping. Heating foods such as cereals or crackers to remove excessive moisture.

Cutting in. The combining of a solid fat with dry ingredients by a horizontal motion with knives or mixer. A fat is thus combined with dry ingredients with the least amount of blending.

Dicing. Cutting into cubes.

Dredging. Coating or sprinkling a food with flour or other fine substance.

Egging and Crumbing. Dipping a food into diluted, slightly beaten egg, and dredging with crumbs. This treatment is used to prevent soaking of the food with fat or to form a surface easily browned.

Folding. Combining ingredients by using two motions, cutting vertically through the mixture, and turning over and over by sliding the implement across the bottom of the mixing bowl with each turn.

Fricasseeing. Cooking by browning in a small amount of fat, then stewing or steaming. This method is most often applied to fowl or veal cut into pieces.

Frizzling. Cooking in a small amount of fat to produce a food that is crisp and brown with curled edges.

Frying. Cooking in hot fat. The food may be cooked in a small amount of fat (also called sautéing or pan frying), or in a deep layer of fat (also called deep-fat frying).

Glacéing. Coating with a thin sugar sirup cooked to the crack stage. It may also refer to a less concentrated mixture containing thickening, and used for coating certain types of rolls or pastries.

Grilling. Cooking by direct heat.

Grinding. Changing a food to small particles.

Kneading. Manipulation with a pressing motion accompanied by folding and stretching.

Larding. The insertion of small strips of fat (lardoons) into or on top of uncooked lean meat or fish, to give flavor or prevent dryness.

Marinating. Placing a food into a marinade (usually an oil-acid mixture, such as French dressing).

Melting. Liquefying by the application of heat.

Mincing. Cutting or chopping food into very small pieces—not so fine and regular as grinding, yet finer than those produced by chopping.

Mixing. Uniting two or more ingredients.

Pan-Broiling. Cooking, uncovered, on hot metal, such as a fry pan. The fat is removed as it accumulates. Liquid is never added.

Pan-Frying. Cooking in a small amount of fat. (See *Frying.*)

Parboiling. Partially cooking a food by boiling, the cooking being completed by another method.

Parching. Browning by the application of dry heat usually applied to grains of corn.

Paring. Cutting off the outside covering, usually with a knife.

Peeling. Stripping off the outside covering.

Planking. Cooking or serving a food, usually fish or steak, on a hot wooden board or plank made especially for this purpose.

Poaching. Cooking in a hot liquid, the original shape of the food being retained.

Pot-Roasting. Cooking large cuts of meat by braising.

Reconstituting. Restoring concentrated foods to their normal state, usually by adding water. Applied to such foods as dry milk (for fluid milk) or frozen orange juice (for liquid juice).

Rehydration. Cooking, soaking, or using other procedures with dehydrated foods to restore water lost during drying.

Roasting. Cooking uncovered by dry heat. The term is usually applied to meat.

Sautéing. Cooking in a small amount of fat. (See *Frying*).

Scalding. Heating a liquid to a point just below boiling.

Scalloping. Baking food, usually cut into pieces and covered with a liquid or sauce and crumbs. The food and sauce may be mixed together or arranged in alternate layers in a baking dish, with or without crumbs. *Escalloped* is a synonymous term.

Scoring. Making shallow lengthwise and crosswise slits on the surface of meat.

Searing. Browning the surface of meat by the application of intense heat for a short time.

Simmering. Cooking in a liquid in which bubbles form slowly and break just below the surface. The temperatures range from 85° C. (185° F.) to a temperature just below the boiling point.

Steaming. Cooking in steam with or without pressure. Steam may be applied directly to the food, as in a steamer, or to the vessel, as in a double boiler.

Steeping. The process of extracting flavors, colors, or other qualities by adding boiling water and allowing the mixture to stand. The mixture is always just below the boiling point.

Stewing. Simmering in a small amount of liquid.

Stirring. Mixing food materials with a circular motion. Food materials are blended or made into a uniform consistency by this process.

Toasting. The application of direct heat until the surface of the food is browned.

Whipping. Rapid beating to increase volume by the incorporation of air.

PART TWO
RECIPES

RECIPES

General Information

YIELD

The recipes in this book provide servings for 50 people unless otherwise stated. It is recognized that many factors affect the probable yield, portioning possibly one of the most important. Yield also will vary with the type of food service, the clientele, and the skill of the employee serving the food.

Dippers numbered according to yield per quart and ladles for different portion weights are helpful in serving. The yield of dippers and ladles, given on p. 32, is based on level portions, so there could be variations if the food is liquid or very thick and if the server rounds or heaps the food into the dipper. If serving spoons are used, guidelines should be marked on the food in the pan or a portion weighed or measured to determine the correct quantity to serve.

A pan 12 x 20 x 2 in. has been indicated for many recipes in this book, as it is an accepted counter pan size. For some entrées, 2 12 x 20 x 2 in. pans were specified, especially in those having a crusty or crumb topping. For breads, gelatin salads, cakes, and other desserts that are to be cut into servings, the yield has been given as 48 rather than 50 because of ease of cutting. In some institutions where larger portions are needed a pan 12 x 20 x 2 in. may yield only 32 or 40 servings.

Bun pans 18 x 26 in. are often preferred for sheet cakes, rolls, jelly rolls, and cookies. A 9-in. round 2-layer cake is calculated to yield 14–16 servings, although an 8-in. pie will give only 6 servings. All recipe yields vary according to desired portion size, pan size, and the institutional policies of quality, i.e., whether broken or corner pieces are to be served.

The cooking time given in each recipe is based on the size of pan indicated and the amount of food in the pan. If a smaller or larger pan is used, the cooking time should be adjusted accordingly. The number of pans placed in the oven at one time may also affect the length of baking time.

VARIATIONS AND NOTES

Variations and notes have been placed at the bottom of many recipes. A variation may have one or more ingredients replaced, added, or deleted from the basic recipe. A note will include explanations and alternate methods of preparation.

WEIGHTS AND MEASURES

Quantities of most dry ingredients weighing more than 1 oz. are given by weight, and all liquids are indicated by measure. If measures are used in place of weights, a table of fractional equivalents can be referred to on p. 33. A table giving measure equivalents of weights 1–16 oz. of commonly used foods will assist in quick conversion of small quantities given in the recipes. For conversion of other foods, see p. 19. Careful weighing and measuring of ingredients are essential for a satisfactory product. Weights given are for food as purchased (A.P.) unless otherwise stated. If the weight is for edible portion, it is designated as E.P.

INGREDIENTS USED IN STANDARDIZING RECIPES

Flour. In flour mixtures, the exact ratio between the flour and liquid will vary with the kind of flour. Cake flour was used in cake recipes, and all purpose flour in other recipes.

Baking Powder. Sodium-aluminum-sulphate type baking powder (double acting) was used in all recipes.

Eggs. Fresh shell eggs weighing approximately 2 oz. each were used in the preparation of recipes.

Fats. High ratio and/or hydrogenated fats were used in cake and pastry recipes. Butter or margarine was used in cookies and most sauce recipes. Solid fats, such as butter, margarine, and hydrogenated fats, were used interchangeably in recipes that specify only "fat." Unsaturated fat, including corn and vegetable oil, was used in recipes that specify salad oil.

Increasing and Decreasing Recipes

It may be necessary to adapt the recipes in this book to meet the needs of individual situations. The following methods are presented as guidelines for increasing or decreasing recipe yields.

DIRECT READING TABLES

Three direct reading tables for increasing or decreasing recipes are provided. Table 1 (p. 39) is to be used when ingredients are stated in weights and when yields (known and desired) are divisible by 25. Tables 2 and 3 are based on ingredient measurement and recipe yields divisible by 25 (Table 2, p. 44) or 8 (Table 3, p. 49). These tables can be used together for recipes that include ingredients expressed in both weight and measurement.

FACTOR METHOD[1]

For recipes, as for soups or puddings, that do not need to be in quantities divisible by 25 or developed for stated pan sizes, the factor method may be preferred. To use this method:

1. Divide the *desired* yield by the *known* yield to obtain a basic **factor**.
2. Wherever possible, convert ingredients to weight.[2]
3. Multiply weights by the **factor**.
4. To check adjustment, total the original weights and multiply by the **factor**. This should equal the total of the adjusted weights.

ABBREVIATIONS USED IN RECIPES

f.d.	few drops
f.g.	few grains
t.	teaspoon
T.	tablespoon
c.	cup
pt.	pint
qt.	quart
gal.	gallon
oz.	ounce
lb.	pound
° F.	degrees Fahrenheit
A.P.	as purchased
E.P.	edible portion

[1] Adapted from *Standardizing Recipes for Institutional Use*. The American Dietetic Association, 1967.

[2] See Food Weights and Approximate Equivalents in Measure (p. 19), Guide for Rounding off Weights and Measures (p. 58), or Ounces and Decimal Equivalents of a Pound (p. 38) if using the decimal system.

APPETIZERS

Appetizers include hors d'oeuvres, canapés, cocktails, and soups, and are served at the beginning of a meal to stimulate the appetite. They should be attractive in appearance, pleasing in flavor, and well seasoned.

Hors d'Oeuvres and Canapés

Hors d'oeuvres are relishes served at the beginning of the meal. They may be canapés, olives, stuffed celery, deviled eggs, pickles, radishes, cheese, fish, sausages, or a combination. Hors d'oeuvres may be arranged on individual plates and served as the first course, or a tray containing a variety may be passed prior to seating the guests.

Canapés are made by spreading a well-seasoned mixture of eggs, cheese, fish, or meat on a canapé base and garnishing with a bit of some colorful or interesting food. A well-seasoned canapé mixture is often served in a bowl, accompanied by crisp crackers or chips. Guests "dip" into the mixture to make their own canapés.

HORS D'OEUVRES

Apple–Cheese. Core and cut crisp tart red apples into wedges. Dip in fruit juice to prevent discoloration. Spread with a bit of Roquefort cheese softened with cream, and spear each wedge with a toothpick. Arrange sections close together in a circle around a whole red apple.

Carrot Curls. See p. 317.

Cheese Puffs. Prepare Cream Puffs (p. 209) and drop on baking sheet by level teaspoonful. Combine 8 oz. cream cheese, 4½-oz. can deviled ham, 1 t. grated onion, 1 T. horseradish, ½ t. Worcestershire sauce, and ¼ t. pepper. Blend until smooth. Fill each tiny puff with cheese mixture (5 doz.).

Cheese Straws. See p. 113.

Cherry Tomatoes. Select uniform firm cherry tomatoes; wash, chill, and serve whole.

Chicken or Fish Puffs. Fill tiny cream puffs with chicken or fish salad.

Cocktail Wieners. Broil small cocktail-size wieners. Spear with cocktail picks and serve immediately.

Ginger–Cheese Balls. Combine 8-oz. package cream cheese, 2½ oz. crumbled Roquefort cheese, 2 T. candied ginger, shredded, and 2–4 T. cream. Mix well. Chill thoroughly. Make into small balls. Roll in chopped pecans.

Ham–Cheese Wedges. Spread 6 thin Pullman slices of ham or luncheon meat with whipped cream cheese and stack. Chill, cut into small wedges. Spear with cocktail picks.

Hot Cheese Balls. Prepare small cheese balls, using recipe on p. 295. Serve hot on cocktail picks with chilled tomato juice.

Hot Cheese Canapés. Combine 4 oz. sharp grated Cheddar cheese, ⅛ t. salt, and f.g. cayenne. Spread on toasted canapé base. Sprinkle with sesame seed. Toast and serve hot.

Cheese Wafers. Blend 4 oz. grated sharp Cheddar cheese and 8 oz. butter or margarine. Add ½ t. Worcestershire sauce, 6 oz. flour, ½ t. salt, and f.g. cayenne pepper, and mix thoroughly. Form into 1-in. roll. Wrap in waxed paper and chill for several hours. Slice in ¼-in. slices and bake on ungreased baking sheet for 12–15 min at 375° F.

Melon Cubes. Cut fresh honeydew, cantaloupe, or other melon into cubes. Dip in lemon juice and spear with cocktail picks.

Parsleyed Olives. Use a smooth cheese spread to cover small pimiento-stuffed olives. Roll in minced parsley and spear with colored cocktail picks.

Party Cheese Ball. Combine 3 oz. cream cheese, 4 oz. Blue cheese, 6 oz. sharp Cheddar cheese, 1 T. onion juice, f.d. Worcestershire sauce. Add 1 T. finely cut candied ginger if desired. Mix until smooth. Shape into a ball. Cover with pecans and chill. Serve in center of plate surrounded with crisp assorted crackers. Cheese mixture may also be formed into a long roll, wrapped in waxed paper, and chilled several hours. Slice and serve on crackers.

Pineapple–Shrimp. Spear a small whole shrimp and a pineapple cube on a cocktail pick. Serve with a cheese dip.

Strawberries. Arrange whole, perfect strawberries, with stems, around a bowl of sour cream.

Stuffed Celery. Cut prepared celery into 3-in. lengths and stuff with cream cheese and Roquefort dip, or pimiento cheese.

Stuffed Burr Gherkins. Place a whole almond in a half burr gherkin to form an "acorn," or stuff gherkin with red cherry.

Stuffed Cucumber. Pare cucumber and scoop out center. Fill with ham or shrimp mixture. Chill. Cut into ½-in. slices.

Stuffed Olives. Use ripe or green olives. Prepare thin carrot sticks about 3 in. long and pull 2 or 3 through center of each large pitted olive. Place in ice water to crisp.

CANAPÉS

Canapé bases may include bread slices, cut into various shapes with cookie or sandwich cutter, and toasted or sautéd on one side; thin slices of pan rolls, toasted or sautéd; crisp thin crackers, wafers, corn or potato chips, bread sticks, tiny plain or cheese biscuits, small pancakes, or puff pastry shells. A combination of these makes interesting canapé bases and offers a wide variety for the hors d'oeuvres tray. Suggested canapé spreads and dips follow:

Anchovy. Combine and blend 4 T. anchovy paste, 4 T. cream cheese, 2 T. minced chives, 1 t. lemon juice, and 1 T. soft butter. Spread on canapé bases. Garnish with watercress and/or riced yolk and egg white.

Avocado–Shrimp. Mash 2 soft avocados; season with 1 T. lemon juice, 1 T. minced onion, and f.g. salt. Spread on crackers or canapé bases and top each with small whole shrimp.

Crabmeat and Parmesan Cheese. Mix 1 c. crabmeat, 1 T. onion browned lightly in butter, ¼ c. Parmesan cheese, and mayonnaise to moisten. Spread on canapé bases. Garnish with thin strips of red pepper or pimiento.

Chicken or Ham. Combine 2 c. chicken or ham, finely chopped, with creamed butter seasoned with ½ t. curry powder or chutney. Spread on canapé bases. Garnish with watercress and/or paprika.

Cheese–Mushroom. Sauté a 4-oz. can mushrooms, drained, in 4 T. of butter or margarine. Add ¼ c. heavy cream, few drops of onion juice, salt, pepper, and ¾ c. Cheddar cheese. Mash to a paste. Spread toasted bread rounds with creamed butter and then cheese-mushroom mixture. Garnish with grated cheese and thinly sliced ripe olives.

Carrot. Combine ½ c. ground raw carrot with 1 grated hard-cooked egg, a few drops of onion juice, ½ t. lemon juice, and enough French dressing to moisten. Spread on canapé base. Garnish with thinly sliced stuffed olive or parsley.

Crab or Lobster. Moisten crab or lobster meat with mayonnaise. Add finely cut celery if desired. Pile on canapé base spread with sweet butter.

Crabmeat or Lobster with Egg. Mash 1 6-oz. can crabmeat or lobster. Add 2 chopped hard-cooked eggs, ½ t. prepared mustard, 2 T. mayonnaise, 1 T. lemon juice, ½ t. curry powder. Blend. Spread on canapé base.

Deviled Ham. Blend 3 oz. of canned deviled ham and 1 T. of mayonnaise. Spread on canapé bases that have been toasted on one side. Garnish with parsley.

Pâté de foie gras (or Liverwurst). Mash ½ lb. liverwurst; add 1 t. lemon juice, ½ t. Worcestershire sauce, and cream to moisten. Spread on canapé bases. Garnish with outside border of riced hard-cooked egg yolks mixed with mayonnaise to moisten and season, and an inside border of finely chopped hard-cooked egg whites. Sprinkle with chopped parsley.

Sardine. Mash and bone 3 oz. sardines. Add 2 T. lemon juice and French dressing to moisten. Spread canapé bases with creamed butter and then with sardine mixture. Garnish with riced egg yolk in center and a border of chopped hard-cooked egg whites.

Avocado Dip. Mash 2 ripe avocados and blend with 1 c. cultured sour cream, ¼ t. salt, 1 t. onion juice, 2 T. prepared horseradish. Serve with cooked chilled shrimp.

California Dip. Combine 1 pt. cultured sour cream with 1 1½-oz. package dry onion soup. Blend thoroughly. Serve with crackers, potato or corn chips.

Cheddar Cheese Dip. Blend 4 oz. sharp Cheddar cheese, grated, with 2 t. minced green onion, ½ c. mayonnaise, and ¼ t. salt. Just before serving add ¼ c. chopped crisp bacon. Garnish with ¼ c. chopped toasted almonds. Serve with crisp crackers.

Cheese Bowl. Mix 2 c. cottage cheese, 1 c. grated sharp Cheddar cheese, 2 T. horseradish, 3 finely chopped young green onions, f.g. cayenne, and 2 T. mayonnaise. Serve in bowl with crisp salty crackers.

Clam Dip. Combine 1 7-oz. can minced clams, 1 c. cottage cheese, 1 8-oz. package cream cheese, 2½ oz. Blue cheese, 2 t. lemon juice, 1½ t. Worcestershire sauce, ½ t. salt, f.d. Tabasco sauce. Thin with clam juice or cream. Blend well. Serve with crisp crackers, potato or corn chips.

Cream Cheese Dip. Blend 3 oz. cream cheese, 2 oz. crumbled Blue cheese, 1 t. onion juice, ⅛ t. salt, ⅛ t. pepper, f.d. Tabasco sauce, 2 T. cream. ¼ c. chopped pecans may be added. Serve with potato chips or pretzels.

Guacamole Dip. Mash 2 ripe avocados; add 1 T. lemon or lime juice, ½ t. salt, 1 T. finely grated onion, ½ t. chili powder, 1 ripe tomato, peeled and mashed. Mix well. Spread ¼ c. mayonnaise over top of mixture in a thin layer to prevent discoloration. Serve with potato chips or Melba toast.

Roquefort Dip. Blend 6 oz. cream cheese with 1 oz. Roquefort cheese; then fold in 1 c. whipped cream. Serve in bowl, garnish with paprika.

Tuna–Pineapple Dip. Blend 1 6½-oz. can tuna, 9 oz. drained crushed pineapple, 8 oz. cream cheese, and 3 T. pineapple juice. Serve in bowl with potato chips.

Cocktails

Cocktails are made of pieces of fruit, fruit or vegetable juices, carbonated or alcoholic beverages, or a combination of these. They may also be made of sea food, such as oysters, shrimp, crab, or lobster, and served with a highly seasoned sauce.

FRUIT CUP OR COCKTAIL SUGGESTIONS[1]

Avocado. Cut avocado into cubes. Serve in small glasses with sauce made of 1 part catsup, 2 parts orange juice, and a few drops of onion juice.

Avocado–Fruit. Cut avocado into sections. Combine with pineapple chunks and grapefruit sections. Chill.

Cantaloupe–Berry. Combine melon balls with berries. Place in sherbet glasses and chill.

Crab Meat. Line cocktail glasses with lettuce. Fill with alternate layers of crab meat, chopped celery, or diced avocado and cocktail sauce (p. 380).

Cranberry–Ginger Ale. Add sugar to cranberry purée. Chill. Add an equal amount of chilled ginger ale. Serve in cocktail glasses. Garnish with a sprig of mint or paper-thin slices of orange.

Cranberry–Grapefruit. Arrange grapefruit sections in cocktail glasses. Cover with chilled cranberry juice.

Frosted Fruit Cup. Pineapple cubes, grapefruit and orange sections or berries topped with lime ice.

Fruit Coconut. Combine diced orange sections, pineapple, and shredded coconut. Chill.

Grape–Melon. Mix seedless grapes, diced honeydew melon, cubed orange sections, lemon juice, and sugar. Chill. Serve in sherbet glasses.

Grapefruit, broiled. Cut grapefruit in halves and remove centers and seeds. Cut fruit from skin with a sharp knife. Add 1 t. butter and 1 oz. sugar to each center. Broil in a hot oven until fruit turns a golden brown.

---

[1] Ginger ale may be used as liquid in recipes designated as "cups."

Honeydew. Combine chilled pineapple tidbits and juice with honeydew melon balls, seedless grapes, and a little grenadine sirup. Place a grape or ivy leaf under cocktail dishes.

Melon Cup. Cut small round balls from heart of ripe watermelon, cantaloupe, or honeydew melon, or use a combination of the three. Chill thoroughly. Cover with chilled ginger ale.

Mint Cup. Cubes of fresh or canned pineapple and pear with mint or lime ice.

Minted Pineapple. Just before serving, mix 2 No. 10 cans of pineapple tidbits and 1 lb. mints (white, soft). Garnish with a maraschino cherry.

Orange Cup. Orange sections with orange ice or orange sections sprinkled with powdered sugar, covered with pineapple and lemon juice, and garnished with mint leaf.

Oyster. Drain small oysters. Chill and serve in cocktail cups with cocktail sauce (p. 380) and wedge of lemon.

Papaya. Add chopped papaya, salt, and sugar to fresh grapefruit juice. Chill. Serve in frappé glasses. Garnish with cherries.

Pineapple Cup. Cubes of fresh pineapple and whole fresh strawberries.

Raspberry Cup. Fresh raspberries topped with raspberry ice.

Red Raspberry or Strawberry. Prepare fresh berries. Add sugar. Chill. Place in cocktail dishes. Add lime juice and garnish with mint leaves.

Rhubarb–Strawberry. Cut rhubarb into pieces. Cook, sweeten. Chill. Combine with strawberries.

Sherbet. Place no. 16 dipper of lime, pineapple, lemon, orange, or raspberry sherbet in a chilled sherbet dish. Pour 2 T. orange juice or ginger ale over sherbet just before serving.

Shrimp. Line cocktail glasses with lettuce. Add cooked shrimp, either whole or cut into pieces, depending on size. Serve with cocktail sauce (p. 380).

Shrimp–Avocado–Grapefruit. Arrange avocado wedges, grapefruit sections, and shrimp in lettuce lined cocktail glasses. Serve with cocktail sauce (p. 380).

Strawberry. Arrange a few green leaves on each plate. Form a mound of powdered sugar in the center. Around the sugar arrange 5 or 6 large unhulled strawberries.

Strawberry Cup. Fresh strawberries topped with strawberry ice.

Vegetable. Separate raw cauliflower into small flowerets. Mix with chili sauce, lemon juice, Worcestershire sauce, Tabasco sauce, salt, and celery cut very fine. Garnish with parsley.

For fruit and vegetable juice cocktails, see "Beverages," pp. 87–97.

BEVERAGES

Coffee

Coffee in an institutional food service is most often made in an urn, vacuum coffee maker, or percolator. The type of equipment will determine the method and the grind of coffee to be used. Regardless of the method used, certain precautions should always be observed.

1. The coffee must be accurately measured or weighed, fresh, and of a satisfactory blend and grind.
2. The water must be freshly drawn, freshly boiled, and accurately measured.
3. Coffee should be held at a temperature of 185° to 190° F. and never allowed to boil.
4. Care of equipment is of utmost importance for a satisfactory brew. The urn or other equipment should be cleaned immediately after each use, following instructions that come with the equipment.

The number of servings per pound of coffee will vary with the quality of the coffee bean, equipment used, and the cup size. A pound of high-quality coffee properly made should yield on the average 52 4½-oz. servings, using a 6-oz. cup; 47 5-oz. servings, using a 6½-oz. cup; or 39 6-oz. servings, using an 8-oz. cup.

Hot Coffee

Yield: 2½–3 gal.

Amount	Ingredient	Method
1 lb.	Coffee	Use proper blend and grind for coffee maker used.
2½–3 gal.	Water	Use method recommended by manufacturer of coffee maker.

Variation:
Instant Coffee. Use 3 oz. instant coffee or 2 oz. freeze dried to 2½–3 gal. boiling water. Dissolve the coffee in a small amount of boiling water and add to the remaining hot water. Keep hot just below the boiling point.

Hot Coffee (Steeped)

Yield: 2½–3 gal.

Amount	Ingredient	Method
1 lb.	Coffee, regular grind	Tie coffee loosely in a cloth bag.
2½–3 gal.	Water, cold	Immerse bag in water. Heat to boiling point.
		Boil 3 min. Test. When coffee is of desired strength remove coffee bag.
		Cover and hold over low heat to keep at serving temperature.

Note:
For an extra clear brew, beat an egg and one cup of water together and stir into coffee until dampened. Then proceed as above.

Iced Coffee

Yield: 3–3½ gal.

Amount	Ingredient	Method
3–3½ gal.	Water	Make coffee by any method desired.
2 lb.	Coffee	Cover. Cool at room temperature. Do not refrigerate.
10–15 lb.	Ice, chipped or cubed	Fill 12-oz. glasses with ice just before serving; add coffee.

Notes:
1. 4–5 oz. instant coffee and 3 gal. water may be used in place of the brewed coffee.
2. Coffee to be served iced should be stronger than for hot coffee.

Tea

Tea is made by the process of infusion, in which boiling water is poured over tea leaves or tea bags and the mixture is allowed to stand until the desired concentration is reached. A stainless steel or earthenware container is preferable for brewing tea. Freshly drawn cold water, heated just to the boiling point, should be used.

Hot Tea

Yield: 2 gal.

Amount	Ingredient	Method
2 1-oz.	Tea bags	Place tea bags in a stainless steel, enamel, or earthenware container.
2–2½ gal.	Water, boiling	Add water. Steep for 3 min. Remove bags.

Notes:
1. If bulk tea is used, tie loosely in a bag.
2. The amount of tea to be used will vary with the quality.
3. ¾–1 oz. instant tea may be used in place of the tea bags. The exact amount will vary according to the strength desired.

Iced Tea

Yield: 3 gal.

Amount	Ingredient	Method
6 1-oz.	Tea bags	Place tea bags in stainless steel, earthenware, or enamel container.
1 gal.	Water, boiling	Add boiling water. Steep 4–6 min.
2 gal.	Water, cold	Remove bags. Pour hot tea into cold water.
10–15 lb.	Ice, chipped or cubed	Fill 12-oz. glasses with ice. Pour tea over ice just before serving.

Notes:
1. Always pour the hot tea concentrate into the cold water. Do not refrigerate or ice the tea prior to service.
2. 1–1½ oz. instant tea may be used in place of the tea bags.
3. 6–7 lemons may be cut in eighths to serve with the tea.

Spiced Tea

Yield: 1½ gal.

Amount	Ingredient	Method
1½ gal.	Water, boiling	Mix all ingredients except tea.
1 lb. 8 oz.	Sugar	Simmer 20 min.
¼ c.	Lemon juice and 1 rind, grated	Strain.
1 c.	Orange juice and 1 rind, grated	
4 t.	Cloves, whole	
8	Cinnamon sticks	
1 1-oz.	Tea bag	Add tea bag and let steep 5 min. Remove tea bag. Serve hot.

Variation:
Russian Tea. Use only 1¼ gal. water. Add 1 qt. grape juice when adding other juice.

Cocoa and Chocolate

Cocoa

Yield: 2½ gal.

Amount	Ingredient	Method
1 lb. 8 oz.	Sugar	Mix dry ingredients.
8 oz.	Cocoa	Add water and mix until smooth.
½ t.	Salt	Boil approximately 3 min. or to form a thin sirup.
1 qt.	Water	
2¼ gal.	Milk, hot	Add sirup to milk.
1 t.	Vanilla	Just before serving, add vanilla and beat well with a wire whip.

Notes:
1. A marshmallow or 1 t. whipped cream may be added to each cup if desired.
2. Cocoa sirup may be made in amounts larger than this recipe and stored in the refrigerator. To serve, add 1 qt. cocoa sirup to each 2 gal. of hot milk.

Variations:
1. *Hot Chocolate.* Substitute 10 oz. of chocolate for cocoa.
2. *Instant Hot Cocoa.* Dissolve 2½ lb. cocoa powder in 2 gal. boiling water.

French Chocolate

Yield: 3 gal.

Amount	Ingredient	Method
1 lb. 2 oz. 3 c.	Chocolate Water, cold	Combine chocolate and water. Cook over direct heat about 5 min., stirring constantly. Remove from heat. Beat with a rotary beater until smooth.
2 lb. 8 oz. ½ t.	Sugar Salt	Add sugar and salt to chocolate mixture. Return to heat. Cook over hot water 20–30 min. or until thick. Chill.
3½ c.	Whipping cream	Whip cream. Fold into cold chocolate mixture.
2½ gal.	Milk, hot	To serve, place 1 rounded T. chocolate mixture in each serving cup. Add hot milk to fill cup. Stir well to blend. Serve immediately.

Notes:
1. The milk must be kept very hot during the serving period.
2. The chocolate mixture may be stored for a short time in the refrigerator.

Punch

Frozen and canned juices are most often used as the base for punch and for vegetable drinks prepared in institutional food services. Fruit juices, such as lemon, orange, pineapple, cranberry, and the several nectars, are combined in varying proportions to produce a drink of the desired flavor and concentration.

Lemonade (p. 92) or Foundation Fruit Punch (p. 93) may be used as a base for many other fruit drinks by the addition of fresh, frozen, canned, or powdered juices of the desired flavor. The amount of sugar needed will vary with the sugar concentration of the added juice and individual preference. A sugar sirup for sweetening punch is made from 2–2½ lb. sugar and 1 qt. water, heated to the boiling point and cooled. If time does not permit making the sirup, the sugar may be added directly to the punch and stirred until sugar is dissolved.

Punch most often is served iced but may be served hot if desired. Ingredients for making iced punch should be refrigerated and the chilled ingredients combined well in advance of serving time. If a carbonated beverage, such as ginger ale, is to be used it should be chilled and added just before serving. A block of ice placed in the punch bowl is a satisfactory way of icing the punch. However, ice cubes and ring molds of ice are often used because of their availability and the opportunity they offer for color effects. Ring molds made with lemonade will accent flavor of other juices and will not dilute the flavor of the punch.

Decorative ice cubes are easily made by filling an ice cube tray with pastel colored water or fruit juice. A red cherry added to each ice cube section before freezing will add color. Ice ring molds may be made by arranging alternate slices of orange, lemon, and unstemmed strawberries or cherries in the ring molds. Sprigs of mint may be added as a garnish. Water is added to fill the mold ¾ full and frozen. The ring is unmolded and placed upside down in the punch bowl.

The amount of punch or iced beverage to prepare will depend on the size of the punch cup or glass, on the number of guests to be served, and whether guests will be offered second servings. Service from a punch bowl will require slightly more punch than if it is to be poured from a pitcher for individual service. It is always desirable to have on hand unopened cans of the main punch ingredients to facilitate serving a larger crowd than anticipated.

Most recipes in this book were developed for 2–2½ gal. punch. Each gallon will yield 30–35 4-oz. (½ c.) portions. Punch cups vary in size from 3 oz. to 6 oz., so it is important that the size be considered in determining the correct amount of punch to prepare.

Lemonade

Yield: 3 gal.

Amount	Ingredient	Method
1¼ qt.	Lemon juice (approx. 30 lemons)	Mix lemon juice and sugar.
2 lb. 8 oz.	Sugar	Add water. Stir until sugar is dissolved.
2¼ gal.	Water, cold	Chill.

Notes:
1. Lemonade makes a good base for fruit punch.
2. Three 6-oz. cans undiluted frozen lemon juice may be substituted for fresh lemon juice. Increase water to 2½ gal.

Foundation Fruit Punch

Yield: 2½ gal.

Amount	Ingredient	Method
2 lb. 8 oz.	Sugar	Mix sugar and water. Bring to boil.
1 qt.	Water	Cool.
3 c. (2 12-oz. cans)	Orange juice, frozen, undiluted	Add juice and water. Chill.
3 c. (2 12-oz. cans)	Lemon juice, frozen, undiluted	
1½ gal.	Water, cold	

Notes:
1. If time does not permit making and cooling sirup, the sugar may be added to the cold punch and stirred until dissolved. Increase cold water to 1¾ gal.
2. Ginger ale may be substituted for part or all of water. Chill and add just before serving.

Variations:
1. *Golden Punch.* Reduce orange and lemon juice to 12 oz. each. Add 2 46-oz. cans of pineapple juice.
2. *Raspberry Punch.* Reduce orange and lemon juice to 18 oz. each. Add 2 12-oz. packages of frozen red raspberries.
3. *Sparkling Grape Punch.* Reduce orange and lemon juice to 12 oz. each. Add 24 oz. frozen grape juice. Just before serving, add 2 20-oz. bottles of ginger ale.

Sparkling Apricot–Pineapple Punch

Yield: 2½ gal.

Amount	Ingredient	Method
3 qt. (2 46-oz. cans)	Apricot nectar	Combine juices and water. Chill.
3 qt. (2 46-oz. cans)	Pineapple juice, unsweetened	
1½ c. (2 6-oz. cans)	Lemon or lime juice concentrate, frozen	
2 qt.	Water	
2 qt.	Ginger ale, chilled	Add ginger ale just before serving.

Ginger Ale Fruit Punch

Yield: 3 gal.

Amount	Ingredient	Method
3 lb.	Sugar	Mix sugar and water. Bring to boil. Cool.
1 qt.	Water	
1½ qt.	Lemon juice	Add remaining ingredients. Chill.
1½ qt.	Orange juice	
1 qt.	Pineapple juice	
1 gal.	Water	
2 qt.	Ginger ale, chilled	Add ginger ale just before serving.

Note:
Lime, orange, or lemon ice may be added to the punch just before serving.

Banana Punch

Yield: 2 gal.

Amount	Ingredient	Method
2 lb.	Sugar	Boil sugar and water for 3 min.
1½ qt.	Water, hot	Cool.
1½ c. (1 12-oz. can)	Orange juice, frozen, undiluted	Combine juices, fruits, and water.
¾ c. (1 6-oz. can)	Lemon juice, frozen, undiluted	Add chilled sugar sirup.
1 qt.	Water, cold	
3 qt. (1 No. 10 can)	Pineapple, crushed	
6 medium	Bananas, ripe, crushed	
1 qt.	Ginger ale, chilled	Add ginger ale just before serving.

Notes:
1. Mixture may be frozen (before ginger ale is added) and held for use later.
2. 2 46-oz. cans of unsweetened pineapple juice and 1 12-oz. can lemonade may be substituted for the crushed pineapple and lemon juice.

Variation:
Banana Slush Punch. Mix and freeze juices, sirup, and crushed bananas. To serve, fill glass about half full of partially frozen slush and add ginger ale.

Rhubarb Punch

Yield: 1½ gal.

Amount	Ingredient	Method
10 lb. 1 gal. 4–5 lb.	Rhubarb, pink Water Sugar	Cut rhubarb into 1-in. pieces. Add water and sugar. Cook below the boiling point until soft. Strain. There should be 1¼ gal. juice. Chill.
1 pt. 1 28-oz. bottle	Pineapple juice Ginger ale	Add chilled pineapple juice and ginger ale just before serving.

Cranberry Punch

Yield: 2½ gal.

Amount	Ingredient	Method
3 qts. 3 qts. (2 46-oz. cans) 1 qt. (1 32-oz. can) 1 qt.	Cranberry juice Pineapple juice Lemonade, frozen, undiluted Water, cold	Mix juices and water. Chill.
3 28-oz. bottles	Ginger ale, chilled	Add ginger ale just before serving.

Chilled Tomato Juice

Yield: 2¼ gal.

Amount	Ingredient	Method
8½ qt. (6 46-oz. cans) ¾ c. 3 T. ½ t. 3 T.	Tomato juice, chilled Lemon juice, fresh Worcestershire sauce Tabasco sauce Celery salt	Mix all ingredients. Chill.

Variation:

Sauerkraut Juice Cocktail. Omit the seasonings and substitute 2 qt. of sauerkraut juice for 2 qt. of tomato juice.

Hot Spiced Tomato Juice

Yield: 2 gal.

Amount	Ingredient	Method
4¼ qt. (3 46-oz. cans)	Tomato juice	Mix all ingredients but consommé.
8 oz.	Onion, chopped	Boil gently about 15 min.
3	Bay leaves	Strain.
12	Cloves, whole	
2 T.	Salt	
1 T.	Mustard, dry	
6	Celery stalks, cut	
1 gal.	Consommé	Add consommé and reheat. Serve hot.

Note:

2 50-oz. cans condensed beef or chicken consommé, diluted with 2 qt. water, may be used.

Spiced Cider

Yield: 2½ gal.

Amount	Ingredient	Method
2½ gal.	Cider	Add sugar and spices (tied loosely in a cloth bag) to the cider.
12 oz.	Brown sugar	
10	Cinnamon sticks	Bring slowly to the boiling point. Boil about 15 min.
2½ T.	Cloves, whole	
2½ T.	Allspice	Remove spices.
½ t.	Mace	Serve hot or chilled.
1 t.	Salt	
f.g.	Cayenne	

Variation:

Cider Punch. Omit spices; substitute 1 qt. reconstituted frozen orange juice and 1 qt. pineapple juice for an equal amount of cider. Garnish with thin slices of orange.

Wassail Bowl

Yield: 2½ gal.

Amount	Ingredient	Method
2 lb. 8 oz.	Sugar	Mix sugar, water, and spices. Boil
2½ qt.	Water	10 min.
½ T.	Cloves, whole	Cover and let stand 1 hr. in a warm
10	Cinnamon sticks	place.
10	Allspice berries	Strain.
5 T.	Crystallized ginger, chopped	
2 qt.	Orange juice, strained	When ready to serve add juice and
1¼ qt.	Lemon juice, strained	cider. Heat quickly to boiling
5 qt.	Apple cider	point.
		Pour over crabapples or small oranges studded with cloves, in a punch bowl.

BREADS

Quick Breads

Quick breads are made with a leavening agent that acts quickly, thus enabling them to be baked at once. This type of bread includes biscuits, muffins, pan breads such as coffee cake and corn bread, loaf breads, and griddle cakes. Most quick breads should be mixed only to blend, with as little handling as possible.

Baking Powder Biscuits

Bake: 15 min.
Oven: 425° F.

Yield: 100 2½-in. biscuits
130 2-in. biscuits

Amount	Ingredient	Method
5 lb.	Flour	Mix dry ingredients (low speed).
5 oz.	Baking powder	
2 T.	Salt	
1 lb. 4 oz.	Fat	Add fat. Mix (low speed) until crumbly.
1¾–2 qt.	Milk	Add milk all at once. Mix (low speed) to form a soft dough. Do not overmix. Dough should be as soft as can be handled. 1. Place one-half of dough on lightly floured board. Knead lightly 15–20 times. 2. Roll to ¾-in. thickness. Cut with a 2½-in. (or 2-in.) cutter. 3. Place on baking sheet ½ in. apart for crusty biscuits, just touching for softer biscuits. Repeat, using remaining dough. 4. Biscuits may be held several hours in the refrigerator until time to bake.

Note:
For variations, see p. 100.

Variations:

1. *Butterscotch Biscuits.* Divide dough into 8 parts. Roll each part into a rectangular sheet ¼ in. thick. Spread with melted butter or margarine and brown sugar. Roll the dough and cut off slices ¾ in. thick. Bake 15 min. at 375° F.
2. *Cheese Biscuits.* Use 4 oz. less fat and add 1 lb. dry grated cheese.
3. *Cinnamon Biscuits.* Proceed as for Butterscotch Biscuits. Spread with mixture of 1 lb. sugar, 2 oz. cinnamon, and 1 lb. raisins.
4. *Corn Meal Biscuits.* Substitute 2 lb. corn meal for 2 lb. white flour.
5. *Drop Biscuits.* Add 1 qt. milk. Drop from spoon onto greased baking sheet.
6. *Filled Biscuits.* Roll dough into a sheet ¼ in. thick. Cut dough with cutter 1¾ in. diameter. Cut out centers of half of the biscuits, using a ¾-in. cutter. Place biscuit ring on a whole biscuit; fill center of each with ½ oz. jam.
7. *Nut Biscuits.* Cut biscuit dough with fancy cutter; sprinkle with 2 c. finely chopped nuts and 1 c. sugar mixed.
8. *Orange Biscuits.* Proceed as for Butterscotch Biscuits. Spread with orange marmalade.
9. *Raisin Biscuits.* Use 6 oz. less fat and ½ c. less milk; add 4 whole eggs, 3 T. grated orange rind, 8 oz. sugar, and 8 oz. chopped raisins.
10. *Shortcake.* Add 8 oz. fat and 8 oz. sugar.
11. *Whole Wheat Biscuits.* Substitute 2 lb. whole wheat flour for 2 lb. white flour.

Plain Muffins

Bake: 25 min.   Yield: 5 doz.
Oven: 400° F.

Amount	Ingredient	Method
2 lb. 8 oz.	Flour	Combine dry ingredients in mixer bowl.
2 oz.	Baking powder	
1 T.	Salt	
6 oz.	Sugar	
4	Eggs, beaten	Add combined eggs, milk, and fat.
1½ qt.	Milk	Mix only to blend (low speed) about 30 sec. Batter still will be lumpy.
8 oz.	Fat, melted, cooled	
		Measure with No. 16 dipper into well-greased muffin pans, about ⅔ full. Batter should be dipped all at once with as little handling as possible but may be refrigerated a short time and baked as needed.

Note:
No. 24 dipper will yield 6½ doz. muffins.

Variations:

1. *Apricot Muffins.* Add 3 c. drained, chopped, cooked apricots to the liquid ingredients.
2. *Bacon Muffins.* Substitute 10 oz. chopped bacon, slightly broiled, and bacon fat for the fat in recipe.
3. *Blueberry Muffins.* Carefully fold 1 lb. blueberries into the batter. Increase sugar to 10 oz.
4. *Cherry Muffins.* Add 2 c. well-drained cooked cherries to liquid.
5. *Corn Meal Muffins.* Substitute 1 lb. white corn meal for 1 lb. flour.
6. *Cranberry Muffins.* Sprinkle 4 oz. sugar over 1 lb. chopped raw cranberries. Fold into batter.
7. *Currant Muffins.* Add 8 oz. chopped currants.
8. *Date Muffins.* Add 1 lb. chopped dates.
9. *Graham Muffins.* Substitute 12 oz. graham flour for 12 oz. white flour. Add 4 T. molasses.
10. *Jelly Muffins.* Drop ¼ to ½ t. jelly on top of each muffin when placed in oven.
11. *Nut Muffins.* Add 10 oz. chopped nuts.
12. *Raisin–Nut Muffins.* Add 6 oz. chopped nuts and 6 oz. chopped raisins.
13. *Spiced Muffins.* Add 1½ t. cloves, 1 t. ginger, and 1 t. allspice to dry ingredients.

Honey Cornflake Muffins

Bake: 20 min.
Oven: 400° F.

Yield: 4 doz.

Amount	Ingredient	Method
8 oz. 11 oz. 4	Fat Honey Eggs, well beaten	Cream fat and honey (low speed). Add eggs. Mix (medium speed) about 30 sec.
1 lb. 12 oz. 2½ oz. 1 t. 1 qt.	Flour Baking powder Salt Milk	Combine dry ingredients. Add alternately with the milk to creamed mixture. Mix only to blend (low speed) about 15 sec.
8 oz.	Cornflakes	Add cornflakes all at once. Stir only enough to mix. Measure with No. 20 dipper into well-greased muffin pans. Bake.

Oatmeal Muffins

Bake: 15–20 min.   Yield: 5 doz.
Oven: 400° F.

Amount	Ingredient	Method
14 oz. 1¼ qt.	Rolled oats Sour milk or buttermilk	Combine rolled oats and sour milk in mixer bowl. Let stand 1 hr.
5 1 lb. 4 oz. 1 lb.	Eggs Brown sugar Fat, melted, cooled	Add eggs, sugar, and fat. Mix 30 sec. Scrape down bowl.
1 lb. 4 oz. 5 t. 2½ t. 2½ t.	Flour Baking powder Salt Soda	Add combined dry ingredients. Mix (low speed) about 15 sec. or only until dry ingredients are moistened. Measure with No. 16 dipper into well-greased muffin pans (⅔ full). Bake.

Note:
No. 24 dipper will yield 7 doz. muffins.

All-Bran Muffins

Bake: 20 min.   Yield: 5 doz.
Oven: 400° F.

Amount	Ingredient	Method
1 lb 8 oz. 3 c. 2¼ qt.	All-Bran Molasses Milk	Combine All-Bran and molasses in mixer bowl. Let stand 15 min.
6 ⅓ c.	Eggs Fat, melted, or oil	Add eggs and fat. Mix (medium speed) 30 sec.
1 lb. 8 oz. 1 T. 2 T.	Flour Salt Soda	Mix dry ingredients and add all at once. Mix (low speed) only to blend, about 15 sec. Measure with No. 16 dipper into well-greased muffin pans. Bake.

Note:
1½ lb. chopped dates, raisins, or nuts may be added for variety.

Griddle Cakes

Yield: 100 cakes 4-in. diameter

Amount	Ingredient	Method
4 lb. 8 oz.	Flour	Combine dry ingredients in mixer bowl.
4 oz.	Baking powder	
2 T.	Salt	
12 oz.	Sugar	
12	Eggs, beaten until light	Add eggs, milk, and fat. Mix (low speed) 30 sec.
3½ qt.	Milk	If batter is thicker than desired, thin with milk.
12 oz.	Fat, melted and cooled, or oil	Use No. 16 dipper to place batter on hot griddle. Bake until surface of cake is full of bubbles. Turn and finish baking.

Variations:
1. *Buttermilk Griddle Cakes.* Add 9 oz. dry buttermilk and 1 T. soda to dry ingredients. Substitute 3½ qt. water for milk.
2. *Blueberry Griddle Cakes.* Add 1 lb. well-drained blueberries to batter after cakes are mixed. Handle carefully to avoid mashing berries.

Griddle Cake Mix

Yield: 12 lb. mix

Amount	Ingredient	Method
9 lb.	Flour	Combine ingredients.
8 oz.	Baking powder	Store in covered container.
¼ c.	Salt	
1 lb. 8 oz.	Sugar	
1 lb. 8 oz.	Instant nonfat dry milk	

Variation:
Buttermilk Griddle Cake Mix. Substitute 1 lb. 2 oz. dry buttermilk for the instant nonfat dry milk and add 2 T. soda.

Note:
For chart for using Griddle Cake Mix, see p. 104.

Chart for Using Griddle Cake Mix

Ingredient	30 *cakes*	50 *cakes*	100 *cakes*	200 *cakes*
Mix	2 lb.	3 lb.	6 lb.	12 lb.
Eggs	4	6	12	24
Water	1 qt.	1½ qt.	3 qt.	1½ gal.
Fat	4 oz.	6 oz.	12 oz.	1 lb. 8 oz.

Waffles

Yield: 6 qts. batter
50–60 waffles

Amount	Ingredient	Method
3 lb. 6 T. 2 T. 4 oz.	Flour Baking powder Salt Sugar	Combine dry ingredients in mixer bowl.
18 2¼ qt. 1 lb.	Egg yolks, beaten Milk Fat, melted, cooled	Add eggs, milk, and fat. Mix (low speed) just enough to moisten dry ingredients.
18	Egg whites	Beat egg whites until stiff but not dry. Fold into batter. Use No. 10 dipper to place batter on preheated waffle iron. Bake about 4 min.

Note:
Serve with Sirup (p. 377), Honey Butter (p. 127), or Creamed Chicken.
Variations:
1. *Bacon Waffles.* Add 1 lb. chopped bacon slightly broiled, and substitute bacon fat for the fat in recipe.
2. *Corn Meal Waffles.* Substitute 12 oz. fine corn meal for 8 oz. flour.
3. *Pecan Waffles.* Add 6 oz. chopped pecans.

Corn Bread

Bake: 35 min.
Oven: 400° F.

Yield: 1 pan 12 x 20 x 2 in.
40 portions 2¼ x 2½ in.
48 portions 2 x 2½ in.

Amount	Ingredient	Method
1 lb. 4 oz.	Corn meal	Combine dry ingredients in mixer bowl.
1 lb. 5 oz.	Flour	
6 oz.	Sugar	
1½ T.	Salt	
2 oz.	Baking powder	
5	Eggs, well beaten	Add eggs, milk, and fat.
1 qt.	Milk	Mix (low speed) only until ingredients
6 oz.	Fat, melted, cooled	are moistened.
		Spread into well-greased baking pan.
		Bake.

Note:
Batter may be baked in corn stick or muffin pans. Reduce baking time to 15–20 min.

Bishop's Bread

Bake: 25 min.
Oven: 400° F.

Yield: 1 bun pan 18 x 26 x 1 in.
60 portions 3 x 2½ in.

Amount	Ingredient	Method
14 oz.	Fat	Cream fat and sugar (medium speed)
2 lb. 12 oz.	Brown sugar	5 min.
2 lb. 8 oz.	Flour	Mix flour, salt, and cinnamon.
2 t.	Salt	Blend with creamed mixture.
1 T.	Cinnamon	Remove 2½ c. of the mixture to sprinkle on top later.
1 lb.	Flour	Mix flour, baking powder, and soda.
4 t.	Baking powder	Add alternately with combined butter-
2 t.	Soda	milk and eggs to creamed mixture.
1¼ qt.	Buttermilk or	Scrape down bowl.
	sour milk	Mix (low speed) about 30 sec. (Batter
4	Eggs, beaten	will not be smooth.)
		Spread into greased bun pan.
		Sprinkle with the 2½ c. brown sugar mixture reserved from second step.
		Bake.

Note:
4½ oz. dry buttermilk and 1¼ qt. water may be substituted for sour milk.

Coffee Cake

Bake: 25 min.
Oven: 400° F.

Yield: 1 pan 12 x 20 x 2 in.
40 portions 2¼ x 2½ in.
48 portions 2 x 2½ in.

Amount	Ingredient	Method
2 lb.	Flour	Combine dry ingredients in mixer bowl.
2⅔ T.	Baking powder	
1 lb. 4 oz.	Sugar	
1 T.	Salt	
4	Eggs, beaten	Add eggs and milk.
3 c.	Milk	Mix (low speed) until dry ingredients
1 lb.	Fat, melted, cooled	are just moistened. Add fat and mix (low speed) for 1 min. Spread into well-greased baking pan.
8 oz.	Butter or margarine	Mix until crumbly. Sprinkle over batter.
1 lb.	Sugar	Bake. Serve warm.
2½ oz.	Flour	
3 T.	Cinnamon	
1 t.	Salt	

Note:
For 18 × 26-in. bun pan, use 1½ times recipe.

Blueberry Coffee Cake

Bake: 45 min.
Oven: 375° F.

Yield: 1 bun pan 18 x 26 x 1 in.
60 portions 3 x 2½ in.

Amount	Ingredient	Method
2 lb. 4 oz. 12 oz. 6	Sugar Fat Eggs	Cream sugar and fat (medium speed) about 10 min. Add eggs and continue mixing about 5 min.
3 lb. 2 oz. 1 T. 3 c.	Flour Baking powder Salt Milk	Combine dry ingredients and add alternately with milk to creamed mixture. Mix (medium speed) about 15 sec.
1 lb. 8 oz.	Blueberries, drained	Carefully fold in well-drained blueberries. Pour into greased bun pan.
8 oz. 4 oz. 4 oz. 2 t. 6 oz.	Brown sugar Sugar, granulated Flour Cinnamon Butter, soft	Combine. Mix to a coarse crumb consistency. Crumble evenly over top of batter. Bake.

Note:
After cake is baked, thin Powdered Sugar Glaze (p. 168) may be drizzled in a fine stream over the top to form an irregular design.

Doughnuts

Fry: 3–4 min.   Yield: 4 doz.
Deep Fat Fryer: 350–375° F.

Amount	Ingredient	Method
3	Eggs, slightly beaten	Mix eggs, sugar, and fat (medium speed) about 10 min.
10 oz.	Sugar	
1½ oz.	Fat, melted and cooled	
1 lb. 10 oz.	Flour	Add combined dry ingredients alternately with the milk.
1 t.	Nutmeg	
1¼ t.	Salt	Mix to form a soft dough (add more flour if dough is too soft to handle).
⅛ t.	Ginger	
3 T.	Baking powder	Chill, roll to ⅜ in. thickness on floured board.
2 t.	Orange rind, grated	Cut with 2½-in. cutter.
1 pt.	Milk	Fry in deep fat.
		Sprinkle with sugar when partly cool.

Variation:
Chocolate Doughnuts. Substitute 4 T. cocoa for 4 T. flour.

Boston Brown Bread

Steam: 1¼–1½ hr.   Yield: 8 round loaves
Steam Pressure: 5–7 lb.   8 slices per loaf

Amount	Ingredient	Method
1 lb.	Cornmeal	Combine dry ingredients in mixer bowl (low speed).
12 oz.	Flour, whole wheat	
12 oz.	Flour, white	
1½ T.	Salt	
1½ T.	Soda	
1½ qt.	Sour milk or buttermilk	Blend milk and molasses. Add all at once to dry ingredients.
2¼ c.	Molasses	Mix (low speed) only until ingredients are blended.
		Fill 8 greased cans 3¼ × 4½ in. ¾ full. Cover tightly with aluminum foil. Steam.

Baked Brown Bread

Bake: 45 min.
Oven: 375° F.

Yield: 7 loaves 4 x 9 in.
12–14 slices per loaf

Amount	Ingredient	Method

1 lb. 8 oz.
4
6 oz.
	Brown sugar
	Eggs
	Fat, melted,
	   cooled
		Mix sugar, eggs, and fat (medium
		   speed) about 5 min.

2 qt. 1¼ c.	Sour milk or buttermilk Molasses	Combine sour milk and molasses.

4 lb.
 	
1 T.
2½ T.
	Flour, whole
	   wheat
	Salt
	Soda
		Mix dry ingredients and add alternately
		   with milk and molasses to first mixture.
		Mix (low speed) about 3 min.
		Divide batter into 7 greased loaf pans,
		   approximately 1½ lb. per pan. Bake.

Variations:
1. *Pecan Brown Bread.* Add 8 oz. chopped pecans.
2. *Prune Brown Bread.* Add 12 oz. chopped, pitted prunes.
3. *Raisin Brown Bread.* Add 12 oz. raisins.

Nut Bread

Bake: 1 hr.
Oven: 375° F.

Yield: 5 loaves 4 x 9 in.
14 slices per loaf

Amount	Ingredient	Method
3 lb. 1 oz. 1 lb. 1 T. 1 lb. 8 oz.	Flour Baking powder Nuts, chopped Salt Sugar	Combine dry ingredients and nuts in mixer bowl (low speed).
6 1½ qt. 4 oz.	Eggs, beaten Milk Fat, melted, cooled	Add combined milk, eggs, and fat. Mix (low speed) only until blended. Divide batter into 5 greased loaf pans. Let stand 30 min. before baking.

Banana Bread

Bake: 50 min.   Yield: 4 loaves 4 x 9 in.
Oven: 350° F.   14 slices per loaf

Amount	Ingredient	Method
1 lb. 10 oz.	Sugar	Cream fat and sugar (medium speed)
10 oz.	Fat	5 min.
5	Eggs	Add eggs and beat 2 min.
1 lb. 10 oz.	Bananas, mashed	Add bananas and beat 1 min.
¾ c.	Milk	Add milk, dry ingredients, and nuts. Mix
2 lb.	Flour	(low speed) 1 min.
2 t.	Salt	Divide batter into 4 greased loaf pans.
4 T.	Baking powder	Let stand 30 min. before baking.
½ t.	Soda	
8 oz.	Nuts, chopped	

Cranberry Nut Bread

Bake: 1 hr.   Yield: 5 loaves 4 x 9 in.
Oven: 350° F.   14 slices per loaf

Amount	Ingredient	Method
2 lb. 8 oz.	Flour	Combine dry ingredients in mixer bowl.
2 lb. 4 oz.	Sugar	
1 oz.	Baking powder	
2 t.	Soda	
2 t.	Salt	
1½ c.	Orange juice	Add orange juice, oil, and water. Mix
½ c.	Salad oil	slightly.
3¾ c.	Water, boiling	Add eggs. Mix (low speed) only until
5	Eggs, beaten	dry ingredients are moistened.
1 lb.	Nuts, chopped	Add nuts, rind, and cranberries.
7 oz.	Orange rind, ground	Mix (low speed) until blended. (Batter still may be lumpy.)
1 lb. 4 oz.	Cranberries, raw, coarsely ground	Divide batter into 5 greased loaf pans. Bake.
		Cool before slicing.

Date–Nut Bread

Bake: 1 hr.
Oven: 350° F.

Yield: 4 loaves 4 x 9 in.
14 slices per loaf

Amount	Ingredient	Method
1 lb. 8 oz. 1½ T. 3¼ c.	Dates, chopped Soda Water, boiling	Add water and soda to dates. Let stand 20 min.
3 oz. 1 lb. 12 oz. 4 1½ T.	Fat Sugar Eggs Vanilla	Cream fat and sugar (medium speed) 5 min. Add eggs and vanilla. Mix 2 min. (medium speed).
2 lb. 1½ t.	Flour Salt	Combine flour and salt. Add alternately with dates to creamed mixture.
8 oz.	Nuts, chopped	Add nuts. Divide batter into 4 greased loaf pans. Bake.

Pumpkin Bread

Bake: 1 hr.
Oven: 350° F.

Yield: 4 loaves 4 x 9 in.
14 slices per loaf

Amount	Ingredient	Method
2 lb. 6 oz. 14 oz.	Sugar Fat	Cream sugar and fat (medium speed) for 5 min.
6 1 lb. 10 oz.	Eggs Pumpkin	Add eggs and pumpkin to creamed mixture. Mix (medium speed) for 8 min. Scrape down bowl.
1 lb. 6 oz. 2 t. 1 t. 2 t. 2 t. 2 t. 2 t. 2 t.	Flour Salt Baking powder Soda Nutmeg Cloves Cinnamon Allspice	Combine dry ingredients and add to pumpkin mixture. Mix 3 min.; scrape down bowl, mix 3 min. Divide batter into 4 greased loaf pans. Bake.

Swedish Timbale Cases

Fry: 2–3 min.   Yield: 50
Deep Fat Fryer: 350–365° F.

Amount	Ingredient	Method
3 1½ c. 1½ t.	Eggs, beaten Milk Oil or melted fat	Mix eggs, milk, and fat.
6 oz. 1 t. 1½ t.	Flour Salt Sugar	Add combined dry ingredients. Stir until smooth. Let stand until air bubbles have come to top. Dip hot timbale iron into batter and fry in deep fat until brown.

Notes:
This recipe may be used for either timbale cases or rosettes.
1. Serve timbale cases filled with creamed chicken or creamed peas.
2. Serve rosettes sprinkled with powdered sugar, heaped with fresh or preserved fruits and garnished with whipped or ice cream; or use the same as timbale cases.

Fritters

Fry: 4–6 min.   Yield: 100
Deep Fat Fryer: 375° F.   2 fritters per portion

Amount	Ingredient	Method
4 lb. 1 T. 4 oz. 2 oz.	Flour Salt Baking powder Sugar	Mix dry ingredients.
12 2 qt. 6 oz.	Eggs, beaten Milk Fat, melted	Combine eggs, milk, and fat. Add to dry ingredients. Mix only enough to moisten dry ingredients. Measure with No. 30 dipper into hot deep fat. Serve with sirup.

Variations:
1. *Apple Fritters.* Add 1 lb. raw apple, peeled and finely chopped.
2. *Corn Fritters.* Add 2 qt. corn, drained.
3. *Fruit Fritters.* Add 1 qt. fruit: banana, drained peach, or pineapple.

Dumplings

Steam: 12–15 min. under pressure   Yield: 100 dumplings

Amount	Ingredient	Method
2 lb. 8 oz. 3 oz. (6 T.) 2 T.	Flour Baking powder Salt	Mix flour, baking powder, and salt.
6 5½ c.	Eggs, beaten Milk	Combine eggs and milk. Add to flour mixture. Mix only until blended. Use No. 24 dipper to drop on trays. Do not cover trays. Serve with meat stew.

Note:
Mixture may be dropped onto hot meat or meat mixture in counter pans and steamed.

Cheese Straws

Bake: 10–15 min.   Yield: 6 doz. 4 x 1-in. straws
Oven: 350° F.

Amount	Ingredient	Method
6 oz. 8 oz. 8 oz. 2 t. 1 t. ¼ t.	Butter or margarine Cheese, sharp, grated Flour Baking powder Salt Cayenne	Cream butter or margarine (medium speed). Add grated cheese and the combined dry ingredients (low speed).
3 2 T.	Eggs, beaten Water	Add eggs and water. Mix (low speed) to form a stiff dough. Chill. Roll ¼ in. thick and cut into strips 4 in. long and 1 in. wide. Place on ungreased baking sheet. Bake.

Variation:
Caraway Cheese Straws. Add 2 t. caraway seeds to flour before mixing.

Yeast Breads

INGREDIENTS

An understanding of the functions of the main ingredients used in yeast-raised doughs is essential to the production of good bread and rolls.

Flour. The flour used for baking must contain enough protein to make an elastic framework of gluten that will stretch and hold the gas bubbles formed as the dough ferments. Bread flour contains more proteins than other flour and is used by bakers who make large quantities of bread. All purpose flour, which contains enough protein to provide the gluten essential to make good rolls and the home-made yeast specialties of most food services, was used in testing these recipes.

Yeast. Either compressed or active dry yeast may be used in yeast doughs. When substituting active dry for compressed yeast, only 50% by weight is required. Active dry yeast does not require refrigeration and remains active a reasonable length of time in cool dry storage. Compressed yeast is perishable and must be held under refrigeration (30–34° F.) and storage is limited to not more than two weeks. It may be frozen to extend its keeping time but must be used immediately after defrosting. Compressed yeast may be softened in lukewarm (95° F.) water or other liquid. Active dry yeast must be softened in water (104° F.–113° F.). Yeast grows best between 80° F. and 85° F. Dough should be kept in this temperature range during fermentation. One of the main purposes of scalding milk is to give warmth to the dough. Dough should be near 80° F. when mixing is completed.

Other Ingredients. Although used in small quantity, other ingredients influence the quality of the finished product. Salt is added mainly for flavor but does help to control the rate of fermentation. Too much salt may cause a firm compact loaf or may kill the yeast if added directly. Too much sugar tends to slow down the action of the yeast. Fat is added to improve flavor, tenderness, browning, and keeping quality. Fat in large amounts, or if added directly to the yeast, will slow its action. Eggs are added for flavor and also to help form a framework. Dry skim milk may be added to the dry ingredients or reconstituted and used as fluid milk. (See p. 64.) The nutritive value of the bread may be increased by the addition of extra quantities of dry milk.

MIXING THE DOUGH

Mixing and kneading are essential in developing a good gluten network. Kneading is accomplished by continuing the mixing process beyond the point of combining. In a mixer this is done with a dough hook or flat beater attachment. The mixing speed and exact length of time will be determined by the type of mixer, the mixer attachment used, and the amount of dough. The last part of the flour should be added gradually to determine if the full amount is needed. It may be necessary to use more or less flour than the recipe specifies. The dough should be soft but not sticky. Dough for rolls is softer than for plain bread. Soft dough makes a lighter and more tender product. The dough is mixed only until it leaves the sides and bottom of the bowl.

Yeast *rolls* usually are shaped after the dough has doubled in volume, although yeast *breads* generally are allowed to rise the second time.

FERMENTATION OF DOUGH

Fermentation begins when the dough is mixed and continues until the yeast is killed by the heat of the oven. The dough must be set in a warm place (79–90° F.), free from drafts, to ferment. The length of the fermentation period depends on the amount of yeast added, the strength of the flour, the amount of sugar added, and the temperature. Temperatures above 140° F. will kill the yeast. Usually 1½ hours are required for the dough to double its bulk the first time. After the dough has doubled, it is punched down to its original bulk. Punching forces out excess carbon dioxide and incorporates oxygen, which allows the yeast cells to grow more rapidly. The yeast cells also are more uniformly distributed, producing an even-textured product with a fine grain. After the dough has been punched down it must be handled lightly to avoid breaking the small air cells that have been formed.

The dough may be retarded at any point during the fermentation process by chilling the dough, as in refrigerator rolls. The dough also may be allowed to rise first, scaled into rolls, and then refrigerated. The baking process may be halted at a time when the rising is complete and before browning occurs, as in brown and serve rolls.

Plain Rolls

Bake: 15–25 min.   Yield: 6 doz. rolls
Oven: 400–425° F.

Amount	Ingredient	Method
4 oz. 3 T. 6 oz.	Sugar Salt Fat	Place sugar, salt, and fat in mixer bowl.
1¼ qt.	Milk, scalded	Add hot milk. Mix (low speed) to blend. Cool to lukewarm.
3 oz. 1 c. 4	Yeast, compressed (or 1½ oz. dry) Water, lukewarm, 80–85° F. Eggs, beaten	Soften yeast in water. Add softened yeast and eggs to milk mixture. Mix (medium speed) until blended.
4 lb. 12 oz. (Variable)	Flour	Add flour to make a moderately soft dough. Mix (low speed) until smooth and satiny. 1. Turn into lightly greased pan, turn over to grease top. Cover. Let rise in a warm place (80° F.) until double in bulk. 2. Punch down. Divide into thirds for ease in handling. Shape into 1½ oz. rolls. 3. Let rise until double in bulk. 4. Bake.

Notes:
1. 3–4 hrs. are required for mixing and rising. For a quicker rising dough, increase yeast to 4 oz. compressed (2 oz. dry).
2. 5 oz. nonfat dry milk plus 1¼ qt. water may be substituted for milk. Combine dry milk powder with sugar and salt.

Variations:
1. *Bowknots.* Roll 1½ oz. portions of dough into strips 9 in. long. Tie loosely into a single knot. (See Fig. 1.)
2. *Braids.* Roll dough ¼ in. thick and cut in strips 6 in. long and ½ in. wide. Cross 3 strips in the middle and braid from center to end. Press ends together and fold under.
3. *Butterhorns.* Proceed as for crescents only do not form a crescent shape.
4. *Caramel Crowns.* Scale dough into balls 1½ oz. each. Roll in melted butter or margarine, then in a sugar and cinnamon mixture. Drop 18 balls into each of 5 greased angel food cake pans, sprinkling each layer with nuts (and raisins if desired). The pan should be about ⅓ full. Let rise until

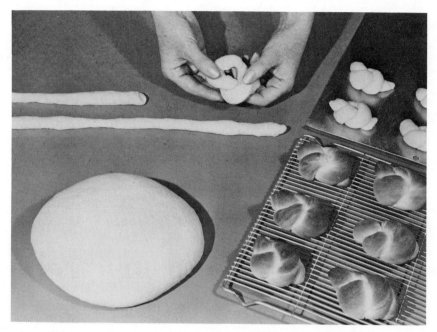

Fig 1. Bowknots. (Courtesy of the Wheat Flour Institute.)

double in bulk. Bake for 35–40 min. at 350–375° F. Immediately loosen from pan with a spatula. Invert pan. After removing from pan, place whole maraschino or glacé cherries on top.

5. *Cloverleaf Rolls.* Pinch off small balls of dough. Fit into greased muffin pans, allowing 3 balls for each roll (See Fig. 2.)

6. *Crescents.* Weigh dough into 12-oz. portions. Roll each into a circle ⅛ in. thick, 8 in. in diameter. Cut into 12 triangles, brush top with melted fat. Beginning at base, roll each triangle, keeping point in middle of roll and bringing ends toward each other to form a crescent shape. Place on greased baking sheet 1½ in. apart. (See Fig. 3.)

7. *Dinner Rolls.* Shape dough into small balls; place on well-greased baking sheet. Cover. Let rise until light. Brush with mixture made of egg yolk and milk—1 egg yolk to 1 T. milk. (See Fig. 4.)

8. *Fan Tan Rolls.* Weigh dough into 12-oz. pieces. Roll out into very thin rectangular sheet. Brush with melted butter. Cut in strips about 1 in. wide. Pile six or seven strips together. Cut 1½-in. pieces and place on end in greased muffin pans. (See Fig. 5.)

9. *Finger or Wiener Rolls.* Divide dough into 2 portions. Roll each piece of dough into a strip 1½ in. in diameter. Cut strips of dough into pieces approximately 1 oz. each (1½ oz. for Wiener Rolls). Round pieces of dough; roll into pieces approximately 4½ in. long. Place in rows on greased baking sheet ½ in. apart.

Fig. 2.   Cloverleaf Rolls. (Courtesy of the Wheat Flour Institute.)

Fig. 3.   Crescents. (Courtesy of the Wheat Flour Institute.)

Fig. 4. Dinner or Pan Rolls. (Courtesy of the Wheat Flour Institute.)

Fig. 5. Fan Tan or Butterflakes. (Courtesy of the Wheat Flour Institute.)

10. *Half-and-half Rolls.* Proceed as for Twin Rolls. Use 1 round plain dough and 1 round whole wheat dough for each roll (p. 121).
11. *Hot Cross Buns.* Divide dough into thirds. Roll ½ in. thick. Cut rounds 3 in. in diameter. Brush top with beaten egg. Score top of bun to make cross before baking or after baking make a cross on top with frosting. (See Fig. 7.)
12. *Parkerhouse Rolls.* Divide dough into thirds. Roll to ⅓-in. thickness. Cut rounds 2–2½ in. in diameter or form 1½-oz. balls. Allow balls to stand for 10 min., then elongate with rolling pin. Crease middle of each roll with dull edge of knife. Brush with melted butter, fold over, press together with palm of hand. (See Fig. 6.)
13. *Poppy Seed Rolls.* (a) Proceed as for Twists. Substitute poppy seeds for sugar and cinnamon. (b) Proceed as for Cinnamon Rolls. Substitute poppy seed for sugar, cinnamon, and raisins.
14. *Ribbon Rolls.* Weigh dough into 12-oz. pieces. Roll ¼ in. thick. Spread with melted butter. Place on top of this a layer of whole wheat dough rolled to the same thickness. Repeat, using the contrasting dough until 5 layers thick. Cut with a 1½-in. cutter. Place in greased muffin pans with cut surface down.
15. *Rosettes.* Follow directions for Bowknots. After tying, bring one end through center and the other over the side.
16. *Sandwich Buns.* Divide dough into 2 portions. Roll each piece of dough into a strip 1½ in. in diameter. Cut strips into pieces approximately

Fig. 6. Parkerhouse Rolls. (Courtesy of the Wheat Flour Institute.)

2 oz. each. Round the pieces into balls. Place balls in rows on greased baking sheet 1½–2 in. apart. Let stand 10–15 min.; flatten balls with fingers to desired thickness or weigh 12-oz. pieces. Roll into 2-oz. balls. Place 35 rolls on a greased bun pan. Flatten with a rolling pin or another bun pan.

17. *Sesame Rolls.* Proceed as for Twin Rolls. Brush top with melted fat and sprinkle with sesame seeds.
18. *Twin Rolls.* Weigh dough into 12-oz. pieces. Roll ⅝ in. thick. Cut rounds 1 in. in diameter. Brush with melted butter or margarine. Place on end in well-greased muffin pans, allowing 2 rounds for each roll.
19. *Twists.* Weigh dough into 12-oz. pieces. Roll ⅓ in. thick, spread with melted butter, sugar, and cinnamon. Cut into strips ⅓ × 8 in., bring both ends together and twist dough.
20. *Whole Wheat Rolls.* Substitute 2 lb. 6 oz. whole wheat flour for 2 lb. 6 oz. white flour. Proceed as for Plain Rolls.

Quick Roll Dough

Bake: 15–20 min.   Yield: 10 doz. rolls
Oven: 400–425° F.

Amount	Ingredient	Method
4 oz.	Yeast, compressed (or 2 oz. dry)	Soften yeast in water.
2 qt.	Water, lukewarm	
12	Eggs	Add eggs and fat. Mix.
8 oz.	Fat, liquid	
7 lb. 4 oz.	Flour (amount variable)	Add dry ingredients. Mix (low speed) until dough is smooth and elastic and leaves side of bowl, 15–20 min.
7 oz.	Nonfat dry milk	
8 oz.	Sugar	Divide dough into 12 equal portions (approximately 1½ lb. each). Let rest a few minutes.
3 T.	Salt	Work with 1 portion at a time. This will be a rather soft dough.
		Shape and place rolls on greased baking sheets and let rise. Bake.

Variations:
See variations for Plain Rolls pp. 116–121.

Refrigerator Rolls

Bake: 15–20 min. Yield: 6 doz.
Oven: 425° F.

Amount	Ingredient	Method
12 oz.	Sugar	Place sugar, fat, salt, and potatoes in mixer bowl.
12 oz.	Fat	
3 T.	Salt	
1½ c.	Potatoes, mashed, hot	
1¼ qt.	Milk, scalded	Add milk. Mix to blend. Cool to lukewarm.
2 oz.	Yeast, compressed (or 1 oz. dry)	Soften yeast in water. Add softened yeast, soda, and baking powder to milk mixture.
1 c.	Water, lukewarm	Add just enough of the flour to make a stiff batter.
1½ t.	Soda	Let rise 15 min.
1 T.	Baking powder	Add remaining flour or enough to make a stiff dough.
4 lb.	Flour	Mix until dough is smooth. Place in a greased container. Grease top. Cover and place in the refrigerator for 24 hrs.
		Remove dough from refrigerator and shape into rolls. Let rise 1–1½ hrs. or until light.
		Bake.

Variations:
See variations for Plain Rolls pp. 116–121.

Basic Sweet Roll Dough

Bake: 20–25 min.　　　　　　　　　　　　　　　Yield: 8 doz.
Oven: 375° F.

Amount	Ingredient	Method
3 c.	Milk, scalded	Combine milk, sugar, fat, and salt in mixer bowl.
1 lb.	Sugar	
1 lb.	Fat	Mix to blend.
3 T.	Salt	Cool to lukewarm.
9	Eggs, beaten	Add eggs.
4 oz.	Yeast, compressed (or 2 oz. dry)	Soften yeast in water. Add softened yeast to milk mixture.
1½ c.	Water, lukewarm	Mix (medium speed) until blended.
5–6 lb. (Variable)	Flour	Add flour. Mix (medium speed) to a smooth dough (5–6 min.). Do not overmix. Dough should be moderately soft.

1. The dough temperature just after mixing should be 78–82° F.
2. Place in lightly greased bowl. Grease top of dough, cover and let rise in warm place until double in bulk, about 2 hrs. (For a quicker rising dough, increase yeast to 6 oz. compressed or 3 oz. dry yeast.)
3. Punch down and let rise again, about 1 hr.
4. Punch down and divide into portions for rolls. Let rest 10 min.
5. Scale about 2 oz. per roll. Shape and let rise until rolls are almost double in bulk.
6. Bake.

Note:
You may substitute 4 oz. nonfat dry milk mixed with flour and 1 qt. water for the fluid milk.

Variations:
1. *Cherry-Nut Rolls.* Add 1 t. nutmeg, 1 t. lemon extract, 1 lb. chopped glacé cherries, and 1 lb. chopped pecans to dough. Shape dough into 1-oz. balls. When baked, cover with glaze made of orange juice and powdered sugar.
2. *Coffee Cake.* Scale 4 lb. dough, roll out to size of sheet pan. Cover top of dough with melted butter or margarine and topping. Butter Crunch Topping:

Blend 1 lb. sugar, 1 lb. butter or margarine, ½ t. salt, 3 oz. honey, and 2 lb. flour together to form a crumbly mixture. Butter Cinnamon Topping: Cream 8 oz. butter or margarine, 1 lb. sugar, 3 T. cinnamon, ½ t. salt. Add 4 beaten eggs and 3 oz. flour and blend. Fruit fillings may also be used.

3. *Crullers*. Roll dough ⅓ in. thick. Cut into strips ⅓ × 8 in. Bring 2 ends together and twist dough. Fry in deep fat after proofing. Frost with Powdered Sugar Glaze (p. 168) or dip in fine granulated sugar.

4. *Danish Pastry*. Roll a 4- or 5-lb. piece of dough into a rectangular shape about ¼ in. thick. Start at one edge and cover completely ⅔ of dough with small pieces of hard butter or margarine. Use from 2 to 5 oz. per lb. of dough. Fold the unbuttered ⅓ portion of dough over an equal portion of buttered dough. Fold the remaining ⅓ buttered dough over the top to make 3 layers of dough separated by a layer of fat. Roll out dough ¼ in. thick. This completes the first roll. Repeat folding and rolling two or more times. Do not allow fat to become soft while working with the dough. Let dough rest 45 min. Make into desired shapes.

5. *Hot Cross Buns*. Add to dough 8 oz. chopped glacé cherries, 8 oz. raisins, 2 T. cinnamon, ¼ t. cloves, and ¼ t. nutmeg. Shape into round buns, 1 oz. per bun. When baked, make a cross on top with powdered sugar frosting. (See Fig. 7.)

6. *Kolaches*. Add 2 T. grated lemon peel to dough. Shape dough into 1-oz. balls. Place on lightly greased baking sheet. Let rise until light. Press down

Fig. 7.   Hot Cross Buns. (Courtesy of the Wheat Flour Institute.)

center to make cavity and fill with 1 t. filling. Brush with melted butter or margarine and sprinkle with chopped nuts. Suggested fillings: Chopped cooked prunes and dried apricots with sugar and cinnamon, poppy seed mixed with sugar and milk, apricot or peach marmalade.
7. *Long Johns.* Roll out dough to a thickness of ½ in. Cut dough into rectangular pieces ½ × 4 in. Proof. Fry in deep fat.
8. *Swedish Braids.* Add to dough 1 lb. chopped candied fruit cake mix, 8 oz. pecans, and ½ t. cardamom seed. Weigh dough into 1¾-lb. portions and braid. When baked, brush with Powdered Sugar Glaze made with milk (p. 168).

Cinnamon Rolls

Bake: 20–25 min.   Yield: 7–8 doz.
Oven: 375° F.

Amount	Ingredient	Method
1 Recipe (10 lb.)	Plain Roll Dough (p. 116) or Basic Sweet Roll Dough (p. 123) (raised and ready for shaping)	Divide dough into 8 portions about 1¼ lb. each. Roll each portion into rectangular strip 9 × 14 × ⅓ in.
12 oz.	Butter or margarine, melted	Spread each strip with butter, then sprinkle with 1 c. of the mixed sugar and cinnamon.
2 lb.	Sugar	Roll as for Jelly Roll (p. 149).
3 T.	Cinnamon	Cut into 1-in. slices. Place cut side down on greased bun pans (2 doz. rolls, 1½ oz. each, per 18 × 26 × 1-in. pan) or in muffin pans. Let rise until doubled in bulk, about 45 min. Bake. After removing from oven, spread tops with Powdered Sugar Glaze (p. 168) made with milk in place of water.

Variations:
1. *Butterfly Rolls.* Cut rolled dough into 2 in. slices. Press each roll across center parallel to the cut side, with the back of a large knife handle. Press or flatten out the folds of each end. Place on greased baking sheet 1½ in. apart. (See Fig. 9.)
2. *Butterscotch Rolls.* Use brown sugar and omit cinnamon, if desired. Cream 8 oz. butter or margarine, 1½ lb. brown sugar, and 1 t. salt. Gradually add 1 c. water, blending thoroughly. Spread 1 T. mixture into each greased muffin pan cup. Place rolls cut side down in pans.

Fig. 8. Cinnamon Rolls. (Courtesy of the Wheat Flour Institute.)

Fig. 9. Cinnamon Butterfly Rolls. (Courtesy of the Wheat Flour Institute.)

3. *Cinnamon–Raisin Rolls.* Use brown sugar and add 8 oz. raisins to filling.

4. *Double Cinnamon Buns.* Proceed as for Butterfly Rolls. Roll sheet of dough from both sides to form a double roll.

5. *Glazed Marmalade Rolls.* Omit cinnamon. Dip cut slice in additional melted butter and sugar. When baked, glaze with orange marmalade mixed with powdered sugar until of a consistency to spread. Apricot marmalade, strawberry jam, or other preserves may be used for the glaze.

6. *Honey Rolls.* Substitute honey filling for sugar and cinnamon. Whip 1 lb. butter or margarine and 1 lb. honey until light and fluffy.

7. *Orange Rolls.* Omit cinnamon. Spread with mixture of 1½ lb. sugar and 1 c. grated orange rind. When baked, brush with glaze made of powdered sugar and orange juice. If desired, use a filling made by cooking 1½ lb. sugar and 6 c. ground whole oranges (about 9 medium-sized ones) until thickened. Cool. Spread on roll dough. A quick filling may be made by combining 12 oz. frozen orange juice and 1½ lb. sugar.

8. *Pecan Rolls.* Proceed as for Butterscotch Rolls. Add 12 oz. pecans to mixture placed in muffin pans. (See Fig. 10.)

9. *Sugared Snails.* Proceed as for Butterfly Rolls, rolling dough thinner before adding sugar filling. Cut rolled dough into slices ¾ in. thick. Place cut surface of each roll in granulated sugar. Place on greased baking sheet ½ in. apart with sugared side up. Allow to stand 10 to 15 min., then flatten before baking.

Fig. 10. Pecan Rolls. (Courtesy of the Wheat Flour Institute.)

Fruit Coffee Rings

Bake: 25–30 min.   Yield: 8 rings
Oven: 375° F.

Amount	Ingredient	Method
10 lb. (1 recipe)	Plain Roll Dough (p. 116) or Basic Sweet Roll Dough (p. 123) (raised and ready for shaping)	Divide dough into 1½-lb. portions. Roll out each portion into a rectangular strip 9 × 14 × ⅓ in.
2 qt.	Filling (see below)	Spread each strip with 1 c. filling. Roll as for cinnamon rolls. Arrange in ring mold or 10-in. tube pan. Cut slashes in dough with scissors about 1 in. apart. Let rise. Bake.

Suggested Fillings:
Apricot Ring. Use 2 qt. Apricot Filling (p. 173).
Cranberry Ring. Use 2 qt. Cranberry Filling (p. 174).
Fig Ring. Use 2 qt. Fig Filling (p. 174).
Honey Ring. Whip 1 lb. butter or margarine and 1 lb. honey until light and fluffy.
Orange Ring. Use 2 qt. orange marmalade.
Prune–Date Ring. Use 2 qt. Prune–Date Filling (p. 173).

Bran Rolls

Bake: 15 min.   Yield: 8 doz.
Oven: 425° F.

Amount	Ingredient	Method
1 lb.	Fat	Combine in mixer bowl.
12 oz.	Sugar	Stir until fat is melted.
1 T.	Salt	Let stand until mixture is lukewarm.
4 oz.	All-Bran	
1 pt.	Water, boiling	
2 oz.	Yeast, compressed (or 1 oz. dry yeast)	Soften yeast in water. Add softened yeast and eggs to bran
1 pt.	Water, lukewarm	mixture.
4	Eggs, beaten	Mix (medium speed) until blended.
3 lb. (Variable)	Flour	Add flour (low speed). Mix until soft dough is formed. 1. Place in lightly greased bowl. 2. Cover and place in refrigerator until chilled. (Dough may be held overnight in refrigerator.) 3. Remove from refrigerator, form balls of dough to half fill greased muffin pans. 4. Let rise 2 hr. Bake.

Raised Muffins

Bake: 20 min.   Yield: 8 doz.
Oven: 350° F.

Amount	Ingredient	Method
9 oz. 12 oz. 3 T.	Fat Sugar Salt	Place fat, sugar, and salt in mixer bowl.
1½ qt.	Milk, scalded	Add milk. Mix (low speed). Cool to lukewarm.
3 oz. 1½ c. 12 2 lb.	Yeast, compressed (or 1½ oz. dry) Water, lukewarm Eggs, beaten Flour	Soften yeast in water. Add softened yeast and eggs to milk mixture. Add flour. Beat (medium speed) 10 min. Let rise in warm place for 1½ hr.
2 lb. 12 oz. (Variable)	Flour	Add remaining flour. Beat until batter is smooth. Use No. 20 dipper to fill greased muffin pans. Let rise until double in bulk (about 1 hr.) Bake.

Butter Buns

Bake: 15–20 min.   Yield: 9–10 doz.
Oven: 400° F.

Amount	Ingredient	Method
1 qt.	Milk	Scald milk and cool until lukewarm.
4 oz.	Yeast, compressed	Add yeast. Let stand to soften.
1 lb.	Sugar	Add sugar and butter or margarine.
1 lb. 8 oz.	Butter or margarine	
12	Eggs, beaten	Add eggs, salt, extract, and flour. Mix thoroughly.
16	Egg yolks, beaten	Let rise until double in bulk.
2 T.	Salt	Use a No. 30 dipper to fill greased muffin tins.
4 t.	Lemon extract	
4 lb. 8 oz.	Flour	Let rise 1 hr.
		Bake.

Note:
You may substitute 2 oz. dry yeast for compressed yeast. Soften dry yeast in
1 c. lukewarm water and decrease milk to 1½ pt.

White Bread

Bake: 30–40 min.
Oven: 400° F.

Yield: 16 1½-lb. loaves

Amount	Ingredient	Method
4–5 oz.	Yeast, compressed (or 2–2½ oz. dry)	Soften yeast in water. Let stand 10 min.
1½ pt.	Water, lukewarm	
10 oz.	Sugar	Add sugar, salt, water, fat, and dry milk.
5 oz.	Salt	Mix (medium speed) until blended.
1 gal.	Water, lukewarm	
12 oz.	Fat, melted	
14 oz.	Nonfat dry milk solids	
15 lb.	Flour	Add flour. Mix (low speed) about 10 min. or until dough is smooth and elastic.
		1. Let rise approximately 2 hrs., or until double in bulk. Knead.
		2. Let rise approximately 1 hr. Knead and divide dough into 16 loaves. (26½ oz. raw dough will yield 1½-lb. loaf.)
		3. Let rise approximately 1½ hr. or until double in bulk.
		4. Bake.

Notes:
1. The dough temperature should be 88°–90° F. when mixed.
2. Fat may be increased to 1 lb. and sugar to 2 oz. if a richer dough is desired.
3. 1¼ gal. fresh milk may be substituted for the water and dry milk.

Variations:
1. *Cinnamon Bread.* After dough has been divided and scaled into loaves, roll into a rectangular sheet. Brush with melted fat; sprinkle generously with cinnamon and sugar. Roll as for jelly roll. Seal edge of dough and place in greased baking pan sealed edge down. Sprinkle top with cinnamon and sugar.
2. *Raisin Bread.* Add 3 lb. of raisins to dough after mixing.
3. *Whole Wheat Bread.* Substitute whole wheat flour for ½ of white flour.
4. *Butter Slices.* Divide dough into thirds. Roll ⅓ in. thick. Cut with 3-in. biscuit cutter. Dip in melted butter or margarine and stand pieces on edge in 4 × 9-in. loaf pans (8 pieces per pan). Let rise and bake. Dough may be shaped into long roll and cut into slices.

Norwegian Christmas Bread

Bake: 40 min.   Yield: 6 loaves 4 x 9 in.
Oven: 350° F.   12–14 slices per loaf

Amount	Ingredient	Method
1 qt. 1 lb. 2 t. 1 t.	Milk Sugar Salt Cardamom seed, crushed	Scald milk. Add sugar, salt, and carda-mom seed. Cool to lukewarm.
3 oz. ½ c.	Yeast, compressed Water, lukewarm	Soften yeast in water and add to milk.
1 lb. 8 oz. 1 lb.	Flour Butter or mar-garine, soft	Add flour and butter. Mix to form a batter. Let stand 15 min.
1 lb. 12 oz. (or more) 12 oz. 6 oz.	Flour Candied cherries (red and green) Pecans, chopped fine	Slice cherries and dust with flour. Add cherries, pecans, and remainder of flour to batter. Mix until a smooth dough is formed. Cover and let rise until double in bulk. Punch down gently. Turn onto lightly floured board. Divide into 6 loaves and shape. Let rise until almost double in bulk (about 40 min.). Bake.

French Toast

Yield: 50 slices

Amount	Ingredient	Method
18	Eggs	Beat eggs.
1½ qt.	Milk	Combine with other ingredients.
1 T.	Salt	
½ c.	Sugar	
50	Bread slices	Dip bread into egg mixture. Do not let bread soak in the egg mixture. Fry in deep fat at 360° F. or on a well-greased griddle until golden brown. Sprinkle with powdered sugar to serve.

Notes:
1. The bread should be at least 3 days old.
2. Unsliced bread may be sliced double thickness, cut into triangles, or left whole, dipped in egg mixture or in thin batter (p. 69), and fried in deep fat.

DESSERTS

Cakes

Cakes are classified as butter cakes and sponge cakes. Butter cakes are usually leavened with baking powder or soda and an acid. True sponge cakes are leavened chiefly by air incorporated in beaten eggs, although modified sponge cakes may have baking powder added. Butter cakes are most often baked as sheet cakes, in layers, or as individual cup cakes; sponge cakes are baked in tube pans or sheets.

A properly balanced formula, correct temperature of ingredients, accurate measurements, controlled mixing of ingredients, proper relationship of batter to pan, and correct oven temperature and baking time are essential to good cake making.

Angel Food Cake

Bake: 50–55 min. at 325° F. *or*   Yield: 3 10-in. cakes
      35 min. at 400° F.
                                    14–16 portions per cake

Amount	Ingredient	Method
2 lb. 8 oz. (5 c.) 1 t. 2 T.	Egg whites Salt Cream of tartar	Beat egg whites (high speed) 1 min. Add salt and cream of tartar Continue beating until egg whites are just stiff enough to hold shape.
1 lb. 8 oz. 1 T.	Sugar Vanilla	Add sugar slowly (medium speed). Add vanilla. Continue beating (high speed) for 2 min. or until mixture will stand in stiff peaks.
12 oz. 12 oz.	Sugar Cake flour	Mix sugar and flour. Gradually add to egg whites (low speed).* Continue mixing 2 min. after last addition. Pour into 3 ungreased tube cake pans. Bake. Immediately upon removal from oven, invert cake to cool.

* To mix by hand, remove bowl from machine and fold sugar–flour mixture into meringue with wire whip or spatula, adding 1 c. at a time. Mix about 5 strokes after each addition.

Note:
Either frozen or fresh egg whites may be used. The frozen egg whites should be approximately 70° F. when whipped.

Variations:
1. *Chocolate Angel Food Cake.* Substitute 1½ oz. cocoa for 1½ oz. flour.
2. *Tutti Frutti Angel Food Cake.* Add chopped candied fruits, dates, and nuts to cake batter.
3. *Orange-filled Angel Food Cake.* Cut cake into 3 slices. Spread Orange Filling (p. 172) between layers, and frost top and sides with Orange Frosting (p. 170).
4. *Gelatin-filled Angel Food Cake.* Cut a slice from top of cake. Remove some from inside, leaving a ¾-in. wall. Fill case with any gelatin mixture. Replace top of cake, cover with icing, and garnish with almonds and cherries.
5. *Frozen Filled Angel Food Cake.* Cut cake into 3 slices. Spread softened strawberry ice cream on first layer and cover with cake slice. Spread second slice with softened pistachio ice cream. Top with remaining slice. Frost top and sides with sweetened whipped cream and toasted coconut. Freeze. Other ice cream or sherbet variations may be used as filling.

Yellow Angel Food
(*Egg Yolk Sponge Cake*)

Bake: 30–45 min.   Yield: 3 10-in. cakes
Oven: 350–375° F.   10–14 portions per cake

Amount	Ingredient	Method
3 c.	Egg yolks	Beat egg yolks.
2 c.	Water, boiling	Add water. Beat (high speed) until light, approximately 5 min.
1 lb.	Sugar, sifted	Add sugar gradually, beating (high speed) while adding.
12 oz. 12 oz.	Cake flour Sugar	Add combined flour and sugar (low speed).
10 oz. 4½ t. 1 t. 3 T. 1 T.	Cake flour Baking powder Salt Lemon juice Lemon rind, grated	Mix flour and baking powder. Gradually add (low speed) to egg mixture alternately with lemon juice and rind.
1 T. 1½ t.	Vanilla Lemon extract	Add flavoring and continue mixing (low speed) 2 min. Pour into 3 ungreased tube cake pans. Bake. Immediately on removal from oven, invert cakes to cool.

Orange Chiffon Cake

Bake: 45–50 min.   Yield: 3 10-in. cakes
Oven: 350° F.   10–14 portions per cake

Amount	Ingredient	Method
1 lb. 8 oz. 1½ oz. (3 T.) 2 t. 1 lb. 3 oz.	Cake flour Baking powder Salt Sugar	Combine dry ingredients (low speed) in mixer bowl.
12 oz. (1½ c.) 1 lb. (2 c.) 1½ c.	Salad oil Egg yolks, beaten Water	Add oil, yolks, and water. Mix (medium speed) until smooth.
1 c. 2 T.	Orange juice Orange rind, grated	Add orange juice and rind gradually. Mix well after each addition, but avoid overmixing.
1 lb. 4 oz. (2½ c.) 2 t. 1 lb. 2 oz.	Egg whites Cream of tartar Sugar	Whip egg whites until foamy. Add cream of tartar, continue beating until egg whites form soft peaks. Add sugar gradually and continue beating until very stiff. Fold gently into the batter. Pour into 3 ungreased tube cake pans. Bake.

Note:
Turn cake upside down as soon as removed from oven. When cake has cooled, remove from pans and frost with Orange Frosting (p. 170).
Variations:
1. *Cocoa Chiffon Cake.* Omit orange juice and rind. Add 5 oz. cocoa to dry ingredients. Increase water to 2⅓ c. Add 1 T. vanilla.
2. *Walnut Chiffon Cake.* Omit orange juice and rind. Increase water to 2⅓ c. Add 2 T. vanilla and 12 oz. finely chopped walnuts. Frost with Burnt Butter Frosting (p. 170).

Plain Cake

Bake: 40–45 min.
Oven: 350° F.

Yield: 1 pan 12 x 20 x 2 in.
40 portions 2¼ x 2½ in.
48 portions 2 x 2½ in.

Amount	Ingredient	Method
1 lb. 9 oz. 2½ T. 10 oz.	Cake flour Baking powder Fat	Mix flour, baking powder, and fat (low speed) 2 min. Scrape down bowl; mix 3 min. more.
1 lb. 14 oz. 1½ t. 1¼ c.	Sugar Salt Milk	Add combined sugar, salt, and milk. Mix (low speed) 2 min. Scrape down bowl; mix 3 min. more.
5 1⅔ c. 1 T.	Eggs Milk Vanilla	Add half of combined egg, milk, and vanilla. Mix (low speed) 30 sec. Scrape down bowl; mix 1 min. Add remaining egg mixture. Mix 1 min. Scrape down bowl; mix 2½ min. Pour into greased baking pan. Bake.

Notes:

1. Use 1½ recipe for 6 9-in. layer pans. Scale 1 lb. 8 oz. into each pan.
2. For cup cakes, measure into muffin pans with No. 30 dipper; yield 6 doz.

Variations:

1. *Boston Cream Pie.* Bake plain cake in sheet pan or in layer pans. Spread with Custard Filling (p. 172). Sprinkle with chopped nuts and serve with whipped cream.
2. *Chocolate Cake.* Omit 6 oz. flour and add 6 oz. cocoa to the flour and fat.
3. *Cottage Pudding.* Cut cake into squares and serve with No. 20 dipper of fruit sauce or other sauce.
4. *Dutch Apple Cake.* After the cake batter is poured into baking pan, arrange 2½ lb. pared sliced apples in rows. Sprinkle over the top ½ c. sugar and 1 t. cinnamon, mixed.
5. *Lazy Daisy Cake.* Mix 9 oz. butter, melted, 1 lb. brown sugar, 1 lb. coconut, and ¾–1 c. cream (enough to moisten to consistency for spreading). Spread over Plain Cake (baked) and brown under broiler or in oven.
6. *Marble Cake.* Divide batter into 2 portions after mixing. To 1 portion add 1 T. cocoa, 1 t. cinnamon, ½ t. cloves, and ½ t. nutmeg. Place spoonsful of batters alternately in cake pans; mix slightly.
7. *Praline Cake.* Substitute chopped pecans for coconut in Lazy Daisy cake.
8. *Spice Cake.* Add 1 T. cocoa, 2 t. cinnamon, ½ t. cloves, and 1 t. nutmeg.
9. *Upside-down Cake.* Place 1 No. 10 can of crushed pineapple (or tidbits), drained, 1 lb. butter or margarine, 1½ lb. brown sugar, and 8 oz. chopped nutmeats in bottom of the cake pan. Pour plain cake batter over mixture. (2½ lb. A.P., cooked dried apricots may be substituted for pineapple.)
10. *Washington Cream Pie.* Double the basic recipe and bake in 12 9-in. layers. Put the layers together with cream or chocolate filling. Sift powdered sugar on top of pie or cover with a thin Chocolate Frosting (p. 166).

Master Cake Mix

Yield: 30 lb. mix

7 12 x 20 x 2-in. cakes

Amount	Ingredient	Method
10 lb. 8 oz.	Cake flour	Mix flour, dry milk, baking powder, salt, and sugar (low speed) 1 min.
1 lb. 12 oz.	Nonfat dry milk	
8 oz.	Baking powder, double acting	
2 oz.	Salt	
5 lb. 4 oz.	Sugar	
6 lb.	Sugar	Divide sugar into 2 lb. portions.
4 lb. 14 oz.	Shortening, hydrogenated, emulsified	Cream shortening (medium speed) using flat beater 3 min. Scrape down bowl and beater.
		Add 2 lb. sugar. Cream (medium speed) 1 min. Repeat until all sugar is added. Scrape bowl and beater.
		Add 4 qt. blended dry ingredients. Mix (low speed) 1 min. Repeat once more.
		Lower bowl, add remaining dry ingredients. Blend (low speed) 1 min. while slowly raising mixer bowl. Mix should resemble cornmeal in consistency.
		Store in tightly covered container.

Plain Cake
(*Using Master Cake Mix*)

Bake: 45 min. Yield: 1 12 x 20 x 2-in. cake
Oven: 350° F.

Amount	Ingredient	Method
4 lb. 4 oz.	Master Cake Mix (p. 140)	Place mix in bowl. Add eggs, vanilla, and ½ of the water.
12 oz.	Eggs, whole, frozen or fresh	Mix (low speed) 2 min. Scrape down bowl.
1 T.	Vanilla	Mix (medium speed) 3 min. Scrape bowl and beater.
2½ c.	Water	Add remaining water gradually, mixing (low speed) 2 min. Scrape down bowl and mix (medium speed) 1 min.
		Scale 5 lb. batter in a slightly greased and lined pan. Bake.

Variations:
1. *Spice Cake.* Blend 1½ T. cinnamon, 1 T. nutmeg, 2½ T. cloves, and 1½ t. allspice with cake mix.
2. *Chocolate Cake.* Blend 4 oz. (1 c.) cocoa and 1¾ t. baking soda with mix.

White Cake

Bake: 40–45 min.   Yield: 1 pan 12 x 20 x 2 in.
Oven: 350° F.   40 portions 2¼ x 2½ in.
                                             48 portions 2 x 2½ in.

Amount	Ingredient	Method
1 lb. 8 oz. 1 oz. 12 oz.	Cake flour Baking powder Fat	Mix flour, baking powder, and fat (low speed) 2 min. Scrape down bowl; mix 3 min. more.
1 lb. 8 oz. 1½ t. 1 c.	Sugar Salt Milk	Add combined sugar, salt, and milk. Mix (low speed) 2 min. Scrape down bowl; mix 3 min. more.
8 1¼ c. 1 T.	Egg whites Milk Vanilla	Add half of combined egg whites, milk, and vanilla. Mix (low speed) 30 sec. Scrape down bowl; mix 1 min. Add remaining egg–milk mixture. Mix (low speed) 1 min. Scrape down bowl; mix 2½ min. Pour into greased baking pan. Bake.

Notes:
1. For 6 9-in. layer pans, use 1½ recipe; scale 1 lb. 6 oz. per pan.
2. For cup cakes, increase flour to 1 lb. 14 oz. Use No. 20 dipper to portion.
Variations:
1. *Chocolate Chip Cake.* Add 4 oz. chocolate chips.
2. *Poppy Seed Cake.* Add 4 oz. poppy seed.

Banana Cake

Bake: 25–30 min.   Yield: 3 2-layer cakes (9 in.)
Oven: 350° F.   14–18 portions per cake

Amount	Ingredient	Method
12 oz.	Fat	Cream fat, sugar, and vanilla (medium speed) 10 min.
1 lb. 8 oz.	Sugar	
1 T.	Vanilla	
3 c.	Bananas, mashed	Add bananas and eggs. Mix (medium speed) 5 min.
6	Eggs	
1 lb. 8 oz.	Cake flour	Add combined dry ingredients alternately with sour milk (low speed). Mix (medium speed) 2 to 3 min. Pour into 6 greased layer cake pans. Bake.
1 t.	Salt	
2½ T.	Baking powder	
½ T.	Soda	
¾ c.	Sour milk or buttermilk	

Note:
May be baked in 12 × 20 × 2-in. pan.

Applesauce Cake

Bake: 40–45 min.   Yield: 1 pan 12 x 20 x 2 in.
Oven: 350° F.   40 portions 2¼ x 2½ in.
                                          48 portions 2 x 2½ in.

Amount	Ingredient	Method
12 oz.	Fat	Cream fat and sugar (medium speed) 10 min.
1 lb. 8 oz.	Sugar	
6	Eggs	Add eggs. Mix (medium speed) 5 min.
1 lb. 6 oz.	Cake flour	Add combined dry ingredients alternately with water (low speed).
2 T.	Baking powder	
1½ t.	Salt	
2 t.	Cinnamon	
2 t.	Cloves	
½ t.	Soda	
1 t.	Nutmeg	
1 pt.	Water	
1 pt.	Applesauce	Add remaining ingredients. Mix (low speed) only to blend. Pour into greased baking pan. Bake.
1 lb.	Raisins	
8 oz.	Nuts, chopped	

Note:
This cake is too tender to bake in layers.

Fudge Cake

Bake: 25–30 min.   Yield: 3 2-layer cakes (9 in.)
Oven: 350° F.   14–18 portions per cake

Amount	Ingredient	Method
12 oz.	Fat	Cream fat, sugar, and vanilla (medium
2 lb.	Sugar	speed) 10 min.
1 T.	Vanilla	
6	Eggs	Add eggs and mix (medium speed) 5 min.
5 oz.	Cocoa	Mix cocoa and hot water.
1½ c.	Water, hot	
1 lb. 12 oz.	Cake flour	Mix dry ingredients.
1½ T.	Soda	Add alternately with cocoa and sour milk
1 t.	Salt	to creamed mixture (low speed).
3 c.	Sour milk or buttermilk	Scrape down bowl. Continue mixing until smooth and ingredients are mixed. Pour into 6 greased 9-in. layer pans. Bake.

Variations:
1. *Chocolate Sheet Cake.* Bake cake in a bun pan 18 × 26 × 1 in. or, using ¾ recipe, in a 12 × 20 × 2-in. pan.
2. *Chocolate Cup Cakes.* Portion with No. 20 dipper into muffin pans.

German Sweet-Chocolate Cake

Bake: 35–40 min. Yield: 3 2-layer cakes (9 in.)
Oven: 350° F. 14–18 portions per cake

Amount	Ingredient	Method
1 lb.	Fat	Cream fat and sugar (medium speed)
2 lb.	Sugar	10 min.
8	Egg yolks	Add yolks one at a time. Beat well after each addition.
8 oz.	German sweet chocolate	Melt chocolate in water. Cool.
1 c.	Water, boiling	Add vanilla.
2 t.	Vanilla	Add to creamed mixture.
1 lb. 4 oz.	Cake flour	Add combined dry ingredients alternately with buttermilk (low speed).
1 t.	Salt	
2 t.	Soda	Mix (low speed) until smooth.
2 c.	Buttermilk	Scrape down bowl.
8	Egg whites	Beat egg whites until stiff peaks form. Fold into batter (low speed). Pour into 6 greased layer pans. Bake. When cool, cover with Coconut Pecan Frosting (p. 169).

Pineapple Cashew Cake

Bake: 25–30 min. Yield: 3 2-layer cakes (9 in.)
Oven: 350° F. 14–18 portions per cake

Amount	Ingredient	Method
1 lb. 2 oz.	Butter or margarine	Cream butter or margarine, sugar, and vanilla (medium speed) 8 min.
1 lb. 14 oz.	Sugar	
1 T.	Vanilla	
10	Egg yolks	Add egg yolks in 3 portions, while creaming. Mix 2 min.
1 lb. 14 oz.	Cake flour	Add combined dry ingredients alternately with milk (low speed).
1½ oz.	Baking powder	
1½ t.	Salt	
2¼ c.	Milk	
1 lb.	Pineapple, crushed, drained	Add pineapple. Mix (low speed) only to blend.
10	Egg whites	Beat egg whites until stiff but not dry (high speed). Fold into batter (low speed). Pour into 6 greased layer cake pans. Bake.
8 oz.	Cashew nuts, toasted, chopped	When cool, cover with Pineapple Butter Frosting (p. 169) and sprinkle with toasted cashews.

Burnt Sugar Cake

Bake: 25–30 min.
Oven: 375° F.

Yield: 3 2-layer cakes (9 in.)
14–18 portions per cake

Amount	Ingredient	Method
12 oz. 2 lb.	Fat Sugar	Cream fat and sugar (medium speed) 10 min.
6	Egg yolks	Add yolks and mix 5 min.
1½ c. 1½ c. ½ c. 1 T.	Milk Water Burnt Sugar Sirup (p. 69) Vanilla	Combine liquids.
1 lb. 10 oz. 2 T. 1 t.	Cake flour Baking powder Salt	Combine dry ingredients. Add to creamed mixture alternately with liquids (low speed). Scrape down bowl. Mix 2 min.
6	Egg whites	Beat egg whites until they form soft peaks. Fold into batter (low speed). Pour into 6 greased layer pans. Bake.

Prune Cake

Bake: 25–30 min.   Yield: 3 2-layer cakes (9 in.)
Oven: 360° F.   14–18 portions per cake

Amount	Ingredient	Method
1 lb. 8 oz.	Fat	Cream fat and sugar (medium speed)
2 lb.	Sugar	10 min.
12	Eggs	Add eggs, one at a time, beating after each addition.
1 qt. (1½ lb. A.P.)	Prunes, cooked, pitted, mashed	Add prunes. Mix until blended.
2 lb.	Cake flour	Combine dry ingredients.
1 t.	Salt	Add to creamed mixture (low speed)
4 t.	Soda	alternately with sour cream (low
1 T.	Nutmeg	speed).
1 T.	Cinnamon	Pour into 6 greased layer pans. Bake.
1 T.	Allspice	
1 T.	Cloves	
2 c.	Cultured sour cream	

Note:
When cake is cooled, put two layers together with Prune Filling (p. 173). Spread top with Cream Cheese Frosting (p. 171) or with sifted powdered sugar.

Jelly Roll

Bake: 12 min.   3 rolls (3 pans 12 x 20 in.)
Oven: 375° F.   15–20 slices per roll

Amount	Ingredient	Method
15 1 lb. 8 oz.	Eggs Sugar	Beat eggs (high speed) 1–2 min. Add sugar. Beat 10–15 min.
12 oz. 1 T. 2 T. 1½ t.	Cake flour Cream of tartar Baking powder Salt	Mix dry ingredients. Fold (low speed) into egg-sugar mixture.
2 t.	Lemon juice	Add lemon juice. Mix only to blend, 1 min. Pour into 3 12 × 20-in. pans lined with waxed paper. When baked, turn onto a cloth or heavy paper covered with powdered sugar. Quickly remove waxed paper. Trim edges if hard. Immediately roll cake (tightly). When cooled but not cold, unroll, spread with a thin layer of jelly or Custard Filling (p. 172). Roll firmly and wrap with wax paper until serving time. Sprinkle top with powdered sugar. Slice to serve.

Variation:
Apricot Roll. Cover with Apricot Filling (p. 173) and roll. Cover outside with sweetened whipped cream or whipped topping and toasted coconut.

Chocolate Roll

Bake: 20 min.   Yield: 4 rolls (2 pans 18 x 26 in.)
Oven: 325° F.   13 slices per roll

Amount	Ingredient	Method
24 2 lb. 4 oz.	Egg yolks Sugar	Beat yolks (high speed). Add sugar and continue beating until mixture is lemon colored, thick, and fluffy.
12 oz. 2 T.	Chocolate, melted Vanilla	Add chocolate and vanilla. Blend (low speed).
9 oz. 1 T. 1½ t.	Cake flour Baking powder Salt	Add combined dry ingredients (low speed).
24	Egg whites	Beat egg whites (high speed) until they will form rounded peaks. Fold into cake mixture (low speed). Spread into 2 greased pans 18 × 26 in. lined with heavy waxed paper. When baked, cut each cake in half crosswise. Quickly remove waxed paper and trim edges if hard. Roll and let stand a few minutes. Unroll and spread with Custard Filling (p. 172) or Fluffy Frosting (p. 167) or whipped cream, plain or flavored with peppermint. Roll up securely. Cover with a thin layer of Chocolate Frosting (p. 166).

Variation:
Ice Cream Roll. Spread with a thick layer of vanilla ice cream, soft enough to spread. Roll up securely and wrap in waxed paper. Place in freezer for several hours before serving.

Gingerbread

Bake: 40 min.
Oven: 350° F.

Yield: 1 pan 12 x 20 x 2 in.
40 portions 2¼ x 2½ in.
48 portions 2 x 2½ in.

Amount	Ingredient	Method
10 oz.	Fat	Cream fat and sugar (medium speed)
10 oz.	Sugar	10 min.
2½ c.	Sorghum	Add sorghum and blend (low speed).
1 lb. 10 oz.	Cake flour	Add combined dry ingredients alter-
2½ t.	Cinnamon	nately with the hot water (low speed).
2½ t.	Cloves	
2½ t.	Ginger	
1½ T.	Soda	
1 t.	Salt	
2¾ c.	Water, hot	
5	Eggs, beaten	Add eggs and mix (low speed) 2 min. Pour into greased baking pan. Bake.

Note:
Sprinkle with powdered sugar and serve warm.
Variations:
1. *Almond Meringue Gingerbread.* Cover baked Gingerbread with meringue, sprinkle with almonds, and brown in a moderate oven.
2. *Praline Gingerbread.* Spread baked Gingerbread with topping of 9 oz. butter, melted, 1 lb. brown sugar, 1 lb. chopped pecans, ¾–1 c. cream. Brown under broiler, or return to oven and heat until topping is slightly browned.
3. *Ginger Muffins.* Measure into well-greased muffin pans with No. 24 dipper. Yield 5½ doz.

Orange Cup Cakes

Bake: 20–25 min.   Yield: 4 doz.
Oven: 375° F.

Amount	Ingredient	Method
10 oz. 1 lb. 1 oz.	Fat Sugar	Cream fat and sugar (medium speed) 10 min.
1 T. 5	Vanilla Eggs	Add vanilla and eggs; mix (medium speed) until well blended.
7 oz. 3	Raisins, ground Orange rinds, grated	Add raisins and grated rind. Blend (low speed).
1 lb. 8 oz. ¾ T. 1½ oz. ¾ t. 1¾ c.	Cake flour Soda Baking powder Salt Milk, sour or buttermilk	Add combined dry ingredients alternately with sour milk (low speed). Mix only until smooth. Measure with No. 30 dipper into greased muffin pans. Bake.
6 oz. ¾ c.	Sugar Orange juice	While cakes are hot, brush with sugar and orange juice mixture, or frost with Orange Frosting (p. 170).

Note:
May be baked in loaves.

Fruit Cake

Bake: 2½ hr.   Yield: 4 2-lb. cakes (4 x 9 in.)
Oven: 300° F.   12–14 slices per cake

Amount	Ingredient	Method
8 oz.	Fat	Cream fat and sugar (medium speed)
1 lb.	Sugar	8 min.
4	Eggs	Add eggs. Mix 5 min.
8 oz.	Jelly	Add ingredients in the order listed.
2 t.	Cinnamon	Mix (low speed) only until fruit is
2 t.	Cloves	coated with flour mixture.
2 lb.	Raisins	
1 lb.	Currants	
1 lb.	Dates, chopped	
8 oz.	Nuts, chopped	
1 lb. 4 oz.	Cake flour	
2 t.	Soda	Dissolve soda in cold coffee; add to other
1½ c.	Coffee infusion, cold	ingredients. Mix until blended. Pour into 4 loaf pans lined with 2 layers of heavy waxed paper. Bake.

Notes:
1. May be steamed for 4 hrs.
2. Store in a container with a tight cover. Most fruit cakes improve in flavor if kept about 2 weeks before using.

Cookies

Cookies may be classified as drop and bar cookies, made from a soft dough; and as rolled, refrigerator, pressed, and molded cookies, made from a stiff dough. Almost all cookie doughs may be made in large amounts and stored in the refrigerator or freezer and used as needed.

For drop cookies, use No. 40, 50, or 60 dipper, depending on the desired size. A No. 40 would make a large cookie. A No. 60 might be used for 2 cookies per serving. For a smaller, tea-size cookie, drop dough from the end of a teaspoon or use a No. 100 dipper, if available. Icebox cookies may be sliced with a meat slicer if they have been well chilled.

Avoid overbaking cookies, and always remove from baking sheet onto cooling racks immediately after taking pans out of oven.

Sugar Cookies

Bake: 7 min.   Yield: 7 doz. 2-in. cookies
Oven: 400° F.

Amount	Ingredient	Method
8 oz.	Butter or margarine	Cream butter or margarine and sugar (medium speed) 5 min.
8 oz.	Sugar	
2	Eggs	Add eggs and vanilla. Blend (medium speed) 2 min.
2 t.	Vanilla	
12 oz.	Flour	Add combined dry ingredients. Mix (low speed).
1 t.	Salt	
1 t.	Baking powder	Roll dough ⅛ in. thick on board lightly dusted with a mixture of 1 c. flour and ½ c. sugar. Cut into desired shapes. Place on ungreased cookie sheets. Bake.

Note:
Cookies also may be shaped with cookie press or may be measured with No. 60 dipper onto baking sheet about 1½ in. apart and flattened to ¼-in. thickness with small can dipped in sugar.

Variations:
1. *Coconut Cookies.* Cut rolled dough with a round cookie cutter. Brush each cookie with melted fat and sprinkle with shredded coconut.
2. *Filled Cookies.* Cut dough with a round cutter. Cover half with Fig or Date Filling (pp. 173, 174). Brush edges with milk, cover with remaining cookies. Press edges together with tines of a fork.
3. *Pinwheel Cookies.* Use half of Sugar Cookie recipe. Divide dough into 2 portions. Add 1 square melted chocolate to 1 portion. Roll each into ⅛-in. sheets the same size. Place the chocolate dough over the white dough and press together. Roll as for Jelly Roll. Chill thoroughly. Cut into thin slices.
4. *Ribbon Cookies.* Cut chocolate and plain dough into long strips 1¾ in. wide. Arrange chocolate and plain strips alternately, until 1¼ in. high. Press together. Chill thoroughly. Cut into thin slices.
5. *Wreath Cookies.* Cut rolled dough with a doughnut cutter. Brush with beaten egg and sprinkle with chopped nuts. For Christmas cookies, decorate with candied cherry rings and pieces of citron arranged to represent holly.

Butter Tea Cookies

Bake: 10–12 min.   Yield: 50–75
Oven: 400° F.

Amount	Ingredient	Method
8 oz. 4½ oz. 3 ½ t.	Butter Sugar Egg yolks Vanilla	Cream butter and sugar (medium speed) 5 min. Add egg yolks and vanilla. Mix (medium speed) until blended.
10 oz.	Flour	Add flour and mix (low speed). Chill dough. Shape with cookie press onto ungreased baking pan. Bake.

Variation:
Thimble Cookies. Roll dough into 1-in. balls. Dip in egg white and roll in finely chopped pecans. Bake 3 min. at 325° F., then make indentation in center of cookies and fill with jelly. Bake 10–12 min. longer.

Chocolate Tea Cookies

Bake: 6–10 min.   Yield: 50–75
Oven: 375° F.

Amount	Ingredient	Method
8 oz. 6 oz. 1 2 t.	Butter or mar- garine Sugar Egg Vanilla	Cream butter or margarine and sugar (medium speed) 5 min. Add egg and vanilla. Blend (medium speed).
9 oz. ⅛ t. ½ t. 2 T.	Flour Salt Baking powder Cocoa	Add combined dry ingredients. Mix (low speed). Chill dough. Shape with cookie press onto ungreased baking pan. Bake.

Sandies

Bake: 20 min.   Yield: 8 doz.
Oven: 325° F.

Amount	Ingredient	Method
12 oz.	Butter or margarine	Cream butter or margarine, sugar, and vanilla (medium speed) 5 min.
3 oz.	Sugar	
1 t.	Vanilla	
1 lb. 2 oz.	Flour	Add flour and salt. Mix (low speed).
1 t.	Salt	
1 T.	Water	Add water and pecans.
8 oz.	Pecans, chopped	Chill dough.
		Shape into small balls ¾ in. in diameter or into bars about 1½ in. long and ½ in. thick. If mixture crumbles so it will not stick together, add a small amount of melted butter or margarine.
		Place on lightly greased baking sheet.
		Bake until lightly browned.
		Roll in powdered sugar while still hot.

Fudge Balls

Bake: 10–12 min.   Yield: 6 doz.
Oven: 350° F.

Amount	Ingredient	Method
12 oz.	Flour	Combine flour, sugar, and salt in mixer bowl.
1 lb.	Sugar	
1 t.	Salt	Add fat, chocolate, and coffee. Mix (medium speed) until smooth.
12 oz.	Fat, soft	
4 oz.	Chocolate, melted	
½ c.	Coffee, cold	
8 oz.	Rolled oats, quick, uncooked	Add rolled oats. Mix (low speed) until blended.
6 oz.	Nuts, chopped	Shape dough into balls 1 in. in diameter. Roll in nuts.
		Place on ungreased baking sheet.
		Chill before baking.

Butterscotch Pecan Cookies

Bake: 10–12 min.   Yield: 6 doz.
Oven: 375° F.

Amount	Ingredient	Method
8 oz.	Butter or margarine	Cream butter or margarine and sugar (medium speed) 5 min.
1 lb.	Brown sugar	
2	Eggs	Add eggs and vanilla. Mix (medium speed) until well blended.
2 t.	Vanilla	
12 oz.	Flour	Add flour and pecans. Mix (low speed).
8 oz.	Pecans, chopped	Drop onto greased baking sheet with No. 50 dipper, ⅔ oz. per cookie.

Butterscotch Drop Cookies

Bake: 10–15 min.   Yield: 8 doz.
Oven: 400° F.

Amount	Ingredient	Method
8 oz.	Butter or margarine	Cream butter or margarine and brown sugar (medium speed) 5 min.
1 lb.	Brown sugar	
4	Eggs	Add eggs and vanilla. Mix (medium speed) until well blended.
2 t.	Vanilla	
1 lb. 4 oz.	Flour	Add combined dry ingredients alternately with sour cream. Mix (low speed).
1 t.	Baking powder	
2 t.	Soda	
1 t.	Salt	
2 c.	Cultured sour cream	
8 oz.	Walnuts, chopped	Add nuts. Mix until blended. Chill dough until firm. Drop on greased baking sheet with No. 60 dipper, ½ oz. per cookie. Bake. Cover with Burnt Butter Frosting (p. 170) while still warm.

Variations:
1. *Butterscotch Squares.* Spread batter in 12 × 26-in. pan. Bake 25 min. at 325° F.
2. *Chocolate Drop Cookies.* Add 4 oz. chocolate, melted, to creamed mixture.

Chocolate Chip Cookies

Bake: 10–12 min.   Yield: 8 doz.
Oven: 375° F.

Amount	Ingredient	Method
6 oz. 4 oz. 4 oz.	Fat Granulated sugar Brown sugar	Cream fat and sugars (medium speed) 5 min.
2 1 t.	Eggs Vanilla	Add eggs and vanilla. Mix until well blended.
10 oz. 1 t. 1 t.	Flour Salt Soda	Add combined dry ingredients (low speed).
8 oz. 12 oz.	Nuts, chopped Chocolate chips	Add nuts and chocolate chips. Mix until blended. Drop on greased baking sheet with No. 60 dipper, ½ oz. per cookie. Bake.

Oatmeal Drop Cookies

Bake: 12–15 min.   Yield: 6 doz.
Oven: 375° F.

Amount	Ingredient	Method
6 oz. 8 oz. 2 1 t.	Fat Brown sugar Eggs Vanilla	Cream fat and sugar (medium speed) 5 min. Add eggs and vanilla. Continue to cream until well mixed.
7 oz.	Rolled oats, quick, uncooked	Add oats. Mix (low speed) to blend.
8 oz. 2 t. 1 t. ½ t. 5 T.	Flour Baking powder Salt Soda Milk	Add combined dry ingredients alternately with milk. Mix (low speed) until blended.
6 oz.	Raisins, cooked, chopped	Add raisins. Mix only to blend. Drop on greased baking sheet with No. 50 dipper, ⅔ oz. per cookie. Bake.

Coconut Drop Cookies

Bake: 15–18 min. Yield: 4 doz.
Oven: 325° F.

Amount	Ingredient	Method
1½ c.	Condensed milk, sweetened	Combine all ingredients.
1 lb.	Coconut, flaked	Drop on greased baking sheet with No. 60 dipper, ½ oz. per cookie.
1 T.	Vanilla	Bake.
8 oz.	Nuts, chopped	

Cornflake Kisses

Bake: 15 min. Yield: 6 doz.
Oven: 325° F.

Amount	Ingredient	Method
4	Egg whites	Beat egg whites (high speed) until frothy.
1 lb.	Sugar, sifted	Gradually add sugar. Beat until sugar is dissolved.
4 oz.	Cornflakes	Carefully fold in remaining ingredients.
8 oz.	Nuts, chopped	
3 oz.	Coconut, shredded	Drop on greased baking sheet with No. 60 dipper, ½ oz. per cookie.
1 t.	Vanilla	Bake.

Coconut Macaroons

Bake: 15 min. Yield: 8 doz.
Oven: 325° F.

Amount	Ingredient	Method
8	Egg whites	Beat egg whites and salt (high speed) until foamy.
⅛ t.	Salt	
12 oz.	Granulated sugar	Add sugars gradually. Add vanilla.
12 oz.	Powdered sugar	Continue beating (high speed) until stiff.
2 t.	Vanilla	
1 lb. 6 oz.	Coconut, shredded	Carefully fold in coconut (low speed). Drop on greased baking sheet with No. 50 dipper, ⅔ oz. each. Bake.

Peanut Butter Cookies

Bake: 8 min.   Yield: 5 doz.
Oven: 375° F.

Amount	Ingredient	Method
8 oz. 8 oz. 5 oz.	Fat Sugar Brown sugar	Cream fat and sugars (medium speed) 5 min.
2 1 t.	Eggs Vanilla	Add eggs and vanilla. Continue beating until blended.
9 oz. (1 c.)	Peanut butter	Add peanut butter. Blend (low speed).
8 oz. 1 t. ½ t.	Flour Soda Salt	Add combined dry ingredients. Mix (low speed) until well blended. Form into balls with No. 50 dipper, ⅔ oz. each. Flatten with tines of a fork or with a glass with damp cloth held over it. Bake.

Crisp Ginger Cookies

Bake: 8–10 min.   Yield: 8 doz.
Oven: 375° F.

Amount	Ingredient	Method
1 c. 8 oz.	Molasses Sugar	Combine molasses and sugar. Boil 1 min. Cool.
8 oz. 2	Fat Eggs	Add fat and blend (medium speed). Add eggs and mix well.
1 oz. 12 oz. (or more) ½ t. 1 t. 2 t.	Flour Salt Soda Ginger	Add combined dry ingredients. Mix (low speed) until well blended. Form dough into a roll 2 in. in diameter. Chill thoroughly and slice. (Dough also may be rolled and cut.) Place on greased baking sheet. Bake.

Butterscotch Ice Box Cookies

Bake: 8–10 min.   Yield: 8 doz.
Oven: 400° F.

Amount	Ingredient	Method
8 oz.	Butter or margarine	Cream fats and sugars (medium speed) 5 min.
8 oz.	Fat	
12 oz.	Granulated sugar	
1 lb.	Brown sugar	
4	Eggs	Add eggs and vanilla. Mix (medium speed) 5 min.
2 t.	Vanilla	
2 lb.	Flour	Add combined dry ingredients, dates, and nuts. Mix (low speed) until well blended.
2 t.	Cream of tartar	
2 t.	Soda	
8 oz.	Dates, finely chopped	Place dough on waxed paper. Form into 3 2-lb. rolls. Wrap.
8 oz.	Nuts, chopped	Chill several hours. Slice cookies ⅛ in. thick. Place on ungreased baking pan. Bake.

Oatmeal Crispies

Bake: 12–15 min.   Yield: 8 doz.
Oven: 350° F.

Amount	Ingredient	Method
12 oz.	Flour	Combine flour, salt, and soda in mixer bowl.
2 t.	Salt	
2 t.	Soda	
1 lb.	Fat	Add fat, sugars, eggs, and vanilla. Mix (low speed) about 5 min.
1 lb.	Brown sugar	
1 lb.	Granulated sugar	
4	Eggs	
2 t.	Vanilla	
1 lb.	Rolled oats, quick, uncooked	Add rolled oats and nuts. Mix (low speed) to blend.
8 oz.	Nuts, chopped	Shape dough into rolls 2 in. in diameter. Wrap in waxed paper. Chill overnight. Cut into slices ¼ in. thick. Place 2 in. apart on ungreased baking pan. Bake.

Note:
For smaller cookies, form into 1½-in. roll and slice ⅛ in. thick. Yield: Approximately 25 doz.
Variation:
Oatmeal Coconut Crispies. Add 1 c. flaked coconut.

Brownies

Bake: 25–30 min.   Yield: 1 pan 12 x 20 x 2 in.
Oven: 325° F.   48 portions 2 x 2½ in.

Amount	Ingredient	Method
12	Eggs	Beat eggs (high speed).
2 lb.	Sugar	Add sugar, fat, and vanilla. Mix (medium speed) 5 min.
1 lb.	Fat, melted	
¼ c.	Vanilla	
12 oz.	Cake flour	Add combined dry ingredients. Mix (low speed) about 5 min.
8 oz.	Cocoa	
4 t.	Baking powder	
2 t.	Salt	
12 oz.	Nuts, chopped	Add nuts. Mix to blend. Spread mixture ½ in. thick in pan. Bake. Should be soft to the touch when done. Do not overbake. While warm sprinkle with powdered sugar or cover with a thin layer of mocha or chocolate frosting if desired.

Notes:
1. 3 oz. unsweetened chocolate may be substituted for the cocoa. Add to fat-sugar-egg mixture.
2. 2 lb. chopped dates may be added.
3. For 18 × 26-in. bun pan, use 1½ times the recipe.

Butterscotch Squares

Bake: 25 min.   Yield: 1 pan 12 x 20 x 2 in.
Oven: 325° F.   48 squares 2 x 2½ in.

Amount	Ingredient	Method
8 oz. 1 lb. 4 oz.	Butter or margarine Brown sugar	Cream butter or margarine and sugar (medium speed) 5 min.
5 2 t.	Eggs Vanilla	Add eggs, one at a time, and vanilla. Mix (low speed) until blended.
12 oz. 1 T. ½ t.	Flour Baking powder Salt	Add combined dry ingredients. Mix (low speed) until blended.
6 oz.	Nuts, chopped (optional)	Add nuts. Spread mixture evenly in a greased baking pan. Bake.

Note:
Use twice as much for an 18 × 26-in. pan.

Oatmeal Date Bars

Bake: 45 min.   Yield: 1 pan 12 x 20 in.
Oven: 325° F.   48 bars 2 x 2¼ in.

Amount	Ingredient	Method
13 oz. 1 lb. 6 oz.	Fat Brown sugar	Cream fat and sugar (medium speed) 10 min.
1 lb. 12 oz. 4 t.	Flour Rolled oats, quick uncooked Soda	Add combined dry ingredients. Mix (low speed) until crumbly.
1½ qt.	Date Filling (p. 173)	Spread ⅔ of dough on greased baking pan. Pat down by hand to an even layer. Spread date filling evenly over entire surface. Cover with remainder of dough and pat down. Bake. Cut into bars.

Notes:
1. Crushed pineapple or cooked dried apricots may be used in place of dates in the filling.
2. For a thinner bar, mixture may be spread in a bun pan 18 × 26 in. Use 1½ times filling recipe.

Date Bars

Bake: 25–30 min.
Oven: 350° F.

Yield: 1 pan 18 x 26 in.
96 bars 2 x 2 in.
128 bars 1 x 3 in.

Amount	Ingredient	Method
12 2 lb.	Egg yolks Sugar	Beat yolks (high speed) until lemon colored. Add sugar gradually and continue beating after each addition.
1 lb. ½ t. 1½ T. 3 lb. 1 lb.	Flour Salt Baking powder Dates, chopped Nuts, chopped	Mix flour, salt, and baking powder. Add dates and nuts. Combine with egg–sugar mixture.
12	Egg whites	Beat egg whites (high speed) until they form a soft peak. Fold into batter. Spread evenly in a greased bun pan. Bake. Cut into bars while warm and roll in powdered sugar.

Coconut Pecan Bars

Bake: 30–35 min.
Oven: 350° F.

Yield: 1 pan 18 x 26 in.
96 bars 2 x 2 in.
128 bars 1 x 3 in.

Amount	Ingredient	Method
1 lb. 8 oz. 12 oz. 1 lb. 4 oz.	Butter or margarine Brown sugar Flour	Blend butter or margarine, brown sugar, and flour (low speed) until mixture resembles coarse meal. Press even layer of mixture into bun pan. Bake until light brown, 15–20 min.
8 4 oz. 1 T. 2 t. 8 oz. 2 lb. 8 oz. 1 T. 12 oz.	Eggs, beaten Flour Baking powder Salt Coconut, shredded or flaked Brown sugar Vanilla Pecans, chopped	Combine remaining ingredients to form topping. Spread over baked crust. Bake 20–25 min. Frost with Orange Frosting (p. 170) if desired.

Marshmallow Squares

Yield: 1 pan 12 x 20 in.
48 2 x 2½ in.

Amount	Ingredient	Method
6 oz. 1 lb. 1 t.	Butter or margarine Marshmallows Vanilla	Melt butter or margarine and marsh- mallows over hot water. Add vanilla.
11 oz.	Rice Krispies	Pour marshmallow mixture over Rice Krispies. Mix well. Press ½-in. layer into greased baking pan. Cool and cut into squares.

Variation:
Chocolate Marshmallow Squares. Cover squares with a thin rich chocolate
frosting.

Frostings and Fillings

The amount of frosting to use on a cake will depend on the kind of cake
to be frosted and the individual preferences of the patrons. The following
may serve as a guide:

1–1½ qt. for a 12 x 20-in. sheet cake
2¼–2½ qt. for 3 2-layer cakes
2–2½ qt. for 3 10-in. angel food cakes
2¼–2½ qt. for 18 x 26-in. sheet cake.

Boiled Frosting

Yield: 4½ qt.

Amount	Ingredient	Method
4 lb. 2½ c.	Sugar Water, hot	Combine sugar and water. Stir until sugar is dissolved. Boil without stirring to soft ball stage (238° F.).
8 2 T.	Egg whites Vanilla	Beat egg whites until stiff but not dry. Gradually pour sirup over egg whites while beating. Continue beating until frosting is of consistency to spread. Add vanilla. Spread on cake at once.

Variations:
See Variations of Ice Cream Frosting p. 166.

Ice Cream Frosting

Yield: 2½ qt.

Amount	Ingredient	Method
1 lb. 8 oz. 1 c.	Granulated sugar Water, hot	Combine sugar and water. Boil without stirring to soft ball stage (238° F.).
9 3 oz.	Egg whites Powdered sugar, sifted	Beat egg whites until frothy. Add powdered sugar and beat (high speed) to consistency of meringue. Add hot sirup slowly and continue beating until mixture is thick and creamy.
8 oz. 1 T.	Powdered sugar, sifted Vanilla	Add powdered sugar and vanilla. Beat until smooth. Add more sugar if necessary to make frosting hold its shape when spread.

Note:
This frosting can be kept several days in a covered container in refrigerator.
Variations:
1. *Bittersweet Frosting.* Melt 8 oz. bitter chocolate over water, gradually stir in 3 T. butter; when slightly cool, pour over white frosting to form a design.
2. *Candied Fruit Frosting.* Add 8 oz. chopped candied fruit.
3. *Chocolate Frosting.* Add 8 oz. melted chocolate.
4. *Coconut Frosting.* Frost cake, sprinkle with 4 oz. dry shredded coconut.
5. *Lady Baltimore Frosting.* Use 1¾ qt. Boiled Frosting. Add 1 t. orange juice, 4½ oz. macaroon crumbs, 5 oz. chopped almonds, and 1 c. chopped raisins.
6. *Maple Nut Frosting.* Flavor with maple flavoring; add 6 oz. chopped nuts.
7. *Maraschino Frosting.* Add 8 oz. chopped maraschino cherries.
8. *Peppermint Frosting.* Add 8 oz. finely crushed peppermint candy.

Fluffy Frosting

Yield: 4¼ qt.

Amount	Ingredient	Method
2 lb. 8 oz.	Sugar	Boil sugar, water, sirup and salt until mixture reaches the soft ball stage (238° F.).
1½ c.	Water	
5 T.	Corn sirup, white	
¼ t.	Salt	
10	Egg whites	Beat egg whites (high speed) until stiff but not dry.
1 T.	Vanilla	Gradually add ½ hot sirup to egg whites, beating constantly.
		Cook remaining half of sirup until it forms a hard ball (250° F.).
		Gradually add to first mixture.
		Beat (high speed) until it holds its shape.
		Add vanilla.

Variation:
Fluffy Brown Sugar Frosting. Substitute brown sugar for granulated sugar.

Creamy Frosting

Yield: 1–1½ qt.

Amount	Ingredient	Method
12 oz.	Butter or margarine	Cream butter or margarine (medium speed) 1 min., or until soft.
½ c.	Evaporated milk	Add remaining ingredients gradually.
1 T.	Vanilla	Whip (medium speed) until mixture is smooth and creamy.
2 lb. 8 oz.	Powdered sugar	
2 t.	Salt	

Note:
Milk or cream may be substituted for evaporated milk.
Variations:
1. *Cocoa Frosting.* Increase liquid ¾ c.; add 6 oz. cocoa sifted with sugar.
2. *Lemon Butter Frosting.* Substitute ¼ c. lemon juice for an equal amount of milk, and 1½ T. grated lemon rind for the vanilla.
3. *Mocha Frosting.* Substitute cold coffee for liquid. Add 6 oz. cocoa sifted with sugar.
4. *Orange Butter Frosting.* Substitute ½ c. orange juice for an equal amount of milk, and 1½ T. grated orange rind for the vanilla.

Powdered Sugar Glaze

Yield: 1 qt.

Amount	Ingredient	Method
2 lb.	Powdered sugar	Gradually add water to sugar. Beat until smooth.
¾ c.	Boiling water	
2 t.	Vanilla	Add vanilla and blend. Thin, if necessary, to spread.

Note:
Use for frosting baked rolls or products requiring a thin frosting.

Butter Cream Frosting

Yield: 1 qt.

Amount	Ingredient	Method
1 lb.	Powdered sugar	Combine sugar and eggs. Cook over low heat and beat until lukewarm. Remove from heat.
5	Eggs, beaten	
1 lb.	Butter, unsalted, soft	Add butter. Mix (high speed) until fluffy. Refrigerate several hours before using.

Chocolate Butter Cream Frosting

Yield: 3 qt.

Amount	Ingredient	Method
2 lb.	Butter or margarine, soft	Cream butter (medium speed). Add milk. Blend.
⅔ c.	Evaporated milk	Add sugar gradually. Mix until smooth (medium speed).
2 lb.	Powdered sugar	
8 oz.	Chocolate, unsweetened, melted	Add chocolate and vanilla. Beat (high speed) until light and fluffy.
1 t.	Vanilla	

Pineapple Butter Frosting

Yield: 2½ qt.

Amount	Ingredient	Method
1 lb. 8 oz. 3 lb. ½ t.	Butter or margarine Powdered sugar Salt	Mix butter or margarine, sugar, and salt (medium speed) until creamy.
3	Egg yolks	Add egg yolks. Whip (high speed) until light and fluffy.
1 lb.	Drained, crushed pineapple	Add pineapple and blend (low speed). Keep under refrigeration until ready to use.

Coconut–Pecan Frosting

Yield: 2 qt.

Amount	Ingredient	Method
2 c. 6 1 lb. 8 oz.	Evaporated milk Egg yolks Sugar Butter	Combine milk, yolks, sugar, and butter in double boiler. Cook until thickened.
12 oz. 12 oz. 2 t.	Pecans, finely chopped Coconut, flaked Vanilla	Add pecans, coconut, and vanilla. Cool, then beat well until thick enough to spread.

Mocha Frosting

Yield: 1 qt.

Amount	Ingredient	Method
1 c. 2 oz. 3 oz.	Hot coffee, strong Butter or margarine, soft Cocoa	Add coffee to butter or margarine and cocoa. Mix (medium speed) until blended.
2 lb. ½ t. ½ t.	Powdered sugar Salt Vanilla	Add sugar, salt, and vanilla. Mix until smooth. Add more sugar if necessary to make frosting hold its shape when spread.

Note:
Instant coffee, 1½ T. dissolved in 1 c. hot water, may be used in place of brewed coffee.

Orange Frosting

Yield: 1¼ qt.

Amount	Ingredient	Method
8 oz.	Butter or margarine	Cream butter or margarine.
2 lb. 8 oz.	Powdered sugar, sifted	Add sugar gradually (medium speed). Mix until creamy.
2 T.	Vanilla	Add remaining ingredients. Blend until smooth.
½ t.	Salt	
¼ c.	Orange juice	
¼ c.	Lemon juice	
1 t.	Orange rind, grated	

Ornamental Frosting

Yield: 1 qt.

Amount	Ingredient	Method
8	Egg whites	Beat egg whites until stiff but not dry.
1 lb. 8 oz.	Powdered sugar	Add sugar (low speed). Beat (high speed) to consistency of heavy cream if used for frosting. If used for decorating with a pastry tube, beat until it will retain its shape when drawn to a point.

Notes:
1. This frosting dries quickly when exposed to the air and should be covered with a damp cloth.
2. A teaspoon of lemon juice or vanilla may be added for flavoring if desired.

Burnt Butter Frosting

Yield: 5 c. (Frosting for 8 doz. 2½ in. cookies)

Amount	Ingredient	Method
9 oz.	Butter	Heat butter until golden brown.
1 lb. 8 oz.	Powdered sugar	Blend in sugar.
1 T.	Vanilla	Add vanilla and water. Beat until right consistency to spread.
½ c.	Water, hot	Add more water if necessary.

Cream Cheese Frosting

Yield: 4½ c.

Amount	Ingredient	Method
2 8-oz. pkg. ¼ c.	Cream cheese Cream or milk	Blend cream cheese and cream until smooth (medium speed).
1 lb. 12 oz. 1 T.	Powdered sugar, sifted Vanilla	Add sugar gradually. Whip (high speed) until smooth. Add vanilla and blend.

Note:
This frosting is especially good on Gingerbread (p. 151) and Spice Cake (p. 141).

Variation:
Orange Cheese Frosting. Substitute 1 T. orange juice and 1 T. grated orange rind for vanilla.

Chocolate Cream Filling

Yield: 3 qt.

Amount	Ingredient	Method
2 lb. 4 oz. (3 12-oz. pkg.) 1 c. 8 oz.	Chocolate chips Orange juice or water Sugar	Combine chocolate, orange juice, and sugar. Melt over hot water. Cool.
1½ qt.	Whipping cream	Whip cream and fold into chocolate mixture.

Note:
Use as filling for Orange Cream Puffs (p. 209).

Custard Filling

Yield: 3 qt.

Amount	Ingredient	Method
6 oz. 1 lb. ½ t. 1 pt.	Cornstarch Sugar Salt Milk, cold	Combine dry ingredients. Add cold milk and stir until smooth.
2½ qt.	Milk, hot	Add cold mixture to hot milk, stirring constantly. Cook over hot water until thick.
10 2 t.	Eggs, beaten Vanilla	Add eggs gradually to thickened mixture. Cook 7 min. Remove from heat. Add vanilla. Cool. Spread between layers of cake, 1½ c. per cake.

Notes:
1. Use as a filling for Cream Puff (p. 209), Washington Cream Pie (p. 139), Chocolate Roll (p. 150), and Éclairs (p. 209).
2. To fill 3 9-in. layer cakes use ⅓ recipe.

Lemon Filling

Yield: 1 qt.

Amount	Ingredient	Method
1 lb. 3 c. 2½ oz. ¾ c.	Sugar Water Cornstarch Cold water	Heat sugar and water to boiling point. Gradually add cornstarch blended with cold water. Cook until thickened and clear, stirring constantly.
4	Egg yolks, beaten	Blend in egg yolks. Cook 5–8 min. while stirring.
¾ t. 2 t. ½ c. 2 T.	Salt Lemon rind, grated Lemon juice Butter or margarine	Add remaining ingredients. Stir to blend. Cool. Spread between layers of cake, 1½ c. per cake.

Variation:
Orange Filling. Substitute orange juice for water, and orange rind for lemon rind. Reduce lemon juice to 3 T.

Date Filling

Yield: 1½ qt.

Amount	Ingredient	Method
2 lb.	Pitted dates, chopped	Combine dates, water, and sugar. Cook until mixture is thick.
2¼ c.	Water	Cool.
12 oz.	Sugar	Use as cake or cookie filling.

Note:
6 oz. jelly or ¼ c. orange juice may be used in place of ¼ c. of the water.

Prune Filling

Yield: 1 qt.

Amount	Ingredient	Method
1 pt.	Prunes, cooked, pitted, chopped	Add cream, butter, and eggs to prunes.
1 c.	Cultured sour cream	Heat over hot water.
2 oz.	Butter or margarine	
4	Eggs, beaten	
1 lb.	Sugar	Add mixed dry ingredients.
½ t.	Salt	Cook and stir over hot water until thick.
1 oz. (¼ c.)	Flour	Cool.
		Spread between layers of cake, 1½ c. per cake.

Note:
8 oz. chopped nuts may be added.
Variation:
1. *Apricot Filling.* Substitute dried apricots for prunes.

Prune Date Filling

Yield: 1 qt.

Amount	Ingredient	Method
1 c.	Prunes, cooked, pitted, and chopped	Combine all ingredients. Cook until thick, stirring constantly.
1 c.	Dates, chopped	
1 c.	Water and prune juice	
¼ c.	Lemon juice	
6 oz. (¾ c.)	Sugar	
⅓ c.	Flour	
1 oz.	Butter	

Fig Filling

Yield: 2 qt.

Amount	Ingredient	Method
2 lb.	Figs	Chop figs and soak in water, then cook
2 c.	Water	together.
1 lb.	Sugar	Add sugar, flour, salt, and lemon juice.
4 oz.	Flour	Cook to a paste.
½ t.	Salt	Add butter.
1 c.	Lemon juice	
1 lb.	Butter	

Cranberry Filling

Yield: 2 qt.

Amount	Ingredient	Method
1 lb. 8 oz.	Cranberry relish (p. 342)	Cook all ingredients except butter until thick.
1 No. 2 can	Crushed pineapple	Add butter.
12 oz.	Apples, ground	Use as filling for Cranberry Ring (p. 128).
8 oz.	Sugar	
¼ c.	Flour	
1 oz.	Butter	

Pastry and Pies

A good pie should have a tender, flaky crust and a filling that will just hold its shape. The type of crust produced is partially determined by the method of combining the fat and flour, a flaky crust resulting when fat and flour are mixed until small lumps are formed throughout the mixture. A mealy crust results when fat and flour are mixed thoroughly.

Tenderness depends largely on the kind of flour and amount of fat and water used. Excess fat increases tenderness and excess water gives a tough product. Overmixing after water has been added or use of too much flour when rolling toughens pastry also.

To make a 1-crust pie:
1. Weigh 5 oz. dough for each 8-in. crust.
2. Chill for 10 min.
3. Roll into circle 2 in. larger than pie pan.
4. Fit crust loosely into pan so that there are no air spaces between the crust and the pan.

5. Trim, allowing ½ in. extra to build up edge.
6. For custard type pie, crimp edge, add filling, and bake.
7. For cream or chiffon pies, fit pie crust over inside or outside of pie pans. Crimp edge and prick crust with fork. Bake, cool, and fill. A second pan may be placed over the crust for the first part of baking, then removed and crust allowed to brown. The second pan helps to keep the crust in shape.

To make a 2-crust pie:
1. Scale 5 oz. for bottom crust and 4 oz. for top crust for each 8-in. pie.
2. Roll pastry into circle. Place bottom crust in pan and trim. If desired, leave ½ in. extra crust around edge and fold over to make a pocket of pastry to prevent fruit juices from running out.
3. Add fruit filling and brush edge of bottom crust with water.
4. Cover with top crust, in which slits or vents have been cut to allow steam to escape.
5. Trim, flute, and seal by pressing the two crusts together with the fingertips. Brush top crust with milk. Bake.

Pastry I

Yield: 4½ lb.

Pastry for 8 8-in. 2-crust pies

Amount	Ingredient	Method
2 lb. 1 lb. 8 oz.	Flour Fat	Mix flour and fat (low speed) 1 min.
1½–1¾ c. 1½ T.	Water, cold Salt	Add water and salt. Mix (low speed) only until a dough is formed, about 40 sec. Portion into 5-oz. balls for bottom crust and 4-oz. balls for top crust. Let stand 10 min. in refrigerator before rolling. See above for directions for rolling.

Pastry II[1]

Yield: 50 lbs.

Amount	Ingredient	Method
25 lb.	Flour	Mix flour and fat (low speed) until
18 lb.	Fat	blended.
3¾ qt.	Water, cold	Add water and salt.
12–14 oz.	Salt	Mix (low speed) only until dough will hold together.

Notes:
1. Pastry should be mixed several hours before it is to be used. It may be stored (covered) in refrigerator for several days.
2. Hydrogenated fat was used in this recipe. If lard is used, reduce the amount by ⅛.
3. Use approximately 5 oz. for bottom crust and 4 oz. for top crust for 8-in. pie.
4. See p. 175 for directions for rolling.

[1] Similar to recipe for Pastry I except for quantity.

Graham Cracker Crust

Bake: 5 min.   Yield: 8 8-in. pie shells
Oven: 375° F.

Amount	Ingredient	Method
1 lb. 5 oz.	Graham cracker crumbs	Mix all ingredients. Pat about 5 oz. of crumb mixture evenly
10 oz.	Sugar	into each pie pan.
10 oz.	Butter or margarine, melted	Bake. Fill shells with Cream Pie Filling (p. 182) or Chiffon Pie Filling (p. 187, 188).

Notes:
1. Crusts may be refrigerated several hours instead of baking.
2. Vanilla wafer crumbs may be substituted for graham cracker crumbs.
3. This recipe will make 5 9-in. shells (8 oz. per shell).

Pie Meringue

Bake: 12 min.
Oven: 375° F.

Yield: Meringue for 8 8-in. pies

Amount	Ingredient	Method
16 (2 c.) ½ t. 1 lb.	Egg whites Salt Sugar	Add salt to egg whites. Whip past frothy stage (high speed), approximately 1½ min. Add sugar gradually while beating. Beat until sugar has dissolved. The meringue should be stiff enough to hold peaks but not dry. Spread meringue on filling while it is hot. It should touch all edges of the crust. Brown in oven.

Canned Fruit Pie

Bake: 30 min.
Oven: 425° F.

Yield: 8 8-in. pies
6 portions per pie

Amount	Ingredient	Method
1½ No. 10 can 6 oz.	Fruit, water pack Cornstarch	Drain fruit. Measure liquid and add water to make 1½ qt. Bring 1 qt. of liquid to boiling. Mix remaining ½ qt. liquid with cornstarch, then add gradually while stirring to hot liquid. Cook until thick and clear.
3 lb. 1 T.	Sugar Salt	While still hot, add sugar and salt. Mix thoroughly and bring to boiling point. Add drained fruit and mix carefully. Cool slightly.
4 lb. 8 oz.	Pastry (p. 175)	Measure 3 c. filling into each unbaked pie shell. Moisten edge of bottom crust with water. Cover with perforated top crust. Seal edge, trim and flute edges. Bake.

Notes:
1. May be used for all canned fruit fillings, such as apricot, blackberry, cherry, gooseberry, peach, or raspberry (sugar variable).
2. Other thickening agent may be used; e.g. waxy maize (4½ oz.) or tapioca (7½ oz.). Cold water starches also are available on the market.

Frozen Fruit Pie or Cobbler Guide in Using Frozen Fruit for Pies

Yield: 8 8-in. pies

| Fruit (10 *lb.*) | Sugar° | Thickening | | Seasonings |
		Cornstarch°	Waxy Maize°	
Apples	1 lb. 12 oz.	3 oz.	2½ oz.	Salt, 1 t., Nutmeg, 1 t. Cinnamon, 1 T., Butter, 2 oz.
Apricots	2–2½ lb.	5½ oz.	4 oz.	Cinnamon, 2 t.
Berries	2½–3½ lb.	6½ oz.	5 oz.	Lemon juice, 2 T. Salt, 1 t.
Blueberries	3 lb.	8 oz.	6 oz.	Salt, 1 t., Butter, 2 oz. Lemon juice, 1½ c., Cinnamon, 1 t.
Blue plums	2–2½ lb.	5½ oz.	4 oz.	Salt, 1 t., Butter, 2 oz.
Cherries	2 lb.	7 oz.	5 oz.	Salt, 1 t.
Gooseberries	6 lb.	14 oz.	10 oz.	Salt, ½ t.
Peaches	1 lb. 6 oz.	5½ oz.	4 oz.	Butter, 1 oz., Salt, 1 t. Almond, ¼ t.
Pineapple	2–2½ lb.	5½ oz.	4 oz.	Salt, 1 t.
Rhubarb	2 lb.	7 oz.	5 oz.	Salt, 1 t.
Strawberries	2 lb.	12 oz.	8½ oz.	Lemon juice, ¾ c. Red color, ¾ t.

° The amount of sugar and cornstarch or waxy maize added to the fruit will vary according to the pack of the fruit and individual preferences of flavor and consistency. Frozen fruits packed without the addition of sugar are known as "dry pack." When sugar is added during the freezing process, the ratio is usually 3, 4, or 5 parts by weight of fruit to 1 part by weight of sugar.

Directions. Thaw fruit at room temperature in the unopened original container. When fruit is thawed, drain off the juice. Measure juice and figure the amount of cornstarch or waxy maize needed to thicken it, allowing 2⅓–3 oz. cornstarch or 2–2½ oz. waxy maize for each quart of liquid. If fruit is lacking in juice, water may be added to bring the total liquid to 1½–2 qt. for the 10 lb. fruit, according to the consistency desired. Bring liquid to boiling point. Add sugar and cornstarch or waxy maize, stirring constantly with a wire whip. Add seasonings. Pour over fruit. Use 3 c. filling for each 8-in. pie. Bake 30–40 min. at 425° F. If pies are to be frozen, use waxy maize for thickening.

For cobblers, follow the same procedure as for pies, using less thickening.

Fresh Apple Pie

Bake: 15 min. 425° F.; then   Yield: 8 8-in. pies
30 min. 350° F., or   6 portions per pie
until apples are done.

Amount	Ingredient	Method
12 lb. (E.P.)	Apples, tart, sliced	Combine sugar, flour, and nutmeg.
3 lb. 4 oz.	Sugar	Add to apples and mix carefully.
4 oz.	Flour	
2 t.	Nutmeg	
8 oz.	Butter or margarine, melted	Portion 2 lb. filling into 8 deep pie pans that have been lined with pastry.
4 lb. 8 oz.	Pastry (p. 175)	Add 1 oz. butter or margarine to each pie. Moisten edge of bottom crust. Cover with perforated top crust. Seal edge, trim excess dough and flute edges. Bake.

Variation:

Apple Crumb Pie. Omit top crust. Sprinkle apples with Streusel Topping: Mix 1 lb. flour, 1 lb. 10 oz. sugar, 2 oz. nonfat dry milk, 1 t. salt, cut in 10 oz. butter or margarine and add 6 oz. chopped pecans. Use 1 c. per pie. Bake until apples are done and topping is brown.

Raisin Pie

Bake: 15 min. at 425° F.   Yield: 8 8-in. pies
and then 15 min.   6 portions per pie
at 375° F.

Amount	Ingredient	Method
4 lb.	Raisins, washed	Simmer raisins until plump.
4½ qt.	Water, hot	
2 lb. 4 oz.	Sugar	Add combined sugar, cornstarch, and salt. Cook until thickened.
6 oz.	Cornstarch	Remove from heat.
2 t.	Salt	
6 T.	Lemon juice	Add juice and butter or margarine.
3 oz.	Butter or margarine, melted	Cool slightly.
4 lb. 8 oz.	Pastry (p. 175)	Pour into 8 unbaked pie shells. Cover with pastry. Bake.

Note:

A superior product is obtained if 3 qt. cream are substituted for 3 qt. water.

Dried Apricot Pie

Bake: 30 min.   Yield: 8 8-in. pies
Oven: 450° F.   6 portions per pie

Amount	Ingredient	Method
5 lb.	Apricots, dried	Wash and drain apricots. Cover with hot water; let stand 1 hr. Cook slowly without stirring until tender.
4 lb. 2½ oz. ½ c.	Sugar Cornstarch Water	Combine sugar and cornstarch. Mix with water. Add to apricots a few minutes before done. Continue cooking until juice is clear.
4 lb. 8 oz.	Pastry (p. 175)	Pour into 8 unbaked pie shells. Cover with pastry. Bake.

Variation:
Prune Pie. 8 lb. prunes (cooked and pitted), 1 qt. prune juice, 2 lb. sugar, 8 oz. butter, ½ oz. lemon juice, 4 oz. flour, and 1 t. salt.

Rhubarb Custard Pie

Bake: 30–35 min.   Yield: 8 8-in. pies
Oven: 375° F.   6 portions per pie

Amount	Ingredient	Method
4 lb. 8 oz. 1 t. 4	Sugar Flour Salt Lemon rinds, grated	Mix dry ingredients.
12 7 lb. 8 oz. 2 lb. 8 oz.	Eggs, beaten Rhubarb, fresh, cut fine Pastry (p. 175)	Combine eggs and rhubarb. Add dry ingredients and mix. Fill unbaked pie shells. Bake.

Notes:
1. May be topped with meringue (p. 177).
2. Unbaked pie may be covered with a top crust or a latticed top made of ⅜-in. pastry strips.

Fresh Rhubarb Pie

Bake: 35 min.
Oven: 400° F.

Yield: 8 8-in. pies
6 portions per pie

Amount	Ingredient	Method
10 lb.	Rhubarb, ½ in. pieces	Combine all ingredients. Let stand 30 min.
6 oz.	Tapioca	
5 lb. 8 oz.	Sugar	
2 t.	Salt	
3 T.	Orange rind, grated	
5 oz.	Butter, melted	
4 lb. 8 oz.	Pastry (p. 175)	Put 3 c. filling in each unbaked pie crust. Moisten edges with cold water. Cover with top crust or pastry strips. Press edges together. Bake.

Note:
8 oz. cornstarch or 5 oz. waxy maize may be substituted for tapioca.

Strawberry Pie

Yield: 8 8-in. pies
6 portions per pie

Amount	Ingredient	Method
3 gal.	Strawberries, fresh	Wash and cap berries. Set aside half of the best berries and mash the rest.
3 lb. 12 oz.	Sugar	Mix sugar and cornstarch. Add to mashed berries.
7½ oz.	Cornstarch	
¾ c.	Lemon juice	Cook 5–6 min. or until thick and clear. Add lemon juice. Cool.
2 lb. 8 oz.	Pastry (p. 175)	Add reserved berries, whole or cut. Pour into baked pie shells.
1 qt.	Whipping cream	Whip cream and add sugar. Top each pie with 1 c. whipped cream.
¼ c.	Sugar	

Cream Pie

Bake: 12 min.   Yield: 8 8-in. pies
Oven: 375° F.   6 portions per pie

Amount	Ingredient	Method
3 qt.	Milk	Heat milk to boiling point.
11 oz.	Cornstarch	Mix dry ingredients. Add cold milk and
2 lb. 4 oz.	Sugar	stir until smooth.
2 t.	Salt	Add to hot milk gradually, stirring briskly
1 qt.	Milk, cold	with a wire whip. Cook over hot water until smooth and thick, approximately 10 min.
16	Egg yolks, beaten	Add while stirring a small amount of hot mixture to the beaten egg yolks. Combine all ingredients, stirring constantly. Stir slowly and cook 5–10 min. Remove from heat.
4 oz.	Butter or margarine	Add butter or margarine and vanilla. Pour 3 c. filling into each baked pie shell.
2 T.	Vanilla	Cover with meringue (p. 177).
2 lb. 8 oz.	Pastry (p. 175)	

Variations:
1. *Banana Cream Pie.* Slice 1 large banana in each pie shell before adding cream filling.
2. *Chocolate Cream Pie.* Add 6 oz. cocoa and 3 oz. sugar. Omit 1 oz. cornstarch.
3. *Coconut Cream Pie.* Add 10 oz. toasted coconut to filling and sprinkle 2 oz. coconut over meringue.
4. *Pineapple Cream Pie.* Add 3½ c. crushed pineapple, drained, to cooked filling.
5. *Date Cream Pie.* Add 3 lb. chopped, pitted dates to cooked filling.
6. *Fruit Glazed Pie.* Use frozen blueberries, strawberries, or cherries. Thaw 6 lb. frozen fruit and drain. Measure 1 qt. fruit sirup, adding water if needed to make that amount. Add slowly to a mixture of 4 oz. cornstarch, 6 oz. sugar, and ¾ c. lemon juice. Cook until thick and clear. Cool slightly. Add drained fruit. Spread over cream pies.
7. *Fruit Tarts.* Substitute 2 qt. cream for equal quantity of milk. Fill baked individual pastry shells ⅓ full of cream pie filling; add fresh, canned, or frozen fruits. Cover with whipped cream.
8. *Nut Cream Pie.* Add ½ c. chopped pecans or other nuts.

Butterscotch Cream Pie

Bake: 12 min.
Oven: 375° F.

Yield: 8 8-in. pies
6 portions per pie

Amount	Ingredient	Method
1 lb.	Butter or margarine	Melt butter or margarine; add sugar and mix thoroughly.
2 lb. 8 oz.	Brown sugar	Cook over low heat to 220° F., stirring occasionally.
3 qt.	Milk	Add milk slowly, while stirring. Stir until all sugar is dissolved. Heat mixture to boiling point.
6 oz.	Cornstarch	Combine cornstarch, flour, and salt.
6 oz.	Flour	Add milk and eggs and mix thoroughly.
1 T.	Salt	
1 qt.	Milk, warm	Add to the hot mixture while stirring. Cook until thick.
5	Eggs, whole	
10	Egg yolks	Remove from heat.
2 T.	Vanilla	Add vanilla and butter or margarine. Partially cool.
4 oz.	Butter or margarine	Fill baked pie shells. Cover with meringue (p. 177). Brown.
2 lb. 8 oz.	Pastry (p. 175)	

Note:
Recipe may also be used for pudding. Omit flour, increase cornstarch to 8 oz.

Lemon Pie

Bake: 12 min.   Yield: 8 8-in. pies
Oven: 375° F.   6 portions per pie

Amount	Ingredient	Method
2¼ qt. 2 t. 3	Water Salt Lemon rinds, grated	Heat water, salt, and grated rind to boiling point.
12 oz. 1½ pt.	Cornstarch Water, cold	Mix cornstarch and cold water. Add slowly to boiling water, stirring constantly. Cook until thickened and clear.
3 lb. 8 oz. 1½ c.	Sugar Whole eggs or 16 yolks, well beaten	Add sugar. Remove from heat. Add eggs slowly to hot mixture, stirring constantly. Return to heat. Cook about 5 min. Remove from heat.
3 oz. 1½ c. 2 lb. 8 oz.	Butter or margarine Lemon juice Pastry (p. 175)	Add butter or margarine and lemon juice. Blend. Pour into baked pie shells. Cover with Meringue (p. 177). Brown.

Custard Pie

Bake: 15 min. at 450° F.   Yield: 8 8-in. pies
       20 min. at 350° F.   6 portions per pie

Amount	Ingredient	Method
24 1 lb. 8 oz. 1 t. 2 T.	Eggs Sugar Salt Vanilla	Beat eggs slightly. Add sugar, salt, and vanilla. Mix.
1 gal. 2 lb. 8 oz. 2 t.	Milk, scalded Pastry (p. 175) Nutmeg	Add hot milk, slowly at first, then more rapidly. Pour into unbaked pie shells. Sprinkle nutmeg over top. Bake. The custard filling is done when a knife inserted half the way between the edge and center comes out clean.

Variation:
Coconut Custard Pie. Omit nutmeg and add 1 lb. flaked coconut.

Pumpkin Pie

Bake: 15 min. at 450° F. Yield: 8 8-in. pies
      25 min. at 350° F. 6 portions per pie

Amount	Ingredient	Method
14 2½ qt. (3 No. 2½ cans)	Eggs, beaten Pumpkin	Combine eggs and pumpkin in mixer bowl.
1 lb. 12 oz. 10 oz. ½ T. 1½ T. 1 T.	Granulated sugar Brown sugar Ginger Cinnamon Salt	Add combined dry ingredients.
2¾ qt. 2 lb. 8 oz.	Milk, hot Pastry (p. 175)	Add milk. Pour into unbaked pie shells. Bake. The filling is done when a knife inserted halfway between the edge and center comes out clean.

Notes:
1. Undiluted evaporated milk may be used in place of fresh milk.
2. 1 lb. chopped pecans may be sprinkled over tops of pies after 15 min. of baking. Continue baking.

Praline Pumpkin Pie

Bake: 40–45 min.   Yield: 8 8-in. pies
Oven: 325° F.   6 portions per pie

Amount	Ingredient	Method
2 lb. 8 oz.	Pastry, unbaked (p. 175)	
12 oz.	Pecans, finely ground	Mix pecans, brown sugar, and butter or margarine.
14 oz.	Brown sugar	Pat into unbaked pie shells.
8 oz.	Butter or margarine, soft	Bake 10 min. at 450° F.
16	Eggs, well beaten	Combine eggs, pumpkin, brown sugar, and seasonings.
2 qt.	Pumpkin	Blend in cream. Pour into shells. Bake.
1 lb. 12 oz.	Brown sugar	
5 T.	Flour	
2 t.	Cloves	
1 t.	Mace	
4 t.	Salt	
4 t.	Cinnamon	
4 t.	Ginger	
2 qt.	Coffee cream or undiluted evaporated milk	

Lemon Chiffon Pie

Yield: 8 8-in. pies
6 portions per pie

Amount	Ingredient	Method
1½ oz. 1¾ c.	Gelatin Water, cold	Sprinkle gelatin over water. Let stand 10 min.
21 1 lb. 8 oz. 2 t. 2½ c. 2 T.	Egg yolks Sugar Salt Lemon juice Lemon rind, grated	Beat egg yolks. Add sugar, salt, and lemon juice. Cook over hot water until consistency of custard. Remove from heat. Add softened gelatin. Stir until dissolved. Add lemon rind. Chill until mixture begins to congeal.
21 1 lb. 2 oz. 2 lb. 8 oz.	Egg whites Sugar Pastry (p. 175)	Beat egg whites until frothy. Gradually add sugar and beat until meringue will form soft peaks. Fold into lemon mixture. Fill baked pie shells. Chill.
1 qt. ¼ c.	Whipping cream Sugar	Just before serving, whip cream, add sugar. Spread 1 c. of the whipped cream over each pie.

Variations:
1. *Orange Chiffon Pie.* Substitute 2 c. orange juice for 2 c. lemon juice and 2 T. grated orange rind for 2 T. grated lemon rind.
2. *Lemon Refrigerator Dessert.* Crush 3 lb. 8 oz. vanilla wafers. Spread half of crumbs in bottom of 12 × 20-in. pan. Pour chiffon pie mixture over crumbs and cover with remaining crumbs.
3. *Frozen Lemon Pie.* Increase sugar in custard to 2 lb. Delete sugar from meringue. Beat egg whites, fold into 2 qt. cream, whipped. Fold into chilled lemon mixture. Pour into graham cracker pie shells (p. 176). Freeze and serve frozen.

Chocolate Chiffon Pie

Yield: 8 8-in. pies
6 portions per pie

Amount	Ingredient	Method
1½ oz. 1½ c.	Gelatin Water, cold	Sprinkle gelatin over water. Let stand 10 min.
8 oz. 1½ pt.	Chocolate, unsweetened Water, boiling	Melt chocolate. Add hot water slowly. Stir until mixed. Add gelatin and stir until dissolved.
24 1 lb. 8 oz. 1½ t. 2 T.	Egg yolks, beaten Sugar Salt Vanilla	Combine egg yolks, sugar, and salt. Cook until mixture begins to thicken. Add vanilla and chocolate mixture. Chill until mixture begins to congeal.
24 1 lb. 8 oz. 2 lb. 8 oz.	Egg whites Sugar Pastry (p. 175)	Beat egg whites until frothy. Gradually add sugar and beat (high speed) until meringue will form soft peaks. Fold into chocolate mixture. Pour into baked pie shells and chill.
1 qt. ¼ c.	Whipping cream Sugar	Just before serving, whip cream. Add sugar. Spread 1 c. of the whipped cream over each pie.

Variations:

1. *Frozen Chocolate Chiffon Pie.* Fold in 3 c. cream, whipped. Pile into pastry or graham cracker crust. Spread over tops of pies 1½ c. cream, whipped, sweetened with 3 T. sugar. Freeze. Serve frozen.
2. *Chocolate Peppermint Chiffon Pie.* Cover pie with whipped cream to which has been added 1 lb. crushed peppermint candy sticks.
3. *Chocolate Refrigerator Dessert.* Use ⅔ Chocolate Chiffon Pie recipe. Spread 1 lb. 12 oz. vanilla wafer crumbs over bottom of 12 × 20-in. pan. Pour in chocolate chiffon mixture and cover with 1 lb. 12 oz. crumbs.

Chocolate Sundae Pie

Yield: 8 8-in. pies

6 portions per pie

Amount	Ingredient	Method
2 oz.	Gelatin	Sprinkle gelatin over water. Let stand
1½ c.	Water, cold	10 min.
1 lb.	Sugar	Combine dry ingredients.
1 oz.	Cornstarch	Add slowly to milk while stirring.
½ t.	Salt	Cook 5 min.
3 qt.	Milk, scalded	
22	Egg yolks, beaten slightly	Add egg yolks slowly. Cook 10 min. while gently stirring.
		Remove from heat. Add softened gelatin. Stir until dissolved.
		Chill until mixture begins to congeal.
1 T.	Vanilla	Add flavorings.
2 t.	Almond extract	Carefully fold in egg whites and sugar
22	Egg whites	that have been combined to form a
12 oz.	Sugar	meringue (p. 177).
2 lb. 8 oz.	Pastry (p. 175)	Pour into baked pie shells. Chill until set.
1 qt.	Whipping cream	Just before serving, whip cream. Add
¼ c.	Sugar	sugar. Spread 1 c. of the whipped
8 oz.	Chocolate, grated	cream over each pie. Sprinkle with grated chocolate.

Variation:

Black Bottom Pie. Add 8 oz. melted chocolate to 3 qt. custard. Pour 1½ c. into each baked pie shell. Fold beaten egg whites into partially congealed remaining custard. Pour 2½–3 c. of this mixture over chocolate layer in crusts.

Frozen Mocha Almond Pie

Yield: 8 8-in. pies

6 portions per pie

Amount	Ingredient	Method
6 T.	Gelatin	Sprinkle gelatin over water. Let stand
1½ c.	Water, cold	10 min.
18	Egg yolks	Beat egg yolks.
1 lb. 8 oz.	Sugar	Add sugar, salt, and coffee. Cook over
1 T.	Salt	hot water until mixture coats spoon.
7½ c.	Coffee, hot	Remove from heat. Add softened gelatin. Stir until dissolved.
		Chill until mixture is consistency of unbeaten egg whites.
18	Egg whites	Add cream of tartar to egg whites. Beat until frothy.
1½ t.	Cream of tartar	
1 lb. 8 oz.	Sugar	Add sugar gradually and beat (high speed) until consistency of meringue.
		Fold into gelatin mixture.
3 c.	Whipping cream	Whip cream.
3 c.	Almonds, toasted, chopped	Fold cream, almonds, and vanilla into mixture.
2 T.	Vanilla	Pour into prepared crusts.
1 recipe	Graham Cracker Crusts (p. 176)	
1½ c.	Whipping cream	Whip cream, add sugar and cover top of pies.
3 T.	Sugar	
		Freeze. Serve frozen.

Ice Cream Pie

Brown: 2–3 min. Yield: 8 8-in. pies
Oven: 500° F. 6 portions per pie

Amount	Ingredient	Method
8	Graham Cracker Crusts (p. 176)	Fill crusts with ice cream using 1 qt. per pie. Freeze several hours.
2 gal.	Vanilla ice cream	
24	Egg whites	Add salt to egg whites. Beat until frothy.
¾ t.	Salt	
1 lb. 8 oz.	Sugar	Add sugar gradually, beating constantly, until sugar has dissolved. Add vanilla.
1½ t.	Vanilla	
		Cover pies with meringue. Brown in oven.
		Return to freezer if not served immediately.
1½ qt.	Chocolate Sauce (p. 373)	Serve with chocolate sauce.

Notes:
1. Pastry crust, baked, may be used in place of graham cracker crust.
2. Other flavors of ice cream may be used.
Variation:
Raspberry Alaska Pie. Thicken 3 40-oz. packages frozen raspberries with 6 T. cornstarch. Make thin layers of thickened berries and ice cream in graham cracker crusts, using about half of the berries. Proceed as for Ice Cream Pie. Spoon remaining berries over individual servings of pie.

Pecan Pie

Bake: 40 min. Yield: 8 8-in. pies
Oven: 350° F. 6 portions per pie

Amount	Ingredient	Method
4 lb.	Sugar	Cream sugar, butter, and salt (medium speed) until fluffy.
4 oz.	Butter	
1 T.	Salt	
24	Eggs, beaten	Add eggs and mix well.
1 qt.	Corn sirup, white	Add corn sirup and vanilla. Mix well.
2½ T.	Vanilla	
1 lb. 8 oz.	Pecans	Place 3 oz. pecans in each unbaked pie shell.
2 lb. 8 oz.	Pastry (p. 175)	Pour egg–sugar mixture over pecans. Bake.

Sour Cream Raisin Pie

Bake: 12 min.
Oven: 375° F.

Yield: 8 8-in. pies
6 portions per pie

Amount	Ingredient	Method
2½ qt.	Cultured sour cream	Mix all ingredients except raisins.
2 lb. 12 oz.	Sugar	Cook until thick.
6 oz.	Flour	
3 T.	Cinnamon	
1½ T.	Cloves	
2 T.	Nutmeg	
21	Egg yolks, beaten	
3 lb. 8 oz.	Raisins, cooked	Add raisins.
2 lb. 8 oz.	Pastry (p. 175)	Pour into baked pie shells.
		Top with meringue (p. 177).
		Brown.

Puddings and Other Desserts

Baked Custard

Bake: 45 min.
Oven: 325° F.

Yield: 50 4-oz. portions

Amount	Ingredient	Method
20	Eggs	Beat eggs slightly.
1 lb. 4 oz.	Sugar	Add sugar, salt, and milk.
½ t.	Salt	Mix (low speed) only until blended.
1 qt.	Milk, cold	
1 gal.	Milk, scalded	Add milk and vanilla.
2 T.	Vanilla	Pour into custard cups that have been
2 t.	Nutmeg	arranged in baking pans.
		Sprinkle nutmeg over top.
		Pour hot water around cups. Bake.
		Custard is done when a knife inserted
		in custard comes out clean.

Variations:
1. *Caramel Custard.* Add 1 c. caramelized sugar (p. 73).
2. *Rice Custard.* Use ½ of custard recipe, adding 1 lb. (A.P.) rice, cooked, 1 lb. raisins, and 3 oz. melted butter.
3. *Bread Pudding.* Pour liquid mixture over 1 lb. dry bread cubes and let stand until bread is softened. Add 1 lb. raisins if desired.

Floating Island

Yield: 6 qt.
Portion: ½ c.

Amount	Ingredient	Method
4½ qt.	Milk	Heat milk to boiling point.
1 lb. 4 oz. ½ t.	Sugar Cornstarch Salt	Add combined dry ingredients gradually, stirring briskly with wire whip. Cook over hot water or in heat-controlled kettle until slightly thickened.
24	Egg yolks, beaten	Gradually stir in egg yolks. Continue cooking until thickened, about 5 min.
2 T.	Vanilla	Add vanilla and blend.
24 12 oz.	Egg whites Sugar	Beat egg whites (high speed) past frothy stage, approximately 1½ min. Add sugar gradually, while beating. Beat until sugar has dissolved. Drop meringue by spoonsful onto hot water and bake (375° F.) until set.
		Cool custard slightly and pour into sherbet dishes, or dip, using a No. 10 dipper. Lift meringues from the water with a fork and place on top of portioned custard. Add a dash of nutmeg. Chill before serving.

Vanilla Cream Pudding

Yield: 6 qt.

Portion: ½ c.

Amount	Ingredient	Method
4½ qt.	Milk	Heat milk to boiling point.
1 lb. 8 oz. 8 oz. 2 t. 3 c.	Sugar Flour Salt Milk, cold	Mix dry ingredients. Add cold milk and stir until smooth. Add to the hot milk gradually, stirring briskly with a wire whip. Cook over hot water until smooth and thick, approximately 10 min.
12	Eggs, beaten	Add, while stirring, a small amount of hot mixture to the beaten eggs. Combine all ingredients, stirring constantly. Stir slowly and cook about 5 min. Remove from heat.
2 T. 4 oz.	Vanilla Butter or margarine	Add vanilla and butter. Cover and cool. Serve with No. 10 dipper.

Note:
5 oz. cornstarch may be substituted for flour.

Variations:
1. *Banana Cream Pudding.* Use only ¾ of recipe. Add 12 bananas, sliced, to cold pudding.
2. *Chocolate Cream Pudding.* Add 6 oz. sugar and 8 oz. cocoa.
3. *Coconut Cream Pudding.* Add 8 oz. shredded coconut just before serving.
4. *Pineapple Cream Pudding.* Add 1 qt. crushed pineapple, well drained.

Tapioca Cream

Yield: 6 qt.
Portion: ½ c.

Amount	Ingredient	Method
1 gal. 9 oz.	Milk Tapioca	Heat milk to boiling point. Add tapioca gradually. Cook until clear, stirring frequently.
10 1 lb. 2 t.	Egg yolks, beaten Sugar Salt	Mix egg yolks, sugar, and salt. Add slowly to hot mixture, while stirring. Cook about 10 min. Remove from heat.
10 4 oz. 2 T.	Egg whites Sugar Vanilla	Beat egg whites until frothy. Add sugar and beat (high speed) to form a meringue. Fold egg whites and vanilla into the tapioca mixture. Serve with No. 10 dipper.

Note:
1 lb. instant dry milk and 1 gal. water may be substituted for fluid milk.
Variation:
Fruit Tapioca Cream. Add 1 qt. chopped canned peaches or crushed pineapple, drained. Add ½ t. almond extract for peach tapioca.

Chocolate Cream Pudding

Yield: 6 qt.
Portion: ½ c.

Amount	Ingredient	Method
1 gal.	Milk	Heat milk to boiling point.
2 lb. 6 oz. 6 oz. 3 oz. 1 t. 8 oz.	Sugar Flour Cornstarch Salt Cocoa	Mix dry ingredients. Add to hot milk gradually, while stirring briskly with a wire whip. Cook until thickened (about 10 min.), stirring occasionally. Remove from heat.
8 oz. 2 T.	Butter or margarine Vanilla	Add butter and vanilla. Blend. Cover while cooling to prevent formation of scum. Serve with No. 10 dipper.

Butterscotch Pudding

Yield: 7 qt.
Portion: ½ c.

Amount	Ingredient	Method
3 qt.	Milk	Heat milk to boiling point.
1 lb. 2 oz. 2 lb. 8 oz. 1½ qt.	Flour Brown sugar Milk, cold	Mix flour, sugar, and cold milk until smooth. Add gradually to hot milk. Cook and stir with wire whip until thickened.
18 1½ t.	Eggs, beaten Salt	Add eggs and salt gradually to hot mixture, while stirring. Cook about 10 min. Remove from heat.
1 T. 12 oz.	Vanilla Butter or margarine	Add vanilla and butter or margarine. Chill. Serve with No. 10 dipper.

Lemon Snow

Yield: 1 pan 12 x 20 x 2 in.
Cut 6 x 8
Portion: 2 x 2½ in.

Amount	Ingredient	Method
1 lb. 8 oz. 8 oz. ½ t.	Sugar Cornstarch Salt	Mix sugar, cornstarch, and salt.
2 qt.	Water, boiling	Add boiling water gradually, while stirring with a wire whip. Cook until thickened.
16 6 oz.	Egg whites Sugar	Beat egg whites until frothy. Gradually add sugar and beat until rounded peaks will form. Add hot cornstarch mixture slowly, beating constantly.
1 c. 2 T.	Lemon juice Lemon rind, grated	Add lemon juice and rind. Blend. Pour into pan. Chill. Cut and serve with chilled Custard Sauce (p. 376).

Apricot Whip

Yield: Approximately 4 qt.
Portion: ⅓ c.

Amount	Ingredient	Method
1½ oz. 1½ c.	Gelatin Water, cold	Sprinkle gelatin over water. Let stand about 10 min.
1 c. 1 lb. ¼ c. 1 qt.	Water or apricot juice, boiling Sugar Lemon juice Apricot purée	Add hot liquid. Stir until dissolved. Add sugar, lemon juice, and purée. Mix. Chill. When mixture begins to congeal, beat (high speed) until light.
12 12 oz.	Egg whites Sugar	Beat egg whites until foamy. Add sugar and beat (high speed) to form a meringue. Fold into apricot mixture. Portion into sherbet dishes with No. 12 dipper. Chill. Garnish with whipped cream or whipped topping.

Note:
Raspberries, frozen strawberries, or prune purée may be substituted for apricot purée.
Variation:
Apricot Chiffon Pie. Pour Apricot Whip into graham cracker crusts. Reserve 2 c. crumb mixture to sprinkle over top.

Date Pudding

Bake: 45 min.
Oven: 350° F.

Yield: 1 pan 12 x 20 x 2 in.
Portion: 3 oz.

Amount	Ingredient	Method
2 lb. 1 lb. 1½ oz. 1½ t. 12 oz. 2 lb. 4 oz. 2¼ c.	Sugar Flour Baking powder Salt Nuts, chopped Dates, chopped Milk	Mix dry ingredients, dates, and nuts. Add milk and blend. Pour into a well-greased baking pan.
1 lb. 14 oz. 2 oz. 2¼ qt.	Brown sugar Butter or margarine Water, boiling	Mix sugar, butter or margarine, and water. Pour over cake mixture. Bake.

Royal Rice Pudding

Yield: 6 qt.

Portion: 4 oz.

Amount	Ingredient	Method
1 lb.	Rice	Cook rice (p. 309). Chill.
1 qt.	Pineapple, crushed, drained	Combine remaining ingredients except cream, and add to cooked rice.
8 oz.	Marshmallows, miniature	Mix lightly.
8 oz.	Nuts, chopped	
1 lb. 12 oz.	Powdered sugar	
2 t.	Salt	
1 c.	Maraschino cherries, chopped	
1 qt.	Whipping cream	Just before serving, whip cream and fold into rice mixture. Portion into serving dishes, using No. 12 dipper.

Fudge Pudding

Bake: 45 min.

Oven: 350° F.

Yield: 1 pan 12 x 20 x 2 in.

Portion: 3 oz.

Amount	Ingredient	Method
1 lb. 2 oz.	Flour	Mix dry ingredients (low speed).
1¼ oz.	Baking powder	
1 lb. 12 oz.	Sugar	
1 t.	Salt	
2 oz.	Cocoa	
1 pt.	Milk	Add milk, vanilla, and butter or margarine. Mix until smooth.
2 T.	Vanilla	
9 oz.	Butter or margarine, melted	Add nuts. Spread batter ¾–1 in. thick in pan.
1 lb.	Nuts, chopped	
2 lb. 4 oz.	Brown sugar	Mix sugar, cocoa, and hot water.
3 oz.	Cocoa	Pour over batter. Bake.
2 qt.	Water, hot	

Lemon Cake Pudding

Bake: 45 min.
Oven: 350° F.

Yield: 1 pan 12 x 20 x 2 in.
Cut 6 x 8
Portion: 2 x 2½ in.

Amount	Ingredient	Method
3 lb. 6 oz.	Sugar Butter or margarine	Cream sugar and butter (medium speed) 10 min.
3 oz. 2 t. 2 c. 5 T.	Flour Salt Lemon juice Lemon rind, grated	Add flour, salt, juice, and rind. Blend.
18 3 qt.	Egg yolks, beaten Milk	Add combined egg yolks and milk.
18	Egg whites	Fold in egg whites that have been beaten until they form rounded peaks. Pour into greased pan. Place in pan of hot water. Bake.

Date Roll

Yield: 4 rolls
Portion: 2½ oz.

Amount	Ingredient	Method
2 lb. 2 lb. 2 lb. 8 oz. 8 oz. 6 oz.	Dates, chopped fine Marshmallows, miniature Graham crackers, ground Nuts, chopped Maraschino cherries, chopped	Combine all ingredients except milk. Mix lightly.
1 pt.	Milk	Add milk. Mix only until ingredients are combined. Form into 4 rolls; roll in powdered sugar. Place in refrigerator for 24 hr. Cut each roll into 12 or 13 slices. Serve with Hard Sauce (p. 377) or whipped cream.

Fruit Cobbler

Bake: 30 min.
Oven: 425° F.

Yield: 1 pan 12 x 20 x 2 in.
Cut 6 x 8
Portion: 2 x 2½ in.

Amount	Ingredient	Method
2½ qt.	Fruit juice	Heat juice to boiling point.
6 oz. 1 pt.	Cornstarch Water	Mix cornstarch and water until smooth. Add to hot juice while stirring briskly with a wire whip. Cook until thickened.
2 lb. 8 oz. 1 T.	Sugar Salt	Add sugar and salt. Bring to boiling point.
10 lb.	Fruit, drained, unsweetened or pie pack	Add cooked, drained fruit. Mix carefully. Cool. Pour into greased pan.
2 lb.	Pastry (p. 175)	Cover top of pan with pastry. Seal edges to sides of pan. Perforate top. Bake.

Notes:
1. The amount of sugar will vary with the tartness of the fruit.
2. Use cherries, berries, peaches, apricots, apples, or other fruits.

Variation:

Fruit Slices. Use 2¾ lb. of pastry. Line an 18 × 26-in. pan with part of pastry. Add fruit filling prepared as for cobbler. Moisten edges of dough and cover with crust made of remaining pastry. Trim and seal edges and perforate top. Bake 1–1¼ hr. at 400° F.

Old Fashioned Strawberry Shortcake

Bake: 15 min.
Oven: 450° F.

Yield: 50 individual shortcakes

Amount	Ingredient	Method
2 lb.	Flour	Mix dry ingredients.
⅓ c.	Baking powder	Cut in butter.
2½ t.	Salt	
12 oz.	Sugar	
1 lb.	Butter	
1 pt.	Heavy cream	Mix cream and water. Stir quickly into flour mixture.
1 c.	Water	Drop dough with No. 24 dipper onto ungreased cookie sheets. Place about 2 in. apart to allow for spreading. Bake.
7–8 qts.	Strawberries	Slice or mash strawberries. Sweeten to taste. Pour over shortcakes, or split cakes and serve berries between layers and over the top. Serve with cream.

Baked Apples

Bake: 45 min.
Oven: 375° F.

Yield: 50 apples

Amount	Ingredient	Method
50	Apples	Wash and core apples. Pare down about one fourth of the way from top. Place in baking pan, pared side up.
3 lb.	Sugar	Mix sugar, water, salt, and cinnamon.
1½ pt.	Water, hot	Pour over apples.
1 t.	Salt	Baste occasionally while cooking to glaze.
1 T.	Cinnamon	Bake until tender when tested with a pointed knife.

Notes:
1. Use apples of uniform size, suitable for baking.
2. Amount of sugar will vary with tartness of apples.
3. ½ c. red cinnamon candies may be substituted for cinnamon.
4. Apple centers may be filled with chopped dates, raisins, nuts, or mincemeat.
5. 3 oz. butter may be added to the sirup for flavor if desired.

Applesauce

Yield: 50 3-oz. portions

Amount	Ingredient	Method
15 lbs. (A.P.)	Apples, tart	Pare and core apples. Cut into quarters. Add water.
1 qt.	Water	Cook slowly until soft.
4 lb.	Sugar	Add sugar. Stir until sugar is dissolved. Serve with No. 16 dipper.

Notes:
1. Thin slices of lemon, lemon juice, or 1 t. cinnamon may be added.
2. Peaches or pears may be substituted for apples.
3. Apples may be cooked unpared.
4. Amount of sugar will vary with tartness of apples.

Variation:
Apple Compote. Combine sugar and water, and heat to boiling point. Add apples and cook until transparent.

Apple Crisp

Bake: 45–50 min.
Oven: 350° F.

Yield: 1 pan 12 x 20 x 2 in.
Cut 6 x 8
Portion: 2 x 2½ in.

Amount	Ingredient	Method
10 lb. (E.P.)	Apples, sliced	Mix sugar and lemon juice with apples.
8 oz.	Sugar	
¼ c.	Lemon juice	Arrange in greased pan.
1 lb. 4 oz.	Butter or margarine, soft	Combine remaining ingredients and mix until crumbly.
12 oz.	Flour	Spread evenly over apples.
12 oz.	Rolled oats, quick, uncooked	Bake.
2 lb.	Brown sugar	Serve with whipped cream, ice cream, or cheese.

Variations:
1. *Cherry Crisp.* Substitute frozen pie cherries for apples.
2. *Peach Crisp.* Substitute sliced peaches for apples.
3. *Cheese Apple Crisp.* Add 8 oz. grated cheese to topping mixture.

Apple Dumplings

Bake: 40–45 min.   Yield: 50 dumplings
Oven: 375°–400° F.

Amount	Ingredient	Method
5 lb.	Pastry (p. 175)	Roll to ⅛ in. thickness and cut into 5-in. squares.
12 lb.	Sliced apples, frozen	Place No. 16 dipper of apples in center of each pastry square. Fold corners to center on top of fruit and seal edges together. Place in lightly greased baking pans. Prick top of dumplings.
4 lb. 2 qt. 1 lb. 2 t. 2 t.	Sugar Water, hot Butter or margarine Cinnamon Nutmeg	Make sirup of sugar, hot water, butter, and spices. Pour around dumplings. Bake.

Note:
Fresh or canned fruit may be used. The amount of sugar will vary with the type of fruit.
Variation:
Peach Dumplings. Substitute peaches for apples.

Apple Brown Betty

Bake: 1 hr. (or longer)   Yield: 1 pan 12 x 20 x 2 in.
Oven: 350° F.   Cut 6 x 8
                          Portion: 2 x 2½ in.

Amount	Ingredient	Method
12 lb. (A.P.)	Apples	Pare, core, and slice apples.
3 qt.	Cake (or bread) crumbs	Arrange apples and crumbs in layers in greased baking pan.
1 lb. 8 oz.	Brown sugar	Mix sugar, spices, water, and juice.
1 t.	Cinnamon	Pour a small portion over each layer.
½ t.	Nutmeg	
2 qt. (or less)	Water or fruit juice	
2 T.	Lemon juice	
8 oz.	Butter or margarine, melted	Pour melted butter or margarine over top. Bake. Serve hot with Lemon Sauce (p. 376) or cold with whipped cream.

Notes:
1. 10 lb. canned or frozen apples may be used.
2. The amount of water will vary according to the dryness of the crumbs used.
3. Graham cracker crumbs may be substituted for cake crumbs. 8 oz. nutmeats may be added.
4. Peaches, apricots, or rhubarb may be substituted for the apples.

Pineapple Bavarian Cream

Yield: 1 pan 12 x 20 x 2 in.
Cut 6 x 8
Portion: 2 x 2½ in.

Amount	Ingredient	Method
3 oz.	Gelatin	Sprinkle gelatin over water. Let stand
1 qt.	Water, cold	10 min.
1 No. 10 can	Pineapple, crushed	Heat pineapple and sugar to boiling point.
1 lb. 12 oz.	Sugar	Add gelatin and stir until dissolved.
¼ c.	Lemon juice	Add lemon juice.
		Chill until mixture begins to congeal.
1 qt.	Whipping cream	Whip cream and fold into pineapple mixture.
		Pour into 50 individual molds or 12 × 20 × 2-in. pan.

Note:
May be used for pie filling.
Variations:
1. *Apricot.* Substitute 3 lb. dried apricots (A.P.) or 6 lb. canned apricots for crushed pineapple. (Cook and sieve dried apricots.) Fold 6 beaten egg whites into the whipped cream.
2. *Strawberry Bavarian Cream.* Substitute 6 lb. fresh or frozen sliced strawberries for pineapple.

Pineapple Refrigerator Dessert

Yield: 1 pan 12 x 20 x 2 in.
Cut 6 x 8
Portion: 2 x 2½ in.

Amount	Ingredient	Method
3 lb. 8 oz. 12 oz. 18	Sugar Butter or margarine Egg yolks	Cream sugar and butter or margarine (medium speed) 5 min. Add egg yolks. Continue creaming until well blended.
1½ qt. 1 c.	Pineapple, crushed Cream	Add pineapple and cream. Cook over hot water until thick. Cool.
4 oz. 3 oz.	Nuts, chopped Maraschino cher- ries, chopped	Add nuts and cherries.
3 lb. 8 oz.	Vanilla wafers, crushed	Place a thin layer of crushed wafers in bottom of pan. Fill pan with alternate thin layers of fruit mixture and crushed wafers. Store overnight in refrigerator. Serve with whipped cream or whipped topping.

Note:
Dry cake crumbs or sliced cake may be substituted for the wafers.

English Toffee Dessert

Yield: 1 pan 12 x 20 x 2 in.
Cut 6 x 8
Portion: 2 x 2½ in.

Amount	Ingredient	Method
1 lb. 8 oz.	Vanilla wafers, finely crushed	Mix crumbs, nuts, and butter. Cover bottom of pan with approximately ⅔ of mixture. (Save remaining crumbs for top.)
1 lb.	Nuts, finely chopped	
12 oz.	Butter or margarine, melted	
1 lb. 4 oz.	Butter or margarine, soft	Combine remaining ingredients except egg whites. Mix (medium speed) until smooth and fluffy.
3 lb.	Powdered sugar	
8 oz.	Nonfat dry milk	
16	Egg yolks	
8 oz.	Chocolate, melted	
3 T.	Vanilla	
16	Egg whites	Add egg whites, beaten stiffly. Pour over crumbs in pan. Sprinkle remaining crumbs on top of filling. Place in refrigerator for several hours. Garnish with whipped cream if desired.

Notes:
1. Graham cracker crumbs may be used in place of vanilla wafers.
2. May be made in 8 8-in. pie pans.

Jellied Fruit Cup

Yield: 1 pan 12 x 20 x 2 in.
Cut 6 x 8
Portion: 2 x 2½ in.

Amount	Ingredient	Method
1 lb. 8 oz.	Gelatin, flavored	Pour boiling water over gelatin. Stir
2 qt.	Water, boiling	until dissolved.
2 qt.	Fruit juice or water	Add cold juice or water. Chill.
4–5 lb.	Fruit, drained	Arrange fruit in counter pan, individual molds, or serving dishes. When gelatin begins to congeal, pour over fruit. Refrigerate.

Note:
For detailed instructions on preparation of gelatin, see p. 332.
Suggested Combinations.
1. Orange gelatin, 2 lb. orange sections, 1½ lb. pineapple chunks, 1½ lb. banana cubes.
2. Raspberry gelatin, 2 lb. frozen raspberries, 2 lb. sliced bananas.
3. Strawberry gelatin, 2 lb. frozen strawberries, 1 lb. sliced bananas, 1 lb. pineapple chunks.
4. Lemon gelatin, 2 lb. sliced peaches, 2 lb. mandarin oranges, 8 oz. maraschino cherries.
5. Lime gelatin, 2 lb. canned pear pieces, 2 lb. canned pineapple chunks.

Cream Puffs

Bake: 15 min. at 425° F. then
      30 min. at 325° F.

Yield: 50 large puffs

Amount	Ingredient	Method
1 lb.	Butter or margarine	Melt butter or margarine in boiling water.
1 qt.	Water, boiling	
1 lb. 3 oz.	Flour	Add flour and salt all at once. Beat vigorously.
1 t.	Salt	Remove from heat as soon as mixture leaves sides of pan.
		Transfer to mixer bowl.
		Cool slightly.
16	Eggs	Add eggs one at a time, beating (high speed) after each addition.
		Drop batter with No. 24 dipper onto greased baking sheet. Bake.
		Fill puffs with Custard Filling (p. 172), using a No. 16 dipper. Top with Chocolate Sauce (p. 373) if desired.

Note:
For tea service, small shells may be made with a pastry tube and filled with creamed chicken or chicken salad. Yield: Approximately 200 puffs.
Variations:
1. *Orange Cream Puffs with Chocolate Filling.* Add ½ c. grated orange rind and 2 c. chopped almonds to cream puff mixture. Bake. Fill with Chocolate Cream Pudding (p. 195) or Chocolate Cream Filling (p. 171).
2. *Butterscotch Cream Puffs.* Fill cream puffs with Butterscotch Pudding (p. 196). Top with Butterscotch Sauce (p. 373) if desired.
3. *Éclairs.* Shape cream puff mixture with pastry tube into 4½-in. strips. Bake. Split lengthwise. Proceed as in directions for Cream Puffs.
4. *Ice Cream Puffs.* Fill with vanilla ice cream and serve with Chocolate Sauce (p. 373).

Christmas Pudding

Steam: 45 min. to 1 hr.   Yield: 50 3-oz. portions
      under pressure

Amount	Ingredient	Method
1 lb. 4 oz.	Carrots, raw, grated	Mix ingredients (low speed) until blended.
1 lb. 11 oz.	Potatoes, raw, grated	
1 lb. 4 oz.	Raisins	
1 lb. 4 oz.	Dates, chopped	
2 lb.	Sugar	
1 lb.	Butter or margarine	
12 oz.	Nuts, chopped	
1 lb.	Flour	Add combined dry ingredients. Mix (low speed).
1⅓ T.	Soda	
1 T.	Cinnamon	Measure with No. 16 dipper into greased muffin pans. Cover each filled pan with an empty muffin pan. Steam.
1 T.	Cloves	
1 T.	Nutmeg	
¼ t.	Salt	Serve with Vanilla Sauce (p. 376) or Hard Sauce (p. 377).

Variation:

Flaming Pudding. Dip sugar cube in lemon extract. Place on hot pudding and light just before serving.

Steamed Pudding

Steam: 1 hr. under pressure   Yield: 50 2½-oz. portions

Amount	Ingredient	Method
2½ oz.	Butter or margarine	Cream butter or margarine, sugar, eggs, and molasses (medium speed) until light.
1 lb. 3 oz.	Sugar	
5	Eggs	
2⅓ c.	Molasses	
4½ oz.	Flour	Combine dry ingredients. Add to creamed mixture alternately with milk.
1 T.	Soda	
1 T.	Cloves	
1½ T.	Cinnamon	Mix (low speed) only until blended.
1 lb. 14 oz.	Bread crumbs, dry	
2½ c.	Sour milk or buttermilk	
12 oz.	Raisins	Measure with No. 16 dipper into greased muffin pans. Cover with empty muffin pans. Steam.
8 oz.	Nuts, chopped	Serve puddings hot with Vanilla Sauce (p. 376) or Hard Sauce (p. 377).

Meringue Shells

Bake: 1 hr.   Yield: 50 3-oz. shells
Oven: 275° F.

Amount	Ingredient	Method
28 (3 c.) 1 t. 1 t.	Egg whites Salt Cream of tartar	Add salt and cream of tartar to egg whites. Beat (high speed) until frothy.
3 lb.	Sugar	Add sugar ½ c. at a time, beating (high speed) between each addition until sugar is dissolved and mixture will hold its shape (approximately 20–30 min.). Using No. 10 dipper, place on well-greased and floured baking sheets. Shape into nests with spoon or use pastry tube to form nests. Bake. Serve ice cream or fruit in center; or crush baked meringue and serve on ice cream.

Variations:
1. *Meringue Sticks.* Force mixture through pastry tube to form sticks. Sprinkle with nuts. Bake.
2. *Angel Pie.* Place meringue in well-greased and floured pie pan, about 5 cups per pan. Use spoon and form a nest. After baking, fill each shell with 3 c. of Cream Pie Filling (p. 182), Lemon Pie Filling (p. 184), or Chocolate Pie Filling (p. 182). Then top with a thin layer of whipped cream.

MEAT

The quality of cooked meat will depend on the quality purchased, the storage and handling of meat after delivery, and cooking methods. All meats marketed must meet federal inspection standards for wholesomeness. This includes all processed meat products as well as fresh and frozen meats. Federal grading is on a voluntary basis. Federal and packer-brand grades of meat are based on composite evaluation of conformation, finish, and quality.

Purchasing Meat

Meat for institutional food service is available in carcass, wholesale cuts, fabricated roasts, and portion-ready items. The form in which meat is purchased depends on the policies and size of the institution, the type of service it offers, and its storage and meat-cutting facilities. Fabricated and portion-ready cuts require less storage space, eliminate skilled labor for cutting, and do away with waste. Costs are easily controlled, as the weight and price of each portion are predetermined and only the amount needed is ordered.

Storing Meat

Fresh meat should be unwrapped when delivered and stored on trays or hung on hooks at a temperature of 35° to 40° F., with relative humidity 80 to 90%. It should be used as soon after purchase as possible. The temperature should not fall below freezing, unless frozen meat is being stored.

Frozen meat[1] requires a uniform holding temperature of 0° F. or below. It should be well-wrapped to exclude air and to prevent drying. Frozen meat should not be unwrapped before defrosting in the refrigerator at

---

[1] Unpublished material, National Live Stock and Meat Board, Chicago, Illinois, 1968.

30° to 35° F., at room temperature in front of a fan, or under running water. It is not necessary to defrost meat cuts before cooking, with the exception of steaks and chops that are to be coated for frying or baking.

Meat should be cooked soon after defrosting. Once thawed, it should not be refrozen unless in an emergency and then there will be some sacrifice in juiciness. Cooked meat may be frozen provided it is frozen immediately after cooking and cooling.

Cured, and cured and smoked, meats such as ham and bacon, sausages, and dried beef require refrigerator storage. The limited keeping qualities of ham cannot be overemphasized. There are three principal types of ham on the market:

1. Cook-before-eating ham: Partially cooked in processing and must be kept under refrigeration.
2. Fully cooked ham: Cooked sufficiently so that it may be served without further cooking or may be heated just enough to serve hot. Fully cooked hams require storage at refrigerator temperature before and after heating. Most canned hams, which are also fully cooked, require refrigeration.
3. Old-style cured ham: Fully cured and smoked but not cooked, may be stored without refrigeration.

Commercially processed hams indicate on the label which type they are or to what degree they have been cooked.

Cooking Methods

Meat is cooked either by dry or moist heat. The method used will depend on the grade and location of the cut. Tender cuts of high-grade meat (Prime, Choice, or Good) are usually cooked by dry heat (broiled, roasted, or deepfat fried). Moist heat is used for less tender cuts from the upper grades, and for all lower grade cuts. For the less tender cuts pot roasting, stewing, and cooking under pressure are the preferred cooking methods. Dry-heat cookery does not improve tenderness, and under some conditions reduces it. Cooking with moist heat tends to make meat tender. A low temperature, regardless of the method, is desirable. The degree of doneness affects losses. The percentage loss is smaller in rare meat than in medium or well-done meat, provided other factors are the same.

ROASTING

In roasting, which is a dry-heat method, meat is cooked in an oven, in an open pan, with no moisture added. Meat cuts must be tender to be roasted. In beef these are the less-used muscles, or those attached to the backbone. In veal, pork, and lamb practically any cut may be cooked by this method. Cuts suitable for roasting are given on p. 217.

Meats may be completely or partially defrosted or frozen at the time the cooking process is begun. Roasts that have been partially defrosted before cooking often yield a more satisfactory cooked product than those that remain completely frozen up to the time they are put into the oven. However, when time is a factor, as it is in institutional food service, defrosting meat before cooking is usually the accepted method.

Steps in roasting are:

1. Place the meat, fat side up, on a rack, in an uncovered roasting pan. Do not add water. Salt need not be added before cooking, as the salt does not penetrate more than 1 in.
2. Insert a meat thermometer in the roast so that the bulb rests in the center of the cut, but not in contact with bone or pocket of fat.
3. Cook at constant temperature—350° F. for fresh pork, 300° F. for other meats, including cured meats—until the desired degree of doneness has been reached (see p. 218). Searing a roast is no longer considered necessary and may increase losses. Although flavor may be improved, only the surface of the meat is affected.

Cooking time has been used generally as a guide to the degree of doneness of roasts, but research studies have shown that measuring the internal temperature of the roast with a meat thermometer is the only accurate method (Fig. 11). The length of the cooking period depends on several factors: oven temperature, size and shape of roast, style of cut (boned or bone in), oven load, quality of meat, and the degree of doneness desired. Investigations indicate that the use of metal skewers in roasts may shorten the cooking time.

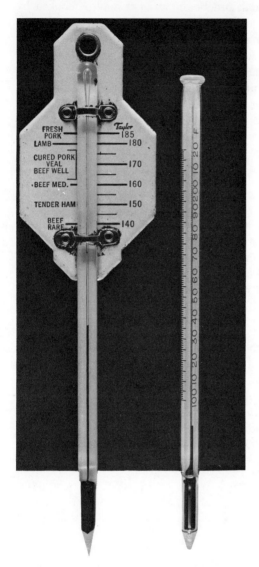

Fig. 11. Two types of meat thermometers used in testing the degree of doneness of meat.

Meat Cuts for Roasting

Beef U.S. Prime, Choice, or Good	Veal	Lamb	Pork	
			Fresh	Smoked
Standing rib	Leg, bone in	Leg, bone in	Ham, bone in	Ham, whole
Rolled rib	Leg, boned and tied	Leg, boned and tied	Rolled ham	Ham, half
Sirloin butt	Loin	Rolled loin	Loin, bone in	Ham, boneless
Loin strip	Rib	Rolled shoulder	Loin, boneless	Rolled ham
Loin points	Rolled shoulder	Rolled breast	Regular pork strip	Picnic
Round			Canadian style pork strips	
Inside (top)				
Outside (bottom)*			Boston butt	Boneless butt
			Picnic shoulder	
Sirloin tip or triangle			Boned and rolled	
Rump*			Cushion style	

Note:

For amount to buy, see p. 7.

* These cuts may be roasted satisfactorily if cooked at a low temperature for a long period of time.

Temperature and Timetable for Roasting Meat

Cut	Approxi- mate Weight Lb.	Oven Tem- pera- ture ° F.	Degree Cooked	End Point Tem- pera- ture ° F.	Min- utes per Lb.	Approxi- mate Total Time Hrs.°
Beef Rib						
Standing 3 rib	6–8	300	rare	140	18–20	2–3
			medium	160	22–25	2½–3
			well	170	27–30	3–4
Standing 7 rib	23	300	rare	125	11	4
			medium	140	12	4½
			well	150	13	5
Rolled 7 rib	16–18	250	well	150	26	7–8
Lamb						
Leg	6½–7½	300	well	180	30–35	3–4
Rolled shoulder	3–4	300	well	180	40–45	2½–3
Pork, fresh						
Ham (leg)	10–12	350	well	185	30–35	6
Loin, bone in	12–15	300	well	185	16	3–4
Loin, rolled	7–8	350	well	185	11	4
Shoulder, rolled	4–6	350	well	185	35–40	3–3½
Pork, cured (cook before eating)						
Ham, whole	10–14	300		160	15–18	3–3½
Shoulder butt	2–4	300		170	30–35	1–2
Veal						
Leg	7–8	300		170	24	3–3½
Rolled shoulder	9–10	300		170	35–40	6–7

SOURCE. Adapted from *Cooking Meat in Quantity*, 2nd Ed., Revised, National Livestock and Meat Board, Chicago, Illinois, pp. 16–18.

BROILING

Broiling or pan broiling are the usual methods for cooking cuts of meat shown in Timetable for Broiling Meats (p. 219). Veal should not be broiled unless it is fairly mature and well-marbled with fat, and then only loin chops or steaks. Fresh pork should never be broiled.

Oven broiling.

1. Turn the oven regulator to "broil" and preheat.
2. Slash fat edge of meat to prevent curling.
3. Place steaks on a rack 2 to 3 in. from tip of gas flame or from elec-

° For frozen meat, allow approximately double the cooking time here specified.

tric unit. Place 1-in. steaks or chops 2 in. from the heat, and 2-in. steaks or chops 3 in. from the heat.

4. Broil on one side until meat is browned and approximately half done. Season browned side, then turn and brown on the opposite side and cook to the desired degree of doneness. (See below for time.) Season second side. The meat should be turned only once.

Pan broiling.

1. Place meat on a preheated ungreased griddle or heavy frying pan.
2. Cook slowly, turning occasionally. Since the meat is in contact with the hot metal of the pan or griddle, turning more than once may be necessary for even cooking. If the steak is a thick one, reduce the temperature after browning. Griddle broiling requires more attention than true broiling but is more rapid than cooking in some types of broilers.
3. Care should be taken not to puncture the meat with a fork while cooking.
4. Neither water nor fat should be added. Excess fat should be scraped from the griddle as it accumulates.

Time Table for Broiling*

Cut	Approximate Thickness (in.)	Approximate Cooking Time (Min.)		
		Rare	Medium	Well-done
Beef				
Rib, club, T-bone,	1	15	20	30
porterhouse, tenderloin,	1½	25	35	
or sirloin steak	2	35	50	
Ground beef patties	1 (4 oz.)	15	20	
Lamb				
Rib, loin, and	1		12	15
shoulder chops	1½		17	20
or steaks	2		20	25
Ground lamb patties	1 (4 oz.)		20	22
Pork, smoked				
Ham slice, uncooked	½			10–12
	1			16–20
Ham slice, cooked	½			5–6
	1			8–10
Bacon				4–5
Canadian-style bacon	¼			6–8

* For frozen meat, allow approximately double the cooking time here specified.

BRAISING

Braising is a cooking method adapted to the less-tender cuts of meat, particularly the much used muscles and low grades of beef. Certain cuts of veal and thin cuts of pork, such as chops and steaks, are better if braised, although they are tender (see p. 221). The terms pot roasting or fricasseeing also are applied to this method of cooking.

Steps in braising are:

1. Season meat with salt (¼ t. per lb. of meat) and pepper if desired. Meat may be dredged with flour to increase browning.
2. Place meat in a heavy kettle, a roasting pan, or a steam-jacketed kettle. Add fat as needed and brown.
3. Add small amount of water and other liquid; use additional liquid as needed during the cooking. Braising or pot roasting in a steam-jacketed kettle will require more water than pot roasting in the oven. Other liquid, such as meat stock, tomato juice, or cultured sour cream, may be used.
4. Cover; simmer on top of range or bake at 325° F. until tender; or simmer in a steam-jacketed kettle until tender. (See Timetable for Braising Meat.)

Timetable for Braising Meat

Cut	Average Weight or Thickness	Approximate Cooking Time
Beef:		
Pot roast	3–5 lb.	3–4 hr.
Pot roast	5–15 lb.	3–5 hr.
Swiss steak	1–2½ in.	2–3 hr.
Round or flank steak	½ in. (pounded)	45 min.–1 hr.
Stuffed steak	½–¾ in.	1½ hr.
Short ribs	2 × 2 × 2 in. pieces	1½–2 hr.
Fricassee	1–2 in. pieces	2–3 hr.
Beef birds	½ × 2 × 4 in.	1½–2 hr.
Lamb:		
Breast, stuffed	2–3 lb.	1½–2 hr.
Breast, rolled	1½–2 lb.	1½–2 hr.
Shanks	½ lb. each	1–1½ hr.
Neck slices	½–¾ in.	1–1½ hr.
Riblets	¾ × 2½ × 3 in.	2–2½ hr.
Pork:		
Chops or steaks	¾–1 in.	45 min.–1 hr.
Spareribs	2–3 lb.	1½ hr.
Veal:		
Breast, stuffed	3–4 lb.	1½–2 hr.
Breast, rolled	2–3 lb.	2–3 hr.
Cutlets	½ × 3 × 5½ in.	45 min.–1 hr.
Steaks or chops	½–¾ in.	45 min.–1 hr.
Birds	½ × 2 × 4 in.	45 min.–1 hr.

SOURCE. *Cooking Meat in Quantity,* 2nd edition, Revised, National Livestock and Meat Board, Chicago, Illinois, p. 26.

STEWING OR SIMMERING

1. Brown meat if desired and cover with water.
2. Season with salt and pepper. Herbs and spices, used wisely, add to the variety and flavor of stewed meats. Suggested seasonings are carrots, celery, onions, bay leaves, thyme, marjoram, and parsley.
3. Cook in tightly covered heavy utensil or in steam-jacketed kettle below boiling point until tender.

Timetable for Simmering (*Cooking in Liquid*)

Cut	Average Size or Average Weight Lb.	Approximate Cooking Time	
		Min. per Lb.	Total Hr.
Large cuts			
Fresh beef	4–8	40–50	3–4
Corned beef	6–8	40–50	4–6
Fresh pork	Weight desired	30	
Smoked whole ham	12–16	18–20	4–5
Smoked half ham	6–8	25	2½–3½
Smoked picnic ham	4–8	35–45	3–4½
Stew			
Beef	1–2 in. cubes		2–3*
Lamb or veal	1–2 in. cubes		1½–2*

SOURCE. Adapted from *Cooking Meat in Quantity*, 2nd Edition, Revised, National Livestock and Meat Board, Chicago, Illinois, p. 29.

* If cooking in pressure pans, follow timetable of manufacturer.

Meat Recipes

		Swiss Steak	
BEEF			

Bake: 1½ hr.
Oven: 350° F.

Yield: 50 5-oz. portions (A.P.)

Amount	Ingredient	Method
16–18 lb.	Beef round, sliced ¾ in. thick	Cut meat into portions, 3 per lb. Mix flour, salt, and pepper. Pound into meat.
1 lb.	Flour	
¼ c.	Salt	
2 t.	Pepper	
1 lb. 8 oz.	Fat, hot	Brown meat in fat.
3 qt.	Gravy (p. 389)	Place, slightly overlapping, in 2 baking or counter pans. Add 1½ qt. gravy to each pan. Cover pan tightly with aluminum foil. Bake.

Notes:
1. If portioned steaks are used, order boneless beef round, cut 3 per pound, scored twice. This will tenderize steaks, but if scored more than twice, steaks may fall apart when cooked. Dredge steak with flour mixture and brown. Proceed as above.
2. 1 No. 10 can tomatoes may be substituted for the gravy. Add 4 oz. chopped onion.

Variations:
1. *Spanish Steak.* Substitute Spanish Sauce (p. 382) for gravy.
2. *Country Fried Steak.* Use beef round cut ⅜ in. thick. Proceed as for Swiss Steak except for adding gravy. Place steaks on racks in roaster or counter pans. Cover bottom of pan with water, 1½–2 c. per pan. Cover with aluminum foil and bake. Make Cream Gravy (p. 389) to serve with steaks.
3. *Smothered Steak with Onions.* Proceed as for Swiss Steak. Add 3 lb. sliced onions lightly browned.

Pot Roast of Beef

Bake: 4–5 hrs.
Oven: 300° F.

Yield: 50 3-oz. portions
cooked meat

Amount	Ingredient	Method
20 lb.	Boneless beef, chuck, round, or rump	Season meat with salt and pepper. Place in roasting pan in 450° F. oven.
1½ T.	Salt	When browned, add water. Reduce heat to 300° F. Cover. Cook slowly until tender (3–5 hrs.). Add water as necessary.
½ t.	Pepper	Remove meat from pan. Cool ½ hr. before slicing.
2 qt.	Water	Thicken the drippings in the pan with 6½ oz. of flour that has been mixed to a paste with 1½ c. water. Remove excess fat if necessary and add water to make 4 qts. of liquid. Season with 1½ T. salt and ½ t. pepper.

Note:
Meat may be cooked in a steam-jacketed kettle. Brown in a small amount of fat. Add water, salt, and pepper. Cover kettle and cook until tender. Add water as necessary.

Variations:
1. *Beef à la Mode.* About 1½ hr. before serving add: 5 lb. carrot halves; 8-oz. onion, chopped; 4 oz. green pepper, chopped; 3 lb. celery cut into 2-in. strips. Serve a slice of meat with vegetables and a spoonful of gravy on top.
2. *Yankee Pot Roast.* Add 1½ qt. tomato purée, 1 bay leaf to the water used in cooking pot roast.
3. *Savory Pot Roast.* Place roast on heavy aluminum foil in baking pan. Sprinkle 5 oz. dry onion soup mix over meat. Close foil tightly. Bake at 350° F. 3–3½ hr. Open foil and bake ½ hr. longer. Use juice for gravy. Fresh beef brisket may also be cooked by this method. The meat may be brushed with barbecue sauce for the last half hour of cooking.

Corned Beef and Cabbage

Yield: 50 3-oz. portions
cooked meat

Amount	Ingredient	Method
25–30 lb.	Corned beef brisket	Cover meat with water and simmer until tender, 4–5 hr. When done, remove from liquid. Allow to stand 20–30 min. before slicing.
12 lb.	Cabbage, cut into wedges	Cook cabbage (p. 406) in corned beef stock. Serve 1 wedge with 3 oz. sliced meat.

Beef Stew

Yield: 50 6-oz. portions

Amount	Ingredient	Method
12 lb. 8 oz.	Beef, 1-in. cubes	Brown beef in kettle or oven.
3 qt.	Water	Add water and seasonings. Cover
¼ c.	Salt	and simmer 2 hr. Add more
1 t.	Pepper	water as necessary.
2 lb.	Potatoes, cubed	Cook vegetables in steamer or in
2 lb.	Carrots, sliced or cubed	small amount of water in kettle
1 lb.	Onion, cubed	or oven.
1 lb. 8 oz.	Celery, diced	
¼ c.	Salt	
1 t.	Pepper	
5 oz.	Flour	Mix flour and water until smooth. Add to stew and cook until thickened.
1¼ c.	Water	Add vegetables.

Notes:
1. If a higher ratio of meat is desired, use 15 lb. cubed beef; reduce vegetables by 2½ lb. A total of 3 gal. stew is needed to serve 50 6-oz. portions.
2. Veal may be substituted for beef.

Variations:
1. *Beef Pot Pie.* Omit potatoes and add 1 40-oz. package frozen peas. Place cooked stew in 2 greased baking pans or in casseroles. Cover with Pastry (p. 175) or Batter Crust (p. 270). Bake 20–25 min. at 450° F.
2. *Beef Stew with Biscuits.* Place cooked stew in 2 baking pans just before serving. Completely cover with hot Baking Powder Biscuits (p. 99).
3. *Beef Stew with Dumplings.* Drop Dumplings (p. 113) on meat mixture and steam 15–18 min.

Beef Stroganoff

Yield: 50 portions
5 oz. Stroganoff
5 oz. noodles

Amount	Ingredient	Method
10 lb.	Beef round, cut in ¼ in. strips	Brown meat in fat. Add onion and seasonings.
8 oz.	Fat	
1 lb. 4 oz.	Onion, chopped	
2 T.	Salt	
1 t.	Pepper	
2½ qt.	Beef broth, hot	Add broth. Simmer 35–40 min. or until meat is tender.
2 lb. 8 oz.	Mushrooms, sliced, drained	Add mushrooms. Blend sour cream with flour. Add to meat mixture gradually, stirring constantly. Stir until thickened.
2 qt.	Cultured sour cream	
8 oz.	Flour	Serve over noodles.
4 lb. (A.P.)	Noodles	Cook noodles (p. 311).

Note:
For a 4-oz. portion of noodles, cook 3 lb.

Hungarian Goulash

Time: 2½–3 hr.

Yield: 50 8-oz. servings
4 oz. goulash,
4 oz. noodles

Amount	Ingredient	Method
10 lb.	Beef, cubed	Brown beef and vegetables in fat.
1 lb. 8 oz.	Onion, chopped	
1 clove	Garlic, finely chopped	
8 oz.	Fat	
5 oz.	Brown sugar	Combine seasonings and water.
1 T.	Mustard, dry	Add to browned meat.
¼ c.	Paprika	Cover container and simmer 2½–3
⅛ t.	Cayenne pepper	hr. or until meat is tender.
¼ c.	Salt	
1½ c.	Worcestershire sauce	
2 T.	Vinegar	
1 qt.	Catsup	
3 qt.	Water	
1 lb. 4 oz.	Flour	Mix flour and water until smooth.
1 qt.	Water, cold	Add to hot mixture and cook until thickened.
3 lb. (A.P.)	Noodles	Cook noodles (p. 311). Serve 4 oz. ladle goulash over 4 oz. noodles.

Note:
Beef may be browned in a roasting pan in 450° F. oven.

Chop Suey

Yield: 6¼ qt. meat
Portion: 4 oz. chop suey
4 oz. rice

Amount	Ingredient	Method
5 lb.	Beef or veal, ½-in. cubes	Brown meat. Add salt and water. Simmer until tender.
5 lb.	Pork, ½-in. cubes	
¼ c.	Salt	
1 gal.	Water	
4 oz.	Green peppers, chopped (optional)	Add vegetables. Cook 10–15 min. Vegetables should still be crisp.
8 oz.	Onion, chopped	
5 lb.	Celery, sliced	
6 oz.	Cornstarch	Mix cornstarch and water to a smooth paste. Add to hot mixture while stirring.
1 pt.	Water	
3 No. 2 cans	Bean sprouts or Chinese vegetables	Add vegetables and soy sauce.
1–1½ c.	Soy sauce	
3 lb. (A.P.)	Rice	Cook rice (p. 309).
3 No. 2½ cans	Chinese noodles	Serve No. 10 dipper of meat on No. 8 dipper of rice. Garnish with Chinese noodles.

Variation:
Chicken Chow Mein. Substitute cubed, cooked chicken or turkey for veal.

Meat Loaf

Bake: 1½ hr.   Yield: 5 loaves
Oven: 325° F.   Portion: 4 oz.

Amount	Ingredient	Method
8 lb.	Ground beef	Mix all ingredients (low speed) until blended. **DO NOT OVER-MIX.**
2 lb.	Ground pork	
10 oz.	Bread crumbs, soft	Press mixture into 5 loaf pans 4 × 9 in.
2 qt.	Milk	
12	Eggs, beaten	Meat loaf also may be made in 12 × 20 × 4-in. counter pan.
¼ c.	Salt	
2 oz.	Onion, finely chopped	Press mixture into pan. Divide into 4 loaves. Bake 2 hr. at 300° F.
1 t.	Pepper	
f. g.	Cayenne	

Variations:
1. *Vegetable Meat Loaf.* Add 2 c. catsup; 8 oz. each raw carrots, onions, and celery; and 4 oz. green peppers. Grind vegetables. Pour a small amount of tomato juice over loaf before baking.
2. *Sour Cream Meat Loaf.* Add 1 qt. of chopped stuffed olives to meat mixture. Cover the unbaked loaf with 1 qt. cultured sour cream.
3. *Meat Balls.* Measure with No. 8 dipper and shape into balls. Proceed as for Swedish Meat Balls (p. 230), or Meat Balls and Spaghetti (p. 231).
4. *Barbecued Meat Balls.* Measure with No. 8 dipper. Shape into balls. Cover with Barbecue Sauce (p. 382).

Swedish Meat Balls

Bake: 1 hr.   Yield: 100 2½-oz. balls
Oven: 300° F.   Portion: 2 meat balls

Amount	Ingredient	Method
2 lb. 8 oz.	Bread	Soak bread in milk 1 hr.
1½ qt.	Milk	
3 lb.	Ground beef	Add remaining ingredients.
2 lb. 8 oz.	Ground veal	Mix to blend but do not overmix.
2 lb. 8 oz.	Ground pork	Dip with No. 16 dipper. Shape
1 lb. 4 oz.	Potato, raw, grated	into balls. Place in baking pan. Brown in hot oven (400° F.).
12 oz.	Onion, minced	Transfer to 2 12 × 20-in. counter
3 T.	Salt	pans.
2 t.	Pepper	
6 oz.	Meat drippings	Make Cream Gravy (p. 389) from
6 oz.	Flour	meat drippings.
3 qt.	Milk	Pour over meat balls. Bake.
2 t.	Salt	
¾ t.	Pepper	

Note:
Beef may be substituted for veal and pork.

Spanish Meat Balls

Bake: 2½ hr.   Yield: 50 4-oz. balls
Oven: 325° F.

Amount	Ingredient	Method
12 lb.	Ground beef	Mix all ingredients except tomato and water.
12	Eggs, beaten	
2 oz.	Onion, grated	Measure with No. 8 dipper and
2 T.	Salt	form into balls.
1 lb. 2 oz.	Rice, partially cooked	Place in 2 baking pans 12 × 20 × 2 in.
1 lb.	Potatoes, mashed	
4 oz.	Green peppers, chopped	
3 qt.	Tomato purée	Mix purée and water. Pour over
2 qt.	Water	meat balls.
		Cover tightly and bake. Add more liquid if necessary.

Notes:
1. For 2 balls per serving use No. 16 dipper.
2. Spanish Sauce, p. 382 may be substituted for tomato purée.

Meat Balls and Spaghetti

Brown: 20 min. 400° F.
Bake in Sauce: 30 min. 375° F.

Yield: 50 portions
3 meat balls
5 oz. spaghetti

Amount	Ingredient	Method
8 lb.	Ground beef	Mix meat, bread, milk, and seasonings (low speed). **DO NOT OVERMIX.**
4 lb.	Ground pork	
6 slices	Bread, crumbled	
1 pt.	Milk	Dip with No. 24 dipper onto baking sheet.
2 T.	Salt	
2 t.	Pepper	Brown in 400° F. oven. Remove to deep counter pan or roasting pan.
3 qt. (2 50-oz. cans)	Tomato soup	Make sauce of all ingredients and simmer 1½–2 hr.
1¼ qt. (1 46-oz. can)	Tomato paste	Pour over browned meat balls. Cover and cook in 375° F. oven about 30 min.
3½ qt.	Water, boiling	
2 T.	Mustard, prepared	
2 T.	Paprika	
½ c.	Worcestershire sauce	
2 T.	Sugar	
4 cloves	Garlic	
8 oz.	Onion, chopped	
4 lb. (A.P.)	Spaghetti	Cook spaghetti (p. 311). Serve 3 meat balls and sauce over 5 oz. spaghetti.

Note:
If desired mix the cooked spaghetti with the tomato sauce. Place in 2 counter pans, arrange meat balls over top, and bake 20–30 min. at 375° F.

Spaghetti with Meat Sauce

Yield: 50 portions
4 oz. sauce
4 oz. spaghetti

Amount	Ingredient	Method
8 lb.	Ground beef	Brown beef.
5 qt.	Tomato purée (or tomatoes)	Add remaining sauce ingredients. Cook slowly, stirring frequently, until thickened, approximately ½ hr.
1 qt.	Water	
1¾ qt.	Catsup	
1 lb.	Onion, chopped	
2	Bay leaves	
1 t.	Thyme	
1 clove	Garlic	
¼ c.	Worcestershire sauce	
2 t.	Cayenne pepper	
1½ T.	Salt	
4 lb.	Spaghetti	Cook spaghetti (p. 311). Serve 4-oz. ladle of sauce over 4 oz. spaghetti.

Creole Spaghetti

Bake: 45 min.
Oven: 325° F.

Yield: 2 pans 12 x 20 x 2 in.
Portion: 6 oz.

Amount	Ingredient	Method
5 lb.	Ground beef	Brown beef, onion, and green pepper.
6 oz.	Onion, finely chopped	Add purée.
1 lb.	Green pepper, chopped	
3 qt.	Tomato purée (or tomatoes)	
3 lb. (A.P.)	Spaghetti	Cook spaghetti (p. 311).
1 lb. 8 oz.	Cheese, ground	Add sauce. Pour into 2 baking pans. Sprinkle cheese over top. Bake.

Lasagne

Bake: 40–45 min.

Oven: 350° F.

Yield: 2 pans 12 x 20 x 2 in.

Portion: 6 oz.

Amount	Ingredient	Method
12 oz.	Onion, finely chopped	Cook onion and garlic in oil.
5 cloves	Garlic, chopped	Add ground beef. Cook slowly.
½ c.	Oil	
5 lb.	Ground beef	
3 qt.	Tomato sauce	Add tomato sauce, tomato paste,
1 qt.	Tomato paste	and spices. Continue cooking,
1 t.	Pepper	about 30 min., stirring occa-
1 t.	Basil, crumbled	sionally.
1 T.	Oregano, crumbled	
2 lb. 8 oz.	Noodles, lasagne	Cook noodles (p. 311). Drain.
2 gal.	Water	
2 T.	Salt	
2 T.	Oil	
2 lb. 8 oz.	Swiss or mozzarella cheese, grated	Arrange in greased pans: Layer of overlapping noodles
1½ c.	Parmesan cheese, grated	Layer of meat sauce
2 lb. 8 oz.	Cottage cheese, dry or drained	Swiss or mozzarella cheese Parmesan cheese Cottage cheese Repeat: noodles, meat, cheeses, noodles. Spoon remainder of meat sauce on top. Bake.

Beef and Pork Casserole

Bake: 30 min.   Yield: 2 pans 12 x 20 x 2 in.
Oven: 300° F.   Portion: 5 oz.

Amount	Ingredient	Method
4 lb. 4 lb. 1 lb.	Ground beef Ground pork Onion, finely chopped	Brown meat and onion. Drain excess fat.
1 lb. 12 oz. (A.P.) 2 lb. 1½ qt. 1½ qt. 1 T. 1 t.	Noodles, cooked (p. 311) Cheese, Cheddar, grated Tomato soup Water Salt Pepper	Add noodles, cheese, soup, water, and seasonings to meats. Place in 2 baking pans.
1 lb. 2 oz. 5 oz.	Bread crumbs Butter or mar- garine, melted	Combine crumbs and butter or margarine. Cover meat mixture with buttered crumbs. Bake.

American Pizza

Bake: 10–15 min.   Yield: 2 pans 18 x 26 in.
Oven: 450° F.   Portion: 5 oz.

Amount	Ingredient	Method
3 lb. 10 oz.	Flour	Mix dry ingredients.
1½ t.	Salt	
3 T.	Sugar	
1 oz.	Yeast, compressed (or ½ oz. dry yeast)	Soften yeast in water. Add with fat to dry ingredients. Mix (low speed) to form dough.
2⅔ c.	Water, lukewarm	Knead until smooth and elastic. Cover
3 T.	Fat, soft	and let rise 2 hr. Punch down and let rest 45 min. Divide into 2 portions and roll out as thin as possible, stretching to desired shape. Place in 2 greased 18 × 26-in. bun pans. Trim and seal edges.

Topping

Amount	Ingredient	Method
1 qt.	Tomato paste	Mix tomato and seasonings.
1 qt.	Tomato purée	Spread over dough, 1 qt. per pan.
2 t.	Thyme or oregano	
1 T.	Salt	
½ t.	Cumin, ground	
1	Garlic clove, crushed	
2 T.	Chili powder	
2 lb. 8 oz.	Sausage	Partially cook sausage and beef. Drain
2 lb. 8 oz.	Ground beef	off excess fat. Sprinkle evenly over tomato sauce.
2 lb. 8 oz.	Mozzarella cheese, sliced or shredded	Top with cheese. Bake.

Note:
Processed Cheddar cheese may be substituted for Mozzarella. Sweet basil may
be sprinkled over top.

Cheeseburger Pie

Bake: 10 min. at 450° F. (crust)   Yield: 2 pans 12 x 20 x 2 in.
      1 hr. at 350° F.   Portion: 6 oz.

Amount	Ingredient	Method
3 lb.	Pastry (p. 175)	Divide dough in half. Roll to cover bottom and sides of 2 12 × 20 in. baking pans (1½ lb. each). Bake 10 min. at 450° F.
10 lb.	Ground beef	Brown beef; drain excess fat.
3 oz. (¼ c.) 1 T. 2 T. 1 lb. 1 lb. 10 oz.	Salt Pepper Oregano Green pepper, chopped Bread crumbs	Add seasonings and crumbs to ground beef. Spread mixture over baked crusts.
12 3⅓ c. 3 lb. 2 T. 2 T. 2 T.	Eggs, beaten Milk Cheese, shredded Salt Mustard, dry Worcestershire sauce	Combine eggs and milk. Add seasonings and cheese. Spread evenly over meat mixture.
3 c.	Tomato sauce	Distribute 1½ c. sauce unevenly over cheese mixture in each pan. Bake 1 hr. at 350° F.

Stuffed Peppers

Bake: 45 min.–1 hr.
Oven: 350° F.

Yield: 50 5-oz. portions

Amount	Ingredient	Method
25	Green peppers	Wash peppers and remove stem end. Cut in halves and remove seeds. Reserve pepper trimmings for filling. Place in baking pans and steam or parboil for 5–8 min.
9 lb.	Cooked meat, ground	Sauté onion and green pepper trimmings in the fat about 3 min. Add to meat.
4 oz.	Fat	
	Green pepper trimmings	Combine eggs, salt, and milk. Add to meat. Mix.
6	Eggs, beaten	
1½ T.	Salt	
1 pt.	Milk	
6 oz.	Bread crumbs	Using No. 10 dipper, fill each pepper with meat mixture.
4 oz.	Fat, melted	Mix crumbs and fat and sprinkle over tops of peppers.
2 qt.	Tomato juice	Pour juice around peppers. Bake.

Notes:
1. Corn, rice, or spaghetti may be substituted for part of the meat.
2. Fresh ground beef, cooked; Corned Beef Hash (p. 238); or Salmon Loaf Mixture (p. 289) may be used for stuffing.

Meat Croquettes

Fry: 3–4 min.   Yield: 50 3½-oz. croquettes
Temp. 350–375° F.

Amount	Ingredient	Method
4 oz.	Butter or mar-garine	Make Thick White Sauce (p. 385).
3–4 oz.	Flour	
1 qt.	Milk	
1 t.	Salt	
10 lb.	Meat, cooked, ground	Combine meat, onion, white sauce, and salt.
2 oz.	Onion, finely chopped	Dip with No. 12 dipper onto a crumb-covered sheet pan. Chill.
1 T.	Salt	Shape into cylindrical croquettes.
3	Eggs	Dip croquettes into egg and milk mixture. Drain.
1 c.	Milk	
12 oz.	Bread crumbs, fine	Roll in crumbs. Chill 2 hr. before frying. Fry in deep fat.
		Serve with Mushroom Sauce (p. 389) or Tomato Sauce (p. 381).

Note:
If desired, croquettes may be placed on a well-greased sheet pan and baked
1 hr. at 375° F.

Baked Hash

Bake: 1–1¼ hr.   Yield: 2 pans 12 x 20 x 2 in.
Oven: 350° F.   Portion: 6 oz.

Amount	Ingredient	Method
10 lb.	Beef, cooked	Chop or grind meat and vegetables coarsely.
8 lb.	Potatoes, cooked	
1 lb.	Onions	
1 t.	Pepper	Add seasonings and liquid. Mix to blend.
¼ c.	Salt	
2 qt.	Meat stock, gravy, or water	Pour into 2 baking pans. Bake. Serve with No. 6 dipper.

Note:
Raw potatoes, well chopped, or hashed brown potatoes may be used in place
of cooked potatoes. Increase baking time to 1¼–1½ hr.
Variation:
Corned Beef Hash. Substitute cooked corned beef for the cooked beef and de-
crease salt to 2 T.

Meat Roll

Bake: 15 min.
Oven: 450° F.

Yield: 50 5-oz. portions

Amount	Ingredient	Method
2 lb. 8 oz. 2 oz. 1½ T. 2½ oz. 1 qt.	Flour Baking powder Salt Fat Milk	Mix ingredients as for Baking Powder Biscuits (p. 99). Divide dough into 4 portions. Roll each portion ¼ in. thick.
7 lb. 3 c.	Beef or other meat, cooked Gravy, cold	Grind meat. Add gravy and seasoning, as needed. Mix well. Spread 2 lb. meat mixture over each dough portion. Roll as for jelly roll. Slice each roll into pieces 1 in. thick. Place on greased baking sheet. Bake. Serve with hot meat gravy or Mushroom Sauce (3 qt.) (p. 389).

Variations:
1. *Ham Biscuit Roll.* Use ground cooked ham. Serve with Mushroom Sauce (p. 389).
2. *Tuna or Salmon Biscuit Roll.* Substitute tuna or salmon for meat and combine with Thick White Sauce (p. 385). Serve with Cheese Sauce. (p. 385).
3. *Chicken or Turkey Biscuit Roll.* Substitute cooked poultry for meat. Serve with Mushroom Sauce (p. 389).

Creamed Beef

Yield: 6¼ qt.
Portion: ½ c.

Amount	Ingredient	Method
10 lb. ½ c.	Ground beef Onions, chopped	Brown beef and onion.
12 oz. 6 oz. 1½ qt. 1½ qt. 3 T. 1 t.	Fat Flour Meat stock Milk Salt Pepper	Make into Medium White Sauce (p. 385). Add to browned meat. Serve with 4-oz. ladle over toast, biscuits, or baked potato.

Creamed Chipped Beef

Yield: 6¼ qt.

Portion: ½ c.

Amount	Ingredient	Method
2 lb. 8 oz. 1 lb.	Chipped beef Fat	Chop beef coarsely. Brown lightly in fat.

1 lb. 4 oz.
 	
10 oz.
5 qt.
	Butter or
	  margarine
	Flour
	Milk
		Make into Medium White Sauce
		  (p. 385).
		Add chipped beef.
		Add salt and pepper to taste.
		Serve with 4-oz. ladle on toast or
		  with baked potato.

Variations:

1. *Creamed Chipped Beef and Peas.* Reduce beef to 2 lb. and add 1 40-oz. package frozen peas, cooked, just before serving.
2. *Chipped Beef and Noodles.* Add 2 lb. ground cheese to white sauce. Combine with 2 lb. noodles, cooked. Top with buttered crumbs. Bake 30 min. at 350° F.
3. *Chipped Beef and Eggs.* Add 2 doz. hard-cooked eggs, sliced or coarsely chopped. Reduce white sauce to 1 gal.

Chili Con Carne

Yield: 3 gal.

Portion: 1 cup

Amount	Ingredient	Method
3 lb. 1 gal.	Pinto, kidney, or red beans Water, boiling	Wash beans. Add boiling water. Cover and let soak 1 hr. or longer. Cook until tender, approximately 1½ hr.
9 lb. 8 oz. 1½ qt. 2 oz. 3–4 oz. 3 T.	Ground beef Onion, chopped Tomato purée Chili powder Cumin seed, ground Salt Water to make total volume of 3 gal.	Brown beef and onion. Add beef and other ingredients to beans. Simmer about 3 hr.

Notes:
1. If desired, thicken chili by mixing 5 oz. flour and 2 c. cold water. Add to chili mixture and heat until flour is cooked.
2. If canned beans are used, substitute 1½ No. 10 cans.

Variation:

Chili Spaghetti. Use only 5 lb. ground beef. Proceed as for Chili Con Carne. Cook 1½ lb. spaghetti and add to chili mixture just before serving.

VEAL   *Breaded Veal*

Bake: 1½ hr.   Yield: 50 5-oz. portions (A.P.)
Oven: 300° F.

Amount	Ingredient	Method
15 lb.	Veal round, sliced ¼ in. thick	Cut meat into 5-oz. portions. Dredge in flour and salt.
8 oz.	Flour	
3 T.	Salt	
3	Eggs, beaten	Dip veal in mixture of egg and milk. Drain.
1 c.	Milk	
12 oz.	Bread crumbs	Roll in fine bread crumbs.
2 lb.	Fat	Brown meat in hot fat. Place, slightly overlapping, in 2 baking pans 12 × 20 × 2 in. Add about 1 pt. of water to each pan. Cover with aluminum foil. Bake.

Note:
Veal cutlets, 4 or 5 oz. each, may be used.

Veal in Sour Cream

Bake: 2 hr.   Yield: 50 5-oz. portions (A.P.)
Oven: 300° F.

Amount	Ingredient	Method
17 lb. (50 chops cut 3 per lb.)	Veal chops	Mix flour and seasonings. Dredge chops in flour mixture.
8 oz.	Flour	
3 T.	Salt	
1 t.	Pepper	
1 lb. 8 oz.	Fat	Brown chops in hot fat. Place, slightly overlapping, in 2 baking pans.
2 qt.	Cultured sour cream	Mix cream and water. Pour over chops.
2 qt.	Water	Cover with aluminum foil. Bake.

Note:
Veal cutlets, 3 or 4 per lb., may be used in place of veal chops.

Veal Birds

Bake: 2 hr.
Oven: 300° F.

Yield: 50 4-oz. portions

Amount	Ingredient	Method
12 lb. 8 oz.	Veal round, ¼ in. thick	Cut veal into 4-oz. servings.
6 oz.	Fat	Sauté onion and celery in the fat.
¼ c.	Onions, finely chopped	Combine with bread, seasonings, and broth. Mix lightly.
1 c.	Celery, finely chopped	Place No. 16 dipper of bread mixture on each piece of meat. Roll
3 lb.	Bread, dry, cubed	and fasten with a toothpick.
½ t.	Pepper	
2 T.	Sage	
2 t.	Salt	
1¼ qt. (variable)	Broth or water	
8 oz.	Flour	Roll each bird in flour and salt mixture. Brown in hot fat.
3 T.	Salt	
2 lb. 8 oz.	Fat	Place in 2 baking pans. Add 1 pt. water to each pan. Cover with aluminum foil. Bake.

Note:
Beef, pork, or veal cutlets, 4 per lb., may be substituted for the veal round.

Veal Fricassee

Yield: 50 5-oz. portions

Amount	Ingredient	Method
15 lb.	Veal, 1-in. cubes	Dredge veal in flour.
8 oz.	Flour	Brown in hot fat.
1 lb.	Fat	
1 gal.	Water	Add water and salt. Simmer 2 hr. or until meat is tender.
3 T.	Salt	

Variations:
1. *Curried Veal.* Add 2 oz. curry powder when water is added.
2. *Veal Paprika with Rice.* Add ½ c. paprika to flour. Cook 12 oz. minced onions with veal. Add 2 qt. cultured sour cream the last few minutes of cooking. Serve with hot rice.

Mock Drumsticks

Bake: 2 hr.   Yield: 50 4-oz. portions
Oven: 350° F.

Amount	Ingredient	Method
10 lb.	Veal, 1-in. cubes	Place meat on skewers, alternating veal and pork pieces. Use 2 pork and 3 veal on each skewer.
7 lb.	Pork, 1-in. cubes	
50	Skewers	
8 oz.	Flour	Dredge each drumstick in flour and salt.
3 T.	Salt	
3	Eggs	Dip in combined eggs and water. Drain.
1 c.	Water or milk	
12 oz.	Crumbs, fine	Roll in crumbs to cover.
1 lb.	Fat	Brown drumsticks in hot fat. Place in 2 baking pans. Add 1 pt. water to each pan. Cover with aluminum foil. Bake.

Note:
1 fresh mushroom may be placed at each end of skewer before cooking.
Variation:
Barbecued Kabobs. Arrange meat on skewers as above. Dredge in flour and brown in hot fat. Cover with Barbecue Sauce (p. 382). Bake 2 hr. at 350° F.

Veal Patties

Bake: 25–30 min. Yield: 50 5-oz. portions
Oven: 375–400° F.

Amount	Ingredient	Method
12 lb.	Veal, ground	Combine all ingredients carefully.
2 lb.	Salt pork, ground	Do not overmix.
8 oz.	Bread crumbs	Measure with No. 8 dipper. Form into patties. Place on sheet pan.
12	Eggs, beaten	Bake.
3 T.	Salt	
2 t.	Pepper	
1 oz.	Onion, grated	
1½ c.	Milk	

Note:
Wrap with a strip of bacon and fasten with a toothpick if desired.
Variations:
1. *Lamb Patties.* Substitute 14 lb. ground lamb for veal and salt pork. Wrap each pattie with a strip of bacon. Bake approximately 30 min.
2. *Stuffed Meat Cakes.* Place thin slice of onion and tomato between 2 thin meat patties. Press edges together and fasten with a toothpick. Bake approximately 30 min.

PORK ## Deviled Pork Chops

Bake: 1½ hr. Yield: 50 5-oz. portions (A.P.)
Oven: 350° F.

Amount	Ingredient	Method
17 lb.	Pork chops, cut 3 per lb.	Combine chili sauce, water, and seasonings into a sauce.
1½ qt.	Chili sauce	Dip each chop in sauce. Place on baking pan. Bake.
3 c.	Water	
1 t.	Mustard, dry	
3 T.	Worcestershire sauce	
3 T.	Lemon juice	
2 t.	Onion, grated	

Note:
Chops also may be placed on edge, close together, with fat side up. Bake 2–2½ hr.
Variation:
Barbecued Pork Chops. Pour Barbecue Sauce (p. 382) over chops. Bake.

Pork Chops with Dressing

Bake: 1½ hr.   Yield: 50 5-oz. portions
Oven: 350° F.

Amount	Ingredient	Method
16–18 lb.	Pork chops, cut 3 per lb.	Brown chops. Arrange in 2 12 × 20 × 2-in. baking or counter pans.
2 oz.	Salt	Sprinkle with salt.
⅔ recipe	Bread Dressing (p. 280)	Place 2 oz. dressing (No. 16 dipper) on each chop.
3 qt.	Milk	Pour milk over chops. Bake. Baste frequently with milk.

Note:
Dressing may be spread in pan and pork chops placed on top.
Variations:
1. *Stuffed Pork Chops.* Cut pocket in each chop. Fill with dressing and proceed as above. Use ½ Bread Dressing recipe (p. 280).
2. *Baked Pork Chops.* Dredge chops in 8 oz. flour and 4 T. fat mixed. Place on well-greased sheet pan. Bake until thoroughly cooked and browned (approximately 1¼ hr. at 350° F.).
3. *Breaded Pork Chops.* Egg and crumb chops using 3 eggs and 1 c. water (p. 69). Place on greased sheet pans. Pour about 8 oz. melted fat over top of chops. Bake in hot oven (400° F.) until browned—about 20 min. Remove from oven and arrange in partially overlapping rows in 2 counter pans. Add 1 pt. of water to each counter pan and return to the oven. Cook slowly until well done (approximately 1 hr. at 325° F.). Use chops cut 4 per lb.

Barbecued Spareribs

Bake: 2 hr.   Yield: 50 8-oz. portions
Oven: 350° F.

Amount	Ingredient	Method
25 lb.	Pork spareribs or loin back ribs	Brown ribs in oven. Pour off excess fat.
3 qt.	Barbecue Sauce (p. 382)	Pour Barbecue Sauce over ribs. Bake.

Variations:
1. *Barbecued Lamb.* Substitute lamb shanks for spareribs.
2. *Barbecued Shortribs.* Substitute beef or veal shortribs for spareribs.
3. *Sweet-Sour Spareribs.* Brown spareribs for 30 min. in 400° F. oven, or simmer in water 1 hr. Drain and cover with Sweet-Sour Sauce (p. 384). Bake in 350° F. oven until meat is done. Serve with Steamed Rice or Fried Rice with Almonds (p. 309).

Sweet and Sour Pork

Yield: 50 portions
6 oz. pork, 4 oz. rice

Amount	Ingredient	Method
10 lb. 1 c.	Pork, lean, 1-in. cubes Soy sauce	Pour soy sauce over meat. Mix lightly. Let stand at least 1 hr.
12 oz.	Fat	Drain soy sauce; save. Brown meat in hot fat. Drain excess fat.
1 qt. 1 pt.	Broth, chicken or meat	Add broth and drained soy sauce to meat. Simmer until meat is tender, approximately 1 hr.
10 oz. 3 oz. 1½ t. 1½ c. 2 c. ¾ c.	Brown sugar Cornstarch Salt Pineapple juice Vinegar Soy sauce	Combine sugar, cornstarch, and salt. Add pineapple juice, vinegar, and soy sauce. Mix until smooth. Add to meat mixture while stirring. Cook slowly until thickened.
1 lb. 2 lb. 3 lb. 1 No. 10 can	Green pepper strips Onions, medium, cut into eighths Tomatoes, medium, cut into wedges Pineapple chunks, well drained	15 min. before serving, add green peppers and onions and cook gently. Just before serving, add tomato wedges and pineapple chunks. Heat.
3 lb.	Rice (p. 309)	Serve pork over rice.

Glazed Baked Ham

Bake: 4½ hr. at 300° F.
    then ½ hr. at 400° F.
    to glaze

Yield: 50 3-oz. portions

Amount	Ingredient	Method
20 lb.	Ham, whole, cured	Trim excess fat from ham if necessary. Place fat side up on a rack in roasting pan. Do not cover. Bake about 4½ hr. at 300° F. (See timetable p. 218.) If ready-to-eat ham is used, shorten baking time (p. 218).
3 T.	Whole cloves	Remove ham from oven about ½ hr. before it is done. Drain off drippings and trim thin layer of browned fat from entire surface. Score ham fat ¼ in. deep in diamond pattern. Stud with whole cloves. Cover with glaze.

Ham Glaze

Amount	Ingredient	Method
8 oz.	Brown sugar	Combine ingredients for glaze.
2 T.	Cornstarch	Spoon over ham. Repeat if a heavier glaze is desired.
¼ c.	Corn sirup	
2 T.	Pineapple juice	Return ham to hot oven (400° F.) and complete baking.

Note:
Ham may be simmered in kettle for 3 to 4 hrs. then trimmed, glazed, and the cooking completed in oven.

Variations:
1. *Apricot Glaze.* 1 c. apricot jam and ¼ c. fruit juice or enough to cover ham.
2. *Brown Sugar Glaze.* 1 c. brown sugar, 1½ t. dry mustard (or 3 T. prepared mustard), and ¼ c. vinegar.
3. *Cranberry Glaze.* 1¼ c. strained cranberry sauce, or enough to cover.
4. *Honey Glaze.* 1 c. honey, ½ c. brown sugar, and ¼ c. fruit juice. Baste with fruit juice or ginger ale.
5. *Orange Glaze.* 1 c. orange marmalade and ¼ c. spiced peach or orange juice.

Baked Ham Slices

Bake: 2 hr.   Yield: 50 2½-oz. portions
Oven: 325° F.   cooked meat

Amount	Ingredient	Method
18 lb.	Ham, cured, center cut, ½ in. thick	Cut ham into 5-oz. portions. Combine sugar and mustard. Rub over surface of ham slices.
14 oz.	Brown sugar	Place in 2 baking pans 12 × 20
3 T.	Mustard, dry	× 2 in.
2 qt.	Water	Pour combined liquids over ham slices. Cover with aluminum foil. Bake.
1 c.	Pineapple or spiced fruit juice	

Notes:
1. Sliced ham roll may be used.
2. Milk may be substituted for fruit juice.
Variations:
1. *Baked Ham Slices with Pineapple Rings.* When ham is tender, cover with pineapple rings, bake until pineapple is browned.
2. *Baked Ham Slices with Orange Sauce.* Arrange ham slices in counter pan and cover with Orange Sauce (p. 376). Cover with aluminum foil and bake.

Ham Loaf

Bake: 2 hr.   Yield: 5 pans 4 x 9 in.
Oven: 350° F.   Portion: 5 oz.

Amount	Ingredient	Method
4 lb.	Ground cured ham	Combine all ingredients.
4 lb.	Ground veal or beef	Mix (low speed) only until ingredients are blended. **DO NOT OVERMIX.**
4 lb.	Ground fresh pork	Press mixture into 5 loaf pans. (Meat may be baked in 12 × 20 × 4-in. baking or counter pan. Press mixture into pan and divide into 4 loaves. Allow slightly longer baking time than for the individual loaves.)
1 qt.	Milk	
12	Eggs, beaten	
1 t.	Pepper	Cover top of loaves with glaze during last 30 min. of cooking if desired.

Notes:
1. Ground cooked ham may be used.
2. Veal or beef may be omitted, using 8 lb. ground cured ham and 4 lb. ground fresh pork.

Variations:
1. *Glazed Ham Loaf.* Cover top of loaves with a mixture of 1½ lb. brown sugar, 1 c. vinegar, and 1½ T. dry mustard.
2. *Glazed Ham Balls.* Measure with No. 8 dipper and shape into balls. Place on baking pans. Brush with glaze and bake.
3. *Ham Patties with Pineapple.* Measure with No. 8 dipper and shape into patties. Top with slice of pineapple and clove. Pour pineapple juice over patties and bake.
4. *Ham Patties with Cranberries.* Spread pan with Cranberry Sauce (p. 343). Place ham patties on sauce and bake.

Ham and Egg Scallop

Bake: 30–40 min.   Yield: 2 pans 12 x 20 x 2 in.
Oven: 400° F.   Portion: 5 oz.

Amount	Ingredient	Method
1 lb.	Butter or margarine	Make into Medium White Sauce (p. 385).
8 oz.	Flour	
1 T.	Salt	
3¾ qt.	Milk	
4 lb.	Ham, chopped	Fill 2 greased baking pans with alternate layers of ham, eggs, and white sauce.
36	Eggs, hard cooked, sliced	
12 oz.	Bread crumbs	Sprinkle buttered crumbs over top of ham and egg mixture. Bake.
3 oz.	Butter or margarine, melted	

Variation:
Ham and Sweetbread Casserole. Cut ham into cubes. Substitute 4 lb. sweetbreads, cooked and cubed, for eggs.

Creamed Ham

Yield: 6¼ qt.
Portion: ½ c.

Amount	Ingredient	Method
1 lb.	Butter or margarine	Make into Medium White Sauce (p. 385).
6 oz.	Flour	
1 gal.	Milk	
6 lb.	Ham, cooked, cubed	Add ham and heat slowly for approximately 20 min.
To taste	Salt	Salt to taste. Serve with 4-oz. ladle over biscuits, toast, spoon bread, cornbread, or cheese soufflé.

Note:
Chopped celery, sliced mushrooms, or chopped hard-cooked eggs may be added.

Oven-Fried Bacon

Bake: 6–8 min.   Yield: 50 slices
Temp. 375° F.

Amount	Ingredient	Method
50 slices (2½–3 lb.)	Bacon (17–20 slices per lb.)	Arrange bacon slices on bun pans. Bake without turning until crisp. Pour off accumulating fat if necessary. Drain on paper towels or place in perforated pans for serving.

Cheese-Stuffed Wieners

Bake: 30 min.   Yield: 100 wieners
Oven: 350° F.   Portion: 2 wieners

Amount	Ingredient	Method
8 lb. 4 oz.	Weiners, 12 per lb.	Split wieners lengthwise, but do not cut completely through.
3 lb. 1 qt.	Cheddar cheese Pickle relish	Cut cheese into strips about 3½ in. long. Place a strip of cheese and about ½ T. relish in each wiener.
4 lb. 4 oz.	Bacon, 24–26 slices per lb.	Wrap a slice of bacon around each wiener. Secure with a toothpick. Bake.

Note:
1 slice of bacon may be wrapped around 2 wieners.
Variations:
1. *Barbecued Wieners.* Leave wieners whole. Place in counter pans. Cover with Barbecue Sauce (p. 382) and bake about 30 min. at 400° F. Add more sauce as necessary.
2. *Wieners and Sauerkraut.* Steam wieners or cook in boiling water. Serve with sauerkraut.

Sausage Rolls

Bake: 20 min.
Oven: 400° F.

Yield: 50 rolls
Portion: 1 roll, ¼ c. gravy

Amount	Ingredient	Method
12 lb. 8 oz.	Sausages, link	Partially cook sausages. Save fat for gravy.
2 lb. 8 oz.	Flour	Make into biscuit dough (p. 99).
3 oz.	Baking powder	Divide dough into 2 portions. Roll
1½ T.	Salt	each portion to ½-in. thickness
1 lb.	Fat	and cut into 3 × 4-in. rectangles.
1 qt.	Milk	Place 2 sausages in the center of each piece of dough and fold over. Bake.
6 oz.	Sausage fat	Make into gravy (p. 389).
6 oz.	Flour	Serve 2-oz. ladle of gravy over each
2 t.	Salt	sausage roll.
½ t.	Pepper	
3 qt.	Water or meat stock	

Variation:
Pigs in Blankets. Substitute wieners for link sausages. Serve with Cheese Sauce (p. 385).

Scrapple

Yield: 5 pans 4 x 9 in.

Amount	Ingredient	Method
8 lb.	Pork, fresh	Boil pork, water, and salt until meat falls to pieces. Add water as necessary.
6 qt.	Water	
¼ c.	Salt	
3 lb.	Corn meal, yellow	Remove meat and bones from liquid. Remove bones and gristle from meat.
		Finely chop meat and return to liquid (about 1¼ gal.).
		Add corn meal slowly, while stirring constantly.
		Boil 5 min., place in steamer and cook 3 hr.
		Turn into 5 loaf pans to mold.
		Cut into ½-in. slices. Dip in flour. Fry until brown and crisp on both sides.

Note:

8 lb. pork sausage may be substituted for fresh pork. Cook in 1½ gal. water, skim excess fat, then add corn meal and cook until thick. Pour into loaf pans.

Braised Tongue

Yield: 50 4-oz. portions

Amount	Ingredient	Method
20 lb.	Tongue	Wash tongues. Cover with water and simmer until tender, 3–4 hr. Remove skin. Place in pan.
4 oz. 5 oz. 4 oz.	Onion, chopped Carrots, finely diced Celery, finely diced	Add vegetables to meat.
10 oz. 5 oz. 3 qt. 3 T. 2 t.	Fat Flour Meat stock Salt Pepper	Melt fat, add flour and stir until smooth. Add stock gradually while stirring. Add salt and pepper. If soup base has been used to make stock, less salt should be used. Cook until thickened. Pour sauce over tongue. Simmer about 2 hr., turning meat occasionally. Cut tongue into thin slices. Pour sauce over slices and serve.

Note:
Tongue may be sliced after it has been simmered and skin removed, and served with the other ingredients made into a sauce.
Variation:
Spiced Tongue. Substitute 5 t. allspice, 1 T. whole cloves, and 3 bay leaves for vegetables. Serve cold.

Liver with Spanish Sauce

Bake: 1 hr.   Yield: 50 3½-oz. portions
Oven: 350° F.

Amount	Ingredient	Method
10 lb.	Liver, sliced, cut 5 per lb.	Dredge liver in seasoned flour. Brown in hot fat.
8 oz.	Flour	
3 T.	Salt	
2 t.	Pepper	
1 lb. 8 oz.	Fat	
1 recipe	Spanish Sauce (p. 382)	Place liver in 2 baking pans. Pour Spanish Sauce over liver. Cover with aluminum foil. Bake until tender.

Note:
Soaking liver in milk before cooking improves the flavor.
Variations:
1. *Liver and Onions.* Cover browned liver with 4 lb. onions, sliced, and 2 qt. water. Bake until tender.
2. *Liver and Bacon.* Dredge liver and flour and fry in bacon fat. Top each serving with 1 slice crisp bacon.
3. *Braised Liver.* Cover with sauce used for Braised Tongue (p. 255).

Baked Heart with Dressing

Bake: 1 hr.   Yield: 50 6-oz. portions
Oven: 300° F.   3 oz. heart,
                                                        3 oz. dressing

Amount	Ingredient	Method
20 lb.	Heart, beef	Wash, split hearts. Cut away arteries and gristle.
2 gal.	Water	
8 oz.	Onion	Add water, onion, and spices.
4 T.	Peppercorns	Simmer until almost tender (about
6	Bay leaves	3 hr.). Drain. Reserve broth for gravy.
⅔ recipe	Bread Dressing (p. 280)	Slice heart into 3-oz. portions. Place in 2 12 × 20 × 2-in. baking or counter pans. To serve, place 3-oz. portion sliced heart over No. 10 dipper of dressing. Cover with gravy made from broth. Use cornstarch for thickening for a clear gravy.

Sweetbread Cutlets

Fry: 3–4 min.   Yield: 50 3-oz. cutlets
Temp.: 375° F.

Amount	Ingredient	Method
12 lb (A.P.)	Sweetbreads	Soak sweetbreads 30 min. in cold
1½ qt.	Water	water. Drain.
2 T.	Salt	Boil gently in water, vinegar, and
1 t.	Vinegar	salt for 20–30 min. Drain. Plunge into cold water.
		Remove connective membrane.
		Chop coarsely.
8 oz.	Mushrooms, chopped	Add mushrooms and seasonings.
3 T.	Salt	
1 t.	Pepper	
5 T.	Lemon juice	
½ t.	Nutmeg	
8 oz.	Butter or margarine	Make Thick White Sauce (p. 385), of butter, flour, salt, and milk.
8 oz.	Flour	Add eggs and mix.
2 t.	Salt	Combine with sweetbread mixture.
2 qt.	Milk	
8	Eggs, slightly beaten	Measure with No. 12 dipper onto sheet pan covered with thin layer of crumbs. Chill.
6	Eggs, slightly beaten	Shape into cutlets. Egg and Crumb (p. 69). Chill 2 hr. before frying.
12 oz.	Bread crumbs	Fry in deep fat.
1 c.	Milk	

Variation:
Chicken Cutlets. Substitute cooked chicken for sweetbreads.

POULTRY

Purchasing Poultry

Poultry for institution food services usually is purchased in the eviscerated or ready-to-cook state. Whether it is cut up or whole, frozen or fresh, will depend on the class of poultry concerned and the preferences of the buyer. Most types of ready-to-cook poultry are available as parts and in whole, halved, and quartered forms. Some kinds, usually turkeys, also are available as boneless roasts. The ready-to-cook birds require no further processing.

All poultry sold in interstate commerce must have been examined for wholesomeness under United States Government supervision in officially approved processing plants. Most of the poultry in market channels is graded, and all classes are available in U. S. Grades A, B, and C. Grade A birds present the best appearance, but the grade to purchase will depend on the use and price differential. All poultry is highly perishable and extreme caution regarding cleanliness should be exercised in preparation, cooking, cooling, storage, and serving of poultry products.

There is a trend toward purchasing custom-cut, ready-for-the-pan chicken parts, such as whole or half breasts, legs, or thighs. Many institutions find it advantageous to purchase chicken parts, although there is some price differential between custom-cut pieces and whole poultry. Each portion in the package is of identical weight; there is no waste, and the cost of each portion is easily determined. Such a method of purchase makes it possible to order only the amount needed.

Turkeys range in size from 8 to 30 lb. ready-to-cook weight. Larger birds yield more meat in proportion to bone weight than do smaller ones.

The summary[1] of a study undertaken to determine the yield and palatability of the whole and cut-up turkeys both from the thawed and frozen state of birds weighing 20 to 24 pounds each showed that the yield, cutting quality, and palatability of the thawed and frozen birds were not

[1] Lois H. Fulton, Gladys I. Gilpin, and Elsie H. Dawson, "Turkeys, Roasted from Frozen and Thawed States," Journal of Home Economics 59, 728–731 (1967).

significantly different. Average cooking time was reduced from 25 to 63 percent by cutting into pieces, quarters, and halves; the yield and palatability of cut turkey were as good or better than the whole turkey.

Frozen birds may be of the same high quality as unfrozen. Freezing does not change the original quality but maintains it under proper processing and storage conditions. In young birds and broilers, the freezing temperature may darken the bones; but other than appearance, there are no detrimental effects as a result of freezing. The purchase of fresh or frozen poultry depends on the preference of the buyer, the facilities of the institution, and the availability of poultry in local markets.

Cooking started in the frozen state will take approximately 1½ times the total time allowance for thawed poultry. Once thawed, poultry may be kept safely no longer than 24 hours at 38° F. before cooking. It should never be refrozen. To defrost frozen poultry, use one of the following procedures:

1. Place wrapped in a refrigerator. A turkey 18 pounds or over, will require a thawing time of 48 to 72 hours; less than 18 pounds, 24 to 48 hours.

2. Place in original wrap, under a stream of cold water, 5 to 8 hours depending on size of the bird.

Cooking Methods

Recommended cooking methods for various classes of poultry are given in the following table:

Cooking Methods for Poultry

Kind of Poultry	Class	Average Ready to Cook Weight (Lb.)	Cookery Method	Per Capita Allowance Ready-to-Cook
Chicken	Broiler or fryer	1½–3	Barbecue, fry, or broil	¼–½ bird
	Capon	5–7	Roast	¾–1 lb.
	Roaster	3–5	Roast	¾–1 lb.
	Fowl or hen	3–5	Stew or fricassee	½–¾ lb.
Turkey	Fryer–roaster	4–8	Barbecue, fry, or broil	¼–½ bird
	Young hens or toms	10–18	Roast	¾–1 lb.
	Heavy hens or toms	18–30	Roast	¾–1 lb.
	Roast, boned and tied, raw	13 (approximately)	Roast	4–5 oz.
	Roast, cooked	8–10	Slice and heat in broth or heat in an uncovered pan	2½–3 oz.
	Roll, ready to cook	7–9	Roast	4–5 oz.
Duck		4–6	Roast	¾–1 lb.
		6–10	Roast	¾–1 lb.

Note:
For cooked yields, see p. 263.

BROILING

Only young tender chickens, 2½ lb. or under, or 3–5 lb. ready-to-cook turkeys should be broiled. Split each bird in half lengthwise, or into quarters, depending on size. Fold wing tip back onto cut side with the thick part around the shoulder joint. Brush with melted fat. Season each piece with salt and pepper, and place, skin side down, on broiler. Place broiler 7 in. below source of heat, as chicken and turkey should broil slowly. Turn and brush with fat while broiling in order to brown and cook evenly. The time required to cook chicken varies from 50 to 60 min., and 1 to 1¼ hr. for turkey.

DEEP-FAT FRYING

Cut 13 1¾–2 lb. broiler–fryers into pieces of desired serving size. Roll chicken in seasoned flour; or dredge in flour, dip in egg and water mixture, then roll in crumbs (p. 69). Fry in deep fat 12–15 min. at no more than 330° F.

PAN-FRYING

Cut 13 2–2½ lb. broiler–fryers into pieces. Roll chicken in seasoned flour (1 lb. flour, 2 T. salt, 1 T. paprika or poultry seasoning) and brown in a skillet containing ½ in. of hot fat. Reduce heat and cook slowly until tender—usually about 45–60 min. Cooking time depends on size of pieces. Turn as necessary to assure even browning and doneness.

OVEN-FRYING

Cut 13 2–2½ lb. broiler–fryers into pieces. Melt 1 lb. fat on bun pan. Combine 1 lb. flour, 2 c. dry milk, 1–2 t. paprika, and 2 T. salt. Dredge each chicken part in flour mixture and roll in fat on pan. Place pieces close together, skin side down, in 1 layer. Bake 1 hr. at 350° F. This method should result in browning with no turning.

STEWING OR SIMMERING

Cover fowl with water and add 2 t. salt for each 4–5 lb. bird. Cover kettle closely and simmer fowl until tender, approximately 2½ hr. Do not boil. When meat is to be used in jellied loaves, salads, or creamed dishes, add to cooking water for additional flavor 1 carrot, 1 medium onion, 1 stalk of celery, 2 or 3 cloves, and 2 whole peppercorns for each bird. For cooking in a steamer, place whole or parts of birds in a solid steamer pan. Cook until tender, following instructions of the manufacturer.

If cooked fowl is to be held it must be cooled immediately. The fowl may be boned to save refrigerator space. Place meat in a shallow pan and refrigerate at 38° F. or below. Cooked poultry should be used no later than the second day after it is cooked.

ROASTING

For large quantity cookery, it usually is recommended that poultry be roasted unstuffed and that dressing be baked separately. If turkey is to be stuffed, *mix the stuffing just before it is needed.* Do not prepare dressing or stuff the bird in advance. Follow this order of procedure in preparing a roaster:

1. Prepare bird. Remove pin feathers and singe if necessary. Wash well inside and out.

2. Salt inside and outside of bird.

3. Brush with soft fat or oil.

4. Place bird on a rack in a shallow baking pan, breast up.

5. Baste with fat and hot water (4 oz. fat to 1 qt. hot water) if desired. Drippings also may be used for basting.

6. Roast at 325° F. to an internal temperature of 185° F. Insert meat thermometer in center of inside thigh muscle. Allow approximately 15–18 min. per lb. for a 20-lb. unstuffed turkey. Allow approximately 30 min. per lb. for a 5-lb. chicken. If thermometer is not available, test doneness by moving drumstick. It moves easily at the thigh joint when done.

7. To roast a boneless turkey roast place on rack in an open pan. Roast at 325° F. until a meat thermometer inserted in center registers 170–175° F., or follow cooking directions on package.

Timetable for Roasting Unstuffed Birds

Purchased Ready-to-Cook Weight Lb.	Oven Temperature ° F.	Interior Temperature ° F.	Guide to Total Cooking Time Hrs.
6–8	325	185	3–3½
8–12	325	185	3½–4½
12–16	325	185	4½–5½
16–20	325	185	5½–6½
20–24	325	185	6½–7

SOURCE. *Homemaker's Turkey Handbook.* National Turkey Federation, p. 5. Rev. May, 1968.

Yield of Standard Portions Obtainable from Various Sizes of Turkeys

Ready-to-Cook Weight Lb.	Cooked Yield Lb.	Number of Portions		
		2 Oz.	3 Oz.	5 Oz.
10–12	4½	36	22	12
12–14	4½	42	26	15
14–16	6	48	30	18
16–17	6⅔	54	32	20
17–18	7⅓	59	37	23
18–20	8	64	40	25
26–30	13½	108	67	40

SOURCE. *Turkey Handbook,* National Turkey Federation, p. 31.

The yield of fowl and turkey is influenced by the method of preparation and service, and the size of portions desired. A fowl weighing 4 to 4½ lb. ready-to-cook will yield approximately 1 qt. (1¼ lb.) cooked edible meat.

Poultry Recipes

Chicken à la Maryland

Bake: 2½–3 hr.　　　　　　　　　　Yield: 50 3-oz. portions (cooked meat)
Oven: 325° F.

Amount	Ingredient	Method
35 lb. (A.P.) (8 4–4½ lb. hens)	Chicken	Cut chicken into desired pieces. Roll in flour and salt. Brown in hot fat.
12 oz.	Flour	
2 T.	Salt	
1 lb.	Fat	
3 qt.	Cream, thin	Arrange pieces of chicken close together in baking pans. Cover with cream. Bake.

Variation:
Paprika Chicken. Omit cream. Add 2 large onions, diced and browned in hot fat, 4 c. water or chicken stock, 4 egg yolks mixed with 4 c. cultured sour cream, and ¼ c. paprika. Bake.

Barbecued Chicken

Bake: 1½–2 hr.　　　　　　　　　Yield: 52 portions (¼ fryer)
Oven: 325° F.

Amount	Ingredient	Method
35 lb. (13 2–2½ lb. fryers)	Chicken	Cut fryers into quarters or pieces as desired.
2 T.	Salt	Season with salt.
1 lb.	Fat, melted	Roll chicken in melted fat and place on bun pans. Brown in oven.
1 recipe	Cooked Barbecue Sauce (p. 382)	Pour sauce over chicken. Bake 1 hr.

Fricassee of Chicken

Bake: 1½–2 hr.
Oven: 325° F.

Yield: 50 3-oz. portions (cooked meat)

Amount	Ingredient	Method
35 lb. (A.P.) (8 4–4½ lb. hens)	Chicken	Cut chicken into desired pieces. Dip each piece in seasoned flour. Brown in hot fat.
12 oz.	Flour	Remove to roasting pan (or steam
2 T.	Salt	kettle) and cover with boiling
1 t.	Pepper	water.
1 lb.	Fat	Cook slowly, adding more water if necessary.
10 oz.	Fat	When tender, remove chicken from
6 oz.	Flour	stock.
3½ qt.	Chicken broth	Make gravy, using liquid in which chicken was cooked. Serve over chicken.

Variation:

White Fricassee of Chicken. Do not brown chicken. Stew until tender. Remove from liquid. Boil liquid until concentrated. Add milk or cream to make 1½ gal., thicken to make a Medium White Sauce (p. 385). Beat constantly while pouring sauce gradually over 10 beaten egg yolks. Season to taste. Add chicken.

Chicken Tahitian

Brown 30 min., bake 35–40 min.
Oven: 350° F.

Yield: 52 portions (¼ fryer)

Amount	Ingredient	Method
35 lb. (A.P.) (13 2–2½ lb. fryers)	Chicken, cut into quarters	Melt fat in baking pan. Arrange chicken in pans in single layer.
12 oz.	Fat	Brown in oven.
4 6-oz. cans	Frozen orange juice, undiluted	Combine juice, butter or margarine, ginger, and soy sauce.
1 lb.	Butter or margarine	Brush chicken with orange mixture. Bake. Baste with orange mixture
2 T.	Ginger	until chicken is glazed.
2 T.	Soy sauce	Serve with Steamed Rice (p. 309) and garnish with slivered almonds and avocado wedges.

Creamed Chicken

Yield: 50 5-oz. portions

Amount	Ingredient	Method
5 lb. (4 4½–5 lb. hens)	Cooked chicken	Cut chicken into cubes.
1 lb. 12 oz.	Chicken fat or butter	Make as Medium White Sauce (p. 385).
1 lb. 4 oz.	Flour	Add chicken. Cook until chicken is
3 qt.	Chicken stock	thoroughly heated.
2¼ qt.	Milk	
2 T.	Salt	

Variation:
Chicken à la King. Add 12 chopped, hard-cooked eggs, 8 oz. shredded pimiento, and 1 lb. chopped sautéed mushrooms.

Chicken Cutlets

Fry: 3–4 min.
Deep-Fat Fryer: 360–375° F.

Yield: 50 3-oz. cutlets

Amount	Ingredient	Method
6 lb. (5 4½–5 lb. hens)	Cooked chicken	Finely chop chicken.
12 oz.	Chicken fat or butter	Make as Thick White Sauce (p. 385).
6 oz.	Flour	
2 T.	Salt	
1 pt.	Milk, cold	
1 qt.	Chicken stock, hot	
8	Eggs, beaten	When sauce is thickened, add eggs. Stir to blend. Cook 10 min. Add chicken. Mix lightly. Measure with No. 12 dipper onto lightly greased sheet pan. Chill.
4	Eggs	Flatten into oval or kidney-shaped
1 c.	Milk	cutlets. Dip in egg and crumbs
12 oz.	Bread crumbs	(p. 69). Chill not less than 2 hrs. before frying. Fry in deep fat.

Scalloped Chicken

Bake: 30–40 min.
Oven: 350° F.

Yield: 2 pans 12 × 20 × 2 in.
Portion: 6 oz.

Amount	Ingredient	Method
5 lb. (4 4½–5 lb. hens)	Cooked chicken	Cut chicken into cubes.
1 lb.	Chicken fat or butter	Make as Medium White Sauce (p. 385).
8 oz.	Flour	
1 gal.	Chicken stock	
1½ T.	Salt	
12	Eggs, beaten	When thick and smooth, add eggs, stirring constantly.
⅔ recipe	Bread Dressing (p. 280)	Place layer of dressing in 2 baking pans, layer of sauce, layer of chicken, another layer of sauce. Cover with buttered crumbs. Bake.
6 oz.	Cracker crumbs, coarse	
3 oz.	Butter or margarine, melted	

Chicken Turnovers

Bake: 25–30 min.
Oven: 400° F.

Yield: 50 4-oz. portions

Amount	Ingredient	Method
5 lb. (4 4½–5 lb. hens)	Cooked chicken	Cube or coarsely chop chicken.
6 oz.	Chicken fat or butter	Make as Thick White Sauce (p. 385).
4 oz.	Flour	When thick, add chicken.
1 T.	Salt	
1 qt.	Chicken broth	
5 lb. (50 rounds)	Pastry (p. 175), cut with 6-in. cutter	Place No. 20 dipper of chicken mixture on each pastry round. Fold rounds over and seal by pressing edges together with a fork. Bake. Serve with chicken gravy or mushroom sauce (1 gal.).

Hot Chicken Salad

Bake: 25–30 min.   Yield: 2 pans 12 × 20 × 2 in.
Oven: 350° F.   or 50 individual casseroles
                     Portion: 5 oz.

Amount	Ingredient	Method
6 lb. (5 4½–5 lb. hens)	Cooked chicken, diced	Toss chicken and other ingredients together lightly.
4 lb.	Celery, diced	Place in 2 pans (or in individual casseroles, using No. 8 dipper).
6 T.	Onion, chopped	
1 lb.	Almonds, browned and chopped	
3 T.	Lemon rind, grated	
¾ c.	Lemon juice	
1½ t.	Pepper	
1 qt.	Mayonnaise	
3 lb.	Cheese, grated	Sprinkle cheese, then potato chips over top of salad mixture. Bake.
12 oz.	Potato chips, crushed	

Chicken Loaf

Bake: 1½ hr.   Yield: 5 loaves 4 × 9 in.
Oven: 325° F.   Portion: 5 oz.

Amount	Ingredient	Method
1 lb.	Rice	Cook rice (p. 309).
7 lb. (6 4½–5 lb. hens)	Cooked chicken, diced	Combine chicken, cooked rice, pimiento, and onion. Mix lightly.
6 oz.	Pimiento, chopped	
2 oz.	Onion, grated	
16	Eggs, beaten	Add remaining ingredients. Mix only until blended.
1½ T.	Salt	Divide into 5 greased loaf pans or a 12 × 20 × 4-in. baking pan. Bake.
1 t.	Pepper	
2 qt.	Chicken broth, cold	
1 qt.	Milk	Serve with Chicken Gravy (p. 389) or Mushroom Sauce (p. 389).
1 lb.	Bread crumbs, soft	

Note:
Turkey or tuna may be used in place of chicken.

Chicken Pie

Bake: 12–15 min.
Oven: 450° F.

Yield: 50 8-oz. casseroles or
2 pans 12 × 20 × 2 in.

Amount	Ingredient	Method
6 lb. (5 4½–5 lb. hens)	Cooked chicken, cubed	Place in each of 50 8-oz. baking dishes: 2 oz. chicken, 1 oz. potato, 1 T. peas, and ⅓ c. chicken gravy.
3 lb. 8 oz. (E.P.)	Potatoes, cubed, partially cooked	
2 lb.	Peas, fresh or frozen	
1 gal.	Chicken gravy (p. 389)	
1 recipe	Batter Crust (p. 270)	Cover each casserole with ½ c. batter crust.

Notes:
1. Pastry rounds or biscuits may be used instead of Batter Crust.
2. Chicken pie may be made in 2 12 × 20 × 2-in. baking or counter pans. Combine 3 lb. chicken, 1 lb. 12 oz. potatoes, 1 lb. peas, and 2 qt. chicken gravy for each pan. Cover with biscuits, pastry, or batter crust.

Batter Crust for Chicken or Meat Pot Pies

Bake: 12–15 min.   Yield: 6 qt.

Oven: 450° F.   Portion: ½ c. per pie

Amount	Ingredient	Method
2 lb. 4 oz. 1½ oz. (3 T.) 1 T. ¼ c.	Flour Baking powder Salt Sugar	Combine dry ingredients.

2 qt.
18
 	
4 oz.
	Milk
	Egg yolks,
	  beaten
	Butter or mar-
	  garine
		Combine milk, egg yolks, and but-
		  ter or margarine.
		Add to dry ingredients. Stir only
		  enough to mix.

18	Egg whites	Beat egg whites until stiff. Fold into batter.
		Pour ½ c. batter over contents of each individual casserole. Pour around edges and then in center to form a thin covering over meat or chicken mixture. If using for 12 × 20 × 2-in. pans, pour 3 qt. batter over each pan.

Note:

Batter may be refrigerated until needed. Thin mixture with cold milk if too thick.

Chicken Soufflé

Bake: 1 hr. or until set
Oven: 325° F.

Yield: 2 pans 12 × 20 × 2 in.
Portion: 5 oz.

Amount	Ingredient	Method
5 lb. (4 4½–5 lb. hens)	Cooked chicken	Dice chicken.
1 lb.	Butter or chicken fat	Make as Thin White Sauce (p. 385).
4 oz.	Flour	
1½ T.	Salt	
1 t.	Pepper	
2½ c.	Chicken broth, cold	
3¾ qt.	Milk	
1 lb.	Bread crumbs	Add crumbs and egg yolks. Mix well after each addition.
24	Egg yolks, beaten	Add chicken. Mix lightly.
24	Egg whites	Beat egg whites until they form a rounded peak. Fold into chicken mixture. Pour into 2 pans 12 × 20 in. Bake. Serve with Bechamel Sauce (p. 383) or Mushroom Sauce (p. 389).

Note:
Ham, turkey, or tuna may be substituted for the chicken.

Chicken Timbales

Bake: 30 min. or until firm   Yield: 50 4½-oz. timbales
Oven: 350° F.

Amount	Ingredient	Method
1 lb.	Butter or margarine	Melt butter or margarine.
12 oz.	Bread crumbs, dry	Add bread crumbs and milk. Cook 5 min., stirring constantly.
2½ qt.	Milk	
5 lb. 6 oz. (4 4½–5 lb. hens)	Chicken, cooked, chopped	Add chicken, eggs, and seasonings. Stir until mixed. Pour into 50 custard cups.
32	Eggs, beaten slightly	Bake as custard in pans of hot water.
1½ T.	Salt	Serve with Bechamel Sauce (p. 383). Garnish with riced egg yolk.
1 t.	Pepper, white	

Variations:
1. *Ham Timbales.* Substitute ham for chicken; omit 2 t. salt.
2. *Vegetable Timbales.* Substitute 3 finely chopped or puréed vegetables for chicken. Serve with Cheese Sauce (p. 385).

Chicken Croquettes

Fry: 3–4 min.   Yield: 50 3-oz. croquettes
Deep-Fat Fryer: 360–375° F.

Amount	Ingredient	Method
5 lb. (4 4½–5 lb. hens)	Cooked chicken	Chop chicken finely.
1 lb. 8 oz. 3 qt.	Rice Chicken stock	Cook rice in chicken stock.
3 T. 1 t. 1 T. 2 T.	Salt Celery salt Lemon juice Onion juice	Add seasonings to rice and mix lightly.
6 oz. 1 pt. 1 pt.	Flour Chicken stock, cold Chicken stock, hot	Make a smooth paste of flour and cold chicken stock. Add to boiling stock. Stir and cook until thick. Add sauce and chicken to rice. Mix well. Measure with No. 12 dipper onto greased sheet pan. Chill. Shape into croquettes, roll in egg and crumb (p. 69). Chill at least 2 hr before frying. Fry in deep fat.

Note:
May be baked about 30 min. in 400° F. oven.

Chicken and Noodles

Bake: 30 min.
Oven: 350° F.

Yield: 2 pans 12 × 20 × 2 in.
Portion: 4 oz.

Amount	Ingredient	Method
2 lb. 8 oz. 2 gal.	Noodles Chicken stock	Heat chicken stock to boiling. Add noodles and reheat to boiling. Cook approximately 20 min. or until tender. Remove noodles from stock and place in 2 greased pans.
5 lb. (4 4½–5 lb. hens)	Chicken, cooked, cubed	Add chicken to noodles.
10 oz. 6 oz. 3 qt. 1 T. 1 t.	Chicken fat or butter Flour Chicken stock or milk Salt Pepper	Make as Medium White Sauce (p. 385). Pour over chicken and noodles. Mix. Bake.

Variation:
Pork and Noodle Casserole. Substitute 10-lb. (A.P.) pork shoulder, diced and cooked, for chicken.

Chicken Tetrazzini

Bake: 30 min.
Oven: 450° F.

Yield: 2 pans 12 × 20 × 2 in.
Portion: 6 oz.

Amount	Ingredient	Method
5 lb. (4 4–4½ lb. hens)	Chicken, cooked, cubed	Combine chicken, mushrooms, pimiento, and parsley.
1 lb.	Mushrooms, sliced, drained	
1 c.	Pimiento strips	
2 T.	Parsley, chopped	
12 oz.	Butter or margarine	Sauté onions in butter. Blend in flour and salt.
6 oz.	Onion, finely chopped	Add milk; cook and stir until smooth and thick.
6 oz.	Flour	
2 T.	Salt	
3 qt.	Milk, hot	
2 lb.	Spaghetti	Cook spaghetti (p. 311).
8 oz.	Cheese, shredded	Place ½ of spaghetti in each of two baking pans. Add ½ of chicken mixture, then ½ of white sauce to each pan. Sprinkle cheese over top. Bake.

Variations:
1. *Turkey Tetrazzini.* Substitute turkey for chicken.
2. *Tuna Tetrazzini.* Substitute tuna for chicken.

Chicken and Rice Casserole

Bake: 1 hr.   Yield: 2 pans 12 × 20 × 2 in.
Oven: 350° F.   Portion: 6 oz.

Amount	Ingredient	Method
5 lb. (4 4½–5 lb. hens)	Cooked chicken	Dice chicken.
4 lb.	Rice	Cook rice (p. 309).
8 oz. 4 oz. 2½ qt. 2 qt. 2 T.	Chicken fat or butter Flour Milk Chicken broth Salt	Make into Medium White Sauce (p. 385).
1 lb. 12 oz. 8 oz. 4 oz.	Mushrooms, sliced Almonds, shredded Pimiento, chopped	When sauce is thickened, add mushrooms, almonds, and pimiento.
12 oz. 4 oz.	Bread crumbs Butter or margarine	Arrange in layers in 2 lightly greased baking pans the rice, chicken, and sauce. Sprinkle with buttered crumbs. Bake.

Turkey Casserole

Bake: 25–30 min.   Yield: 50 6-oz. portions
Oven: 350° F.

Amount	Ingredient	Method
6 lb. (1 14–16 lb. turkey)	Cooked turkey	Dice turkey.
1 lb.	Butter or turkey fat	Make sauce of fat, flour, and turkey stock.
1 lb. 8 oz.	Flour	Add soup and blend.
3 qt.	Turkey stock	
2 50-oz. cans	Cream of mush-room soup	
6 oz.	Onion, chopped	Cook onion and celery for 3 min.
4 lb. (E.P.)	Celery, chopped	Combine all ingredients.
3 lb.	Cashews, toasted	Portion into individual casseroles or into 2 pans 12 × 20 × 2 in. Bake. To serve, garnish with mandarin oranges.

Turkey Divan

Bake: 12–15 min.
Oven: 400° F.

Yield: 50 5-oz. portions
(3 oz. broccoli, 2 oz. turkey)

Amount	Ingredient	Method
10 lb. (E.P.)	Broccoli spears, fresh or frozen	Cook broccoli (p. 406). Drain well. Arrange in 3-oz. servings in 2 12 × 20 in. counter pans.
8 oz.	Butter or margarine, melted	Pour butter over broccoli. Sprinkle with salt, pepper, and cheese.
2 T.	Salt	
½ t.	Pepper	
9 oz.	Parmesan cheese, grated	
7 lb.	Turkey roll, cooked	Slice turkey in 2 oz. portions. Arrange turkey slices over broccoli. Serving will be easier if edges of turkey slices are tucked under the broccoli portions.
12 oz.	Butter or margarine	Make into Medium White Sauce (p. 385). Add egg yolks. Pour over turkey and broccoli. Bake.
6 oz.	Flour	
1½ T.	Salt	
3 qt.	Milk	
1 c.	Egg yolks, slightly beaten	

Note:
Turkey or chicken broth may be substituted for part of milk in sauce; salt may then be reduced.

Curried Chicken

(*for Singapore Curry*)

Yield: 50 6-oz. portions

Amount	Ingredient	Method
8 4½–5 lb.	Hens	Cook hens (p. 261). Remove meat from bones and cut in pieces. There should be about 10 lb. cooked chicken meat.
1 lb.	Butter or chicken fat	Make sauce of fat, flour, and chicken broth.
1 lb. 4 oz.	Flour	Add curry powder. Add salt and
5 qt.	Chicken broth	pepper to taste.
2 oz.	Curry powder	Add diced chicken and stir gently. Let set to blend flavors. Taste and add more seasonings, as the chicken takes up the curry flavor. It should be quite yellow and have a distinct curry flavor.
5 lb.	Rice	Cook rice (p. 309). This will allow
50 servings	French fried onion rings	very generous servings of rice. Serve curried chicken over rice,
10 lb.	Tomatoes, sliced	with accompaniments. See p.
15 lb.	Bananas, sliced or cut in chunks	507 for directions for serving.
2 No. 10 cans	Pineapple chunks	
2 lb.	Coconut	
1 lb.	Salted peanuts	
2 1-lb. jars	Chutney	

Note:
Shrimp, veal, lamb, or a combination of chicken and pork may be used.

Bread Dressing (or Stuffing)

Bake: 30–45 min.   Yield: 2 pans 12 × 20 × 2 in.
Oven: 325–350° F.   Portion: 4 oz.

Amount	Ingredient	Method
6 lb.	Dry bread, cubed	Add seasonings to bread. Sauté onion and celery in fat until tender.
1½ T.	Salt	
1 t.	Pepper	Add to bread mixture. Mix lightly.
1 oz.	Sage	
4 oz.	Onion, minced	
8 oz.	Celery, chopped (optional)	
2½ qt.	Broth (or water)	Add liquid, fat, and eggs. Avoid overmixing as this causes the dressing to be soggy and solid. Place in 2 greased baking pans 12 × 20 × 2 in. Bake.
8 oz.	Fat, melted (chicken or other)	
6	Eggs, beaten	

Notes:
1. The amount of liquid (water, stock, or milk) will depend on the dryness of the bread.
2. Approximately 4–5 lb. stuffing is required for a 20-lb. turkey.
3. This dressing may be used for fish, veal, or pork or as a stuffing for veal birds.

Variations:
1. *Apple Stuffing.* Substitute 12 oz. finely chopped apples for 6 oz. bread cubes. Add 4 oz. chopped celery.
2. *Chestnut Stuffing.* Substitute 1¼ lb. cooked chestnuts, chopped, and 8 oz. chopped celery for 6 oz. bread cubes. Substitute milk for water.
3. *Corn Bread Stuffing.* Substitute 4½ lb. corn bread crumbs for 4½ lb. bread cubes. Add 6 oz. minced onion, 12 oz. chopped celery. Omit sage. 6 hard-cooked eggs, chopped, may be added.
4. *Mushroom Stuffing.* Substitute 2 lb. mushrooms fried in butter for 6 oz. bread cubes. Omit sage.
5. *Nut Stuffing.* Add 2 c. chopped almonds or pecans that have been browned lightly in 4 oz. melted fat. Substitute 1 pt. of milk for 1 pt. of other liquid.
6. *Oyster Stuffing.* Substitute 1½ lb. oysters for 6 oz. bread cubes. Add 1 lb. cooked ham, minced, and ½ bay leaf, minced.
7. *Raisin Stuffing.* Add 1 lb. washed seedless raisins.
8. *Sausage Stuffing.* Substitute 2 lb. sausage for 8 oz. bread cubes. Add 1 lb. tart apples, chopped, and 3 oz. green pepper, minced.

FISH

Selection and Cooking of Fresh Fish

The most common forms of fresh or frozen fish in the markets are whole (undrawn), drawn (entrails removed), dressed (scaled and eviscerated), steaks (cross-sectional slices of larger fish), fillets (boneless side of fish cut lengthwise), butterfly fillets (two sides of fish corresponding to two single fillets held together by uncut flesh), and sticks (pieces of fish from fillet blocks cut into uniform portions). Many kinds of fish are available in breaded portion-ready form. Shellfish, clams, crabs, lobsters, oysters and scallops also add variety and interest to the institutional menu.

U. S. grade standards have been developed by the United States Department of Interior for 14 different fishery products. These standards provide yardsticks of quality as do U. S. grade standards for many other food products. Grade A products, top or best quality, are uniform in size, practically free from blemishes and defects, are in excellent condition and possess good flavor. Grade B means good quality, may not be as uniform in size or as free from blemishes as Grade A, but this grade is quite suitable for most purposes. Grade C signifies fairly good quality and fish that are wholesome and that may be as nutritious as higher grades. Only fishery products packed under continuous in-plant inspection of U.S.D.I. are permitted to use the prefix "U.S." to the grade designation.

Fish may be cooked in many ways, but some methods are more suitable for certain varieties than others. The Fish Buying and Cooking Chart (p. 282) shows not only the preferred method of cookery, but also the usual market forms in which fish may be purchased. Overcooking should be avoided in any method of cooking fish.

POACHED OR STEAMED FISH

Place fillets or thick slices of fish in a flat baking pan and cover with liquid. This may be acidulated water, court bouillon, fish stock, milk, or milk and water. Cover with parchment or oiled paper. Cook in a moderate

Fish Buying and Cooking Chart

Fish	Type	Bake	Boil or Steam	Broil	Fry	Market Forms
Bass, sea	Lean	Good		Best	Good	Whole, drawn, fillet
Bluefish	Lean	Best		Good	Fair	Whole, drawn
Catfish	Lean	Fair			Best	Whole, dressed
Cod	Lean	Best	Fair	Good	Good	Drawn, dressed, steaks, fillets
Flounder	Lean	Good		Good	Best	Whole, fillets
Haddock	Lean	Good	Fair	Best	Good	Drawn, fillets
Halibut	Lean	Good	Fair	Best	Good	Drawn, steaks, fillets
Herring	Fat	Fair		Best	Good	Whole
Mackerel	Fat	Good	Fair	Best		Whole, drawn, fillets
Pike	Lean	Good		Fair	Best	Whole, dressed, fillets
Pompano	Fat	Good		Best	Fair	Whole
Salmon	Fat	Best	Fair	Good		Drawn, dressed, steaks, fillets
Shad	Fat		Best		Good	Whole, drawn
Smelts	Fat			Good	Best	Whole
Snapper, red	Lean	Best	Good	Good		Drawn, dressed, fillets
Sole	Lean	Fair		Good	Best	Whole, fillets
Swordfish	Lean	Good		Best		Dressed, steaks
Trout	Fat	Fair		Good	Best	Drawn, dressed, fillets
Whitefish	Fat	Good		Best	Fair	Whole, drawn, dressed, fillets
Whiting	Lean		Good	Good	Best	Whole, drawn, dressed, fillets

SOURCE. Adapted from *Basic Fish Cookery,* Test Kitchen Series No. 2, Fish and Wildlife Service, United States Department of the Interior, Washington, D.C., 1959.

oven (350° F.) or in a steamer until fish loses its transparent appearance or until bones may be removed easily. Drain. Allow about 10 min. per pound for cooking whole fish or 10 min. for cooking fillets cut 4 to the pound. Avoid overcooking. Serve with a sauce.

Acidulated water. Use 1 T. salt and 3 T. lemon juice or vinegar for each quart of water.

Court bouillon. Add to 1 gal. of water ¾ c. chopped carrots, ¾ c. sliced onions, ¾ c. chopped celery, 3 T. salt, ½ c. vinegar, 2 or 3 bay leaves, 6 peppercorns, 9 cloves, and 3 T. butter or margarine. Boil gently for 20–30 min. Strain to remove spices and vegetables.

BROILED FISH

Wipe fish fillets or steaks as dry as possible. Brush both sides with oil or melted butter or margarine. Season with salt and pepper and sprinkle with paprika. Lay fish on a pan covered with aluminum foil. Thick pieces of fish should be placed further from the flame than thinner pieces. Broil, turning skin side up just long enough to crisp and brown. Serve with lemon, melted butter, and chopped parsley.

FRIED FISH

Use small whole fish, fillets, or steaks. Season with salt and pepper, roll in flour or corn meal, or a combination of both, and cook in a small amount of fat. Dip in egg and crumbs (p. 69) if fish is to be fried in deep fat. Fry 4–6 min. at 375° F. Fried fish should be served at once while crisp. If it must be held, arrange fish in counter pans and place uncovered in 250° F. oven until serving time.

BAKED FISH

Dip fish steaks or fillets in melted fat, then in flour. Season with salt and pepper. Place a thin slice of lemon on each piece. Bake at 450° F. until lightly brown and tender, 20–25 min. Sprinkle with paprika or chopped parsley before serving.

Selection and Cooking of Shellfish

Among the common varieties of shellfish used as food are clams, oysters and scallops, and the crustaceans, crab, lobsters, and shrimp. These may be purchased fresh, frozen, and canned, in various forms. Shrimp and crab are now freeze-dried.

CLAMS

Clams may be purchased alive in the shell, shucked, and canned. Shucked clams are marketed fresh or frozen in gallons and in No. 10 cans as whole, minced, or made into chowder.

CRABS

Crabs may be purchased alive, cooked in the shell, or as chilled, frozen, canned, or freeze-dried crab meat. Soft-shelled crab usually are parboiled, dipped in egg and crumbs (p. 69), pan-fried or cooked in deep fat. Cooked hard-shelled crabs are chilled, the shells broken apart, and the meat removed to be used in cooked dishes or salads. One 2-pound crab yields about ¾ pound of cooked body and leg meat.

LOBSTERS

Lobsters may be purchased alive in the shell; frozen; fresh-cooked, chilled, canned, and frozen lobster meat; and frozen lobster tails. To prepare frozen lobster tails follow instructions on the package. Lobster meat, frozen or canned, may be used for salads and in cooked dishes. Live lobsters only are broiled or boiled.

OYSTERS

Oysters are available in many markets in the shell, fresh and frozen, shucked, and canned. Shucked oysters are in far greater demand in institution food services than those in the shell. Because they are grown in water that may easily be contaminated and because they frequently are eaten raw, they are subject to strict sanitary inspection by the Public Health Service. After they are purchased they should be held at freezing temperatures no longer than 10 days before use.

Oysters are not ordinarily washed before using. If washing seems necessary, care should be taken to remove the oysters from the water quickly, so that they do not become soaked or waterlogged. They should be inspected and any bits of shell removed. When making oyster stew (p. 402), add butter to oysters and heat only until edges begin to curl, then add to hot milk. Serve at once. To fry, dip oysters in egg and crumbs (p. 69) before frying.

SCALLOPS

The adductor muscle or "eye" that holds together the shells of the scallop is removed, cut into pieces, and marketed fresh or frozen in gallon containers. The large deep sea scallops weigh 8 pounds to a gallon and have a count of 110 to 170. Scallops also may be purchased breaded and ready-to-cook.

SHRIMP

Raw or green shrimp should be washed carefully. Cover with water and bring to a boil. Let simmer 3 min. in water to which have been added 1½ t. salt to each quart, 2 bay leaves, and mixed spice. Drain. Remove shell and dark vein from the center back of each shrimp. To fry, dip peeled and cleaned raw or cooked shrimp in batter, or egg and crumb (p. 69). Fry in deep fat 3–5 min. at 350–365° F. Cooked shrimp may be purchased either in the shell or peeled and cleaned ready to use. Freeze-dried shrimp now available in most markets is a convenience item in quantity food service production. One No. 10 can weighs 13¼ oz. and is the equivalent of 7 pounds of raw green headless shrimp.

Guide to Purchasing Shellfish

Fish	Count or Weight per Unit of Measure	Usual Market Form	Purchase Unit
Clams, hard-shell	80 per bushel	In shell, live	Per 100 or bu.
	100–125 per gal.	Shucked, fresh or frozen	Per gal. or lb.
Clams, soft-shell	45 per bushel	In shell, live	Per 100 or bu.
	350–500 per gal.	Shucked	Per 100 or bu.
Crabs, all kinds	4 oz.-20 lb.	Live, frozen, or	
	(varies with kind)	fresh-cooked	Per lb. or doz.
Crabmeat, cooked E.P.			
Blue	1-lb. tins	Fresh or frozen	Per lb.
Dungeness	5-lb. tins	Fresh or frozen	Per lb.
King	1- and 5-lb. cartons	Frozen	Per lb.
Lobster	1¼–2 lb. each	Whole, live	Per lb.
Lobster tails, Australian	5–24 oz. each	In shell	Per lb.
or South African		Frozen raw	
Oysters (Eastern)			
Counts	160 or less per gal.	Shucked, fresh	Per gal.
Extra select	161–210 per gal.	or frozen	
Select	211–300 per gal.		
Standard	301–500 per gal.		
Shell oysters			
Half shell	800–900 per barrel	Live	Per 100 or barrel
Contuit	600–700 per barrel		
Scallops, bay	150–200 per gal.	Fresh or frozen	Per lb. or gal.
Deep-sea	18–25 per gal.		
	(8 lb. per gal.)		
Shrimp, in shell, headless	Under 15 per lb.	Frozen raw	Per lb.
Jumbo	15–20 per lb.		
Large	21–25 per lb.		
Large-medium	26–30 per lb.		
Medium	31–42 per lb.		
Shrimp, peeled and deveined			
Jumbo	15–20 per lb.	Frozen raw	Per lb.
Large	21–25 per lb.		
Large-medium	26–30 per lb.		
Medium	30–50 per lb.		
Shrimp, cooked, peeled,			
and deveined			
Jumbo	35–40 per lb.	Fresh or frozen	Per lb.
Large	40–50 per lb.		
Medium	50–60 per lb.		
Shrimp, breaded	15–20 per lb.	Frozen raw	Per lb.
Fantail or round	21–25 per lb.		

SOURCE. Adapted from *Fresh and Frozen Fish Buying Manual,* Fish and Wildlife Service, Circular No. 20, United States Department of the Interior, Washington, D.C., 1954.

Fish Recipes

Baked Fish Fillets

Bake: 25 min.
Oven: 400° F.

Yield: 50 4–4½ oz. portions

Amount	Ingredient	Method
15 lb.	Fish fillets	Cut fish into 50 portions.
1 lb.	Fat, melted	Mix fat, salt, pepper, and lemon juice.
1 T.	Salt	
1 t.	Pepper, white	Dip each portion into seasoned fat.
½ c.	Lemon juice	
14 oz.	Flour	Dredge fish with flour.
2 oz.	Butter or margarine, melted	Place close together in single layer in greased baking pan.
¾ c.	Milk	Mix butter or margarine and milk and pour over fillets. Bake.

Scalloped Oysters

Bake: 30 min.
Oven: 400° F.

Yield: 2 pans 12 × 20 × 2 in.
Portion: 5 oz.

Amount	Ingredient	Method
6 qts.	Oysters	Drain oysters, saving liquor. Remove any bits of shell.
3 qt.	Cracker crumbs	Mix crumbs, butter, and seasonings.
1 lb.	Butter or margarine, melted	Spread one third over bottoms of 2 greased baking pans.
1½ T.	Salt	Cover with half of the oysters; repeat with crumbs and oysters.
½ t.	Paprika	
½ t.	Pepper	
1 qt.	Milk or cream	Mix milk or cream and oyster liquor. Pour over top of oysters.
1½ pt.	Oyster liquor (or milk)	Cover with remaining crumbs. Bake.

Note:
2 c. finely chopped, partially cooked celery may be added.

Deviled Crab

Bake: 15 min.   Yield: 50 3-oz. portions
Oven: 400° F.

Amount	Ingredient	Method
5 lb.	Crab meat, flaked	Combine lemon juice, eggs, and seasonings.
4 T.	Lemon juice	
1½ T.	Salt	Add to crab meat. Mix lightly.
2 t.	Pepper	
f.g.	Cayenne	
5	Eggs, beaten	
1 T.	Worcestershire sauce	
2 T.	Onion juice (optional)	
12 oz.	Butter or margarine	Make Thick White Sauce (p. 385) of butter, flour, and milk.
8 oz.	Flour	Add mustard.
2 qt.	Milk	Combine sauce and crab mixture. Mix lightly.
1½ t.	Mustard, prepared	Fill individual casseroles or shells.
8 oz.	Bread crumbs	Sprinkle with buttered crumbs. Bake.
4 oz.	Butter or margarine, melted	

Note:
Croquettes may be made from this mixture.

Creole Shrimp with Rice

Yield: 50 portions
3 oz. Creole shrimp
4 oz. rice

Amount	Ingredient	Method
3 oz.	Fat	Brown onion and celery in fat.
6 oz.	Onion, chopped fine	
12 oz.	Celery, chopped fine	
3 T.	Flour	Add flour, salt, and water. Mix until smooth.
1½ T.	Salt	
1 pt.	Water	Cook 15 min.
1½ qt.	Tomatoes	Add tomatoes, vinegar, and sugar.
6 T.	Vinegar	
2 T.	Sugar	
5 lb. (E.P.)	Shrimp, cooked, peeled, and deveined	Add shrimp to sauce.
4 lb. 8 oz.	Rice	Cook rice (p. 309). Serve shrimp with No. 12 dipper, over No. 8 dipper rice.

Note:
If raw shrimp are used, purchase 10–12 lb. Cook as directed on p. 284.

Salmon Loaf

Bake: 1¼ hr.
Oven: 325° F.

Yield: 5 loaves 4 × 9 in.
Portion: 3½ oz.

Amount	Ingredient	Method
3 c. 1 lb.	Milk, scalded Bread cubes, soft	Mix milk and bread cubes.
8 lb. 1½ T. 1 t. 2 ½ c. 15	Salmon, flaked Salt Paprika Lemon rinds, grated Lemon juice Eggs, beaten	Add salmon and other ingredients. Mix lightly. Place in 5 greased loaf pans. Set pans in hot water to bake.

Note:

For a lighter-textured product, beat egg whites separately and fold into salmon mixture.

Salmon Croquettes

Fry: 4 min.
Deep-Fat Fryer: 375° F.

Yield: 100 2½-oz. croquettes

Amount	Ingredient	Method
12 oz. 9 oz. 1 t. 1½ qt.	Butter or margarine Flour Salt Milk	Make into Thick White Sauce (p. 385). Cool.
8 lb.	Salmon	Remove skin and bones from salmon. Flake and add to white sauce.
6 oz. 3 T. 7 oz.	Cornflakes Onion juice Pimiento, chopped	Add cornflakes, onion juice, and pimiento to salmon mixture. Mix carefully. Measure with No. 30 dipper onto a greased baking sheet. Chill. Shape croquettes cylindrically.
8 2 c. 1 lb. 8 oz.	Eggs Milk or water Bread crumbs	Dip croquettes in egg and milk mixture. Roll in crumbs. Fry in deep fat. Serve with Egg Sauce (p. 385).

Note:

The croquettes may be baked about 30 min. in a 400° F. oven; or the mixture may be shaped into patties and baked or pan-fried in a small amount of fat.

Scalloped Salmon

Bake: 25 min.
Oven: 375° F.

Yield: 2 pans 12 × 20 × 2 in.
Portion: 4 oz.

Amount	Ingredient	Method
1 lb.	Butter or margarine	Make into Medium White Sauce (p. 385).
12 oz.	Flour	
1½ T.	Salt	
½ t.	Pepper	
1 gal.	Milk	
¼ c.	Parsley, chopped	Add parsley, onion juice, and celery salt.
2 t.	Onion juice	
1 t.	Celery salt	
10 lb.	Salmon, flaked	Arrange salmon, sauce, and crumbs in layers in 2 baking pans.
8 oz.	Bread crumbs	
4 oz.	Crumbs	Sprinkle buttered crumbs over top. Bake. Serve with No. 10 dipper.
4 oz.	Butter or margarine, melted	

Note:
Diced hard-cooked eggs and frozen peas are good additions.
Variation:
Scalloped Tuna. Substitute tuna for salmon.

Salmon and Potato Chip Casserole

Bake: 20 min.
Oven: 375° F.

Yield: 2 pans 12 × 20 × 2 in.
or 50 casseroles
Portion: 5 oz.

Amount	Ingredient	Method
8 oz.	Butter or margarine	Melt butter or margarine, add flour, and stir until blended.
5 oz.	Flour	Add soup and cook until mixture is thickened.
2 50-oz. cans	Cream of mushroom soup	
8 lb.	Salmon, flaked	Arrange salmon, potato chips, and sauce in layers in casseroles or in 2 baking pans. Bake.
2 lb. 8 oz.	Potato chips, coarsely crushed	

Variation:
Tuna and Potato Chip Casserole. Substitute tuna for salmon.

Tuna-Cashew Casserole

Bake: 30–40 min.　　　　　　　　Yield: 2 pans 12 × 20 × 2 in.
Oven: 350° F.　　　　　　　　　　Portion: 5 oz.

Amount	Ingredient	Method
8 lb.	Tuna, flaked	Arrange ingredients in layers in 2
6 oz.	Onion, finely chopped	greased baking pans, with noodles as top layer. Bake.
8 oz.	Celery, diced	
1 lb. 8 oz.	Cashews	
2 50-oz. cans	Cream of mushroom soup	
1 No. 10 can	Chinese noodles	

Variation:
Chicken–Cashew Casserole. Substitute diced cooked chicken for tuna.

Tuna and Noodles

Bake: 45 min.　　　　　　　　　　Yield: 2 pans 12 × 20 × 2 in.
Oven: 350° F.　　　　　　　　　　Portion: 5 oz.

Amount	Ingredient	Method
2 lb.	Noodles	Cook noodles until tender (p. 311).
5 lb.	Tuna	Flake tuna and add to noodles.
8 oz.	Butter or margarine	Make into Medium White Sauce (p. 385).
4 oz.	Flour	Add to tuna and noodles.
1½ T.	Salt	Divide into 2 greased baking pans.
2 qt.	Milk	Bake 30 min.
1 lb.	Cheese, grated	Sprinkle cheese over the noodles. Bake 15 min. longer.

Variation:
Tuna and Rice. Substitute rice for the noodles.

Creamed Tuna

Yield: 7½ qt.
Portion: 4 oz.

Amount	Ingredient	Method
12 oz.	Butter or margarine	Make into Medium White Sauce (p. 385).
6 oz.	Flour	
1 gal.	Milk	
6 T.	Worcestershire sauce (optional)	Add remaining ingredients. Mix.
¼ t.	Cayenne	
1 T.	Salt	
9	Eggs, hard-cooked, chopped	
6 oz.	Green pepper, chopped	
6 oz.	Pimiento, chopped	
5 lb.	Tuna, flaked	When ready to serve, add flaked tuna to the sauce and reheat. Serve with 4-oz. ladle on toast or biscuits.

Note:
Other cooked fish may be substituted for tuna.
Variations:
1. *Creamed Tuna and Celery.* Substitute 1 lb. diced cooked celery for 1 lb. tuna.
2. *Tuna Rarebit.* Use 4 lb. tuna; add 1½ lb. shredded cheese.
3. *Creamed Salmon.* Substitute salmon for tuna.

GARNISHES FOR FISH
1. Parsley, chopped or sprig.
2. Lemon wedges, plain or with edges dipped in paprika or chopped parsley.
3. Thin slices of lemon or orange, plain or notched.
4. Small lettuce cup filled with cole slaw or cranberry sauce.
5. Small green pepper cups with tartar sauce.
6. Black, green, or stuffed olives and a bit of salad green.
7. Celery hearts or celery curls and radish roses.
8. Carrot curls or strips, onion ring, green onions, or pickled onions.
9. Tomato slices, wedges, or small whole cherry tomato and parsley sprig.
10. Cucumber slices, peeled and fluted, or unpeeled and accented with pimiento strips.
11. Slices of hard-cooked egg, chopped egg, riced egg yolk, or ½ stuffed egg.

12. Latticed pickled beets.
13. Lemon butter balls. Mint leaves.
14. Sautéed button mushrooms.
15. Toasted croutons.
16. Spiced whole apricot or crabapple.
17. Shredded toasted almonds.
18. Sprig of frosted white grapes or sprigs of green or red grapes.

CHEESE, EGGS, AND CEREALS

Cheese Balls

Fry: 2–3 min.
Deep-Fat Fryer: 360° F.

Yield: 150 balls
50 portions, 3 balls each

Amount	Ingredient	Method
4 lb. 8 oz. 4 oz. 1 T. f.g.	Cheese, grated Flour Salt Cayenne	Mix cheese, flour, and salt.
24	Egg whites	Beat egg whites until stiff. Fold into cheese mixture. Shape into balls 1–1¼ in. diameter or dip with No. 30 dipper. Chill.
3 1 c. 12 oz.	Eggs Milk Bread crumbs	Egg and crumb (p. 69). Chill for several hours. Fry in deep fat.

Notes:
1. Serve 3 balls in center of hot buttered pineapple ring.
2. For serving as first-course accompaniment, use half the recipe and shape into balls ½–¾ in. in diameter. Yield: 150 balls.
3. For 2 balls per portion, use No. 24 dipper; yield: 40 portions.

Cheese Croquettes

Fry: 3–4 min.   Yield: 50 3-oz. croquettes
Deep-Fat Fryer: 360° F.

Amount	Ingredient	Method
8 oz.	Butter or mar- garine	Make into Thick White Sauce (p. 385).
8 oz.	Flour	
2 qt.	Milk	
32	Egg yolks, beaten	Add eggs, cheese, and seasonings. Stir until cheese is melted.
2 lb.	Cheese, diced	Measure with No. 16 dipper onto greased pans. Chill.
1½ T.	Salt	
1 T.	Paprika	Shape. Chill several hours.
16	Egg whites	Beat egg whites and water slightly.
½ c.	Water	Dip each croquette in egg mixture and roll in crumbs. Chill.
1 lb.	Bread crumbs	Fry in deep fat.

Cheese Fondue

Bake: 50–60 min.   Yield: 3 pans 10 × 12 in.
Oven: 350° F.   Portion: 4 oz.

Amount	Ingredient	Method
4½ qt.	Milk, scalded	Add butter and seasonings to milk.
4 oz.	Butter or mar- garine, melted	Pour over bread. Cool slightly.
1½ t.	Mustard	
1 T.	Salt	
f.g.	Cayenne	
3 lb. 8 oz.	Bread cubes, soft	
4 lb. 8 oz.	Cheese, shredded	Add cheese and egg yolks. Mix un-til blended.
24	Egg yolks, beaten	
24	Egg whites	Beat egg whites until stiff. Fold into cheese mixture. Pour into 3 greased pans 10 × 12 in. Set pans in hot water. Bake.

Cheese Soufflé

Bake: 50 min.
Oven: 350° F.

Yield: 3 pans 10 × 12 in.
Portion: 2½ oz.

Amount	Ingredient	Method
2½ qt. 10 oz. 2 T.	Milk, hot Tapioca, minute Salt	Add tapioca and salt to milk, stirring constantly. Cook 15 min. Stir frequently during first 5 min.
3 lb. 24	Cheese, ground Egg yolks, beaten	Add cheese and egg yolks. Stir until cheese is melted.
24	Egg whites	Beat egg whites. Fold into cheese mixture. Pour into 3 greased pans 12 × 12 in. Set pans in hot water. Bake. Serve with Spanish Sauce (p. 382), Shrimp Sauce (p. 386), or Creamed Ham (p. 251).

Variation:
Mushroom Soufflé. Add 1 lb. chopped mushrooms and 5 oz. chopped green peppers to uncooked mixture. Serve with Bechamel Sauce (p. 383).

Cheese Soufflé
(*with White Sauce Base*)

Bake: 1 hr.
Oven: 300° F.

Yield: 2 pans 12 × 20 × 2 in.
Cut 6 × 4

Amount	Ingredient	Method
1 lb.	Butter or margarine	Make into Thick White Sauce (p. 385).
8 oz.	Flour	
2½ qt.	Milk	
1 t.	Salt	
32	Egg yolks	Add egg yolks, stir and cook.
1 lb. 4 oz.	Cheese, shredded	Add cheese and stir until smooth. Remove from heat.
32	Egg whites	Add cream of tartar to egg whites. Beat until stiff.
1½ t.	Cream of tartar	Fold into cheese mixture. Pour into 2 greased pans. Bake. Serve with Cheese Sauce (p. 385) or Shrimp Sauce (p. 386).

Macaroni and Cheese

Bake: 35 min.
Oven: 350° F.

Yield: 2 pans 12 × 20 × 2 in.
Portion: 5 oz.

Amount	Ingredient	Method
2 lb. 8 oz.	Macaroni	Cook macaroni (p. 311). Drain.
2 gal.	Water, boiling	Pour into 2 baking pans.
2 T.	Salt	
8 oz.	Butter or margarine	Make into Medium White Sauce (p. 385)
6 oz.	Flour	
2 T.	Salt	
3 qt.	Milk, hot	
3 lb.	Cheese, sharp, shredded	Add cheese to sauce. Pour over macaroni.
12 oz.	Bread crumbs	Sprinkle with buttered crumbs. Bake.
4 oz.	Butter or margarine, melted	

Notes:
1. Cheese may be mixed with macaroni, then covered with white sauce.
2. Fresh tomato sections, slivers of green pepper or pimiento may be added for variety.

Corn Rarebit

Yield: 50 3½-oz. portions

Amount	Ingredient	Method
4 oz.	Onion, chopped	Brown onion in fat.
6 oz.	Butter or margarine	
1 qt.	Milk	Add milk. Heat to boiling point.
1 pt.	Milk	Blend flour and seasonings with milk.
6 oz.	Flour	
2 T.	Salt	Add gradually to hot mixture, stirring constantly.
f.g.	Cayenne	
1 lb. 8 oz.	Cheese, sharp, shredded	Add cheese and green pepper. Cook over hot water until cheese is melted.
3 oz.	Green pepper, chopped	Add corn.
1 No. 10 can	Corn (whole grain), hot, drained	Serve immediately with No. 8 dipper on split toasted buns.

Variation:

Hot Corn Sandwich. Substitute 1 qt. tomato purée for milk and pimiento for green pepper. To hot cheese–corn mixture, add 2 c. beaten egg yolks. Continue cooking, stirring constantly, until yolks are cooked. Serve immediately on split toasted buns.

Directions for Cooking Eggs

Method	Directions	Cooking Time
Hard-cooked:		
Steamer I	Place eggs in solid steamer pan or counter pan. Cover with cold water. Steam at 5-lb. pressure. Plunge at once into cold water.	25–30 min.
Steamer II	Place eggs in shallow perforated pans. Steam at 5-lb. pressure. Plunge at once into cold water.	15–18 min.
Steamer III	Break eggs into lightly greased pan. Eggs should be thick enough in pan so whites come up to level of yolks. For 4 doz. eggs, use pan 12 × 20 × 2 in; for 1 doz. use pan 5 × 12 × 2 in. This method is suitable when eggs are to be chopped.	13–15 min.
Kettle	Place eggs in wire baskets. Lower into kettles of boiling water. Simmer.	30 min.
Soft-cooked:		
Kettle	Place eggs in kettle, cover with cold water. Bring to full rolling boil. Remove eggs from boiling water. Run cold water over eggs for a few seconds.	
Poached:		
Steamer	Break eggs into water in shallow counter pans. Steam at 5-lb. pressure.	3–5 min.
Top of range	Break eggs one at a time into sauce dishes. Line up dishes on trays. Carefully slide eggs into boiling water in skillets or shallow pans. Keep water at simmering temperature. Remove eggs with slotted spoon or turner.	5–7 min.
Fried:		
Top of range	Break eggs into sauce dishes. Slide carefully into hot fat in skillets or on griddle. Cook over low heat, carefully basting eggs until of desired hardness. If eggs are to be served on hot counter, drain well before removing to counter pans.	
Oven	Heat fat in counter pans or skillets. Carefully slide eggs into fat. Bake at 400° F.	5–7 min., or until of desired hardness

Scrambled Eggs

Yield: 50 3-oz. portions

Amount	Ingredient	Method
75 1½ qt. 2 T.	Eggs Milk, hot Salt	Break eggs into mixer bowl. Beat slightly (medium speed). Add hot milk and salt. Beat until blended.
8 oz.	Butter or margarine	Melt butter or margarine in skillet or steam-jacketed kettle. Pour in egg mixture. Cook over low heat, stirring occasionally, until of desired consistency. Serve with No. 10 dipper.

Notes:
1. *Steamer Method.* Melt 4 oz. butter or margarine in each of two steamer or counter pans. Pour egg mixture into pans. Steam for 6–8 min. at 5-lb. pressure until desired degree of hardness.
2. *Oven Method.* Melt 4 oz. butter or margarine in each of 2 counter or baking pans. Pour egg mixture into pans. Bake approximately 20 min. at 350° F., stirring once after 10 min. of baking.

Variations:
1. *Scrambled Eggs and Cheese.* Add 1 lb. grated Cheddar cheese.
2. *Scrambled Eggs and Ham.* Add 1 lb. 4 oz. chopped cooked ham.
3. *Scrambled Eggs and Chipped Beef.* Add 1 lb. chopped chipped beef.

Omelet

Bake: 45 min.	Yield: 2 pans 12 × 20 × 2 in.
Oven: 325° F.	Portion: 3 oz.

Amount	Ingredient	Method
12 oz.	Butter or margarine	Make into Thick White Sauce (p. 385).
8 oz.	Flour	
2 T.	Salt	
½ t.	Pepper, white	
3 qt.	Milk	
24	Egg yolks, beaten	Add egg yolks and mix well with a wire whip.
24	Egg whites	Beat egg whites until they form rounded peaks. Fold into egg yolk mixture. Pour into 2 baking pans. Set pans in hot water. Bake.

Variations:
1. *Bacon Omlet.* Fry 1½ lb. diced bacon; substitute bacon fat for butter in white sauce. Add diced bacon to the egg mixture.
2. *Cheese Omelet.* Add 12 oz. grated cheese before placing pans in oven.
3. *Ham Omelet.* Add 3 lb. finely diced cooked ham.
4. *Jelly Omelet.* Spread 2 c. tart jelly over cooked omelet.
5. *Spanish Omelet.* Serve with Spanish Sauce (p. 382).

Chinese Omelet

Bake: 45 min.   Yield: 2 pans 12 × 20 × 2 in.
Oven: 325° F.   Portion: 4 oz.

Amount	Ingredient	Method
4 oz.	Butter or mar-garine	Make butter, flour, salt, and milk into Medium White Sauce (p. 385).
2 oz.	Flour	
1 t.	Salt	Add cheese and blend.
1 qt.	Milk	
1 lb.	Cheese, shredded	
24	Egg yolks	Beat egg yolks until light and fluffy.
1 t.	Mustard	Add seasonings.
2 T.	Salt	Add to cheese sauce. Stir until smooth.
1 t.	Paprika	
2 lb. (A.P.)	Rice	Cook rice (p. 309). Add to sauce.
24	Egg whites	Beat egg whites until they form a soft peak. Fold into rice mixture. Pour into 2 greased pans. Bake. Serve with Cheese Sauce (p. 385) or Tomato Sauce (p. 381).

Potato Omelet

Bake: 1 hr.   Yield: 2 pans 12 × 20 × 2 in.
Oven: 325° F.   Portion: 5 oz.

Amount	Ingredient	Method
50	Bacon slices	Arrange bacon, slightly overlapping, in baking pan. Cook in oven until crisp. Remove from pans.
9 lb. (E.P.)	Potatoes, cooked, diced	Brown potatoes slightly in bacon fat. Remove to 2 greased baking pans.
36 3 T. 1 t. f.g. 3 qt.	Eggs, beaten Salt Pepper Cayenne Milk, hot	Combine eggs, milk, and seasonings. Pour over potatoes. Bake. Serve as soon as removed from oven with a slice of crisp bacon on top of each serving.

Variation:
Potato–Ham Omelet. Omit bacon. Add 4 lb. diced cooked ham to potatoes. Reduce salt to 1 T.

Egg Foo Yung

Yield: 50
Portion: Egg Foo Yung, 3–4 oz.
Sauce, 2 oz.

Amount	Ingredient	Method
1 lb.	Mushrooms, shredded	Drain mushrooms and bean sprouts. Save juice.
1 No. 10 can	Bean sprouts, shredded	Fry vegetables 2 min. in fat.
1 lb. 8 oz.	Onions, shredded	
8 oz.	Green peppers, shredded	
8 oz.	Fat	
1 lb.	Ham, cooked, shredded	Combine ham and eggs. Add to vegetables. Mix.
40	Eggs, beaten	Use No. 10 dipper to place mixture on hot grill or frying pan. Brown well on 1 side, fold in half. Serve with following sauce.
2 oz.	Cornstarch	Combine cornstarch and soya sauce into a smooth paste.
1½ c.	Soy sauce	
2 qt.	Vegetable juice, hot	Add vegetable juice. Cook until thickened.

Note:
Roast pork, chicken, or bacon may be used in place of ham; green onions in place of shredded onions.

Creamed Eggs

Yield: 50 5-oz. portions

Amount	Ingredient	Method
1 lb.	Butter or mar- garine	Make into Medium White Sauce (p. 385).
8 oz.	Flour	
1 gal.	Milk	
1½ T.	Salt	
¼ t.	White pepper	
75	Eggs, hard-cooked (p. 300), sliced	When ready to serve, pour hot sauce over eggs. Mix carefully. Reheat.

Variations:
1. *Curried Eggs.* Substitute chicken broth for milk and add 2 T. curry powder. May be served with steamed rice or chow mein noodles.
2. *Eggs à la King.* Substitute chicken stock for milk and add 1 lb. mushrooms that have been sautéed, 12 oz. chopped green peppers, and 8 oz. chopped pimiento.
3. *Scotch Woodcock.* Add 1 lb. sharp cheese to white sauce and blend. Cut eggs in half lengthwise and place in pans. Pour sauce over eggs. Cover with buttered crumbs. Bake until heated through and crumbs are brown.
4. *Goldenrod Eggs.* Reserve 25 egg yolks to mash or rice, and sprinkle over top of creamed eggs.

Egg Cutlets

Fry: 3 min.
Deep-Fat Fryer: 375° F.

Yield: 50 3-oz. cutlets

Amount	Ingredient	Method
12 oz.	Butter or mar- garine	Make into Very Thick White Sauce (p. 385).
10 oz.	Flour	
3 T.	Salt	
2 qt.	Milk	
48	Eggs, hard-cooked, coarsely ground	Add sauce to eggs. Mix. Portion with No. 12 dipper onto a greased sheet pan. Chill. Shape into cutlets. Chill.
6	Eggs	Dip in egg and crumbs (p. 69).
1 c.	Milk	Chill 2 hours. Fry in deep fat.
12 oz.	Bread crumbs	

Deviled Eggs

Yield: 50 portions
(2 halves each)

Amount	Ingredient	Method
50	Eggs, hard-cooked (p. 300)	Peel eggs. Cut in half lengthwise. Arrange whites in rows on a tray.
½ c.	Milk, hot	Mash yolks. Add milk and mix until blended.
1½ c.	Mayonnaise or cooked salad dressing	Add remaining ingredients and mix until smooth.
1 T.	Salt	Refill whites with mashed yolks, using approximately 1½ T. for each half egg white.
¾ T.	Mustard, dry	
½ c.	Vinegar	

Notes:
1. Pastry bag may be used to fill egg whites. Yolk mixture should be smooth and creamy. Use plain or rose tube.
2. 6 oz. finely chopped pimientos may be added to yolk mixture.

Hot Stuffed Eggs

Bake: 30 min.
Oven: 325° F.

Yield: 50 eggs
Portion: 2 halves

Amount	Ingredient	Method
50	Eggs, hard-cooked (p. 300)	Cut eggs lengthwise. Remove yolks and mash.
3 oz.	Butter or margarine, melted	Add butter, ham, and seasonings. Mix thoroughly.
2 t.	Salt	Refill whites.
⅛ t.	Cayenne	Arrange in 2 baking pans 12 × 20 × 2 in.
1 T.	Prepared mustard	
1 lb.	Ham, minced	
12 oz.	Butter or margarine	Make into Medium White Sauce (p. 385).
8 oz.	Flour	Pour over eggs. Bake.
1½ T.	Salt	
1 gal.	Milk	
¼ c.	Parsley, chopped	Sprinkle parsley over the eggs just before serving.

Note:
Tuna may be substituted for the ham.

Baked Egg and Bacon Ring

Bake: 25 min. or until firm   Yield: 50 portions
Oven: 350° F.

Amount	Ingredient	Method
50 (2–2½ lb.)	Bacon slices	Arrange bacon around inside of 50 baking cups (or muffin pans), fat side up.
50	Eggs	Place in hot oven until fat is clear. Remove from oven.
		Break an egg into each cup. Return to oven. Bake until eggs are firm.

Baked Eggs with Cheese

Bake: 25 min. or until firm   Yield: 50 eggs
Oven: 350° F.

Amount	Ingredient	Method
50	Eggs	Break eggs into greased custard cups or muffin pans.
3 oz.	Butter or margarine	Make into Thin White Sauce (p. 385).
1½ oz.	Flour	
1½ qt.	Milk	
1½ t.	Salt	
4 t.	Salt	On top of each egg, place: sprinkle of salt, 2 T. cheese, 2 T. white sauce, and buttered crumbs.
1 lb. 8 oz.	Cheese, grated	
8 oz.	Buttered crumbs	Set cups in pan of hot water. Bake.

Note:
For variety, place a thin slice of raw tomato in the bottom of each cup.

Rice

Yield: 6 qt. cooked rice

Amount	Ingredient	Method
3¾ qt.	Water, boiling	*Top of range method.*
2 T.	Salt	Add salt, fat, and rice to boiling
2 T.	Fat or oil	water.
3 lb.	Rice, converted	Stir and cover tightly.
		Cook on low heat 15 min.
		Remove from heat and let stand covered 5–10 min.
		Steamer or oven method.
		Place rice in baking pan 12 × 20 × 2 in.
		Add salt and fat to boiling water and pour over rice.
		Stir and cover pans tightly.
		Bake at 350° F. oven or steam at 5 lb. pressure for 30–35 min.
		Remove from oven or steamer and let stand covered 5 min.

Notes:
1. Addition of fat or oil is optional. It tends to prevent foaming and boiling over.
2. 1 lb. uncooked rice yields 2 qt. cooked rice.

Variations:
1. *Green Rice.* Cook 3 lb. rice. Add 6 lb. finely chopped raw or frozen spinach, 3 T. onion juice and 2 qt. Medium White Sauce (p. 385). Bake 30–40 min. at 325° F.
2. *Fried Rice with Almonds.* Cook together for 5 min. 4 oz. chopped onion and 4 oz. chopped green pepper in 1 c. salad oil. Add 6 qt. cooked rice (3 lb. before cooking), 1 T. pepper, 1 t. garlic salt, salt to taste, ½ c. soy sauce, 2 lb. blanched slivered almonds. Mix and bake until thoroughly heated.
3. *Curried Rice.* Cook 8 oz. minced onion in 8 oz. butter or margarine. Add 3 lb. rice and stir until fat is absorbed. Add 3 T. curry powder, 1½ T. salt, and 3 qt. boiling water. Boil 10 min. Add 2 qt. hot milk and cook over water until rice is tender. Serve with Veal Stew (p. 243), Creamed Chicken (p. 266), Creamed Eggs (p. 306), or Creamed Tuna (p. 292).
4. *Rice Pilaff.* Brown 2 lb. rice in 1 lb. butter or margarine. Add 1 gal. water and 1½ T. salt. Cook for 30 min. in steamer. Add 1 lb. green pepper, 10 oz. onion, and 8 oz. pimiento, chopped. Bake at 350° F. for 15 min.

Rice Croquettes

Fry: 3–4 min.   Yield: 50 portions
Deep-Fat Fryer: 375° F.   1 croquette per portion

Amount	Ingredient	Method
3 lb. 3 qt. 2 qt. 2 oz. (3 T.)	Rice Milk, hot Water, hot Salt	Add rice to salted hot liquid. Cook until tender (p. 309).
18 2 oz.	Eggs, beaten Fat, melted	Add eggs and fat to hot rice. Cook until eggs are done (10–15 min.) Measure with No. 10 dipper onto a greased sheet pan. Chill 2 hr. Shape, egg and crumb (p. 69). Chill. Fry in deep fat.

Note:
Serve with Cheese Sauce (p. 385), Creamed Ham (p. 251), or Chicken (p. 265).

Spanish Rice

Bake: 1 hr.   Yield: 2 pans 12 × 20 × 2 in.
Oven: 350° F.   Portion: 5 oz.

Amount	Ingredient	Method
2 lb. 8 oz.	Rice	Cook rice (p. 309).
1 gal. 1 lb. 4 oz. 2½ oz. 3 T.	Tomatoes Green pepper, chopped Pimiento, chopped Salt	Add tomatoes and seasonings. Mix.
1 lb. 8 oz. 1 lb.	Bacon, chopped Onion, chopped	Sauté bacon and onions together. Add to rice mixture. Mix carefully. Pour into 2 greased baking pans. Bake.

Notes:
1. The bacon may be omitted and 5 lb. of ground beef added.
2. 2 qts. tomato purée, diluted with 2 qt. water, may be used in place of the tomatoes.

Cooking Macaroni, Spaghetti, or Noodles

Yield: 2¼–2½ gal.
Approximately 50
5-oz. portions

Amount	Ingredient	Method
4 lb.	Macaroni, spaghetti, or noodles	*Top of range* Add macaroni, spaghetti, or noodles to boiling salted water. Stir.
3 gal.	Water, boiling	Reheat to boiling temperature. Cook about 15 min.
¼ c.	Salt	Drain. Rinse with hot water to remove excess starch.
¼ c.	Oil (optional)	*Steamer method* Divide macaroni, spaghetti, or noodles into two steamer pans.
		Add 1½ gal. boiling water, 2 T. salt, and 2 T. oil to each.
		Steam for 12 to 15 min. at 5-lb. pressure.

Note:
Addition of oil is optional. It tends to prevent foaming.

Noodle Ring

Bake: 30 min.
Oven: 350° F.

Yield: 4 large ring molds or
2 baking pans 12× 20 × 2 in.

Amount	Ingredient	Method
1 lb. 12 oz.	Noodles	Cook noodles (p. 311).
6 qt.	Water or broth	Drain.
2 T.	Salt	
8 oz.	Bread crumbs, soft	Add remaining ingredients and mix lightly.
4 oz.	Onion, finely chopped	Pour into 4 large greased ring molds or 2 greased baking pans
2 oz.	Green pepper, finely chopped	12 × 20 × 2 in. Place molds in pan of hot water. Bake.
3 oz.	Pimiento, finely chopped	Serve with Creamed Chicken (p. 266), Creamed Ham, (p. 251),
2 t.	Parsley	or Creamed Tuna (p. 292).
12	Eggs, beaten	
1 qt.	Milk	
1 t.	Paprika	

Variations:

1. *Rice Ring.* Substitute 1 lb. of rice for noodles.
2. *Noodle Casserole.* Cook noodles in chicken broth. Add 5 lb. large-curd cottage cheese, 4 oz. grated onion, ⅓ c. Worcestershire sauce, 2½ c. dry bread crumbs, 1 T. salt, and 1½ qt. cultured sour cream. Place in greased pan, cover with 2½ c. grated Parmesan cheese, and bake 30–35 min. at 350° F.
3. *Poppy Seed Noodles.* To 4 lb. noodles, cooked, add 12 oz. butter or margarine, melted, ⅓ c. poppy seeds, and 12 oz. chopped toasted almonds. Mix lightly.

Spoon Bread

Bake: 1 hr.
Oven: 350° F.

Yield: 2 pans 12 × 20 × 2 in.
Portion: 4 oz.

Amount	Ingredient	Method
5¾ qt. 1 lb. 12 oz. 3 T.	Milk Cornmeal Salt	Scald milk. Add cornmeal and salt, stirring briskly with a wire whip. Cook 10 min., or until thick.
25 6 oz. 2 oz.	Eggs, beaten Fat, melted Baking powder	Add eggs slowly while stirring. Add fat and baking powder. Stir to blend. Pour into 2 greased pans 12 × 20 × 2 in. or 8 casseroles (1 lb. 12 oz. to each). Place in pans of hot water. Bake.

Note:
Serve with crisp bacon, Creamed Chicken (p. 266), or Creamed Ham (p. 251).

SALADS

Preparation of Salad Ingredients

FRESH FRUIT

Apples. Wash, pare, core, remove bruises and spots. If the skins are tender and the desired color, do not pare.

To dice, cut into rings and dice with sectional cutter. Drop diced pieces into salad dressing, lemon, pineapple, or other acid fruit juice to prevent discoloration. If diced apple is placed in fruit juice, drain before using in a salad.

To section, cut into uniform pieces, so the widest part of the section is not more than ½ in. thick. Remove core from each section. If the peeling has not been removed, score it in several places to facilitate cutting when it is served. Prevent discoloration by the same method as for diced apples, only do not use salad dressing.

Apricots. Cut into halves or sections and remove seed. Remove skins if desired.

Avocados. If hard, ripen at room temperature. Peel, cut into halves or quarters, and remove seed. Slice, dice, or cut into balls. Dip into French dressing or lemon juice to prevent discoloration. Peel shortly before serving.

Bananas. Remove skins and soft or discolored parts. Cut into strips, sections, wedges, or slices. Dip each piece into pineapple, other acid fruit juice, or salad dressing to prevent discoloration.

Cantaloupes and Other Melons. Pare, dice, cut into balls with a French vegetable cutter, or cut into uniform wedges or strips.

Cherries and Grapes. Wash, drain, halve, and remove seeds. To frost, brush with slightly beaten egg white. Sprinkle with sugar. Let dry before using.

Grapefruit. For sections select large grapefruit, wash and dry. Cut off a thick layer of skin from the top and bottom. Place grapefruit on cutting board, start at the top, and cut toward the board. Always cut with a downward stroke and deeply enough to remove all the white membrane. Turn grapefruit with the left hand. When paring is completed and pulp is exposed, remove sections by cutting along the membrane of one section to the center of the fruit. Turn the knife and force the blade along the membrane of the next section to the exterior of the fruit. Repeat for each section.

Oranges. Pare, section as grapefruit, or slice or dice.

Peaches. Peel or submerge in boiling water for a few minutes and remove skins. Chill. Cut into halves, wedges, or slices. Remove skins only a short time before using. Drop into acid fruit juice to prevent discoloration.

Pears. Pare and remove core and seeds a short time before serving. Cut into halves, wedges, or slices.

315

Pineappple. Twist out top. Cut into 5–7 slices, crosswise. Pare each slice and cut out eyes. Remove hard center and cut each slice into cubes. If sugar is added let stand several hours before serving.

CANNED FRUIT

Select whole pieces uniform in size and shape and with a firm appearance. Drain. If cubes or sections are desired, cut into pieces uniform in size and shape with well-defined edges. Pieces should not be too small

DRIED FRUIT

Prunes. Size 20–30. Wash in warm water. Add boiling water to prunes. Cover tightly and let stand about 12 hours. Do not drain. Add sugar and cook slowly without stirring for about 30 min. or until tender and glazed. Pour into a shallow pan to cool.

Raisins. Add hot water and let stand until cool. Wash, drain well. Add to salad ingredients or dressing.

MEAT, FISH, CHICKEN, EGGS, CHEESE, AND NUTS

Meat. Cut cooked meat into ⅓-in. cubes. Marinate. Mix just before serving.

Fish. Cook, remove skin and bones. Flake. Marinate if desired. Mix with dressing just before serving.

Chicken. Cook, remove skin, gristle, and bone. Cut into ⅓-in. cubes. Marinate if desired. Mix with dressing and other ingredients just before serving.

Eggs. Hard-cook (p. 300). Use whole, halved, sliced, or sectioned. Slice or mince whites. Force yolks through ricer.

Cheese. Grate, cut in tiny cubes, or put through a ricer or pastry tube.

Nuts. Heat in hot oven to freshen if desired. Use whole, shredded, or chopped.

Blanched Almonds. To blanch almonds, cover with boiling water and let stand until skins will slip. Drain. Cover with cold water and rub off skins. Place skinned almonds between dry clean towels to remove water.

Toasted Almonds. Spread blanched almonds in a shallow pan in a thin layer. Heat at 250° F., stirring occasionally until nuts are light brown in color.

VEGETABLES

Whether used raw or cooked, strive to preserve shape, color, flavor, and crispness of vegetables.

Asparagus. Cook and marinate tips.

Beans, dry. Cook, keeping beans whole (p. 409).

Beans, green. Leave whole or cut lengthwise. Wash, cook, and marinate.

Beets. Wash, cook, peel, remove any blemishes. Cut into desired shape and marinate.

Cabbage. Remove outer leaves. Wash heads, cut into 4–6 pieces. Remove center stalk. Shred remaining portions as desired with a long sharp knife or shredder. Crisp in ice water 15–30 min.

Carrots. Pare and remove blemishes. Cut into wedges, rounds, or strips. Grind, shred, or cook; then cut into desired shapes and marinate. For carrot curls, see Relishes, p. 317.

Cauliflower. Remove all leaves and cut away dark spots. Separate into flowerets, leaving 1 in. stem. Soak in salt water (1 oz. salt or ⅓ c. vinegar per gal.). Cauliflower may be cooked and marinated, or it may be marinated and served raw.

Celery. Separate outer stalks from heart. (Outer stalks may be used for soup.) Wash, trim, and remove strings, bruised, and blemished parts. To dice, cut lengthwise. Several stalks may be cut at one time. Place on a board and cut crosswise with a French knife. For celery curls, see p. 317.

Celery Cabbage. Remove outer leaves and wash. Shred as lettuce or cut into 1–2 in. slices.

Chives. Remove roots and any objectionable portions. Wash. Drain. Cut leaves crosswise with a sharp knife or scissors.

Cucumbers. Wash and pare, or score lengthwise with a fork. Crisp and let stand in salted ice water 15 min. Cut into slices or wedges.

Green Peppers. Wash, remove seeds and stems. Cut into rings or strips; dice or chop.

Onions. Pour water over onions to cover. Under water, remove wilted leaves, outer layer of the bulb, firm root end, and all bruised or decayed parts. Cut as desired.

Peas. Shell. Cook and marinate. Drain before using.

Potatoes. Pare in electric peeler. Remove remaining skin, eyes, and bruised parts by hand. Cut into ½-in. cubes and cook; or wash, cook with skins on, peel, and dice. Marinate 2 hr. before using.

Tomatoes. Wash and peel. If skins are difficult to remove, place in a wire basket and dip in boiling water until the skins begin to loosen. Dip in cold water and remove skins. Chill.

Turnips. Remove tops, wash, pare by hand. Shred or cut into fine strips.

RELISHES

Carrot Curls. Cut long, paper-thin slices. Roll each strip around finger, fasten with toothpick, and chill in ice water for several hours.

Carrot Sticks. Cut carrots into thin strips. Chill in ice water for several hours.

Celery Curls or Fans. Cut celery into 2½-in. lengths. Make lengthwise cuts ⅛ in. apart and about 1 in. in length on one or both ends of celery strips. Place in ice water about 2 hr. before serving.

Celery Rings. Cut celery into 2-in. lengths and then into pieces ⅛ in. thick. Place in ice water for several hours. Each strip of celery will form a ring.

Green Pepper Rings. Remove stem and seeds. Cut into thin slices.

Green Pepper Sticks. Cut pepper lengthwise into narrow strips.

Radish Roses. Cut off root end of radish with sharp knife. Leave an inch or two of the green stem. Cut 4 or 5 petal-shaped slices around the radish from cut tip to center. Place radishes in ice water, and petals will open.

Radish Accordions. Cut long radishes not quite through into 10–12 narrow slices. Place in ice water. Slices will fan out accordion-style.

SALAD GREENS

Chicory. See Endive.

Endive. Wash, remove objectionable portions. Drain, place in plastic bag, and refrigerate.

Escarole. See Endive.

Head Lettuce. Remove ragged and objectionable leaves from head. For a garnish, cut out stem end or core. Hold inverted head under running cold water until the leaves are loosened. Do not soak. Turn heads right side up to drain. Separate the leaves, and stack 6 or 7 leaves in a nest. Invert the nest and pack in a covered container or plastic bag. Place in refrigerator 2 hr. or more to complete crisping.

Leaf Lettuce. Wash, drain, place in plastic bag and refrigerate.

Romaine. See Leaf Lettuce.

Spinach. Remove tough stems. Examine leaves and discard all dry, yellow, wilted, or slimy leaves. Wash first in warm, then in cold water, as many times as necessary to remove sand. Crisp and use as a salad green.

Watercress. See Endive.

Making the Salad

1. Use only clean, cold, and crisp salad greens. Vegetables most often used for salad garnish are several types of lettuce, endive, chicory, escarole, parsley, romaine, spinach, and watercress. Red and green cabbage, celery, celery cabbage, carrot, and green pepper also may be used. Break or cut salad greens.

2. Cut fruits and vegetables into generous wedges, slices, or cubes for an attractive salad. Each piece should retain its identity.

3. Drain fruit or any ingredients surrounded by liquid.

4. When desired, marinate each ingredient separately with a well-seasoned French dressing.

5. Drain and toss ingredients together lightly, if a mixed salad. Add tomato sections or juicy fruits just before serving to avoid wilting salad greens.

6. Set up salads as follows:

(a) Arrange chilled plates on large trays or in rows on the table. Select china, if possible, that will add to the attractiveness of the salad.

(b) Place salad green on plates. Place a lettuce cup so that the frilly edge is at the back and top of the salad. The leaf should not extend over the edge of the plate.

(c) Build from the back to the front, with the salad green as a base. To give height, chopped lettuce may be placed in the lettuce cup under such salad ingredients as fruit or vegetables slices, asparagus tips, or gelatin ring molds.

(d) Top salad lightly with some material that will give accent in color and flavor, if desired.

(e) Select a dressing that will enhance the flavor of the salad ingredients. Add salad dressing just before serving (sprinkle, do not pour), or pass for individual service. For a green salad, 1–1½ pints is ample allowance for 50 servings.

Serving the Salad

Salads may be used as:

1. A first course in a dinner menu: fruit or sea food.
2. A main course of a luncheon: meat, fish, poultry, cheese.
3. An accompaniment to the main course of a dinner or luncheon: salad greens with vegetables, fruit, or combination.
4. A second course in a dinner menu: fruit or vegetable.

ACCOMPANIMENTS FOR SALADS USED AS A SEPARATE COURSE

Breads:
Hot breads, buttered: biscuits, rolls, muffins.
Crisp breads: bread sticks, cracker, Melba toast, hard rolls.
Sandwiches (small): rolled, ribbon, or open face; banana, date, nut, or orange bread.

Cheese:
Cream cheese balls, plain or rolled in nuts or parsley.
Toasted cheese crackers, cheese straws.

Miscellaneous Crisp Materials:
Celery curls, celery hearts, stuffed celery, or radish roses.
Olives, plain, stuffed, or ripe.
Pickles, sweet, sour, dill, burr gherkins, fans, rounds.
Potatoes, chips or latticed, shoestring.
Salted nuts.

Fruit Salads

Apple Celery Salad

Yield: 5 qt.

Portion: ⅓ c.

Amount	Ingredient	Method
1 pt.	Mayonnaise or Cooked Salad Dressing (p. 347–349)	Combine mayonnaise and whipped cream.
½ c.	Cream, whipped (optional)	
8 lb. (E.P.)	Apples, tart (peeled or unpeeled)	Dice apples. Add to dressing as soon as diced to prevent apples turning dark.
2 lb. (E.P.)	Celery, chopped	Add celery, salt, sugar, and marsh-mallows.
1½ T.	Salt	
6 oz.	Sugar (optional)	Mix lightly until all ingredients are coated with dressing.
8 oz.	Marshmallows, cut (optional)	Serve with No. 12 dipper.

Variations:

1. *Waldorf Salad.* Add 8 oz. chopped walnuts just before serving.
2. *Apple–Fruit Salad.* Use 3 lb. cubed pineapple, 2 lb. cubed oranges, sliced peaches, or grapes, and 5 lb. apples.
3. *Apple–Date Salad.* Substitute 2 lb. cut dates for celery.
4. *Apple–Carrot Salad.* Use 6 lb. diced apples, 3 lb. shredded carrots, and only 1 lb. chopped celery.
5. *Apple–Cabbage Salad.* Use 6 lb. diced apples and 4 lb. crisp shredded cabbage. Omit celery.

Spiced Apple Salad

Yield: 50 portions

Amount	Ingredient	Method
50 (approximately 12 lbs.)	Apples	Core and peel apples. Leave whole unless apples are large; then cut in half crosswise. Place apples in a flat pan.
6 lb.	Sugar	Combine sugar, water, and seasonings. Boil about 5 min. to form a thin sirup.
2 qt.	Water	
1 c.	Vinegar	
½ t.	Red coloring	Pour over apples.
1 oz.	Stick cinnamon or a few drops of oil of cinnamon	Cook on top of range until tender. Turn while cooking. Cool.
1 oz.	Whole cloves	
8 oz.	Celery, chopped	Fill centers of apples with celery– nut mixture.
4 oz.	Nuts, chopped	
¾ c.	Mayonnaise	
½ t.	Salt	

Note:
Select apples that will hold their shape when cooked.

Fruit Salad

Yield: 4¼ qt.
Portion: ⅓ c.

Amount	Ingredient	Method
6 lb.	Pineapple, cubed	Drain fruit.
2 lb.	Cherries, Royal Anne or Bing, seeded	Combine carefully. Serve with No. 12 dipper.
6 lb.	Peaches, cubed	
12	Oranges, peeled and diced	

Note:
Other fruit combinations may be used (see pp. 323).

Grapefruit–Orange Salad

Yield: 50 portions

Amount	Ingredient	Method
16 (size 40)	Grapefruit	Pare and section fruit (p. 315).
17 (size 56)	Oranges	For each salad use 2 sections of orange and 3 sections of grapefruit. Arrange alternately on garnish.

Note:
For other citrus fruit combinations, see pp. 323.
Variation:
Grapefruit–Orange–Avocado Salad. Place avocado sections between grapefruit and orange sections.

Frozen Fruit Salad

Yield: 4¼ qt.
Portion: 4 oz.

Amount	Ingredient	Method
1 oz.	Plain gelatin	Sprinkle gelatin over water. Soak 10 min.
½ c.	Water, cold	
1¾ c.	Orange juice	Combine juices and heat to boiling point.
1¾ c.	Pineapple juice	Add gelatin. Stir to dissolve. Cool until slightly congealed.
1 c.	Mayonnaise	Combine whipped cream and mayonnaise.
1 pt.	Cream, whipped	Fold into the slightly congealed gelatin mixture.
1 lb. 12 oz.	Pineapple, diced, drained	Fold in fruit. Pour into molds and freeze.
1 lb. 8 oz.	Orange sections, cut in halves	
1 lb. 8 oz.	Peaches, sliced, drained	
2 lb.	Bananas, diced	
12 oz.	Pecans, chopped	
8 oz.	Maraschino cherries	
8 oz.	Marshmallows, diced	

Notes:
1. Salad may be frozen in counter pans and cut in squares.
2. Other combinations of fruit (a total of 5–6 qt.) may be used.

FRUIT SALAD COMBINATIONS[1]

Apple
1. Apples, celery, Malaga grapes. Chantilly Dressing.
2. Apples, grapes, bananas, pineapple. Fruit Dressing.
3. Apples, bananas, pineapple. Mayonnaise.
4. Apples, celery, dates. Combination Dressing.
5. Apples, pineapple, Tokay grapes. Chantilly Dressing.
6. Apples, grapes, bananas, pineapple, oranges, lemon juice. Chantilly Dressing.
7. Apples, oranges, dates, marshmallows. Combination Dressing.
8. Apples, celery, grapefruit. Mayonnaise.
9. Apple, orange, and pear sections. French Dressing.
10. Apple, orange, and pear mixed with Mayonnaise.
11. Avocado half, filled with Waldorf Salad (p. 320), Tomato Aspic (p. 335), Chicken Salad (p. 337), or fish salad (Shrimp or Lobster, pp. 338–339).
12. Red apple wedges, grapefruit or orange sections, and avocado on leaf lettuce. Thick French Dressing.
13. Waldorf salad served on a slice of pineapple, garnished with maraschino cherry and sprig of parsley.

Banana
1. Bananas, grapes, pineapple chunks, marshmallows. Fruit Dressing.
2. Diced banana, pineapple chunks, pear, and peach. Whipped Cream Dressing.
3. Banana sliced lengthwise, orange, and grapefruit sections. Celery Seed Dressing.
4. Banana and orange sections arranged alternately on Bibb lettuce. French Dressing.
5. Banana cut in thirds crosswise and lengthwise, rolled in thin cooked dressing and chopped nuts or cornflakes. Arrange with thin slices of orange.

Grapefruit
1. Grapefruit sections arranged alternately with orange or apple sections. French Dressing.
2. Grapefruit sections with tomato sections and ½ slice pineapple. French Dressing.
3. Grapefruit, fresh pear, and orange sections arranged on lettuce, radiating from center; cream cheese in center, topped with cherry. French Dressing.
4. Five grapefruit sections arranged on endive and garnished with pomegranate seeds. Celery Seed Dressing.
5. Three sections of grapefruit and orange placed on a lettuce leaf, garnished with avocado. Poppy Seed Dressing.
6. Grapefruit sections and avocado wedges, garnished with fresh strawberries. French Dressing.

[1] See p. 347 for salad dressing recipes.

Melon
1. Honeydew melon wedges garnished with watermelon balls. Honey Fruit Dressing.
2. Melon spear, orange slices, garnished with small cluster of grapes. French Dressing.

Orange
1. Orange slices, Bermuda onion rings, cream cheese balls rolled in chopped nuts. French Dressing.
2. Orange and avocado sections, halves of Ribier grapes. French Dressing.

Peach
1. Peach half stuffed with cream cheese balls, cottage cheese, chopped dates, stuffed prunes, Waldorf Salad, or toasted slivered almonds.
2. Peach half, filled with blueberries, garnished with mint sprig. French Dressing.

Pear
1. Pear half stuffed with cream cheese, cottage cheese, or shredded Cheddar cheese.
2. Pear half, with frosted blueberries in center, fresh plum-slice garnish.

Pineapple
1. Diced pineapple, marshmallows, white grapes, and nuts. Fruit Dressing.
2. Diced pineapple, celery, white grapes. Whipped Cream Dressing.
3. Pineapple slice with cream cheese ball in center. French Dressing.
4. Pineapple slice, orange slice, and apricot half arranged in pyramid style, garnished with maraschino cherry. Celery Seed Dressing.
5. Fresh pineapple, honeydew, and cantaloupe wedges, garnished with whole fresh strawberries. Celery Seed Dressing.

Prune
1. Large cooked prunes stuffed with cream cheese or orange sections. Mayonnaise or Celery Seed Dressing.

Vegetable Salads

Tossed Green Salad

Yield: 9 lb.
Portion: 1 c.

Amount	Ingredient	Method
6 lb.	Head lettuce	Break or cut lettuce into pieces.
3 lb.	Leaf lettuce or Bibb lettuce	Just before serving, toss lightly with French Dressing (p. 350).
1¼ qt.	French Dressing	

Note:
Any combination of salad greens may be used. Serve in individual salad bowls.
Variations:
1. *Green Salad Bowl.* To 7 lb. Tossed Green Salad, add 4 sliced cucumbers, 3 bunches sliced radishes. Garnish with 6 lb. tomato wedges, 2 wedges per salad. Serve with French, Roquefort, or Thousand Island Dressing.
2. *Combination Fresh Vegetable Salad.* To 5 lb. Tossed Green Salad, add 1 lb. cauliflowerets; 3 bunches radishes and 2 cucumbers, sliced; 2 lb. red cabbage, shredded; 1 lb. celery, 4 oz. green peppers, and 1 lb. celery cabbage, coarsely chopped. Serve with French, Roquefort, or Thousand Island Dressing.
3. *Salad Greens with Grapefruit.* Serve 8 lb. Tossed Green Salad in individual bowls. Garnish each with 3 sections pink grapefruit. Serve with Poppy Seed or French Dressing.
4. *Hawaiian Tossed Salad.* To 8 lb. Tossed Green Salad, add sections from 8 grapefruit, 8 oranges, 4 avocados, and 1 fresh pineapple, cubed. Serve with Honey-Orange Dressing.
5. *Chef's Salad Bowl.* Place 6 lb. mixed salad greens in bowls. Arrange 6 lb. meat (turkey, tongue, ham) and 3 lb. Cheddar cheese, cut Julienne or in cubes, over top of salad. Garnish with green pepper ring, carrot curl, and tomato wedges. Serve with French or Roquefort Dressing.
6. *Russian Salad.* Mix 4 lb. head lettuce, 2 bunches sliced radishes, and 1 lb. crisp, clean spinach leaves broken into pieces. Fill individual salad bowls ⅔ full. Top each salad with 1 oz. ham or luncheon meat, 2 oz. turkey, and 1 oz. Cheddar cheese, cut into strips. Garnish with quarters of hard-cooked egg and tomato wedges. Serve with Thousand Island Dressing.
7. *Bacon and Chicken Salad.* To 6 lb. mixed salad greens, add 5 lb. cooked chicken or turkey cut in strips. Mix lightly and portion into salad bowls. Sprinkle 4 lb. chopped crisply cooked bacon over top of salads. Serve with choice of dressing.

Cabbage Salad

Yield: 4¼ qt.
Portion: ⅓ c.

Amount	Ingredient	Method
7 lb.	Cabbage, shredded	Add salad dressing to shredded
1 qt.	Cooked Salad Dressing (p. 349)	cabbage. Mix lightly. If dressing is too thick, add cream to thin.
1½ T.	Salt	Mix just before serving so cabbage does not lose its crispness. Serve with No. 12 dipper.

Variations:
1. *Cabbage–Apple Salad.* Use 4 lb. shredded cabbage. Add 3 lb. diced unpeeled red apples.
2. *Cabbage–Carrot Salad.* Substitute 2 lb. shredded carrots for 2 lb. shredded cabbage.
3. *Cabbage–Pineapple–Marshmallow Salad.* Add 2 lb. diced pineapple, 1 lb. diced marshmallows, 1 pt. whipped cream, and 1 pt. Mayonnaise. Omit Cooked Salad Dressing.
4. *Cole Slaw.* Add 3 c. sugar and 3 c. vinegar mixed. Omit salad dressing. 1 T. celery seed may be added.
5. *Creamy Cole Slaw.* Use 2 c. mayonnaise, 2 c. sweet or sour cream, ½ c. vinegar, ½ c. sugar.
6. *Red Cabbage–Celery Salad.* Use 3 lb. shredded green cabbage and 3 lb. red cabbage. Add 1 lb. diced celery and approximately 1 qt. Sour Cream Dressing (p. 352). Omit cooked salad dressing.

Sauerkraut Salad

Yield: 50
Portion: No. 12 dipper
(⅓ cup)

Amount	Ingredient	Method
1 No. 10 can	Sauerkraut	Combine all ingredients. Refrigerate for at least 12 hours.
1 lb.	Carrots, grated	Serve with No. 12 dipper.
12 oz.	Celery, diced	
8 oz.	Onion, chopped	
1 lb.	Green pepper, chopped	
1 lb. 8 oz.	Sugar	

Note:
Sauerkraut may be cut with scissors before combining with other ingredients.

Carrot Raisin Salad

Yield: 4¼ qt.

Portion: ⅓ c.

Amount	Ingredient	Method
6 lb. 8 oz.	Carrots, raw, coarsely ground or shredded	Mix all ingredients lightly. Serve with No. 12 dipper.
8 oz.	Raisins	
1 T.	Salt	
1 pt.	Mayonnaise	
1 pt.	Cooked Salad Dressing	

Variations:

1. *Carrot–Coconut Salad.* 1 lb. toasted coconut may be substituted for raisins.
2. *Carrot–Celery Salad.* Omit raisins. Use 5 lb. ground carrots. Add 2 lb. chopped celery and 2 oz. sugar.
3. *Carrot–Celery–Apple Salad.* Substitute 3 lb. diced apples for 2 lb. ground or shredded carrots.
4. *Carrot–Celery–Cucumber Salad.* Use 4½ lb. shredded carrots, 1½ lb. chopped celery, and 1½ lb. chopped cucumbers.

Carrifruit Salad

Yield: 5 qt.

Portion: ⅓ c.

Amount	Ingredient	Method
4 lb. 8 oz.	Carrots, shredded	Mix ingredients lightly.
9 oz.	Marshmallows, cut	
2 lb. 12 oz.	Pineapple, tidbits, drained	
8 oz.	Coconut, flaked	
2¼ c.	Mayonnaise	Add mayonnaise blended with cream. Mix carefully. Serve with No. 12 dipper.
¾ c.	Cream	

Stuffed Tomato Salad

Yield: 50 portions

Amount	Ingredient	Method
50 (approximately 12 lb.)	Tomatoes	Peel tomatoes. Remove core and part of pulp from each. Combine tomato pulp with chopped cabbage, celery, and pickle. Add mayonnaise and salt. Mix lightly.
1 lb.	Cabbage, chopped fine	
1 lb.	Celery, chopped fine	
8 oz.	Sweet pickle, chopped	
1 c.	Mayonnaise	
1 T.	Salt	
1½ T.	Salt	Sprinkle salt in tomato cavities. Stuff each tomato with approximately 2 T. (No. 30 dipper) of the vegetable mixture.

Notes:
1. Tomatoes may be cut into fourths to within ½ in. of bottoms. Spread apart. Sprinkle with salt and fill with salad mixture.
2. Fish, egg, or chicken salad may be substituted for vegetable mixture.
Variations:
1. *Tomato–Shrimp Salad.* Fill tomato cups with Shrimp Salad (p. 338). Omit lettuce in Shrimp Salad recipe.
2. *Tomato–Cottage Cheese Salad.* Substitute 6 lb. cottage cheese, seasoned, for vegetable mixture. Fill tomato cups, using No. 20 dipper.

Sliced Cucumber and Onion in Sour Cream

Yield: 4¼ qt.
Portion: ⅓ c.

Amount	Ingredient	Method
4 lb. 4 oz.	Cucumbers	Cut cucumbers and onions in thin slices.
9 oz.	Onions	
3 c.	Cultured sour cream	Blend rest of ingredients to form a thin cream dressing. Pour over cucumbers and onions. Mix lightly.
3 c.	Mayonnaise	
1½ t.	Salt	
3 T.	Sugar	
¾ c.	Vinegar	

Note:
This cream dressing also may be served as a dressing for lettuce.

Potato Salad

Yield: 6½ qt.
Portion: 4 oz.

Amount	Ingredient	Method
15 lb. (E.P.)	Potatoes	Cook potatoes until tender. Dice.
2 c. 1½ T. ½ c.	French dressing Salt (or more) Vinegar, mild	Add combined dressing, salt, and vinegar. Mix carefully while potatoes are warm. Marinate until cold.
12 4 oz. 6 oz. 1 lb. 8 oz. 8 oz. 2 c.	Eggs, hard-cooked, diced Green peppers, chopped Pimiento, chopped Celery, diced Onion, chopped Pickles, chopped Mayonnaise	Add remaining ingredients. Mix carefully. Allow to season at least 1 hr. before serving. Serve with No. 10 dipper.

Hot Potato Salad

Yield: 50 6-oz. portions

Amount	Ingredient	Method
15 lb.	Potatoes	Dice potatoes and steam until tender.
1 lb. 3 oz. 6 oz. 16 1½ qt.	Bacon Onion, chopped Green pepper, chopped Eggs, hard-cooked, diced Mayonnaise	Add crisp bacon, vegetables, and mayonnaise to potatoes just before serving. Serve hot with No. 6 dipper.

Notes:
1. *Hot Vegetable Sauce* (p. 381) may be substituted for mayonnaise, or half mayonnaise and half cooked salad dressing may be used.
2. Bacon may be omitted.

Brown Bean Salad

Yield: 4¼ qt.
Portion: ⅓ c.

Amount	Ingredient	Method
2 No. 10 cans	Beans, brown or kidney, drained	Mix all ingredients. Allow to season at least 1 hr. before serving.
18	Eggs, hard-cooked, diced	Serve with No. 12 dipper.
1 lb.	Pickles, chopped (or pickle relish)	
4 oz.	Onion, minced	
1 lb. 4 oz.	Celery, diced	
4 oz.	Green pepper, chopped	
½ c.	Vinegar	
3 T.	Salt	
1 qt.	Salad dressing	

Note:
4 lb. dried beans, cooked, may be substituted for canned beans.

Triple Bean Salad

Yield: 5 qt.
Portion: ⅓ c.

Amount	Ingredient	Method
1 No. 10 can	Green beans, French style	Drain beans well.
2 No. 2½ cans	Wax beans, cut	
2 No. 2½ cans	Kidney beans	
1 lb. 8 oz.	Onion, thinly sliced	Combine vegetables and seasonings. Cover. Marinate overnight in refrigerator.
1 c.	Green pepper, diced	
3 c.	Vinegar	
1 lb. 8 oz.	Sugar	
¼ c.	Soy sauce	
4 T.	Celery salt	
2 t.	Salt	
2 t.	Pepper	
1 c.	Salad oil	Just before serving, drain vegetables well. Add oil and toss lightly. Serve with No. 12 dipper.

VEGETABLE AND SALAD COMBINATIONS[1]

Asparagus
1. Three asparagus tips through a ring of green pepper placed on a slice of tomato. Bibb lettuce garnish. Mayonnaise.
2. Asparagus tips on shredded lettuce, garnished with sliced hard-cooked egg and pimiento strip. French Dressing.

Green Beans
1. Cooked green beans mixed with chopped small green onions and thinly sliced radishes. Thick French Dressing.
2. Marinated whole green beans, garnished with pimiento strips. French Dressing.

Beets
1. Sliced pickled beets and hard-cooked eggs arranged on lettuce. Mayonnaise.
2. Julienne beets and celery on endive. French Dressing.
3. Sliced cooked beets, Bermuda onion rings, quartered hard-cooked eggs, arranged on shredded lettuce. French Dressing.

Cucumbers
1. Thin slices of cucumber on slices of tomato, arranged on a lettuce leaf. Tarragon Dressing.
2. Thin slices of cucumber and Bermuda onion marinated. Vinaigrette Dressing.

Peas
1. Cooked peas, diced cheese, celery, pickle, and pimiento. Combination Dressing.

Spinach
1. Chopped raw spinach, combined with hard-cooked eggs, garnished with crumbled crisp bacon. Tarragon Dressing.

Tomatoes
1. Tomato and avocado slices, arranged alternately on endive. French Dressing.
2. Tomato sections and marinated broccoli spears. French Dressing.
3. Tomato sections garnished with watercress. French Dressing.

[1] See pp. 347–353 for Salad Dressing recipes.

Gelatin Salads

Fruit Gelatin Salad

Yield: 1 pan 12 × 20 × 2 in.
40 portions 2¼ × 2½ in.
48 portions 2 × 2½ in.

Amount	Ingredient	Method
1 lb. 8 oz.	Gelatin, flavored	Pour boiling water over gelatin.
2 qt.	Water, boiling	Stir until dissolved.
2 qt.	Fruit juice or water, cold	Add juice or cold water. Chill.
4–5 lb.	Fruit, drained	Place fruit in counter pan. When gelatin begins to congeal, pour over fruit. Place in refrigerator to congeal.

Notes:

1. For quick preparation, dissolve 24 oz. flavored gelatin dessert in 1½ qt. boiling water. Measure 2½ qt. chipped or finely crushed ice, then add enough cold water or fruit juice to cover ice. Add to gelatin and stir constantly until ice is melted. Gelatin will begin to congeal at once. Speed of congealing depends on proportion of ice to water and size of ice particles.
2. One or more canned, frozen, or fresh fruits, cut into desired shapes and sizes, may be used. Fresh or frozen pineapple must be cooked before adding to gelatin salad.
3. Fruit juice may be used for part or all of the liquid.
4. If unflavored granulated gelatin is used, soak 2½ oz. plain gelatin for 10 min. in 1 pt. cold water. Add 3½ qt. boiling fruit juice and 1 lb. sugar.

VARIATIONS OF GELATIN SALAD

Jellied Vegetable Salad. Substitute vegetables for fruit. Add 1 t. salt and substitute ½ c. vinegar for ½ c. fruit juice. Use water or vegetable juice for remainder of liquid. If unflavored gelatin is used, add 1 T. salt and 1 c. vinegar or lemon juice.

Applesauce Mold. Add 24 oz. lime gelatin to 3 qt. boiling hot applesauce and stir until dissolved. Add 1 qt. ginger ale and pour into salad molds or 12 × 20-in. pan.

Autumn Salad. Dissolve 24 oz. orange gelatin in 2 qt. hot water. Add 2 qt. cold liquid, 2½ lb. sliced fresh peaches, and 2½ lb. fresh pears.

Cabbage Parfait. Dissolve 24 oz. lemon gelatin in 2 qt. hot water. Blend in 1 qt. mayonnaise, 1 qt. cold water, 1 c. vinegar, 2 t. salt. Chill until mixture is partially congealed, then beat until fluffy. Add 2 qt. finely shredded cabbage, 1 qt. radish slices, 1 qt. diced celery, 1 c. chopped green pepper, and ½ c. minced onion.

Cranberry Ring Mold. Dissolve 24 oz. cherry or raspberry gelatin in 2 qt. hot water. Add 3 lb. fresh or frozen cranberry relish, 1 lb. chopped apples, and 1 lb. crushed pineapple or 1 No. 10 can whole cranberry sauce and 6 oranges, ground. Pour into individual ring molds or 12 × 20-in. pan.

Frosted Cherry Salad. Dissolve 24 oz. cherry gelatin in 2 qt. hot water. Add 2 qt. cold fruit juice, 3 lb. drained, pitted red cherries and 2 lb. crushed pineapple. When congealed, frost with cream cheese and chopped toasted almonds.

Frosted Lime Mold. Dissolve 24 oz. lime gelatin in 2 qt. hot water. Add 2 qt. cold fruit juice and when mixture begins to congeal, add 2 qt. crushed pineapple, 2½ lb. cottage cheese, 8 oz. diced celery, 4 oz. chopped pimiento, and 4 oz. nutmeats. When congealed, frost with mixture of 4 lb. cream cheese blended with ½ c. mayonnaise.

Molded Grapefruit Salad. Dissolve 24 oz. lime gelatin in 2 qt. hot water. Add 2 qt. cold fruit juice, sections from 15 grapefruit, or 2 3-lb. cans frozen grapefruit sections.

Jellied Citrus Salad. Dissolve 24 oz. lemon or orange gelatin in 2 qt. hot water. Add 2 qt. cold water, sections from 15 oranges and 8 grapefruit; or 4 No. 2 cans mandarin oranges and 3-lb. can frozen grapefruit sections.

Jellied Waldorf Salad. Dissolve 24 oz. raspberry or cherry gelatin in 2 qt. boiling water. Add 1 c. red cinnamon candies and stir until dissolved. Add 2 qt. cold liquid. When mixture begins to congeal, add 2 qt. diced apple, 3 c. finely diced celery, and 2 c. chopped pecans.

Molded Pear Salad. Dissolve 24 oz. lime gelatin in 2 qt. hot water. Add 2 qt. cold fruit juice and 50 pear halves.

Molded Pineapple–Cheese Salad. Dissolve 24 oz. lemon gelatin in 2 qt. hot liquid. Add 2 qt. cold fruit juice, 1 lb. grated Cheddar cheese, 3 lb. drained crushed pineapple, 3 oz. chopped green pepper or pimiento, and 4 oz. finely chopped celery.

Molded Pineapple–Cucumber Salad. Dissolve 24 oz. lime gelatin in 2 qt. hot liquid. Add 2 qt. cold fruit juice, 3 lb. drained crushed pineapple, 1½ lb. diced cucumber, and 4 oz. finely chopped pimiento.

Molded Pineapple Relish. Dissolve 24 oz. lemon gelatin in 2 qt. hot liquid. Add 2 qt. cold fruit juice, 4 lb. pineapple tidbits, and 1½ c. pickle relish.

Molded Pineapple and Rhubarb Salad. To 4 lb. frozen rhubarb, add 2 lb. sugar and 1 qt. water. Cook 5 min. Add 4 lb. pineapple tidbits and 24 oz. strawberry gelatin dissolved in juice from rhubarb and pineapple. Add enough water to make 4 qt.

Raspberry Ring Mold. Dissolve 24 oz. raspberry gelatin in 2 qt. hot liquid. Add 2 qt. cold raspberry juice, 3 lb. frozen raspberries, and 2 lb. cantaloupe or watermelon balls. Pour into individual ring molds.

Spicy Apricot Mold. To sirup drained from 2 No. 10 cans peeled apricot halves, add 1 c. vinegar, 6 pieces stick cinnamon, and 1 T. whole cloves. Simmer 10 min. Remove spices and add enough hot water to make 1 gal. liquid. Combine with 24 oz. orange gelatin and congeal. Sliced peaches may be substituted for apricots.

Sunshine Salad. Dissolve 24 oz. lemon gelatin in 2 qt. hot liquid. Add 2 qt. cold fruit juice, 3 lb. drained crushed pineapple, and 8 oz. grated raw carrot.

Ribbon Gelatin Salad. Dissolve 24 oz. raspberry gelatin in 1 gal. hot water. Divide into 3 equal parts. Pour ⅓ into 12 × 20-in. pan and chill. Add 1 lb. cream cheese to another third and whip to blend; pour on the first part when it is congealed. Return to the refrigerator until it too is congealed, then top with remaining portion.

Swedish Green-top Salad. Dissolve 24 oz. lime gelatin in 1½ qt. boiling water. Pour into 12 × 20-in. pan. Dissolve 12 oz. orange gelatin in 1 qt. boiling water and stir until dissolved. While mixture is still hot, add 1½ lb. marshmallows and stir until melted. When cool, add 12 oz. cream cheese, 1½ c. mayonnaise, and ½ t. salt. Fold in 1 pt. cream, whipped. Pour over congealed lime gelatin and return to refrigerator to chill.

Under-the-Sea Salad. Dissolve 24 oz. lime gelatin in 1 gal. hot water. Divide into two parts. Pour one part into a pan and chill. When it begins to congeal, add 3 c. sliced pears or drained crushed pineapple. To the remaining gelatin mixture, add 1 lb. cream cheese, whipping until smooth. Pour over first portion.

Cucumber Soufflé Salad. Dissolve 24 oz. lime or lemon gelatin in 1½ qt. hot water. Add 2 qt. ice and water. Chill until partially set. Whip until fluffy. Add 3 c. mayonnaise and ⅓ c. lemon juice. Fold in 1 gal. chopped cucumbers (10–12 cucumbers).

Ginger Ale Fruit Salad

Yield: 1 pan 12 × 20 × 2 in.
40 portions 2¼ × 2½ in.
48 portions 2 × 2½ in.

Amount	Ingredient	Method
1 lb. 8 oz.	Gelatin, lemon flavored	Pour boiling water over gelatin. Stir until gelatin is dissolved.
2 qt.	Water, boiling	Cool.
2 qt.	Ginger ale	Add ginger ale.
1 lb.	Grapes (or white cherries)	When liquid begins to congeal, add remaining ingredients.
12 oz.	Celery, chopped fine	Pour into counter pan or into individual molds. Place in refrigerator to congeal.
1 lb.	Apples, cubed	
1 No. 10 can	Pineapple, diced	
¼ c.	Lemon juice	

Note:
Cider may be used in place of ginger ale.

Bing Cherry Salad

Yield: 1 pan 12 × 20 × 2 in.
40 portions 2¼ × 2½ in.
48 portions 2 × 2½ in.

Amount	Ingredient	Method
1 lb. 8 oz.	Gelatin, raspberry or cherry flavored	Pour boiling water over gelatin. Stir until dissolved. Cool.
1 qt.	Water, boiling	Add water and juice.
3½ qt.	Water and cherry juice	Chill until mixture begins to congeal.
2 No. 2½ cans	Bing cherries, pitted	Add cherries, pecans and olives.
8 oz.	Pecans, chopped	Pour into counter pan or into 50 individual molds. Place in refrigerator to congeal.
2 c.	Stuffed olives, sliced (optional)	

Notes:
1. 9 oz. cream cheese, rolled into small balls, may be added with cherries and pecans to gelatin mixture.
2. Omit stuffed olives. Add 1 No. 10 can crushed pineapple, drained.

Tomato Aspic

Yield: 1 pan 12 × 20 × 2 in.
40 portions 2¼ × 2½ in.
48 portions 2 × 2½ in.

Amount	Ingredient	Method
4 oz.	Gelatin, plain	Sprinkle gelatin over water. Soak 10 min.
1 qt.	Water, cold	
4 qt.	Tomato juice	Combine tomato juice and seasonings. Boil 5 min. Strain.
2	Onions, small	Add gelatin. Stir until dissolved.
1	Bay leaf	
4	Celery stalks	
8	Cloves, whole	
2 t.	Mustard, dry	
14 oz.	Sugar	
1 T.	Salt	
2 c.	Vinegar or lemon juice	Add vinegar or lemon juice. Pour into counter pan or ring molds. Place in refrigerator to congeal.

Note:
If ring molds are used, recipe will yield approximately 75 servings. Centers may be filled with cole slaw, cottage cheese, crab salad, or lobster salad.

Perfection Salad

Yield: 1 pan 12 × 20 × 2 in.
40 portions 2¼ × 2½ in.
48 portions 2 × 2½ in.

Amount	Ingredient	Method
1 lb. 10 oz.	Gelatin, lemon flavored	Pour boiling water over gelatin. Stir until dissolved.
1 qt.	Water, boiling	
2½ qt.	Water, cold	Add cold liquids and seasonings.
1 c.	Vinegar	Stir until sugar is dissolved. Chill.
1 c.	Lemon juice	
1½ T.	Salt	
1 lb.	Sugar	
1 lb. 8 oz. (E.P.)	Cabbage, chopped	When liquid begins to congeal, add
10 oz.	Celery, chopped	vegetables.
4 oz.	Pimiento, chopped	Pour into counter pan. Place in
4 oz.	Green pepper, chopped	refrigerator to congeal.
1 T.	Paprika	

Jellied Beet Salad

Yield: 1 pan 12 × 20 × 2 in.
40 portions 2¼ × 2½ in.
48 portions 2 × 2½ in.

Amount	Ingredient	Method
1 lb. 8 oz.	Gelatin, lemon flavored	Pour boiling water over gelatin. Stir until dissolved.
2 qt.	Water, boiling	
1 qt.	Beet juice (or water)	Add beet juice, vinegar, salt, and onion juice.
1 c.	Vinegar, mild	Chill.
2 T.	Salt	
3 T.	Onion juice	
6 T.	Horseradish	When mixture begins to congeal,
2 lb. 8 oz.	Celery, finely diced	add horseradish and vegetables.
2 lb. 8 oz.	Beets, diced or chopped	Pour into counter pan. Place in refrigerator to congeal.

Luncheon Salads

Chicken Salad

Yield: 6¼ qt.
Portion: ½ c.

Amount	Ingredient	Method
5 lb. (4 4½–5 lb. hens)	Cooked chicken (p. 261)	Cut chicken meat into ½-in. cubes.
12	Eggs, hard-cooked, diced	Add remaining ingredients. Mix lightly.
3 lb.	Celery, diced	Chill.
2 T.	Salt	Serve with No. 10 dipper.
1 t.	Pepper, white	
3 c.	Mayonnaise	
4 t.	Lemon juice	

Notes:
1. The marinating of cubed chicken with ⅔ c. French Dressing (p. 350) for 2 hr. will improve the flavor.
2. Just before serving, 8 oz. toasted almonds, white cherries, ripe olives, pineapple chunks, sweet pickle or cucumbers may be added.
3. Turkey may be substituted for chicken.
4. Canned or frozen chicken or turkey may be used.

Variation:
Chicken Salad in Cranberry or Raspberry Ring Mold. Fill center of individual cranberry or raspberry ring molds (p. 333) with chicken salad.

Shrimp Salad

Yield: 6¼ qt.
Portion: ½ c.

Amount	Ingredient	Method
6 lb.	Shrimp, cooked and cut into ½ in. pieces	Prepare shrimp and vegetables. Place in bowl.
2 lb.	Celery, diced	
1 lb.	Cucumber, diced	
1 head	Lettuce, chopped (optional)	
3 c.	Mayonnaise	Combine mayonnaise and seasonings.
2 T.	Lemon juice	
2 t.	Salt	Add to shrimp and vegetables. Mix lightly. Chill.
1 t.	Paprika	
2 t.	Mustard, prepared	Serve with No. 10 dipper in lettuce cup.

Notes:
1. If shrimp are small, they may be left whole.
2. 1 doz. hard-cooked eggs, coarsely chopped, may be added; reduce shrimp to 5 lb.
3. May be garnished with tomato wedges or served in a tomato cup.

Shrimp-Rice Salad

Yield: 50 4–5 oz. portions

Amount	Ingredient	Method
1 lb.	Rice, long grain	Cook rice (p. 309).
1¼ qt.	Water	Chill.
1 T.	Salt	
5 lb. (E.P.)	Shrimp, cooked, chilled	Combine cooked rice, shrimp, celery, and green peppers.
1 lb. 8 oz.	Celery, sliced crosswise, thin	
1 lb.	Green peppers, sliced in thin strips	
1 c.	Vinegar	Combine seasonings.
½ c.	Salad oil	Pour over shrimp–rice mixture.
2 T.	Worcestershire sauce	Marinate at least 3 hr.
2 T.	Sugar	Just before serving, add pineapple tidbits.
1 T.	Salt	Serve with No. 8 dipper on lettuce leaf.
2 t.	Curry powder	
¾ t.	Ginger	
½ t.	Black pepper	
3 lb. (3 No. 2½ cans)	Pineapple tidbits, drained	

Crab Salad

Yield: 4¼ qt.
Portion: ⅓ c.

Amount	Ingredient	Method
10 6½-oz. cans	Crab, coarsely flaked (or 4 lb. fresh or frozen crab meat)	Combine ingredients lightly. Chill. Serve with No. 10 dipper.
⅓ c.	Lemon juice	
30	Eggs, hard-cooked, chopped	
1 pt.	Ripe olives, sliced	
1 lb.	Almonds, blanched, slivered (optional)	
1 qt.	Mayonnaise	

Notes:
1. Olives may be deleted and 1–1½ lb. diced cucumbers added.
2. If desired, omit mayonnaise and marinate with French Dressing (p. 350).
Variation:
Lobster Salad. Substitute lobster for crab.

Tuna Salad

Yield: 6¼ qt.
Portion: ½ c.

Amount	Ingredient	Method
8 lb.	Tuna, flaked	Combine ingredients lightly.
1 lb. 8 oz.	Celery, chopped fine	Chill. Serve with No. 10 dipper.
1 lb. 8 oz.	Cucumber, diced	
12	Eggs, hard-cooked, chopped	
1 c.	Sweet pickle, chopped	
1 qt.	Mayonnaise	

Variations:
1. *Tuna–Apple Salad.* Substitute tart, diced apples for cucumbers.
2. *Salmon Salad.* Substitute salmon for tuna.

Macaroni Salad

Yield: 1 gal.
Portion: ⅓ c.

Amount	Ingredient	Method
2 lb. 8 oz.	Macaroni, elbow	Cook macaroni (p. 311). Drain. Chill.
2 lb.	Cheddar cheese, diced or shredded	Add remaining ingredients. Mix lightly.
1 lb. 8 oz.	Sweet pickle, chopped (or pickle relish)	Chill Serve with No. 12 dipper.
18	Eggs, hard-cooked, chopped	
2 lb.	Celery, chopped fine	
1½ T.	Salt	
1 qt.	Mayonnaise	

Note:
Spaghetti or shell macaroni may be substituted for elbow macaroni.

Cottage Cheese Salad

Yield: 1 gal.
Portion: ⅓ c.

Amount	Ingredient	Method
6 lb.	Cottage cheese, dry	Combine ingredients lightly.
3 lb.	Tomatoes, peeled, diced	Chill.
		Serve with No. 12 dipper.
4 oz.	Green peppers, chopped	
1 lb.	Celery, diced	
1 lb.	Cucumber, diced	
8 oz.	Radishes, diced	
3 T.	Salt	
1½ pt.	Mayonnaise (use less if cheese contains cream)	

Salad Plate Combinations

FRUIT

1. Cranberry ring mold, cantaloupe and watermelon balls in center; 3 slices honeydew melon cut ¾ in. thick; cluster of white grapes; Honey Fruit Dressing (p. 353); small rolled cinnamon bread sandwich; lettuce garnish.

2. Fiesta Fruit Plate: 3 pineapple chunks; ⅓ banana, cut in strips and rolled in cream dressing and chopped nuts; 4 grapefruit and 3 orange sections; ½ fresh pear. Garnish with avocado and lettuce. Fill fluted baking cup with No. 16 dipper of raspberry sherbet and place in center of plate as it is served. Serve with Ginger Muffins (p. 151).

3. Frozen Fruit Salad Mold (p. 322) in lettuce cup; pear half on thin slice of whole orange; peach half and large prune stuffed with cream cheese; finger (chicken) sandwich. Garnish with parsley or mint.

4. Two honeydew melon sections; small cluster of red grapes; peach half, rounded side up, ½ orange, thinly sliced; pineapple spears; ⅓ c. fresh strawberries; raisin bread and cream cheese sandwich, cut into thirds; watercress garnish.

5. Cottage cheese, No. 12 dipper; peach half with Royal Cranberry Sauce (p. 343) in center; ½ banana with dressing and chopped nut garnish; 2 figs; pineapple ring; lettuce garnish; All-Bran Muffin (p. 102).

6. Cottage cheese, No. 12 dipper; grapefruit and orange sections; Apple Salad (p. 320), topped with ½ red maraschino cherry; Celery Seed Dressing (p. 352); Nut Bread Sandwiches (p. 109), 2-in. squares cut diagonally.

MEAT, FISH, POULTRY, AND EGGS
1. Baked pullman-style ham, 2 1½-in. slices rolled; 2 tomato slices in lettuce cup; ½ deviled egg, ripe olive garnish. Small hard roll.
2. Baked Ham, 2 2½-oz. slices; Potato Salad, No. 12 dipper, in lettuce cup; green pepper ring; ½ hard cooked egg; carrot and celery strips.
3. Baked Ham, 2½-oz slice; ½ cubed banana, dipped in Whipped Cream Dressing; peach half with cream cheese center; 1 Italian prune; lettuce and parsley garnish. Toasted English Muffin.
4. Cold sliced turkey and baked ham sliced, 2½ oz. each; Bing Cherry Gelatin Mold (p. 335) in lettuce cup; cheese stuffed celery; carrot curls. Banana Nut Bread (p. 110) sandwich strips.
5. Cold roast pork, 2½-oz. slice; Applesauce Mold (p. 332); Potato Salad, No. 12 dipper; radish roses and lettuce garnish.
6. Cold roast beef, 2 oz. slice; Macaroni Salad (p. 340), No. 12 dipper, with green pepper ring; sliced tomatoes, 3 oz.; cucumber slices, 1½ oz.; lettuce garnish.
7. Cold cuts, 2 oz., American Cheese, 1 oz.; Three Bean Salad (p. 330), No. 12 dipper; lettuce wedge, ⅛ head; cucumber slices, 1½ oz.; lettuce garnish.
8. Tuna Salad (p. 340), No. 12 dipper, stuffed olive garnish; pineapple ring topped with a No. 16 dipper Waldorf Salad (p. 320), ½ maraschino cherry; potato chips, ¾ oz.; lettuce and parsley garnish.
9. Deviled egg, 2 halves; chilled canned salmon, 2 oz.; potato chips; lemon wedge, curly endive garnish.
10. Egg Salad (p. 365), No. 12 dipper; 2 tomato wedges, 2 oz. each; ripe olive garnish; 3 asparagus spears; Cucumber Butter Sandwich strips (p. 362); lettuce garnish.
11. Avocado half filled with chicken or shrimp salad, No. 12 dipper; spiced peach, sliced tomatoes, lettuce garnish.

Relishes

Cranberry Relish (Raw)

Yield: 1 gal.

Portion: ¼ c.

Amount	Ingredient	Method
4 (size 72)	Oranges, unpeeled	Grind fruit.
4 lb.	Cranberries, raw	
6 lb.	Apples, cored	
3 lb.	Sugar	Add sugar and blend. Chill 24 hr. Serve with No. 16 dipper as a relish or salad. If using as a salad, drain before serving.

Cranberry Sauce

Yield: 1 gal.
Portion: ¼ c.

Amount	Ingredient	Method
4 lb.	Cranberries	Wash cranberries. Discard soft berries.
4 lb.	Sugar	
1 qt.	Water	Add sugar and water. Cover, boil gently until skins burst. Do not overcook.
		Serve with No. 16 dipper.

Note:
Make sauce at least 24 hr. before using. Cranberries may be puréed before adding sugar.
Variation:
Whole Cranberry Sauce. Make sirup of sugar and 2 qt. water. Boil 10 min., add cranberries, cover and boil until skins burst.

Royal Cranberry Sauce

Yield: 1 gal.
Portion: 2½ T.

Amount	Ingredient	Method
2 lb.	Cranberries	Wash cranberries. Discard soft berries.
2 lb.	Sugar	
1 pt.	Water, hot	Add sugar and hot water to cranberries. Cover and simmer until tender. Cool.
2 (size 72)	Oranges, chopped	When cool, add remaining ingredients.
1 lb.	Apples, tart, chopped	
1 lb.	White grapes, seeded	Serve with No. 24 dipper as a relish.
1 lb.	Pineapple, diced	
4 oz.	Pecans, chopped	

Note:
The sauce will keep for several weeks if placed in a covered jar in a refrigerator.

Buttered Apples

Yield: 7 qt.
Portion: ½ c.

Amount	Ingredient	Method
13 lb. (E.P.)	Apples	Cut apples into sections. Remove cores. Arrange in pan.
8 oz.	Butter or margarine	Mix remaining ingredients. Pour over apples.
1 pt.	Water, hot	Cover and simmer until apples are tender, approximately 1 hr.
1 lb. 8 oz.	Sugar	
1½ T.	Salt	

Notes:
1. A more attractive product is obtained if apple sections are arranged in a serving pan and steamed until tender, butter or margarine and sugar sprinkled over the top, and then baked for 15–20 min.
2. Hot buttered apples often are served in place of a vegetable.

Variations:
1. *Cinnamon Apples.* Cut apples into rings. Add cinnamon drops (redhots) for flavor and color.
2. *Apple Rings.* Cut rings of unpared apples, steam until tender, add sugar and butter or margarine and bake 15 min.

Cabbage Relish

Yield: 1 gal.
Portion: ⅓ c.

Amount	Ingredient	Method
6 lb.	Cabbage	Grind or shred vegetables.
9 oz.	Green peppers	
1 lb. 12 oz.	Carrots	
1 qt.	Cultured sour cream	Combine remaining ingredients. Add to vegetables and mix lightly. Serve with No. 12 dipper.
2 T.	Salt	
9 oz.	Sugar	
1 c.	Vinegar	

Variation:
Cucumber Relish. Substitute 8 lb. finely diced cucumber for cabbage, carrots, and peppers. Season with salt, pepper, and lemon juice. Fold in sour cream and chill. Serve in lettuce cup; garnish with thin slice of red radish or sprig of parsley.

Beet Relish

Yield: 3 qt.
Portion: 1 T.

Amount	Ingredient	Method
1 qt. (2 No. 2½ cans)	Beets, cooked, chopped	Combine beets and cabbage.
12 oz.	Cabbage, raw, shredded	
1 lb.	Sugar	Mix remaining ingredients and add to vegetables.
1 t.	Salt	Chill 24 hr.
1 c.	Horseradish	Serve with No. 60 dipper as a relish with meat.
4 oz.	Onion, chopped fine	
2 c.	Vinegar	

Pickled Beets

Yield: 2 gal.
Portion: ⅓ c.

Amount	Ingredient	Method
2 qt.	Vinegar, mild	Mix vinegar, sugar, and spices.
1 lb.	Brown sugar	Heat to boiling point. Boil 5 min.
8 oz.	Sugar	
1 t.	Salt	
½ t.	Pepper	
1 t.	Cinnamon	
1 t.	Cloves	
1 t.	Allspice	
10 lb. (E.P.) or 2 No. 10 cans	Beets, cooked, sliced	Pour hot, spiced vinegar over beets. Chill.

Note:
Add onion rings if desired.

SALAD DRESSINGS

Mayonnaise

Yield: 1 gal.

Amount	Ingredient	Method
8 (or 4 whole eggs)	Egg yolks	Place egg yolks, salt, paprika, and mustard in mixer bowl. Mix well.
3 T.	Salt	
2 t.	Paprika	
2 T.	Mustard, dry	
¼ c.	Vinegar	Add vinegar and blend.
2 qt.	Salad oil	Add oil very slowly, beating steadily (high speed) until an emulsion is formed. Oil may then be added, ½ c. at a time (and later 1 c. at a time), beating well after each addition.
¼ c.	Vinegar	Add vinegar after the 2 qt. of oil have been added. Beat well.
2 qt.	Salad oil	Continue beating and adding oil until all oil has been added and emulsified.

Note:
The addition of oil too rapidly or insufficient beating may cause the oil to separate from the other ingredients, resulting in a curdled appearance. Curdled, or broken mayonnaise, may be reformed by adding it (a small amount at a time and beating well after each addition) to 2 well-beaten eggs or egg yolks. It also may be reformed by adding it to a small portion of good mayonnaise.

Mayonnaise with Cooked Base

Yield: 3 gal.

Amount	Ingredient	Method
1 lb. 2 c. 2 qt.	Cornstarch Water, cold Water, boiling	Mix cornstarch and water to a smooth paste. Add boiling water, stirring vigorously with a wire whip. Cook until mixture is clear. Pour into mixer bowl. Beat until cool.
20 (or 12 whole eggs)	Egg yolks	Add eggs, ¼ at a time, while beating (high speed).
3 T. ¼ c. 2 t. 2 c.	Salt Mustard, dry Paprika Vinegar	Add seasonings. Mix well. Add vinegar.
1 gal.	Salad oil	Gradually add oil, 1 c. at a time. Beat well (high speed) after each addition. (See Mayonnaise recipe, p. 347.)
2 c. 1 gal.	Vinegar Salad oil	Add vinegar, then add oil slowly, beating constantly.

VARIATIONS OF MAYONNAISE

Blue Cheese Dressing. Mix 6 oz. blue cheese with 3 c. Mayonnaise and ¼ c. cream or milk. Add a few drops Tabasco sauce.

Campus Dressing. Combine 3 T. chopped parsley, 2 T. chopped green pepper, and ¼ c. finely chopped celery with 1 qt. Mayonnaise.

Chantilly Dressing. Whip ¾ c. heavy cream and fold in 3 c. Mayonnaise.

Combination. Combine 2 c. Mayonnaise and 2 c. cooked Salad Dressing.

Cranberry Dressing. Blend 2½ c. Mayonnaise and 2 c. jellied cranberries, beaten until smooth. Fold in 1 c. whipped cream just before serving.

Egg Dressing. Chop 4 hard-cooked eggs and combine with 1 qt. Mayonnaise.

Egg and Green Pepper Dressing. Combine 6 chopped, hard-cooked eggs, 2 T. finely chopped green pepper, 1 T. onion juice, and a few grains cayenne with 3½ c. Mayonnaise.

Garden Dressing. Add 1 qt. cultured sour cream, ¼ c. sugar, 1 T. salt, f.g. pepper, 1 c. minced green onion, 1 c. sliced radishes, 1 c. chopped cucumber, 1 c. minced green peppers to 2 c. Mayonnaise.

Honey-Cream Dressing. Blend 1 oz. cream cheese, ⅔ c. strained honey, ¼ c. lemon or pineapple juice, ¼ t. salt. Fold in 3½ c. Mayonnaise.

Roquefort Dressing. Add 1 c. French Dressing, 4 oz. Roquefort cheese, and
1 t. Worcestershire sauce to 3 c. Mayonnaise.

Russian Dressing. Add 1 c. chili sauce, 1 T. Worcestershire sauce, 1 t. onion
juice, f.g. cayenne to 1 qt. Mayonnaise.

Sour Cream–Roquefort Dressing. Add 1 c. cultured sour cream, 2 T. lemon
juice, 2 t. grated onion, ½ t. salt, 4 oz. Roquefort cheese, crumbled fine, to
2 c. Mayonnaise.

Thousand Island Dressing. Add 1½ oz. minced onion, 3 oz. chopped pimiento,
1¾ c. chili sauce, 10 chopped hard-cooked eggs, 1 t. salt, ½ c. chopped
pickles or olives, f.g. cayenne to 7 c. Mayonnaise.

Whipped Cream Dressing. Add 1 pt. cream, whipped, to 1 qt. Mayonnaise.

Cooked Salad Dressing

Yield: 3 gal.

Amount	Ingredient	Method
3 lb.	Sugar	Combine dry ingredients.
1 lb. 8 oz.	Flour	Add water and stir until a smooth
6 oz.	Salt	paste is formed.
3 oz.	Mustard, dry	
1 qt.	Water	
1 gal.	Milk, hot	Add hot milk and water, stirring
2 qt.	Water, hot	continuously while adding.
		Cook 20 min., or until thickened.
1 lb.	Butter or mar-garine	Add butter or margarine and vinegar.
3 qt.	Vinegar, hot	
50 (2 lb. 12 oz.)	Egg yolks, beaten	Add cooked mixture slowly to egg yolks, stirring briskly. Cook 7–10 min.
		Remove from heat and cool.

Note:
25 whole eggs may be substituted for egg yolks, and hot water for hot milk.

Variations:
1. *Combination Dressing.* Combine 2 c. Cooked Salad Dressing and 2 c. Mayonnaise (p. 347).
2. *Egg Dressing.* Add 4 chopped hard-cooked eggs, ½ c. chopped pimiento,
   and ¼ c. chopped pickles to 1 qt. Cooked Dressing.
3. *Whipped Cream Dressing.* Add 1 pt. cream, whipped to 1 qt. Cooked Salad
   Dressing.

French Dressing

Yield: 3 qt.

Amount	Ingredient	Method
3 T.	Salt	Combine dry ingredients in mixer bowl.
2 T.	Mustard, dry	
2 T.	Paprika	
1 T.	Pepper	
2 qt.	Oil	Add oil, vinegar, and onion juice. Beat (high speed) until thick and blended.
1 qt.	Vinegar	
4 t.	Onion juice	This is a temporary emulsion which separates rapidly. Beat well or pour into a jar and shake vigorously just before serving.

Note:
An egg white beaten into each quart of dressing just before using will keep it from separating.

Variations:
1. *California Dressing.* Add 2 c. mashed avocado, 2 T. lemon juice, and 1 t. salt to 3 c. French Dressing.
2. *Catsup Dressing.* Blend 1 c. catsup with 3 c. French Dressing.
3. *Chiffonade Dressing.* Add 4 t. chopped parsley, 1 oz. chopped red pepper or pimiento, 1 oz. chopped onion, 1½ oz. chopped green pepper, and 4 chopped hard-cooked eggs to 3 c. French Dressing.
4. *Mexican Dressing.* Add 2½ oz. chopped green pepper, ¾ c. chili sauce, and 1 oz. chopped onion to 3 c. French Dressing.
5. *Piquante Dressing.* Add 2 t. mustard, ½ t. Worcestershire sauce, 2 t. onion juice to 1 qt. French Dressing.
6. *Roquefort Cheese Dressing.* Add slowly, 3 c. French Dressing to 4 oz. Roquefort cheese, finely crumbled. Whip dressing slowly into cheese. You may also mix 1 c. heavy cream with cheese before adding French Dressing.
7. *Tomato Dressing.* Add 4 oz. sugar, 1 t. onion juice, and 1½ c. tomato soup to 3 c. French Dressing.
8. *Vinaigrette Dressing.* Add ¾ c. chopped pickle, ½ c. chopped green olives, 6 T. chopped parsley, 1 t. onion juice, 2 T. capers, to 3 c. French Dressing.

Thick French Dressing

Yield: 1½ qt.

Amount	Ingredient	Method
2 lb.	Sugar	Combine sugar and seasonings in
2 T.	Paprika	mixer bowl.
4 t.	Mustard, dry	
2 T.	Salt	
1½ t.	Onion juice	
1⅓ c.	Vinegar	Add vinegar. Mix well.
1 qt.	Salad oil	Gradually add oil in small amounts. Beat well after each addition.

Note:
If a dressing of the usual consistency is desired, use only 8 oz. sugar.
Variations:
1. *Poppy Seed Dressing.* Add ½ c. poppy seed.
2. *Celery Seed Dressing.* Add ½ c. celery seed.

French Dressing, Semipermanent

Yield: 1¼ qt.

Amount	Ingredient	Method
4 t.	Gelatin, plain	Soften gelatin in cold water.
4 T.	Water, cold	Dissolve in boiling water.
½ c.	Water, boiling	Chill.
4 t.	Mustard, dry	Mix dry ingredients in mixer bowl.
4 t.	Paprika	
3 T.	Sugar	
f.g.	Red pepper	
2 T.	Salt	
1 qt.	Salad oil	Add oil slowly while beating (high speed).
1 c.	Vinegar	Add vinegar slowly. Beat (high speed) 5 min. Add gelatin.

Celery Seed Fruit Dressing

Yield: 2 qt.

Amount	Ingredient	Method
1 lb. 8 oz.	Sugar	Mix dry ingredients.
⅓ c.	Cornstarch	Add vinegar. Cook until thickened
2 T.	Mustard, dry	and clear.
2 T.	Salt	Cool to room temperature.
2 T.	Paprika	
2 c.	Vinegar	
1 t.	Onion juice	Add onion juice to cooked mixture.
1 qt.	Salad oil	Add oil slowly while beating (high speed).
2 T.	Celery seed	Add celery seed. Serve with any fruit salad combination.

Variation:
Poppy Seed Dressing. Add poppy seed in place of celery seed.

Sour Cream Dressing

Yield: 2 qt.

Amount	Ingredient	Method
16	Eggs, beaten	Mix eggs and sour cream.
1 qt.	Cultured sour cream	
2 lb.	Sugar	Mix sugar, flour, and water until smooth.
1½ oz.	Flour	
1 c.	Water	Add to the cream and egg mixture.
1 pt.	Vinegar	Add vinegar. Cook until thick. Stir as necessary.

Notes:
1. Dressing may be stored several days in refrigerator.
2. 1 pint cream, whipped, may be added before serving.
Variation:
Sweet-Sour Cream Dressing. Combine 1 qt. cultured sour cream, ½ c. sugar, 2 t. salt, and ½ c. vinegar. May be combined with shredded cabbage or served over tomatoes, cucumbers, or any fruit combination.

Fruit Salad Dressing

Yield: 5 qt.

Amount	Ingredient	Method
1 qt. 1½ pt. 1 pt.	Pineapple juice Orange juice Lemon juice	Heat juices to boiling point.
2 lb. 5 oz. 16	Sugar Cornstarch Eggs, well beaten	Mix sugar and cornstarch. Add to hot mixture while stirring with a wire whip. Add eggs. Cook until thickened.
1 pt.	Whipping cream	Whip cream and fold in just before serving. Serve with fruit salads.

Honey French Dressing

Yield: 2 qt.

Amount	Ingredient	Method
4 t. 1 t. 4 t.	Dry mustard Salt Celery seed or poppy seed	Mix mustard, salt, and celery seed in large mixing bowl.
2 c. 1¼ c. ¼ c. 1 T. 1 qt.	Honey Vinegar Lemon juice Grated lemon Salad oil	While mixing, add remaining ingredients in given order. Pour into covered jar. Refrigerate.

Chilean Dressing

Yield: 1½ qt.

Amount	Ingredient	Method
1 pt. 1 c. 4 oz. 2 t. 4 T. 1 pt. 1 c.	Salad oil Vinegar Sugar Salt Onion, chopped fine Chili sauce Catsup	Combine all ingredients. Beat (low speed) until well blended. Store in covered container. Shake or beat well before serving.

SANDWICHES

Sandwiches may be hearty and substantial, approximating a meal, or light and dainty, as an accompaniment to tea. They are made of one or more slices of bread, spread with one or more kinds of filling. The closed sandwich is made by spreading one slice of bread with a filling and covering it with a second slice. The open-faced sandwich is made by spreading a slice of bread with filling and decorating it.

Sandwich Ingredients

1. *Bread.* Bread is used in sandwiches to provide a variety of color, flavor, texture, and shape. Cracked wheat, graham, whole wheat, white, rye, pumpernickel, French, Italian, or Boston Brown bread are most often used for the substantial type of sandwich. Hamburger, frankfurter, hard, and soft rolls, submarine, or Vienna buns also are popular for hearty sandwiches. Tea sandwiches are made from white or whole wheat bread, or from nut, orange, raisin, date, banana, or cranberry bread.

A Pullman or sandwich loaf is used for most sandwiches. The bread should be sliced ⅛- to ¼-in. thick, depending on the type of sandwich to be made.

2. *Butter or Margarine.* Butter or margarine should be softened or whipped for easy spreading. To whip butter, place in mixer bowl and allow to stand at room temperature until soft enough to mix. A half cup of milk or boiling water per pound of butter may be added gradually while whipping to increase the volume. Mix first on low speed and then whip on second and high speed until fluffy. A savory spread for meat and fish sandwiches may be made by adding minced cucumber, spices, onion, prepared mustard, chopped chives, parsley, or pimiento to the whipped butter. Butter or margarine need not always be used on sandwiches when a rich filling is used. However, butter helps to prevent fillings from soaking into the bread and improves the flavor. 8 oz. butter or margarine or 1 c. mayonnaise should spread one side of 50 sandwiches.

3. *Fillings.* Sandwich filling may be made of chopped meats, poultry,

355

fish, cheese, vegetables, jellies, nuts, or fruits. One of these ingredients or a combination of them is usually mixed with mayonnaise, salad dressing, or cream.

Soft mixed fillings should be measured with a spoon or small dipper to insure a uniform amount in each sandwich.

If slices of meat or cheese are used for filling, the slices should be even in thickness and the same size as the bread upon which they are to be placed. One to 2 oz. very thin sliced meat give greater volume and may be more tender than one thick slice.

4. *Garnishes.* The garnishes to be used depend upon the type of sandwich. Lettuce, parsley, watercress, and other salad greens, olives, pickles, pimiento, green peppers, radishes, nuts, paprika, and cheese are often used as garnishes for various types of sandwiches (p. 363).

Making Sandwiches

PLAIN SANDWICHES
1. Have filling, garnish, and butter prepared.
2. Arrange fresh bread in rows, preferably 4 rows of 10 slices each.
3. Spread all bread slices out to the edges with softened butter or margarine.
4. Portion filling with dipper or spoon on alternate rows of bread and spread to the edges or arrange sliced filling to fit sandwich.
5. If lettuce is used, arrange leaves on filling.
6. Place plain buttered slices of bread on the filled slices.
7. Stack several sandwiches together and cut with a sharp knife.
8. To keep sandwiches fresh, place in sandwich bags or waxed paper. Or place sandwiches in storage pans on damp towel covered with waxed paper and cover completely with more waxed paper and a damp towel.
9. Refrigerate until serving time.

Simple sandwiches may be made more attractive by cutting into rounds, triangles, or small squares.

TEA SANDWICHES
Checkerboard Sandwiches (Fig. 12):
Use whole wheat and white bread, cut about ½ in. thick, and desired filling.
Ribbon Sandwiches (Fig. 13):
Rolled Sandwiches (Pinwheels) (Fig. 14):
Use unsliced Pullman bread. See Fig. 14 for directions.

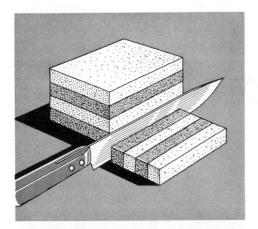

(a) For each stack, alternate 2 slices whole wheat and 2 slices enriched white bread, filling with desired spread.

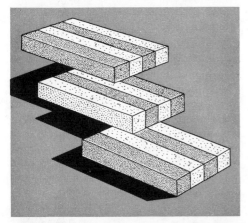

(b) Cut each stack in ½-in. slices. Then put 3 alternating slices together as shown, using a "butter" or spread as filling.

(c) Chill for several hours. Remove from refrigerator, and with sharp knife immediately slice into checkerboard slices, ½ in. thick. (Courtesy Good Housekeeping Institute, "Sandwich Manual," 1951.)

Fig. 12. Checkerboards

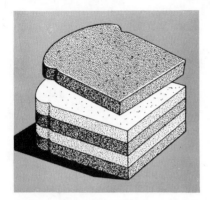

(a) Using fresh or day-old bread, stack alternately 3 slices whole wheat and 2 enriched white bread, filling with one or more spreads (pp. 362–363).

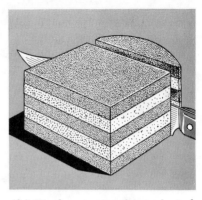

(b) Firmly press together each stack of slices. Then with sharp knife, using a sawing motion, slice crusts from all sides of each stack.

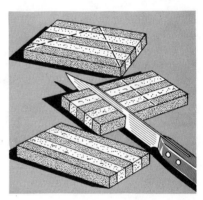

(c) Arrange stacks in shallow pan; cover with waxed paper and moist cloth. Chill for several hours. Cut in ½-in. slices. (d) Cut each slice into thirds, halves, or triangles, as shown above. Arrange on plates. (Courtesy Good Housekeeping Institute, "Sandwich Manual," 1951).

Fig. 13.   Ribbon Sandwiches

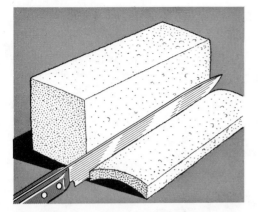

(a) Place loaf of fresh or day-old unsliced, enriched white bread on cutting board; then with long, sharp knife (or bread knife) slice off all crusts except bottom one.

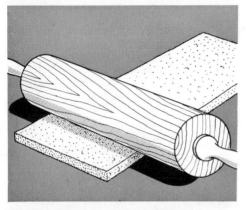

(b) With crust side of loaf to the left, cut into lengthwise slices, ⅛ to ¼ in. thick, as shown above. Now run rolling pin over each slice, starting at narrow end. This makes the bread easy to handle, less likely to crack.

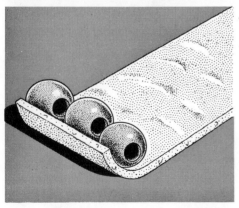

(c) Spread each slice to the edge with softened butter or margarine; then cover with one of the spreads on p. 362. If desired, place 3 stuffed olives or gherkins, a frankfurter, or 2 Vienna sausages across short end.

Fig. 14.   Rolled Sandwiches (Pinwheels).

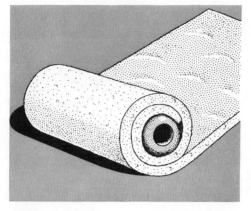

(d) Starting at the end with the stuffed olives or other filler mentioned above, roll up each slice tightly as for a jelly roll, being careful to keep sides in line. Tight rolling makes for easier slicing and neat pinwheels with distinct markings.

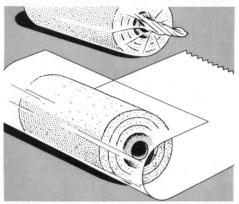

(e) Wrap rolls individually in waxed paper or aluminum foil, twisting ends securely. Chill several hours or overnight. Rolls may be made ahead of time, then wrapped and frozen. Let thaw for about 45 min. before slicing.

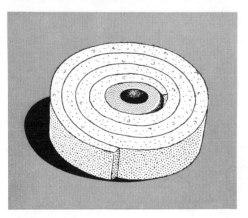

(f) Cut chilled rolls into ¼–½-in. slices. Lift with broad spatula onto serving plate or trays. Cover with waxed paper, then moist cloth, and chill for use later. May be toasted just before serving. (Courtesy Good Housekeeping Institute, "Sandwich Manual," 1951.)

Open Sandwiches

Cut slices of bread ¼ in. thick into rounds, hearts, stars, diamonds, crescents, squares, or any desired shape. Spread with creamed butter, then with filling, and decorate. The filling may be ham and sliced cheese, chicken, tuna, shrimp, lobster, or crab salad, or other fillings (p. 362). Open sandwiches may be decorated with a variety of garnishes (p. 356) such as parsley, sliced olives, sliced radishes, pickles, nuts, and pimiento. A few suggestions for open sandwiches follow:

1. Place a thin slice of tomato on a round of buttered bread. Garnish with mayonnaise and a sprig of parsley, or butter the edges of the bread and roll in chopped parsley.

2. Spread bread cut into diamond shapes with butter and cream cheese. Garnish with pimiento or green peppers.

3. Place thin slices of American cheese on crisp crackers. Add a dash of salt and pepper and place under the broiler until the cheese has melted. Garnish with paprika and serve hot.

4. Spread bread cut in heart shapes with a mixture of chopped almonds, maraschino cherries, and whipped cream.

5. Mix chopped walnuts, candied ginger, and mayonnaise. Cut bread into tiny squares and garnish with a half walnut and bit of paprika.

6. Mix ground American cheese, butter, lemon juice, Worcestershire sauce, paprika, cayenne, and onion juice. Spread on rounds of rye bread. Garnish with stuffed olive slices.

For additional sandwich spreads, see pp. 362-363.

FREEZING SANDWICHES

When making sandwiches to be frozen for later use, certain precautions need to be taken. Bread should be spread with butter or margarine, rather than mayonnaise or salad dressing. Fillings such as minced chicken, meat, egg yolks, fish, or peanut butter freeze well, but sliced cooked eggs and some vegetables, such as tomatoes and parsley, should not be frozen.

Wrap large closed sandwiches individually. Pack tea-sized closed sandwiches in layers in freezer boxes; or place in any suitable box and over-wrap with moisture vapor-proof material. Place open-faced sandwiches on cardboard or trays, wrap as for closed sandwiches. Wrap ribbon, rolled or other loaf sandwiches, uncut.

Sandwiches will thaw in 1–2 hr., shorter for open-face. Outer wrapping should not be removed until sandwiches are partly thawed. If sandwiches are not served immediately after thawing, they should be held in the refrigerator until serving time.

GRILLED AND TOASTED SANDWICHES

Many ingredients may be combined to make suitable fillings for toasted or grilled sandwiches. For a grilled sandwich, the filling is placed between 2 slices of bread, the outside is brushed with butter or margarine, and the sandwich is browned on the grill, in a hot oven, or under a broiler. Fillings for a grilled sandwich may include cheese, meat, fish, or poultry salads, or a combination of fillings, as in a Reuben sandwich.

Bread for toasted sandwiches may be toasted before or after filling is added, although a crisp ingredient like lettuce is added after the sandwich is toasted. Toasted sandwiches may be either closed or open faced. A few suggestions for toasted sandwiches follow:

1. Thinly sliced tomato, broiled bacon, lettuce, and salad dressing.
2. Chicken livers, mashed, crisp bacon, and salad dressing.
3. Sliced cheese, sliced ham, and prepared mustard.
4. Sliced cheese, tomato, and mayonnaise.
5. Sliced corned beef, Swiss cheese, lettuce, on rye bread.
6. Meat, fish, or poultry salads.

Sandwich Filling Suggestions

1. Dates, figs, raisins, orange, ground.
2. Peanut butter and Cheddar cheese, mixed.
3. Hard-cooked eggs and olives, chopped, grated cheese and mayonnaise, mixed.
4. Sliced cold boiled tongue and mayonnaise.
5. Cucumber, chopped and mixed with creamed butter.
6. Dates, lemon juice, and nuts, minced.
7. Sliced tomato and mayonnaise.
8. Cream cheese, minced dried beef, mixed with mayonnaise and seasoned with horseradish, grated onion, and mustard.
9. Cream cheese and chopped chives.
10. Cream cheese, chopped preserved ginger, mixed.
11. Cabbage and carrot, chopped fine, mixed with salad dressing.
12. Grated carrots, chopped nuts, and mayonnaise, mixed.
13. Cottage cheese and chopped green onions on rye bread.

Sandwich Recipes

Sandwich Spread

Amount	Ingredient	Method
1 lb.	Butter or margarine	Whip butter or margarine (high speed) until fluffy.
½ c.	Light cream	Add cream.
1 T.	Mustard	Fold in remaining ingredients.
1½ qt.	Mayonnaise	Use as a spread for a meat or cheese
1 c.	Pickle relish	sandwich.

Chicken Salad Sandwiches

Yield: 50 sandwiches

Amount	Ingredient	Method
4 lb.	Cooked chicken, chopped	Combine filling ingredients.
4 oz.	Almonds, chopped, toasted	
2 t.	Salt	
8 oz.	Celery, chopped fine	
¼ c.	Vinegar	
1 c.	Mayonnaise	
100 slices	Bread	Portion filling with No. 24 dipper.
2–3 heads	Lettuce	Assemble filling, bread, and lettuce (p. 356).

Tuna Salad Sandwiches

Yield: 50 sandwiches

Amount	Ingredient	Method
4 lb.	Tuna, flaked	Combine filling ingredients.
6	Eggs, hard-cooked	
¼ c.	Lemon juice	
1 t.	Onion juice	
1 c.	Mayonnaise	
1 c.	Cooked Salad Dressing (p. 349)	
100 slices	Bread	Portion filling with No. 20 dipper.
2–3 heads	Lettuce	Assemble filling, bread, and lettuce (p. 356).

Note:
1 c. chopped pickle may be added.

Meat Salad Sandwiches

Yield: 50 sandwiches

Amount	Ingredient	Method
4 lb.	Meat, cooked, finely chopped	Combine filling ingredients.
4 oz.	Celery, chopped fine	
8 oz.	Olives or pickles, chopped	
1 c.	Mayonnaise	
1 c.	Cooked Salad Dressing (p. 349)	
¼ c.	Vinegar	
1 t.	Salt	
100 slices	Bread	Portion filling with No. 20 dipper.
2–3 heads	Lettuce	Assemble filling, bread, and lettuce (p. 356).

Ham Salad Sandwiches

Yield: 50 sandwiches

Amount	Ingredient	Method
4 lb.	Ham, cooked, coarsely ground	Combine filling ingredients.
8 oz.	Pickles, chopped	
2 oz.	Pimiento, chopped	
1 c.	Mayonnaise	
1 c.	Cooked Salad Dressing (p. 349)	
100 slices	Bread	Portion filling with No. 20 dipper.
2–3 heads	Lettuce	Assemble filling, bread, and lettuce (p. 356).

Note:
6 hard-cooked eggs, chopped, may be added.

Egg Salad Sandwiches

Yield: 50 sandwiches

Amount	Ingredient	Method
3 doz.	Eggs, hard-cooked, chopped	Combine filling ingredients.
2 c.	Mayonnaise	
2 c.	Pickle relish	
2 t.	Salt	
½ c.	Pimiento, chopped	
100 slices	Bread	Portion filling with No. 24 dipper.
2–3 heads	Lettuce	Assemble filling, bread, and lettuce (p. 356).

Submarine Sandwiches

Yield: 50 sandwiches

Amount	Ingredient	Method
50	Submarine or Vienna buns	Split buns, leaving hinged.
½ lb.	Butter or margarine	Whip butter until fluffy.
¼ c.	Light cream	Add cream.
3 c.	Mayonnaise	Lightly blend in remaining ingredients.
¼ c.	Mustard, prepared	
½ c.	Pickle relish	Spread on open sides of buns.
1 lb. 12 oz.	Salami, ½-oz. slices	Arrange on each bun ½ oz. each of 3 kinds of meat, 2½-oz. triangles of cheese, 2 slices of tomato, and 2 slices of dill pickle.
1 lb. 12 oz.	Spiced ham, ½-oz. slices	
1 lb. 12 oz.	Ham, pullman, ½-oz. slices	
3 lb. 2 oz.	American cheese, 1-oz. slices cut diagonally	
2 doz. medium	Tomatoes, fresh, sliced	
1 qt.	Dill pickle slices, well drained	

Note:
Other meats, as turkey, ham, corned beef, or pork may be used.

Bacon and Tomato Sandwiches

Yield: 50 sandwiches

Amount	Ingredient	Method
4 lb. (100 slices)	Bacon	Cook bacon (p. 252).
100 slices	Bread	Spread 50 slices of bread with mayonnaise, place 2 cooked bacon slices, 2 thin slices of tomato, and a lettuce leaf on each.
1 c.	Mayonnaise	
8 oz.	Butter or margarine	
7 lb.	Tomatoes, sliced	
2–3 heads	Lettuce	Top with remaining 50 slices of bread, which have been spread with whipped butter or margarine.

Oven-Baked Hamburgers

Bake: 15–20 min.
Oven: 400° F.

Yield: 50 4-oz. portions

Amount	Ingredient	Method
12 lb.	Ground beef	Combine all ingredients.
3	Eggs, beaten	Measure with No. 10 dipper and flatten into patties.
2 c.	Milk	Place on lightly greased baking sheet. Bake.
2 c.	Bread crumbs, soft	
2 T.	Salt	
2 t.	Pepper	
4 oz.	Onion, chopped	
50	Hamburger buns	Serve patties on hot buns.

Variation:
Barbecued Hamburgers. Place browned hamburgers in baking pans. Pour Barbecue Sauce (p. 382) over patties. Cover with aluminum foil and bake 20–25 min.

Western Sandwiches

Yield: 50 4-oz. portions

Amount	Ingredient	Method
10 lb.	Ground beef	Brown beef and onion.
8 oz.	Onion, chopped	
1 qt.	Tomato purée	Add remaining ingredients.
2 T.	Salt	Simmer 20–30 min.
2 t.	Paprika	
2 t.	Dry mustard	
2 T.	Worcestershire sauce	
2 t.	Chili powder	
50	Hamburger buns	Serve with No. 10 dipper on buns.

Hot Meat Sandwiches

Yield: 50 sandwiches

Amount	Ingredient	Method
8 lb.	Roast beef or pork, cooked	Cut meat into thin slices. Place 2½ oz. meat on each slice
50 slices	Bread	of bread.
2½ qts.	Gravy (p. 389)	Cover with gravy.

Note:
Meat may be covered with additional slice of bread if desired. Then cover entire sandwich with gravy.

Variation:
Hot Turkey Sandwich. Substitute roast turkey or turkey roll for meat.

Reuben Sandwich

Yield: 50 sandwiches

Amount	Ingredient	Method
100 slices	Rye Bread	Spread No. 100 dipper (scant 2 t.) dressing on bread.
1 pt.	Thousand Island dressing, Mayonnaise, or Sandwich Spread (p. 363)	Place 1 oz. corned beef on bread. Place 2 T. sauerkraut on meat.
4 lb. (E.P.)	Corned beef, cooked, sliced thin	Place 1-oz. slice of cheese on sauerkraut.
1½ qt.	Sauerkraut, well drained	Cover with top slice of bread.
3 lb. 2 oz.	Swiss cheese, 1-oz. slices	
1 lb.	Butter or margarine, melted	Brush sandwich with melted butter or margarine. Grill.

Runza

Bake: 25–30 min.
Oven: 400° F.

Yield: 56 sandwiches

Amount	Ingredient	Method
DOUGH:		
1¼ oz.	Yeast, dry	Sprinkle yeast over water. Let stand 5 min.
2 qt.	Water, warm	
14 oz.	Sugar	Add sugar, salt, and flour.
1 oz. (1½ T.)	Salt	Beat (medium speed) until smooth.
2 lb. 6 oz.	Flour	
8	Eggs	Add eggs and shortening. Continue beating.
5 oz.	Shortening, melted	
5 lb. 8 oz.	Flour	Add flour (low speed) to make a soft dough. Knead 5 min. Cover and let rise until double. Punch down. Divide dough in 4–5 portions. Roll out. Cut into 4 × 6-in. rectangles (3 oz. dough). Place ⅔ c. (No. 6 dipper) filling on dough.

		Fold lengthwise and pinch edges of dough securely to seal. Place on baking sheet with sealed edges down. Bake 10 min.
1 2 T.	Egg yolk Water	Combine yolk and water. Remove runzas from oven. Brush with glaze. Return to oven for 15–20 min.

FILLING:

8 lb.	Ground beef	Brown and drain beef.
2 lb. 2 lb. 3 oz.	Cabbage Onion, chopped	Steam cabbage and onion until slightly underdone.
¼ c. 2 oz. 1 t. 1 t. 1 t. 2 t.	Worcestershire sauce Salt Pepper Savory Chili powder Seasoned salt	Add seasonings and vegetables to ground beef. Mix lightly.

Oven Picnic Buns

Bake: 20 min.   Yield: 50 buns
Oven: 325° F.   (2 ¾ oz. filling)

Amount	Ingredient	Method
3 lb. 2 lb.	Bologna, cubed Cheese, grated	Combine bologna and cheese.
2 c. 1 c. 1 c. ½ c. ¼ c. 2 t.	Pickle relish Chili sauce Mayonnaise Mustard, prepared Onion, grated Salt	Combine remaining ingredients. Mix lightly with bologna and cheese.
50	Sandwich buns	Fill split buns with mixture, using No. 16 dipper. Wrap each in foil (or place in 12 × 20 × 2-in. pan and cover securely with foil). Heat.

Hot Tuna Buns

Bake: 15–20 min.
Oven: 350° F.   Yield: 50 sandwiches

Amount	Ingredient	Method
4 lb.	Tuna	Combine all ingredients.
1 lb. 8 oz.	Cheddar cheese, shredded	
18	Eggs, hard-cooked, chopped	
½ c.	Green pepper, chopped	
¼ c.	Onion, chopped	
¾ c.	Stuffed olives, chopped	
¾ c.	Sweet pickle, chopped	
3 c.	Mayonnaise	
50	Hamburger or coney buns	Fill buns, using No. 16 dipper. Place in counter pan, cover with aluminum foil. Bake.

Variation:
Hot Luncheon Sandwiches. Substitute any ground prepared luncheon meat for tuna, omitting green pepper and olives, and adding ½ c. prepared mustard.

Hot Chipped Beef and Cheese Sandwiches

Bake: 3–5 min.   Yield: 50 sandwiches
Oven: 350° F.

Amount	Ingredient	Method
12 oz.	Butter or margarine	Make into Medium White Sauce, (p. 385).
1 oz.	Flour	
2 c.	Milk	
2 lb.	Beef, chipped, shredded	Add remaining ingredients. Cook 2 min.
¼ c.	Horseradish	
1 T.	Mustard	
50 slices	Bread, toasted and buttered	Place No. 30 dip of mixture on bread.
3 lb. 2 oz.	Cheddar cheese, sliced	Cover with 1 slice cheese. Bake.

Grilled Cheese Sandwiches

Yield: 50 sandwiches

Amount	Ingredient	Method
100 slices	Bread	Make sandwiches.
3 lb. 2 oz.	Cheese, 1-oz. slices	Brush both sides with butter or
1 lb.	Butter or margarine, melted	margarine.
		Grill on hot griddle until golden brown on both sides.

Notes:
1. Cheese may be ground and the following ingredients added to make a spread: 2 T. prepared mustard, ½ c. chili sauce, 1 c. mayonnaise.
2. Salad mixtures such as chicken, ham, tuna, and egg salad are satisfactory fillings for grilled sandwiches.

Variations:
1. *Toasted Cheese Sandwiches.* Assemble cheese sandwiches, place on greased baking sheet, and broil until brown. Invert on second greased baking sheet and broil on other side until brown.
2. *Oven-Baked Cheese Sandwiches.* Assemble cheese sandwiches and place on greased baking sheet. Cover with second greased baking sheet. Bake in 400° F. oven 10 min.
3. *French Fried Cheese Sandwiches.* Dip in batter (p. 69) and fry in deep fat 1–2 min. at 375° F.

Cheese Sandwiches

Yield: 50 sandwiches

Amount	Ingredient	Method
3 lb. 8 oz.	Cheese, ground	Combine filling ingredients.
1 pt.	Salad dressing or cream	
2 t.	Salt	
f.g.	Cayenne	
4 oz.	Butter or margarine	
100 slices	Bread	Portion filling with No. 24 dipper. Assemble filling and bread (p. 356).

Variation:
Pimiento Cheese Sandwiches. Add 1 c. chopped pimiento.

Peanut Sandwiches

Yield: 50 sandwiches

Amount	Ingredient	Method
2 lb.	Peanuts, shelled, ground	Mix peanuts and butter or margarine. Fold whipped cream and salt into mayonnaise.
6 oz.	Butter or margarine, soft	Combine with peanut butter.
1 c.	Cream, whipped	
1 c.	Mayonnaise	
1 T.	Salt	
100 slices	Bread, cracked wheat	Portion filling with No. 24 dipper. Assemble filling, bread, and lettuce (p. 356).
2 heads	Lettuce	

Variation:
Peanut Butter Sandwiches. Substitute 4 lb. peanut butter for peanuts. Omit cream.

SAUCES

Dessert Sauces

Butterscotch Sauce

Yield: 1¼ qt.

Amount	Ingredient	Method
1 lb.	Brown sugar	Combine sugar, sirup, and water.
1⅓ c.	Corn sirup	Cook to soft ball stage, (240° F.).
⅔ c.	Water	Remove from heat.
6 oz.	Butter or margarine	Add butter or margarine and marshmallows. Stir until melted. Cool.
2 oz.	Marshmallows	
1⅓ c.	Evaporated milk	When cool, add milk.

Chocolate Sauce

Yield: 1½ qt.

Amount	Ingredient	Method
12 oz.	Sugar	Mix dry ingredients.
2 oz.	Cornstarch	Add cold water gradually to form
1 t.	Salt	a smooth paste.
3 oz.	Cocoa	
1 c.	Water, cold	
3½ c.	Water, boiling	Add boiling water slowly while stirring. Boil 5 min. or until thickened. Remove from heat.
6 oz.	Butter or margarine	Add butter or margarine. Stir to blend. Serve hot or cold on puddings, cake, or ice cream.

Hot Chocolate Sauce

Yield: 1¼ qt.

Amount	Ingredient	Method
8 oz.	Butter or mar- garine, soft	Cream butter or margarine and powdered sugar over hot
1 lb. 8 oz.	Powdered sugar	water.
1¼ c.	Evaporated milk	Add evaporated milk and cook
8 oz.	Chocolate, chipped or melted	slowly 30 min.
		Add chocolate. Stir until blended.
		Serve on vanilla or peppermint ice cream.

Note:
This sauce may be stored in refrigerator. Heat over hot water before serving. If too thick or grainy, add evaporated milk before heating.

Hot Mincemeat Sauce

Yield: 5 qt.

Amount	Ingredient	Method
1½ qt.	Water	Combine water, sugar, and rind.
3 lb. 8 oz.	Sugar	Cook to soft ball stage, (240° F.).
2 T.	Orange rind, grated	
1 No. 10 can	Mincemeat	Add mincemeat and orange juice.
½ c.	Orange juice	Boil about 10 min.
		Serve hot over vanilla ice cream.

Note:
Sirup may be omitted and hot mincemeat served on the ice cream.

Oriental Sauce

Yield: 1 qt.

Amount	Ingredient	Method
2 lb.	Sugar	Dissolve sugar in hot water.
1½ pt.	Water, hot	Add juice and rinds cut into long,
2 T.	Lemon juice	thin strips.
¼ c.	Orange juice	Cook until rinds are clear.
1	Lemon rind	
1	Orange rind	
6 oz.	Candied ginger	Cut ginger into thin strips and add to hot mixture. Cook to soft ball stage, (234° F.). Remove from heat.
4 oz.	Almonds, blanched, slivered	Add almonds. Serve cold over vanilla ice cream.

Melba Sauce

Yield: 2½ qt.

Amount	Ingredient	Method
2½ qt.	Red raspberries, frozen, and juice	Defrost berries. Add combined sugar and cornstarch.
¼ c.	Sugar	Cook until clear.
3½ T.	Cornstarch	
2½ c.	Currant jelly	Add jelly. Cool. Serve over vanilla ice cream or lime sherbet.

Note:

Peach Melba is made by pouring 3 T. of this sauce over a scoop of vanilla ice cream placed in the center of a canned or fresh peach half. It also may be served over sherbet.

Custard Sauce

Yield: 5 qt.

Amount	Ingredient	Method
14 oz. 2 oz. ½ t. 1 pt.	Sugar Cornstarch Salt Milk, cold	Mix dry ingredients. Add cold milk. Mix until smooth.
3 qt.	Milk, hot	Add cold mixture to hot milk gradually while stirring.
10 2 T.	Egg yolks, beaten Vanilla	Add egg yolks. Cook over hot water until thickened (about 5 min.). Remove from heat and add vanilla. Cool. Serve over cake-type puddings or over cubed oranges or bananas.

Lemon Sauce

Yield: 2 qt.

Amount	Ingredient	Method
2 lb. 3 oz. ½ t. 2 qt.	Sugar Cornstarch Salt Water, boiling	Mix dry ingredients. Add boiling water. Cook until clear.
5 oz. 2 T.	Lemon juice Butter or margarine	Add lemon juice and butter or margarine. Serve hot with Steamed Pudding (p. 211), Bread Pudding (p. 192), or Rice Pudding (p. 198).

Variations:
1. *Vanilla Sauce.* Omit lemon juice and reduce sugar to 1¼ lb. Add 2 T. vanilla.
2. *Nutmeg Sauce.* Omit lemon juice and reduce sugar to 1 lb. Add ¾ t. nutmeg.
3. *Orange Sauce.* Substitute Orange Juice for lemon juice.

Hard Sauce

Yield: 3⅓ c.

Amount	Ingredient	Method
8 oz.	Butter	Cream butter (medium speed).
2 T.	Water, boiling	Add water and continue to cream.
1 lb. 3 oz.	Powdered sugar	Add sugar gradually. Blend.
½ t.	Lemon extract	Add lemon extract.
		Place in refrigerator to harden.
		Serve with Christmas Pudding (p. 210) or Steamed Pudding (p. 211).

Variations:

1. *Strawberry Hard Sauce.* Omit lemon extract and water. Add ¾ c. fresh or frozen strawberries.
2. *Cherry Hard Sauce.* Add ½ c. chopped maraschino cherries.

Brown Sugar Hard Sauce

Yield: 1 qt.

Amount	Ingredient	Method
12 oz.	Butter	Cream butter (medium speed).
1 lb. 4 oz.	Light brown sugar, sifted	Add brown sugar gradually. Cream well.
¾ c.	Whipping cream	Whip cream. Fold cream and vanilla into creamed mixture.
2 t.	Vanilla	Chill.
		Serve with Christmas Pudding (p. 210) or Steamed Pudding (p. 211).

Brown Sugar Sirup

Yield: 2 gal.

Amount	Ingredient	Method
5 lb.	Brown sugar	Combine all ingredients.
5 lb. 8 oz.	Granulated sugar	Stir and heat until sugar is dissolved.
1 c.	Corn sirup	
2½ qt.	Water	Serve hot or cold on griddle cakes,
4 oz.	Butter or margarine	fritters, or waffles.

Meat and Vegetable Sauces

Hollandaise Sauce

Yield: 12 servings

Amount	Ingredient	Method
2 oz. 1½ T. 3	Butter Lemon juice Egg yolks	Place butter, lemon juice, and egg yolks over hot water (not boiling). Cook slowly, beating constantly.
2 oz.	Butter	When first portion of butter is melted, add second portion and beat until mixture thickens.
2 oz. f.g. f.g.	Butter Salt Cayenne	Add third portion of butter and seasonings. Beat until thickened. Serve immediately. Serve with fish or green vegetables, such as asparagus or broccoli.

Notes:
1. If sauce tends to curdle, add hot water, a teaspoon at a time, stirring vigorously.
2. It is recommended that this sauce be made only in small quantity.

Mock Hollandaise Sauce

Yield: 2 qt.

Amount	Ingredient	Method
6 oz. 3 oz. 1½ qt. 1 t. ½ t. f.g.	Butter Flour Milk Salt Pepper Cayenne	Melt butter or margarine. Add flour; stir until smooth. Add milk gradually, stirring constantly. Cook until smooth and thickened. Add seasonings.
12 1 lb. ½ c.	Egg yolks, unbeaten Butter Lemon juice	Add 1 egg yolk at a time, a little butter, and a little lemon juice until all are added. Beat well.

Tartar Sauce

Yield: 1¾ qt.

Amount	Ingredient	Method
1 qt.	Mayonnaise	Mix all ingredients.
1 c.	Pickles, chopped	Serve with fish.
¼ c.	Green pepper, chopped	
¼ c.	Parsley, chopped	
1 c.	Green olives, chopped	
1 T.	Onion, minced	
¼ c.	Pimiento, chopped	
½ c.	Vinegar or lemon juice	
Few drops	Worcestershire sauce	
Few drops	Tabasco sauce	

Cucumber Sauce

Yield: 2¾ c.

Amount	Ingredient	Method
2 c.	Cucumber	Peel cucumbers: remove seeds. Grate or chop finely.
1 T.	Onion, grated	Combine and add remaining ingredients.
1 T.	Vinegar	
1½ T.	Lemon juice	Serve cold with fish.
1 c.	Cultured sour cream	
½ t.	Salt	
Dash	Red pepper	

Mustard Sauce

Yield: 2½ c.

Amount	Ingredient	Method
2 T.	Sugar	Mix dry ingredients.
½ t.	Salt	Add eggs, water, and vinegar.
2 t.	Mustard, dry	Cook over hot water until thick.
2	Eggs, beaten	
2 T.	Water	
4 T.	Vinegar	
1 oz.	Butter or margarine	Add butter. Stir until melted. Cool.
1 pt.	Whipping cream	Whip cream and fold into cooked mixture. Serve cold with pork, beef, or ham roast.

Apple–Horseradish Sauce

Yield: 3 c.

Amount	Ingredient	Method
1 c.	Applesauce, sieved	Fold applesauce and horseradish into mayonnaise.
1 c.	Horseradish	Serve with ham.
1 c.	Mayonnaise	

Note:
Whipped cream may be substituted for Mayonnaise if served at once.

Cocktail Sauce

Yield: 2 qt.

Amount	Ingredient	Method
1 qt.	Chili sauce	Mix all ingredients.
1 pt.	Catsup	Chill.
1 c.	Lemon juice	Serve over clam, crab, lobster, oyster, or shrimp.
2 T.	Onion juice	
2½ c.	Celery, chopped fine	
5 t.	Worcestershire sauce	
6 T.	Horseradish	
Few drops	Tabasco sauce	

Hot Vegetable Sauce

Yield: 2½ qt.

Amount	Ingredient	Method
1 lb. 4 oz.	Bacon, cubed (or ½ lb. butter or margarine) Flour	Fry bacon until crisp. Add flour. Stir until smooth.

1 lb. 4 oz.
¼ c.
1½ pt.
1½ pt.
	Sugar
	Salt
	Vinegar
	Water
		Mix sugar, salt, vinegar, and water.
		  Boil 1 min.
		Add to fat-flour mixture gradually
		  while stirring.
		Cook over hot water until slightly
		  thickened.
		Use to wilt lettuce or spinach; or
		  with hot potato salad or shred-
		  ded cabbage.

Tomato Sauce

Yield: 2 qt.

Amount	Ingredient	Method
6 oz. 4 oz.	Butter or mar- garine Flour	Melt butter or margarine. Add flour and blend.

2 qt.
4 oz.
 	
2 T.
1 t.
¼ t.
1 t.
	Tomato juice
	Onion, finely
	chopped
	Sugar
	Salt
	Pepper
	Worcestershire
	sauce
		Combine tomato juice and season-
		  ings. Simmer 20 min.
		Add gradually to blended butter
		  and flour, while stirring.
		Cook until thickened.

Spanish Sauce

Yield: 2½ qt.

Amount	Ingredient	Method
4 oz.	Onion, chopped	Sauté onions in fat.
4 oz.	Fat	
2 qt.	Tomatoes, canned	Add remaining ingredients.
1 lb.	Celery, diced	Simmer until vegetables are tender.
8 oz.	Green pepper, chopped	Serve with meat, fish, or cheese dishes.
6 oz.	Pimiento, chopped	
1 T.	Salt	
½ t.	Pepper	
f.g.	Cayenne	

Uncooked Barbecue Sauce

Yield: 1 gal.

Amount	Ingredient	Method
1 No. 10 can	Catsup	Mix all ingredients.
3 c.	Vinegar	Pour over spareribs, shortribs, chops,
12 oz.	Sugar	or lamb shanks. Bake.
4 oz.	Salt	
4 oz.	Onion, grated	

Cooked Barbecue Sauce

Yield: 1½ gal.

Amount	Ingredient	Method
1 No. 10 can	Catsup	Combine all ingredients.
3 qt.	Water	Simmer 10 min.
2 c.	Vinegar	Baste chicken or meat with sauce
2 T.	Salt	during cooking.
1 t.	Pepper	
½ c.	Sugar	
1 t.	Chili powder	
¼ c.	Worcestershire sauce	
1 T.	Tabasco sauce	
½ c.	Onion, grated	
2	Lemons, sliced	

Note:
Sauce also may be used for barbecued hamburgers or to combine with beef, pork, or ham slices for barbecued sandwiches.

Hot Mustard Sauce

Yield: 2 qt.

Amount	Ingredient	Method
2 qt.	Beef broth	Heat broth.
5 oz. 2 T. 2 t. ½ t. ½ c.	Cornstarch Sugar Salt Pepper Water	Blend dry ingredients with cold water. Add gradually to hot broth. Cook and stir until thickened.
2 oz. 4 oz. 2 T. 1 oz.	Mustard, prepared Horseradish Vinegar Butter or margarine	Add remaining ingredients. Stir until blended. Serve hot with boiled beef, fresh or cured ham, or fish.

Bechamel Sauce

Yield: 2 qt.

Amount	Ingredient	Method
1½ qt. 4 2 T. 3 oz. 1	Chicken stock Onion slices Peppercorns Carrots, chopped Bay leaf	Cook stock and seasonings together 20 min. Strain. Save liquid for preparation of sauce. (There should be 1 qt. liquid.)
8 oz. 4 oz. 1 qt. 1 qt. ½ t. ½ t. f.g.	Butter or margarine Flour Seasoned stock (prepared above) Milk, hot Salt White pepper Cayenne	Melt butter or margarine. Add flour, stir until smooth. Add liquids gradually, stirring constantly. Cook until smooth and thickened. Add seasonings. Serve with meat or chicken timbales or soufflés.

Note:
Chicken soup base may be used to prepare chicken stock.
Variation:
Mornay Sauce. Add gradually to 6 c. of hot Bechamel Sauce a few grains of cayenne pepper, 1 c. each of grated Parmesan and Swiss cheese. Let sauce remain over heat until cheese is melted, then remove and gradually beat in 1 c. of butter or margarine. Serve with fish and egg dishes.

Raisin Sauce

Yield: 1¼ qt.

Amount	Ingredient	Method
4 oz.	Sugar	Heat sugar and water to boiling point.
1 pt.	Water	
1 lb.	Raisins, cooked	Add remaining ingredients.
⅓ c.	Vinegar	Simmer 5 min. or until jelly is dissolved.
2 oz.	Butter or margarine	Serve with baked ham.
1 T.	Worcestershire sauce	
1 t.	Salt	
¼ t.	White pepper	
½ t.	Cloves	
⅛ t.	Mace	
1 lb.	Currant jelly	
Few drops	Red coloring, (optional)	

Sweet–Sour Sauce

Yield: 5 qt.

Amount	Ingredient	Method
2 c.	Vinegar	Combine vinegar, water, sugar, soy sauce, and salt.
2 c.	Water	Bring to boil.
8 oz.	Sugar	
¼ c.	Soy sauce	
1 T.	Salt	
4 oz.	Cornstarch	Mix cornstarch and water into a smooth paste.
1 c.	Water, cold	Add to hot liquid. Cook until clear.
8 oz.	Onion, chopped	Sauté vegetables in fat for 5 min.
6 oz.	Celery, chopped	Add vegetables and pineapple to sauce.
6 oz.	Green pepper, chopped	Pour over spareribs or other pork cuts and bake.
4 oz.	Fat	
1 No. 10 can	Pineapple tidbits	

White Sauce

	Ingredients				
Consistency	Milk	Flour	Butter or Margarine	Salt	Uses
Very thin	4 qt.	2 oz.	8 oz.	1½ T.	Cream soup made from starchy foods
Thin	4 qt.	4 oz.	8 oz.	1½ T.	Cream soup made from nonstarchy foods
Medium	4 qt.	8 oz.	1 lb.*	1½ T.	Creamed dishes, gravies
Thick	4 qt.	12–16 oz.	1 lb.*	1½ T.	Soufflés
Very thick	4 qt.	1 lb. 4 oz.	1 lb. 4 oz.*	1½ T.	Croquettes

Method 1. Melt butter or margarine, remove from heat. Add flour; stir until smooth. Add salt, then hot milk gradually, stirring constantly. Cook and stir as necessary, until smooth and thick (15–20 min.).

Method 2. Combine flour with ¼ milk. Add flour-milk paste to remainder of milk (hot). Cook to desired consistency, then add fat and salt.

Method 3. This method is used for making large quantities (more than 4 qt.). Add ¼ milk to the fat-flour mixture; beat until smooth. Add mixture to remaining milk.

Method 4. This method uses a steamer. Make a paste of flour and butter or margarine. Add cold milk until mixture is the consistency of cream. Heat remaining milk; add flour and fat mixture, stirring constantly with wire whip. Place in steamer until flour is cooked; if necessary, stir once during cooking.

* Reduce butter or margarine to 8–10 oz. in medium, thick, and very thick White Sauce when using Method 2.

WHITE SAUCE VARIATIONS

Sauce à la King. Add 12 oz. chopped green pepper and 12 oz. sliced mushrooms, sautéed, and 1 lb. chopped pimiento to 1 gal. Medium White Sauce. Combine with cubed cooked chicken, meats, vegetables, or eggs.

Bacon Sauce. Add 1½ lb. cooked chopped bacon to 1 gal. Medium White Sauce. Use bacon fat in making the sauce. Combine with eggs or vegetables in scalloped dishes.

Cheese Sauce. Add 3 lb. sharp Cheddar cheese (grated or ground), 2 T. Worcestershire sauce, f.g. cayenne pepper to 1 gal. Medium White Sauce. Serve on fish, egg dishes, soufflés, and vegetables.

Egg Sauce. Add 20 chopped hard-cooked eggs and 2 T. prepared mustard to 1 gal. Medium White Sauce. Serve with cooked fish or croquettes.

Golden Sauce. Add 2 c. slightly beaten egg yolks to 1 gal. Medium White Sauce. Serve on fish, chicken, or vegetables.

Mushroom Sauce. Add 1½ lb. sliced mushrooms and 4 oz. minced onion, sautéed in 4 oz. butter or margarine, to 1 gal. Medium White Sauce. Serve over egg, meat or poultry dishes or vegetables.

Pimiento Sauce. Add 1¼ lb. finely chopped pimiento and 2 c. finely chopped parsley to 1 gal. Medium White Sauce. Serve with poached fish, croquettes, or egg dishes.

Shrimp Sauce. Add 4 lb. cooked shrimp, 2 T. prepared mustard, and 2 T. Worcestershire sauce to 1 gal. Medium White Sauce. Serve with fish, eggs, or cheese soufflé.

White Sauce Mix

Yield: 21 lb. mix

Amount	Ingredient	Method
3 lb.	Flour	Blend flour and milk in large (60
9 lb.	Milk, nonfat dry	qt.) mixing bowl.
4 lb. 8 oz.	Fat	Using pastry knife or flat beater,
4 lb. 8 oz.	Butter or margarine	blend fats with dry ingredients until mixture is crumbly, scraping down bowl occasionally. Store in covered containers in refrigerator.
To prepare one gallon white sauce		
1 gal.	Water	Heat water and salt to boiling
1½ oz.	Salt	point.
Thin:		
2 lb. 2 oz.	White sauce mix	Add mix for sauce of desired thickness.
Medium:		
2 lb. 14 oz.	White sauce mix	Stirring with French whip, continue cooking until thickened.
Thick:		
3 lb. 8 oz.	White sauce mix	

Brown Sauce

Yield: 1 gal.

Amount	Ingredient	Method
1 gal.	Meat stock (p. 391)	Add onion and seasoning to meat stock.
8 oz.	Onion, thinly sliced	Simmer about 10 min.
1½ T.	Salt	Strain.
½ t.	Pepper	
1 lb.	Fat	Heat fat and blend with flour.
10 oz.	Flour, browned	Add hot stock while stirring. Cook until thickened.

Variations:

1. *Jelly Sauce.* Add 2 c. currant jelly, beaten until melted, 2 T. tarragon vinegar, and 4 oz. sautéed minced onions to 2 qt. Brown Sauce. Serve with lamb or game.
2. *Mushroom Sauce.* Add 1 lb. sliced mushrooms and 2 oz. minced onions, sautéed, to 2 qt. Brown Sauce. Serve with steak.
3. *Olive Sauce.* Add 1 c. chopped stuffed olives to 2 qt. Brown Sauce. Serve with meat or duck.
4. *Piquante Sauce.* Add 2 oz. minced onions, 2 oz. capers, ½ c. vinegar, ¼ c. sugar, ¼ t. salt, ¼ t. paprika, and ½ c. chili sauce or chopped sweet pickle to 2 qt. Brown Sauce. Serve with meats.
5. *Savory Mustard Sauce.* Add ½ c. prepared mustard and ½ c. horseradish to 2 qt. Brown Sauce. Serve with meats.

Drawn Butter Sauce

Yield: 2 qt.

Amount	Ingredient	Method
2 oz.	Butter or mar- garine	Melt butter or margarine. Add flour and blend.
4 oz.	Flour	Gradually add hot water while stir-
2 qt.	Water, hot	ring. Cook 5 min.
1 t.	Salt	When ready to serve, add salt and butter.
6 oz.	Butter, cut into pieces	Beat until blended. Serve with green vegetables, fried or broiled fish, or egg dishes.

Variations:
1. *Almond Butter Sauce.* Add 4 T. lemon juice and 1 c. toasted slivered almonds just before serving.
2. *Lemon Butter Sauce.* Add 1 T. grated lemon rind and 4 T. lemon juice just before serving. Serve with fish, new potatoes, broccoli, or asparagus.
3. *Maitre D'Hotel Sauce.* Add 4 T. lemon juice, 4 T. chopped parsley, and 8 egg yolks, well beaten.
4. *Parsley Butter.* Add 1½ c. minced parsley just before serving. Serve with fish, potatoes, or other vegetables.

Meuniere Sauce

Yield: 3 c.

Amount	Ingredient	Method
1 lb. 4 oz.	Butter or mar- garine	Heat butter until lightly browned. Add onion and brown slightly.
2 oz.	Onion, minced	
½ c.	Lemon juice	Add juice and seasonings.
1 T.	Worcestershire sauce	Serve hot over broccoli, Brussels sprouts, green beans, spinach, or cabbage.
1 T.	Lemon rind, grated	
1 t.	Salt	

Note:
½ c. toasted sliced almonds may be sprinkled over top of vegetable.

Mushroom Sauce

Yield: 4½ qt.

	Method
iced	Sauté mushrooms in butter. Add flour and blend. Add chicken stock and cream while stirring. Stir and cook until thick. Add salt.

1 lb. slivered almonds. Serve over rice as an

lb. grated Cheddar cheese. Serve over aspar-

Pan Gravy

Yield: 1 gal.

	Method
	Add flour to fat and blend. Add salt and pepper. Add water or stock gradually, stirring constantly. Cook until smooth and thickened.

and brown in the fat.
or water or stock.
ppings for fat and chicken broth for liquid.
ped.
lb. thinly sliced onions in fat before adding

ed carrots, 4 oz. chopped celery, and 12 oz.
or meat stock.

A home without Books
is like a room without windows.

CALGARY

DOWNTOWN

CHINOOK-RIDGE

VANCOUVER

PARK ROYAL

Evelyn DeMille Books

SOUPS

Soup Recipes

Beef Stock

Yield: 3–4 gal.

Amount	Ingredient	Method
15 lb.	Beef shank, lean	Pour water over beef shanks. Bring
6 gal.	Water, cold	to boiling point.
8 oz.	Onion, chopped	Add vegetables and seasonings.
8 oz.	Celery, chopped	Simmer until meat leaves bone
8 oz.	Carrot, chopped	(about 4 hr.).
1 T.	Peppercorns	Remove meat, strain, cool, and
2	Bay leaves	skim off fat.
3 oz.	Salt	

Note:

A quick beef stock may be made by adding concentrated beef soup base to water in amounts given in manufacturer's directions. When using this stock for sauces for casseroles, reduce salt by 1 T. per gal. of sauce.

Variations:

1. *Brown Stock.* Allow 10 lb. beef shank to stand 30 min. in cold water. Heat slowly to boiling point. Simmer 2 hr. Add vegetables which have been browned with remaining meat. Add seasonings. Simmer 3 hr.
2. *Chicken Stock.* Substitute 4 4–4½ lb. hens, cut up, for beef shank.
3. *Alphabet Soup.* To 3 gal. Beef Stock, add 2 T. celery salt, ¼ t. pepper, 4 oz. grated onions, 6 oz. grated carrots, and 10 oz. alphabet noodles. Cook until added ingredients are tender. Serving: 1 c.
4. *Barley Soup.* To 3 gal. Beef Stock, add 1¾ lb. barley. Cook until barley is done. Serving: 1 c.
5. *Beef Vegetable Soup.* To 3 gal. Beef Stock, add 3 lb. freshly ground beef, 5 oz. chopped celery, 5 oz. chopped carrots, 3 oz. chopped onions, 12 oz. peas, and 8 oz. rice (if desired). Cook until ingredients are tender. Serving: 1 c.
6. *Beef Noodle Soup.* To 3 gal. Beef Stock, add 1½ lb. (A.P.) noodles. Cook until noodles are tender. Serving: 1 c.

7. *Beef Rice Soup.* To 3 gal. Beef Stock, add 1½ lb. (A.P.) rice. Cook until rice is done. Serving: 1 c.

8. *Beef Vermicelli Soup.* To 3 gal. Beef Stock, add 1½ lb. (A.P.) spaghetti or vermicelli and cook until tender. Serving: 1 c.

9. *Creole Soup.* To 2¼ gal. Beef Stock, add 1 No. 10 can tomatoes, 1 lb. shredded green peppers, 1 lb. chopped onions, 1 lb. cooked shell macaroni, 2 oz. salt (may vary), ¼ t. pepper, and 4 bay leaves. Cook until ingredients are tender. Serving: 1 c.

10. *French Onion Soup.* To 3 gal. Beef Stock, add 8 lb. onions, thinly sliced and sautéed in 12 oz. fat; 3 oz. flour, blended with fat and onions; 3 T. Worcestershire sauce; salt and pepper to taste. Cook until onions are tender. Serving: 1 c. To serve, pour over toasted bread cubes or strips and sprinkle with grated Parmesan cheese.

11. *Julienne Soup.* To 3 gal. Beef Stock, add 2 T. celery salt; 1 lb. carrots, 1 lb. green beans, and 12 oz. celery, cut long and thin; 2 oz. chopped onions; 2 oz. salt (may vary). Cook until vegetables are tender. Serving: 1 c.

12. *Minestrone Soup.* To 3 gal. Beef Stock, add 1 No. 2 can kidney or brown beans, 12 oz. spaghetti, 1 lb. chopped onions, 1 lb. shredded potatoes, 1¾ lb. carrot strips, and 1 oz. chopped parsley. Cook until ingredients are tender. Serving: 1 c.

Vegetable–Beef Soup

Yield: 3 gal.

Portion: 1 cup

Amount	Ingredient	Method
15 lb.	Beef shank, with meat	Add water and seasonings to beef shank.
4 gal.	Water, cold	Bring to boiling point. Simmer 3–4
2	Bay leaves	hr.
3 T.	Salt	Remove meat from bones and chop.
1 lb. 8 oz.	Carrots, cubed	Add vegetables to meat stock.
1 lb. 8 oz.	Celery, chopped	Cover and simmer about 1 hr. Replace water as necessary.
1 lb.	Onion, chopped	place water as necessary.
2 lb.	Potatoes, cubed	Add salt, pepper, and chopped
¼ c.	Salt	meat. Reheat.
1 t.	Pepper	

Bouillon

Yield: 3 gal.

Portion: 1 cup

Amount	Ingredient	Method
8 lb.	Beef, lean	Sear beef. Add bone and water.
4 lb.	Bone, cracked	Let stand 1 hr.
4 gal.	Water, cold	Simmer for 3–4 hr. Replace water as necessary.
8 oz.	Carrots, diced	Add vegetables and seasonings.
8 oz.	Celery, chopped	Cook 1 hr. Strain.
8 oz.	Onion, chopped	Chill overnight.
1	Bay leaf	Remove fat.
1 T.	Peppercorns	
¼ c.	Salt	
3	Egg shells, crushed	Add egg shells and whites to clear the broth.
3	Egg whites, beaten	Bring slowly to boiling point, stirring constantly.
		Boil 15–20 min. without stirring.
		Strain through a cloth.

Variations:

1. *Chicken Bouillon.* Substitute 4 4–4½ lb. hens, cut up, for the beef and bone. Do not sear chicken.
2. *Tomato Bouillon.* To 1½ gal. bouillon, add 4 46-oz. cans tomato juice, 1 oz. chopped onion, 2 oz. sugar, 3 T. salt (may vary), ½ t. pepper, ½ t. cloves, 2 bay leaves, ½ T. peppercorns, ½ t. soda.

Tomato–Rice Soup

Yield: 3 gal.
Portion: 1 cup

Amount	Ingredient	Method
2 gal.	Beef or chicken stock (p. 391)	Heat stock, purée, and salt to boiling point.
1 gal.	Tomato purée	
1½ T.	Salt	
2 oz.	Onion, chopped	Add vegetables and rice.
4 oz.	Green pepper, chopped	Cook until rice is tender.
8 oz.	Rice	
6 oz.	Butter or margarine	Melt butter and add flour. Mix until smooth.
3 oz.	Flour	Add to soup while stirring. Salt to taste.

Note:
If soup base is used to make stock, salt may need to be reduced.
Variation:
Tomato-Barley Soup. Add 1 lb. barley in place of rice.

Pepper Pot Soup

Yield: 3 gal.
Portion: 1 cup

Amount	Ingredient	Method
2 oz.	Onion, chopped fine	Sauté vegetables in butter or margarine until lightly browned, about 15 min.
8 oz.	Green peppers, chopped fine	
6 oz.	Celery, chopped	
3 lb. 8 oz. (E.P.)	Potatoes, diced	
12 oz.	Butter or margarine	
5 oz.	Flour	Add flour. Stir until well blended.
2¼ gal.	Beef or chicken stock, hot (p. 391)	Combine stock, milk, and salt. Add to vegetable mixture, while stirring.
1 qt.	Milk, hot	Add red pepper.
1½ T.	Salt	Keep just below boiling point 30 min.
2 T.	Red pepper, chopped	Serve with Spatzels (p. 402)

Note:
If soup base is used to make stock, salt may need to be reduced.

Rice Soup

Yield: 3 gal.
Portion: 1 cup

Amount	Ingredient	Method
4½–5 qt.	Beef or chicken stock (p. 391)	Add cooked rice, milk, and seasonings to hot stock.
12 oz. (A.P.)	Rice, cooked (p. 309)	
1 gal.	Milk, hot	Garnish with toast rings sprinkled with chopped parsley and Parmesan cheese.
1 t.	Onion juice	
3 T.	Salt	
1 t.	Pepper	
¼ c.	Parsley, chopped	

Note:
If soup base is used to make stock, salt may need to be reduced.

Split Pea Soup

Yield: 3 gal.
Portion: 1 cup

Amount	Ingredient	Method
4 lb. 2 gal.	Split peas Water, boiling	Wash peas. Add boiling water, cover, and soak 1 hr. or longer.
1 4 oz.	Ham bone (or 2 lb. sliced salt pork or bacon ends) Onion, chopped	Add ham bone and onion to peas and water in which they were soaked. Cook 4–5 hrs., or until peas are soft. Remove bone. Add water to make 2½ gal.
4 oz. 2 oz. 2 qt. 2 T. ½ t.	Fat Flour Milk Salt Pepper	Make into Thin White Sauce (p. 385). Add to peas.

Note:
If soup becomes too thick, add hot milk to bring to desired consistency. If a smoother soup is desired, purée peas.

Navy Bean Soup

Yield: 3 gal.
Portion: 1 cup

Amount	Ingredient	Method
3 lb. 1½ gal.	Navy beans Water, boiling	Wash beans. Add boiling water. Cover and let stand 1 hr. or longer.
5 lb.	Ham shanks	Add ham shanks. Simmer until beans are cooked. Remove ham from bones, chop, and add later.
4 oz. 8 oz.	Onion, chopped Celery, diced	Add onion, celery, and water to make a total volume of 3¼ gal. Cook 30 min. Add chopped ham. Season to taste.

Spanish Bean Soup

Yield: 3 gal.

Portion: 1 cup

Amount	Ingredient	Method
5 lb.	Beans, kidney or garbonza	Wash beans. Add boiling water. Cover and let stand 1 hr. or longer.
4½ gal.	Water, boiling	
12 oz.	Onion, chopped	Cook in same water until tender. Purée. Add water to make 1½ gal.
6 oz.	Onion, chopped	Sauté vegetables in butter until slightly browned.
2 oz.	Green pepper, chopped	
2 oz.	Butter or bacon fat	
1½ gal.	Tomato purée	Heat tomato purée and add with seasoning to bean purée.
¼ c.	Salt	
1¼ T.	Pepper	Cook 5 min. to blend ingredients.

Notes:
1. Baked-bean purée may be substituted for kidney bean purée.
2. Ham stock may be used in place of tomato purée. 2 t. saffron may be added if desired.

Basic Sauce for Cream Soup

Yield: 2½ gal. Basic Sauce

Amount	Ingredient	Method
12 oz.	Butter or mar-garine	Make as Thin White Sauce (p. 385). Add vegetables and seasonings as suggested below to make a variety of cream soups.
6 oz.	Flour	
3 T.	Salt	
½ t.	White pepper	
9 qt.	Milk, hot	

Suggestions for Cream Soups

To 1 recipe (2½ gal.) Basic Sauce for Cream Soup for 3 gal. (1 c. portions):

Cream of Asparagus Soup. Add 6½ lb. cooked, chopped asparagus.

Cream of Celery Soup. Add 1½ lb. chopped celery, 8 oz. diced carrots, and 2½ oz. chopped onions cooked in 1 gal. water about 1 hr.

Cream of Corn Soup. Add 3 qt. corn, cream style, and 1 oz. chopped onions.

Cream of Mushroom Soup. Add 2 lb. mushrooms, sliced or chopped. Reduce flour to 4 oz. Chicken stock may be substituted for part of the milk.

Cream of Pea Soup. Add 3 qt. pea purée, 2 oz. minced onions, and 1 oz sugar.

Cream of Potato Soup. Add 12 lb. diced potatoes, 6 oz. chopped onions, and 8 oz. chopped celery which have been cooked in 3 qt. water until soft. Potatoes may be mashed or puréed if desired.

Cream of Spinach Soup. Add 2½–3 qt. chopped, fresh or frozen spinach and 2 oz. grated onions (optional).

Cream of Vegetable Soup. Add 1 lb. chopped celery, 4 oz. chopped onions, 1 lb. diced carrots, 2 lb. diced potatoes, cooked in 1 gal. water, seasoned with 3 T. salt, until soft.

Vegetable Chowder. Add 2 No. 2 cans whole kernel corn, 5 oz. green pepper, and 1 lb. diced cooked bacon or salt pork.

Corn Chowder

Yield: 3 gal.

Portion: 1 cup

Amount	Ingredient	Method
1 lb.	Salt pork or bacon, cubed	Fry pork until crisp. Add onions and cook slowly 5 min.
12 oz.	Onion, chopped	Remove pork and onions from fat.
	Fat, fried from pork	Add flour to pork fat. Blend. Add milk and salt, stirring constantly.
4 oz.	Flour	
2 gal.	Milk	
3 T.	Salt	
5 lb. (E.P.)	Potatoes, cubed, cooked	Add potatoes, corn, pork, and onions.
1 No. 10 can	Corn, whole kernel	

Variation:
Potato Chowder. Omit corn and increase potatoes to 8 lb.

Cream of Tomato Soup

Yield: 3 gal.

Portion: 1 cup

Amount	Ingredient	Method
1½ gal.	Tomato juice	Add onion and bay leaf to tomato juice.
1 oz.	Onion, chopped	
½	Bay leaf	Heat to boiling point.
1 T.	Soda	Add soda.
10 oz.	Butter or margarine, melted	Make into a Very Thin White Sauce (p. 385).
3 oz.	Flour	Just before serving, add tomato mixture gradually, while stirring.
3 T.	Salt	
1 t.	Pepper	
4 oz.	Sugar	
1½ gal.	Milk, hot	

Note:
Chopped parsley and 1 t. whipped cream may be used as a garnish for each serving.

Cream of Chicken Soup

Yield: 3 gal.

Portion: 1 cup

Amount	Ingredient	Method
8 oz.	Chicken fat (or butter)	Make into a Very Thin White Sauce (p. 385).
3 oz.	Flour	
1 gal.	Milk	
1½ T.	Salt	
2 gal.	Chicken stock	Add stock, seasoning, and chopped chicken.
2 t.	Celery salt	
¼ t.	White pepper	
1 lb. 8 oz.	Chicken, cooked, chopped	

Notes:
1. Chicken bouillon or chicken soup base may be added to enhance flavor. Salt may need to be decreased.
2. 1 lb. cooked rice or noodles may be added.

Cheese Soup

Yield: 3 gal.

Portion: 1 cup

Amount	Ingredient	Method
8 oz.	Butter or margarine	Sauté onion in butter or margarine until lightly browned.
8 oz.	Onion, chopped	
4 oz.	Flour	Add flour and cornstarch. Blend.
2 oz.	Cornstarch	Cook 3–4 min.
1 t.	Paprika	Add seasonings and blend.
2 T.	Salt	Add milk and stock slowly, while stirring.
1 t.	White pepper	Cook until thickened.
1 gal.	Milk	
1½ gal.	Chicken stock (p. 391)	
3 c.	Carrots, finely diced, cooked	Add carrots and celery.
3 c.	Celery, finely diced, cooked	
1 lb.	Cheddar cheese, sharp, diced fine	Add cheese just before serving. Blend. Garnish with chopped parsley as served.

Orange Soup (*Ch'en Tzu Keng*)

Yield: 1¾ gal.
Portion: ½ cup

Amount	Ingredient	Method
2 c. 6 oz. 1 t.	Water Sugar Salt	Combine water, sugar, and salt. Heat to boiling point.
2 oz. ½ c.	Cornstarch Water, cold	Add cornstarch and water, mixed to a smooth paste. Cook and stir until clear.
6 qt. 2 oz.	Orange juice Butter	When ready to serve, add orange juice and butter. Reheat and serve at once.

Clam Chowder

Yield: 3 gal.
Portion: 1 cup

Amount	Ingredient	Method
1 gal. fresh or 4 15-oz. cans	Clams	Clean clams. Steam until tender. Drain and chop (save juice).
2 oz. 4 oz.	Onion, chopped Salt pork or bacon, finely cubed	Sauté onion and pork 5 min. until lightly browned. Add to clams.
6 lb. (E.P.) 1 qt. 1 T.	Potatoes, cubed Water Salt	Cook potatoes until tender. Save liquid.
8 oz. 2 oz. 2 gal. 1 t.	Butter or margarine Flour Milk Pepper	Melt butter or margarine. Add flour. Stir until smooth. Add milk gradually, while stirring. Cook until consistency of Very Thin White Sauce. Add clams, onion, salt, pork, potatoes, potato water, and seasoning.

Note:
Juice drained from clams may be substituted for an equal quantity of the milk. Heat and add just before serving.

Oyster Stew

Yield: 3 gal.
Portion: 1 cup

Amount	Ingredient	Method
2½ gal.	Milk	Scald milk.
2½ qt.	Oysters	Heat oysters and butter or margarine only until edges of oysters begin to curl.
8 oz.	Butter or margarine	
3 T.	Salt	About 10 min. before serving time, add oysters and oyster liquor and seasonings to scalded milk. Serve immediately to avoid curdling.
½ t.	Pepper	

Spatzels (Egg Dumplings)

Amount	Ingredient	Method
1 lb. 4 oz.	Flour	Combine dry ingredients.
1 t.	Baking powder	
1½ t.	Salt	
3 c.	Milk	Add combined milk and eggs, all at once, to dry ingredients. Mix to form a soft dough. Drop small bits of dough or press through a colander into 3 gal. hot soup. Cook approximately 5 min.
6	Eggs, whole	

Note:
Soup must be very hot in order to cook dumplings.

GARNISHES FOR SOUP

Cream Soups:
Almonds, shredded, toasted
Bacon, broiled, diced
Cheese, grated
Chives, chopped
Croutons
Fresh mint
Hard-cooked egg white, finely chopped
Hard-cooked egg yolk, riced
Paprika
Parsley, finely chopped
Pimiento, minced, in whipped cream

Stock Soups:
Cheese, grated
Lemon, thin slices
Lime, thin slices
Onion rings
Parsley, finely chopped
Popcorn
Vegetables, diced or shredded

VEGETABLES

Cooking Vegetables

Great care should be given to the preparation of fresh vegetables before cooking or serving raw. This procedure, as well as the cookery, influences the nutritive value, attractiveness, palatability, and color of the finished product. All leafy and stem vegetables should be washed thoroughly and crisped before they are cooked or used raw. Details of preparation of vegetables are given on p. 404.

Fresh or frozen vegetables may be cooked by boiling, steaming, baking, pan- or deep-fat frying. The method used will depend largely on the quality of the product, the amount to be cooked, and the equipment available. To insure a high-quality product, it is important that vegetables be cooked in as small an amount of water as is practicable and as quickly as possible. Water should be brought to a second boil immediately following the addition of vegetables. Add no soda to cooking water.

Vegetables should be cooked in as small a quantity at one time as is feasible for the type of service. The needs of most food services can be met by the continuous preparation of vegetables in small quantities. A small steam-jacketed kettle, if time and pressure are carefully controlled, is highly satisfactory for cooking both fresh and frozen vegetables. It usually is large enough to prevent crowding; it will bring water to a boil quickly after vegetables are added; and it will cook a large or small amount equally well. When a steam-jacketed kettle is not available, top-of-stove cookery or oven cooking may be used. Vegetables may be cooked with satisfactory results in a steamer under pressure if cooked in small quantities and arranged in thin layers in shallow pans. Here, too, the time and temperature must be carefully controlled. Whatever the method used, cook vegetables only until tender. Do not overcook.

Vegetables should be served as soon as possible after cooking and handled carefully to prevent breaking.

PREPARATION OF FRESH VEGETABLES

Asparagus. Cut off tough part of stems. Wash and thoroughly clean remaining portions. Asparagus spears may be tied in bundles of 1–2 lb. each for boiling. For cuts, cut spears into 1-in. pieces.

Beans, green or wax. Wash beans. Trim ends and remove strings. Cut or break beans into 1-in. pieces.

Beans, lima. Shell beans. (Scald pods to make shelling easier.) Wash.

Beet greens. Sort. Cut off tough stems. Wash greens at least 5 times, lifting them out of water each time.

Beets, whole. Remove tops, leaving 2-in. stem on beets. Wash. Do not peel or remove root until beets are cooked.

Broccoli. Cut off tough stalk, ends, and wash. Soak in salted water for ½ hr. if insects are present. Drain. Peel stalks. Cut broccoli lengthwise if thick to speed cooking.

Brussels sprouts. Remove withered leaves and wash thoroughly.

Cabbage. Remove wilted outside leaves. Wash, quarter, and core cabbage. Crisp in cold water, if wilted. Cut in wedges, or shred.

Carrots. Wash, scrape, or pare. Trim ends. Cut as desired.

Cauliflower. Remove outer leaves and stalks. Break into flowerets. Wash. Soak in salted water if insects are present. Drain.

Celery. Wash, trim, cut as desired.

Chard. Sort. Cut off tough stems. Wash greens at least 5 times, lifting them out of water each time.

Collards. Sort and trim. Strip leaves from coarse stems. Wash at least 5 times, lifting them out of water each time.

Corn on cob. Husk. Remove silks. Wash. Do not allow to stand in water.

Eggplant. Peel and cut into slices or pieces.

Kale. Sort. Strip leaves from coarse stems. Wash at least 5 times, lifting out of water each time.

Mustard greens. Sort. Cut off tough stems. Wash greens at least 5 times, lifting them out of water each time.

Okra. Trim stem. Slice or leave whole.

Onions. Peel and wash. Quarter if large, or cut as desired.

Parsnips. Wash. Pare. Quarter lengthwise and cut as desired. Cut core from center if tough and woody.

Peas, green. Shell. Rinse.

Potatoes. Scrub. Cook in skins or pare and remove eyes. Cut into serving size.

Pumpkin. Wash. Cut in half; remove seeds, fiber, and peel. Cut pieces. (If peel is hard and tough, soften by steaming or boiling 10 min.)

Rutabagas. Wash. Pare and cut as desired.

Spinach. Sort and trim. Cut off coarse stems and roots. Wash leaves at least 5 times, lifting out of water each time.

Squash, summer. Wash. Trim and cut as desired.

Squash, winter. Wash. Cut in half; remove seeds, fiber, and peel. Cut into pieces. (If peel is hard and tough, soften by steaming or boiling 10 min.)

Sweet potatoes. Scrub.

Turnip greens. Sort. Cut off tough stems. Wash greens at least 5 times, lifting them out of water each time.

Turnips. Wash. Pare and cut as desired.

BOILING OR STEAMING **FRESH** VEGETABLES
1. Prepare vegetables according to directions given on p. 404.
2. To determine amount to buy, convert ready-to-cook weight to As Purchased weight by using chart on preparation yields (p. 29). A 10-lb. lot of ready-to-cook raw vegetables makes about 50 3-oz. portions when cooked, drained, and seasoned.
3. Schedule cooking of fresh vegetables so they will be served soon after they are cooked.
4. Cook in lots no larger than 10 lb. of prepared raw vegetable. Cook until just tender, no longer than necessary to give a palatable product. For a given vegetable, cooking time will differ according to the method of cookery, variety and maturity of the vegetable, length of time and temperature at which it has been held since harvesting, and its size or the size pieces into which it is cut. See timetable for approximate cooking time (p. 406).

Directions for Boiling
1. Add prepared vegetables to boiling salted water (1⅓ T. salt to amount of water specified in timetable). Bring water quickly back to boiling point; cook uncovered except starchy vegetables such as lima beans.
2. Start timing when water returns to boiling point. Use timetable as a guide. Stir greens occasionally while boiling.
3. Drain cooked vegetables and place in serving pans. Add 8 oz. (1 c.) melted butter or margarine to each 50 portions.

Directions for Steaming
1. Place prepared vegetables in steamer pans. Steam in a compartment steamer using time indicated in timetable. Begin timing when steamer registers 5 lb. pressure.
2. Drain cooked vegetables and add 8 oz. (1 c.) melted butter or margarine and 1⅓ T. salt to each 50 portions.

Timetable for Boiling or Steaming **Fresh** Vegetables
(50 portions, ½ cup each)

Prepared Vegetable	Ready-to-Cook[1] Weight	Boiling Water	Boiling Cooking Time (Minutes)	Steaming Cooking Time (Minutes)
Asparagus, spears	11 lb. 4 oz.	3 qt.	10–25	7–10
cuts	7 lb. 12 oz.	3 qt.	5–15	5–10
Beans, blackeye beans or peas	10 lb. 8 oz.	2½ qt.	30–45	20–40
Beans, green or wax, 1-in. pieces	8 lb. 4 oz.	2½ qt.	15–30	20–30
Beans, lima	9 lb. 4 oz.	2½ qt.	15–25	15–20
Beet greens	11 lb. 12 oz.	Water clinging to leaves.	15–25	15–25
Beets, whole (as purchased)	13 lb. 8 oz.	Water to cover.	45–60	60–75
Broccoli, spears	9 lb. 8 oz.	3 qt.	10–20	7–10
Brussels sprouts	8 lb. 8 oz.	1½ gal.	10–20	5–12
Cabbage, shredded	8 lb. 8 oz.	2 qt.	10–15	5–12
wedges	10 lb. 4 oz.	2 qt.	15–20	12–20
Carrots, whole	9 lb. 12 oz.	2 qt.	20–30	15–30
sliced	9 lb. 12 oz.	2 qt.	10–20	15–30
Cauliflower, flowerets	7 lb. 12 oz.	1½ gal.	15–20	8–12
Celery, 1-in. pieces	9 lb.	1 gal.	15–20	10–15
Chard	13 lb. 12 oz.	Water clinging to leaves.	15–25	15–25
Collards	8 lb. 4 oz.	1 gal.	20–40	15–30
Corn on cob	16 lb. 12 oz. (50 medium ears)	1¼ gal. or to cover.	5–15	8–10
Eggplant, pieces or slices	12 lb. 8 oz.	3 qt.	15–20	10–15
Kale	7 lb.	3 qt.	25–45	15–35
Mustard greens	14 lb. 4 oz.	Water clinging to leaves.	15–25	15–25
Okra, whole	8 lb. 8 oz.	2 qt.	10–15	8–15
Onions, mature, quartered if large	13 lb. 12 oz.	1½ gal.	20–35	20–35
Parsnips, 3-in. pieces	11 lb.	1¼ gal.	20–30	15–20
Peas, green	9 lb. 8 oz.	2 qt.	10–20	10–20
Potatoes, whole	12 lb. 8 oz.			
for dicing	8 lb. 12 oz.			
for slicing	8 lb.	1¼ gal.	30–40	30–45
for mashing	11 lb. 12 oz.			

SOURCE. Quantity Recipe for Type A School Lunches, U.S.D.A. PA 631, Oct. 1965.

[1] To convert to As Purchased weight, see p. 29.

Timetable for Boiling or Steaming **Fresh** *Vegetables*
(50 portions, ½ cup each) continued

Prepared Vegetable	Ready-to-Cook Weight	Boiling Water	Boiling Cooking Time (Minutes)	Steaming Cooking Time (Minutes)
Pumpkin, pieces	15 lb.	1¼ gal.	15–30	15–20
Rutabagas, 1-in. cubes for mashing	10 lb. 4 oz. 14 lb. 8 oz. }	3 qt.	20–30	15–30
Spinach	12 lb.	Water clinging to leaves.	10–20	4–8
Squash, summer, sliced	11 lb. 12 oz.	2 qt.	10–20	8–20
Squash, winter (Hubbard or butter-nut), pieces				
for cubing	14 lb.	1¼ gal.	15–30	15–20
for mashing	15 lb. 8 oz. }			
Sweet potatoes, whole				
for mashing	17 lb. 8 oz.	1¼ gal.	30–45	20–40
for slicing	15 lb. 8 oz. }			
Turnip greens	15 lb.	Water clinging to leaves.	15–25	15–25
Turnips, 1-inch cubes for mashing	11 lb. 8 oz. 14 lb. 8 oz. }	3 qt.	15–20	10–15

BOILING OR STEAMING **FROZEN** VEGETABLES
1. Schedule cooking of frozen vegetables so they will be served soon after they are cooked.
2. 10 lb. frozen vegetables makes about 50 3-oz. portions.
3. Boil vegetables in lots no larger than 10 to 12 lb. (4 2½- or 3-lb. packages). Steam vegetables in lots no larger than 5- to 6-lb. (2 2½- to 3-lb. packages) per steamer pan.
4. Thaw solid pack frozen vegetables long enough to break apart easily.

Directions for Boiling
1. Add vegetables to boiling salted water (1⅓ T. salt to amount of water specified in table for each cooking lot). Cook uncovered except starchy vegetables such as lima beans. Bring water quickly back to a boil.
2. Start timing when water returns to boil.
3. Drain cooked vegetables. Add 8 oz. melted butter or margarine to each 10- to 12-lb. of cooked vegetables.
4. For a creamed vegetable, add 2–3 qt. Thin or Medium White Sauce (p. 385).

Directions for Steaming
1. Place vegetables in steamer pans. Cover winter squash and sweet potatoes with a lid or foil.
2. Steam in compartment steamer using timetable (below). Begin timing when steamer registers 5-lb. pressure.
3. Drain cooked vegetables. Add 4 oz. melted butter or margarine and 2 t. salt to each 5- to 6-lb. of cooked vegetables.

Timetable for Boiling or Steaming **Frozen** Vegetables

Vegetable	Boiling 10–12 lb. Boiling Water (Quarts)	Boiling 10–12 lb. Cooking Time (Minutes)	Steaming 5–6 lb. Cooking Time (Minutes)
Asparagus, cuts and tips	1½	7–10	5–10
Beans, blackeye beans or peas	2	25–30	15–25
Beans, green or wax	1	10–20	10–15
Beans, lima, baby	2	12–15	10–15
Fordhook	2	6–12	12–20
Broccoli, spears	1½	10–15	5–10
cut or chopped	1½	8–20	10–20
Brussels sprouts	1½	10–15	5–10
Carrots	1	8–10	3–5
Cauliflower	1½	10–12	4–5
Collards	1¾	30–40	20–40
Corn, whole kernel	1½	5–10	5–10
Kale	1¾	20–30	15–30
Mustard greens	1¾	20–30	15–20
Okra	1¼	3–5	3–5
Peas and carrots	1	8–10	3–5
Peas, green	1	5–10	3–5
Spinach	1	5–10	5–10
Squash, summer	1	5–10	5–10
Squash, winter			
(in double boiler)		30–40	
(cover with foil)			20–25
Succotash	2	6–15	12–20
Sweet potatoes (cover with foil)			15–20
Turnip greens	1¾	20–30	15–20
Vegetables, mixed	1	12–20	12–20

PREPARATION OF **CANNED** VEGETABLES
1. Schedule heating of canned vegetables so they will be served soon after heating.
2. Prepare in lots of 2 No. 10 cans. This will make approximately 50 portions.

Directions for Heating in Stock Pot or in Steam-Jacketed Kettle
1. Drain off half the liquid; use for soups, gravies, and sauces.
2. Heat vegetables and remaining liquid in a stock pot or steam-

jacketed kettle. Heat only long enough to bring to serving temperature.

3. Drain vegetables and place in serving pans. Add 8 oz. melted butter or margarine.

Directions for Heating in Steamer or Oven
1. Drain off half the liquid, use for soups, gravies, and sauces.
2. Transfer vegetables and remaining liquid to steamer pans and cover. (A 12 × 20 × 2-in. pan will hold 2 No. 10 cans).
3. Heat in steamer at 5-lb. pressure, or 350° F. oven until serving temperature is reached.
4. Drain vegetables and add 8 oz. melted butter or margarine for each lot of vegetables.

PREPARATION OF DRIED VEGETABLES
Wash. Cover vegetable with boiling water. Cover kettle and let stand 1 hr. Cook in same water until tender (about 1 hr.); or cover with cold water and soak overnight.

Vegetable Recipes

Mashed Potatoes

Boil: 30–50 min. or   Yield: 50 5-oz. portions
Steam: 30–45 min.

Amount	Ingredient	Method
12 lb. (E.P.)	Potatoes	Steam or boil potatoes (p. 406). When done, drain and place in mixer bowl. Mash (low speed) until there are no lumps. Whip (high speed) about 2 min.
2–2½ qt.	Milk, hot	Add milk, butter, and salt to potatoes.
8 oz.	Butter or margarine	
3 T.	Salt	Whip (high speed) until light and creamy.

Notes:
1. Potato water may be substituted for part of milk.
2. 8 oz. nonfat dry milk and 2–2½ qt. water may be substituted for the liquid milk. Sprinkle dry milk over potatoes before mashing.
3. 2–2½ lb. dehydrated potatoes may be substituted for 12 lb. raw potatoes. Follow processor's instructions for preparation.
Variation:
Mashed Sweet Potatoes. Use 15 lb. (E.P.) sweet potatoes. Add ½ t. nutmeg.

Scalloped Potatoes

Bake: 1½–2 hr.   Yield: 2 pans 12 × 20 × 2 in.
Oven: 350° F.   Portion: 5 oz.

Amount	Ingredient	Method
12 lb. (E.P.)	Potatoes, pared	Slice potatoes. Place in 2 baking pans.
3 T.	Salt	Sprinkle with salt.
8 oz.	Butter or margarine	Make into Thin White Sauce (p. 385).
4 oz.	Flour	Pour over potatoes.
1 gal.	Milk	
1½ T.	Salt	
6 oz.	Bread crumbs	Sprinkle buttered crumbs over potatoes.
2 oz.	Butter or margarine, melted	

Notes:
1. Potatoes may be partially cooked, and hot white sauce added to shorten baking time.
2. 2 lb. sliced dehydrated potatoes, reconstituted in 2 gal. boiling water and 3 T. salt, may be substituted for the fresh potatoes.

Variations:
1. *Scalloped Potatoes with Onions.* Before baking, cover potatoes with onion rings. About 5 min. before removing from oven, cover potatoes with shredded cheese.
2. *Scalloped Potatoes with Ham.* Add 5 lb. cubed cured ham to white sauce. Cut salt to 1 T.
3. *Scalloped Potatoes with Pork Chops.* Brown chops, season, place on top of potatoes before baking.

VARIATIONS IN POTATO PREPARATION

Au Gratin Potatoes. Cube 12 lb. (E.P.) boiled potatoes (or dice before cooking). Add 1 gal. Medium White Sauce (p. 385) and 2 lb. grated cheese. Place in greased baking pan; top with buttered crumbs. Bake approximately 25 min. at 400° F.

Baked Potatoes. Scrub potatoes of uniform size and remove blemishes. Bake approximately 1 hr. (or until tender) at 400°–450° F. May be served with 1 oz. sour cream and chives or with 2 oz. cheese sauce and chopped green onions.

Cottage Fried Potatoes. Add sliced cold boiled potatoes to hot fat in frying pan. Add salt and pepper. Stir as needed and fry until browned.

Duchess Potatoes. Add melted butter or margarine, a small amount of milk, and beaten egg to mashed or riced potatoes. Mix well. Pile mixture lightly into a greased baking pan. Bake in a moderate oven until set.

Franconia Potatoes. Cook pared uniform potatoes approximately 15 min.; drain and place in pan in which meat is roasting. Bake approximately 40 min., or until tender and lightly browned, basting with drippings in pan or turning occasionally to brown all sides. Serve with roast.

French Baked Potatoes. Select small uniform potatoes and pare. Roll pototoes in melted fat, then in cracker crumbs or crushed cornflakes. Place in shallow pan and bake.

Hashed Brown Potatoes. Add finely chopped boiled potatoes to hot fat in frying pan. Add salt and pepper. Stir occasionally and fry until browned.

Lyonnaise Potatoes. 1. Cook onion slowly in fat without browning. Add seasoned cut, boiled potatoes and cook until browned. 2. Cut potatoes as for French fries. Steam until tender, place in greased baking pan. Cover top with fat and onions. Place in oven and bake until browned.

Lyonnaise Baked Potatoes. Select baking potatoes of medium size. Cut each in 4 crosswise slices; place a slice of onion, salt, pepper, and butter between slices and wrap each in aluminum foil. Bake at 400° F. until potatoes are almost done. Open foil and return to oven to brown tops.

O'Brien Potatoes. Cook cubed potatoes in a small amount of fat with chopped onion and pimiento.

Oven-browned or Rissolé Potatoes. Pare and cut potatoes in uniform pieces. Place in baking pan containing a small amount of fat. Turn potatoes so that all sides are coated with fat. Sprinkle with salt. Bake in hot oven until browned and tender. Turn as necessary for even browning. Potatoes may be parboiled 10–15 min. or browned in deep fat before placing in baking pan, to shorten baking time.

Oven-fried Potatoes. Prepare potatoes as for French fried potatoes. Place in greased shallow pan to make a thin layer and brush with oil or melted fat, turning to cover all sides. Bake 20–30 min. at 450° F., or until browned, turning occasionally. Drain on absorbent paper and sprinkle with salt.

Persillade New Potatoes. Pare and cook uniform small potatoes. Pour over them a mixture of lemon juice and butter, then roll in minced parsley.

Potato Balls. Pare potatoes and cut into balls with a French vegetable cutter. Cook. Season with lemon juice and butter and roll in minced parsley.

Potatoes Continental. Peel and cook small potatoes in meat stock with bay leaves until tender. Drain and season with onion browned in butter. Garnish with minced parsley and paprika.

Potato Croquettes. Mash potatoes, add butter, salt, cayenne, and well beaten egg yolks. Shape into croquettes. Egg and crumb. Chill. Fry in deep fat.

Potatoes in Jackets. Wash medium-sized potatoes and remove any blemishes. Steam until tender and serve without removing skins.

Potato Pancakes. Grate or grind 15 lb. raw potatoes and 4 oz. onion; drain. Add 6 beaten eggs, 8 oz. flour, 3 T. salt, 1 t. baking powder, ¾ c. cream or milk. Drop with No. 20 dipper onto a hot greased griddle. Fry until golden brown on each side. Serve with applesauce.

Potato Rosettes. Force Duchess potatoes through a pastry tube, forming rosettes or fancy shapes. Bake at 350°–400° F. until browned. Use as a garnish for planked steak.

Rissolé Potatoes. See Oven-browned potatoes.

Stuffed Baked (Potatoes in the Half Shell or Double-baked Potato). Cut hot baked potatoes into halves lengthwise (if potatoes are small, cut a slice from one side). Scoop out contents. Mash, season with salt, pepper, butter, and hot milk. Pile lightly into shells, leaving tops rough. Bake until tops are browned. Grated cheese (½ lb.) or pieces of pimiento may be placed over the top. (See recipe for Mashed Potatoes, p. 409.)

French Fried Potatoes

Amount	Ingredient	Method
15–18 lbs.	Potatoes	Pare and cut potatoes into uniform strips from ⅜ to ¼ in. thick. Cover with cold water to keep potatoes from darkening. Just before frying, drain well or dry with paper towels. Fill fry basket about ⅓ full of potatoes. Fry according to method 1 or 2.

Method 1. Half fill fry kettle with fat. Preheat fat to 365° F. Fry potatoes for 6–8 min. Drain. Sprinkle with salt. Serve.

Method 2 (a) BLANCHING. Heat fat to 360° F. Place drained potato strips in hot fat, using an 8 to 1 ratio of fat to potatoes, by weight, as a guide for filling fryer basket. Fry 3–5 min., depending on thickness of potato. (The potatoes should not brown.) Drain. Hold for later browning.

(b) BROWNING. Reheat fat to 375° F. Place about twice as many potato strips in kettle as for first-stage frying. Fry 2–3 min., or until golden brown. Drain; sprinkle with salt if desired. Serve immediately.

Note:
Select a mealy type potato for French frying. For best results, store potatoes at room temperature 2 weeks before frying.

Variations:
1. *Shoestring Potatoes.* Cut potatoes into ⅛-in. strips. Fry 3–10 min. at 325–335° F.
2. *Lattice Potatoes.* Cut potatoes with lattice slicer. Fry 3–10 min. at 350–375° F.
3. *Potato Chips.* Cut potatoes into very thin slices. Fry 3–6 min. at 325° F.
4. *Deep-Fat Browned Potatoes.* Partially cook whole or half potatoes. Fry in deep fat 5–7 min. at 350–375° F.

Glazed or Candied Sweet Potatoes

Bake: 20–30 min.
Oven: 400° F.

Yield: 50 4-oz. portions

Amount	Ingredient	Method
20–25 lb. (A.P.)	Sweet potatoes	Steam or boil potatoes in skins until tender. Peel. Cut into halves lengthwise. Arrange in shallow pans.
1 lb. 12 oz. 1 pt. 8 oz. ½ t.	Brown sugar Water Butter or margarine Salt	Mix sugar, water, butter or margarine, and salt. Heat to boiling point. Pour over potatoes. Bake.

Variations:
1. *Candied with Almonds.* Proceed as for Glazed Sweet Potatoes; increase butter or margarine to 12 oz.; reduce brown sugar to 1½ lb. Add 1 c. dark sirup and 2 t. mace. When partially glazed, sprinkle top with chopped almonds and continue cooking until almonds are toasted.
2. *Glazed with Orange Slices.* Add 4 T. grated orange rind to sirup. Cut 5 oranges into thin slices; add to sweet potatoes when sirup is added.

Sweet Potatoes and Apples

Bake: 45 min.
Oven: 350° F.

Yield: 2 pans 12 × 20 × 2 in.
Portion: 4 oz.

Amount	Ingredient	Method
15 lb. 5 lb.	Sweet potatoes Apples	Cook potatoes in skins. Peel and slice. Pare and slice apples. Place alternate layers of sweet potatoes and apples in baking pans.
1 lb. 8 oz. 2 T. 8 oz. 1 pt.	Brown sugar Granulated sugar Salt Butter or margarine Water	Make a sirup of sugar, salt, butter or margarine, and water. Pour hot sirup over potatoes and apples. Bake.

Notes:
1. 1 lb. coarsely chopped pecans may be added.
2. During last 5 min. of baking, 1 lb. marshmallows may be placed on top.

Variation:
Sweet Potato and Cranberry Casserole. Substitute 3 lb. cooked cranberries for apples; omit brown sugar and add 3 lb. granulated sugar.

Sweet Potato and Almond Croquettes

Fry: 3–4 min.
Temp. 375° F.

Yield: 50 3-oz. croquettes

Amount	Ingredient	Method
15 lb.	Sweet potatoes	Pare, cook, and mash sweet potatoes.
16 2 t. 5 T. 1 T. 1 lb.	Egg yolks, beaten Nutmeg Sugar Salt Almonds, chopped	Add egg yolks, seasonings, and almonds. Mix.
1 lb. 3 1 c.	Cornflakes, crushed Eggs Water or milk	Measure with No. 12 dipper onto tray covered with part of the crushed cornflakes. Chill about 2 hr. Shape into croquettes or patties; dip in egg mixture, and roll in remainder of cornflakes. Fry in deep fat.

Note:
May be baked. Place on greased baking pan. Spread with 8 oz. butter or margarine. Bake 30–45 min. at 350° F.

Baked Tomatoes

Bake: 10–12 min.
Oven: 400° F.

Yield: 50 portions
(½ tomato each)

Amount	Ingredient	Method
25	Tomatoes (5 oz. each)	Wash tomatoes. Cut in halves. Sprinkle each tomato with ⅛–¼ t. salt and pepper or seasoned salt.
6 oz. 2 oz. 6 oz.	Butter or margarine, melted Bread crumbs, coarse Onion, chopped fine	Combine butter or margarine, bread crumbs, and onion. Place 2 t. crumb mixture on each tomato half. Bake.

Variations:
1. *Mushroom-stuffed Tomatoes.* Add 2 lb. sautéed, sliced, or chopped mushrooms to crumb mixture.
2. *Broiled Tomato Slices.* Cut tomatoes in ½-in. slices. Salt, dot with butter, and broil.

French Fried Onions

Fry: 3–4 min.   Yield: 50 3-oz. portions
Deep-Fat Fryer: 350–375° F.

Amount	Ingredient	Method
8 lb. (E.P.)	Onions	Cut onions into ¼-in. slices. Separate into rings.
6	Eggs, beaten	Combine eggs and milk.
2 c.	Milk	Add dry ingredients and mix to
12 oz.	Flour	make batter.
2 t.	Baking powder	Dip onion rings in batter and fry
1½ t.	Salt	in deep fat. Drain.

Variations:
1. *French Fried Cauliflower.* Dip 10 lb. cold cooked cauliflower into batter and fry 3–5 min. at 370° F.
2. *French Fried Eggplant.* Pare, cut into ¼-in. slices or cut in strips as for French Fried Potatoes. Dip in batter and fry 5–7 min. at 370° F.

Buttered Cabbage

Yield: 50 3-oz. portions

Amount	Ingredient	Method
15 lb. (E.P.)	Cabbage	Cut cabbage into wedges or shred
4 gal.	Water, boiling	coarsely.
2 T.	Salt	Cook until tender (p. 406) 15–20 min. Drain.
8 oz.	Butter or margarine, melted	Add butter.

Notes:
1. Cabbage will cook in a shorter time if shredded and will yield a more desirable product.
2. Bacon fat may be used in place of butter. Add it to the water in which cabbage is to be cooked.

Variations:
1. *Creamed Cabbage.* Omit butter or margarine. Pour 2 qt. Medium White Sauce (p. 385) over shredded, cooked, drained cabbage.
2. *Scalloped Cabbage.* Omit butter or margarine. Pour 2 qt. Medium White Sauce over chopped, cooked, drained cabbage. Cover with buttered crumbs. Bake 15–20 min. at 400° F. Shredded cheese may be added.

Hot Slaw

Yield: 1 gal.
Portion: 3 oz.

Amount	Ingredient	Method
1 lb. 5 oz. 1½ T. 4 oz. 2 t.	Sugar Salt Flour Mustard, dry	Mix dry ingredients.
1 qt. 1¼ qt.	Milk, hot Water, hot	Add milk and water while stirring. Cook until thickened.
8 2⅔ c.	Eggs, beaten Vinegar, hot	Add eggs gradually while stirring briskly. Cook 2–3 min. Add vinegar.
12 lb. (E.P.) 4 t.	Cabbage, raw, shredded Celery seed	Pour hot sauce over cabbage just before serving. Add celery seed and mix lightly.

Note:
This sauce also may be used as a cooked salad dressing.

Spanish Green Beans

Yield: 50 3-oz. portions

Amount	Ingredient	Method
8 oz. 6 oz. 4 oz.	Bacon, diced Onion, chopped Green pepper, chopped	Sauté bacon, onion, and green pepper until lightly browned.
4 oz. 2 qt. 1 T.	Flour Tomatoes, hot Salt	Add flour and stir until smooth. Add tomatoes and salt gradually. Stir and cook until thickened.
2 No. 10 cans (or 10 lb.)	Green beans, drained	Add tomato sauce to the green beans. Simmer approximately 30 min.

Variations:
1. *Southern-Style Green Beans.* Cut 1½ lb. bacon or salt pork into small pieces. Add 6 oz. chopped onion and sauté until onion is lightly browned. Add to hot, drained green beans. Serve with boiled ham and corn bread.
2. *Creole Green Beans.* Omit bacon. Sauté onion, green pepper, and 8 oz. celery in 2 oz. butter or margarine. Add 2 oz. sugar to tomatoes.

Spinach Soufflé

Bake: 40 min.
Oven: 350° F.

Yield: 2 12 × 20 × 2 in. pans
Portion: 2½ oz.

Amount	Ingredient	Method
1 lb. 4 oz.	Butter or margarine	Melt butter. Add flour, salt, milk, and sour cream.
8 oz.	Flour	Blend over low heat until smooth, stirring constantly. Remove from heat.
2½ T.	Salt	
1¼ qt.	Milk	
1¼ qt.	Cultured sour cream	
6 lb.	Frozen chopped spinach, thawed and drained	Add spinach, onion, nutmeg, and egg yolks. Mix.
8 oz.	Onion, finely chopped	
1½ T.	Nutmeg	
18	Egg yolks	
18	Egg whites	Beat egg whites until stiff. Fold into spinach mixture. Pour into ungreased counter pans. Bake in pans of hot water until soufflé is set.

Harvard Beets

Yield: 50 3-oz. portions

Amount	Ingredient	Method
1½ qt.	Beet juice	Add bay leaf and cloves to beet
1	Bay leaf	juice. Heat to boiling point.
1 t.	Cloves, whole	
12 oz.	Sugar	Add combined dry ingredients
2 t.	Salt	while stirring briskly. Cook
6 oz.	Cornstarch	until thickened and clear.
4 oz.	Butter or margarine	Add butter or margarine and vinegar.
2 c.	Vinegar	Pour sauce over hot beets.
2 No. 10 cans	Beets, sliced, drained	

Note:
12 lb. fresh beets, cooked, may be substituted for canned beets.
Variations:
1. *Beets with Orange Sauce.* Omit bay leaf and vinegar; add 1½ c. orange juice.
2. *Hot Spiced Beets.* Drain juice from 2 No. 10 cans sliced beets and add 1 T. cloves, 1½ T. salt, ½ t. cinnamon, 1 lb. brown sugar, 8 oz. granulated sugar, and 1 qt. vinegar. Cook 10 min. Pour sauce over beets and reheat.

Baked Beans

Bake: 5–6 hr.
Oven: 350° F.

Yield: 50 5-oz. portions

Amount	Ingredient	Method
5 lb. (A.P.)	Navy beans	Wash beans. Add boiling water.
1½ gal.	Water, boiling	Cover. Let stand 1 hr. or longer. Cook in same water until tender (about 1 hr.). Add more water as necessary.
4 oz.	Salt	Add all ingredients to the beans.
6 oz.	Brown sugar	Blend.
1 t.	Mustard, dry	Pour beans into deep baking pan.
2 T.	Vinegar	Bake.
1 c.	Molasses	
2½ c.	Catsup (optional)	
1 lb.	Salt pork, cubed	

Variation:
Boston Baked Beans. Omit catsup and bake in oven the entire cooking time.

Baked Lima Beans

Bake: 2 hr.
Oven: 350° F.

Yield: 2 pans 12 × 20 × 2 in.
Portion: 5 oz.

Amount	Ingredient	Method
6 lb. 1 gal.	Lima beans Water, boiling	Wash beans. Add boiling water. Cover. Let stand 1 hr. or longer. Cook beans in the same water until tender (about 1 hr.).
4 oz. 8 oz. 1½ T. 1 c.	Pimiento, chopped Bacon fat Salt Molasses	Add seasonings. Pour into 2 baking pans.
1 lb. 8 oz.	Salt pork, sliced	Place salt pork on top of beans. Bake until top is brown (about 1 hr.).

Variations:
1. *Baked Lima Beans with Sausage.* Omit salt pork and bacon fat. Place 6 lb. link sausages on top of beans.
2. *Boiled Lima Beans and Ham.* Omit salt pork and seasonings. Add 5 lb. cured ham, diced, to beans and simmer until tender.

Ranch Style Beans

Bake: 6–8 hr.
Oven: 300° F.

Yield: 50 5-oz. portions

Amount	Ingredient	Method
5 lb. 1½ gal.	Beans, red or pinto Water	Soak beans overnight; drain off water.
2 lb. 8 oz.	Salt pork, 1-in. cubes Water, cold	Add salt pork to beans. Add cold water to cover. Cook slowly until tender.
3–4 pods 2 qt. 8 oz. 1½ T. 1 T. f.g. 2 cloves	Chili peppers Tomatoes, cooked Onion, sliced Salt Pepper Cayenne Garlic, chopped	Soak chili peppers in warm water. Remove pulp from pods and add to beans. Add tomatoes and other seasonings. Cook slowly in kettle an additional 5 hr. or pour into 12 × 20 × 4-in. pan and bake 6–8 hr. at 300° F.

Note:
If chili peppers are not available, 1 oz. of chili powder may be used.

Suggestions for Serving Vegetables[1]

ASPARAGUS

Asparagus with Cheese Sauce. Serve 5 or 6 stalks of cooked asparagus with 1 T. Cheese Sauce (p. 385).

Fresh Asparagus with Hollandaise Sauce. Serve 1 T. Hollandaise Sauce (p. 378) over cooked asparagus.

Creamed Asparagus on Toast. Add 1 gal. Medium White Sauce (p. 385) to 10 lb. (E.P.) asparagus, cooked. Serve on toast.

GREEN BEANS

Green Beans Amandine. Add 8 oz. slivered almonds lightly browned in 8 oz. butter or margarine to 10–12 lb. freshly cooked and drained beans.

French Green Beans. Cook 7½–10 lb. frozen French cut green beans. Drain and season with 1 c. mayonnaise, ¾ c. cultured sour cream, 2 T. vinegar, salt, pepper, and 2 oz. onion sautéed in 2 oz. butter or margarine.

Green Beans and Mushrooms. Add 2 lb. sautéed chopped mushrooms to 7½ lb. cooked, drained beans arranged in a serving pan. Cover with 6 10½-oz. cans cream of mushroom soup. Top with 8 oz. toasted almonds. Bake uncovered about 25 min. at 350° F.

BEETS

Julienne Beets. Shred 8 lb. cooked beets into thin strips. Season with mixture of 8 oz. butter or margarine, ½ c. sugar, 4 t. salt, 1 c. lemon juice.

Beets in Sour Cream. Grate fresh cooked beets and season with a mixture of 1½ c. lemon juice, 1½ T. onion juice, 2 t. salt, and 1¼ c. sugar. Toss lightly. Serve with a spoonful of cultured sour cream on each portion.

BROCCOLI

Almond-Buttered Broccoli. Brown slivered almonds in butter and pour over cooked and drained broccoli.

Broccoli with Hollandaise Sauce or Lemon Butter. Serve cooked spears or chopped broccoli with 1 T. Hollandaise Sauce (p. 378) or 1 t. lemon butter.

CABBAGE

Creole Cabbage. Sauté 8 oz. chopped onion until soft in 1 lb. butter or margarine. Add 3 qt. canned tomatoes, 2 c. chopped green peppers, 12 whole cloves, 1 bay leaf, ¾ c. brown sugar, and 2 t. salt. Simmer about 15 min. Remove cloves and bay leaf. Add this sauce to 10 lb. shredded cabbage cooked 7 min. Mix, reheat, and serve.

Fried Cabbage. Place 1 lb. fat in small steam-jacketed kettle or heavy aluminum pan. Add 13 lb. (E.P.) shredded cabbage and 2 T. salt. Cook about 15 min., stirring frequently.

Cabbage Polonnaise. Arrange 9½ lb. cabbage wedges in baking pans and cover with 3 qt. Medium White Sauce (p. 385). Sprinkle with buttered bread crumbs. Bake about 25 min. at 350° F.

[1] For preparation and detailed cookery methods, see pp. 403–409.

Cabbage au Gratin. Alternate layers of 7-min. cooked coarsely shredded cabbage, Medium White Sauce (p. 385) and grated sharp cheese in a baking pan. Sprinkle with buttered crumbs. (Use 10 lb. cabbage, 3 qt. White Sauce, 12 oz. cheese, 8 oz. crumbs, and 4 oz. butter or margarine.) Bake about 25 min. at 350° F.

CARROTS

Cranberry Carrots. Cut 12½ lb. raw carrots diagonally into 1-in. pieces. Cook. Add 2 T. salt, 8 oz. butter or margarine, and 3 c. cranberry sauce. Reheat.

Candied Carrots. Cut 12½ lb. carrots into 1-in. pieces. Cook until tender but not soft. Melt 12 oz. butter or margarine, add 9 oz. sugar, 1½ T. salt. Add to carrots. Bake 15–20 min. at 400° F. Turn frequently.

Carrots and Celery. Combine 7 lb. carrots and 3 lb. celery sliced about the same thickness. Cook until tender and season with butter or margarine, salt, and pepper.

Mint-glazed Carrots. Peel and cut 12½ lb. carrots into quarters lengthwise, cook until almost tender. Drain. Melt 8 oz. butter or margarine, 8 oz. sugar, 1½ T. salt, and 1 c. mint jelly. Blend. Add carrots and simmer a few minutes.

Savory Carrots. Cook 12½ lb. sliced carrots in a small amount of beef or chicken broth. Remove from broth and season with butter or margarine, salt, pepper, and lemon juice. Sprinkle with chopped parsley.

Lyonnaise Carrots. Arrange 6 qt. cooked carrot strips in baking pan. Add onion that has been cooked until soft in butter or margarine. Place in a 375° F. oven until reheated and lightly browned. Just before serving sprinkle with chopped parsley.

CAULIFLOWER

Cauliflower with Almond Butter. Season 12 lb. freshly cooked cauliflower with 2 c. slivered almonds that have been browned in 8 oz. butter or margarine.

Cauliflower Casserole. Place 12 lb. (E.P.) cooked, drained cauliflowerets in baking pan. Cover with a mixture of 18 eggs, 2 qt. milk, 12 oz. grated cheese, and 1 T. salt. Set in a pan of hot water and bake about 45 min. at 325° F. Serve with Tomato Sauce (p. 381). With crisp bacon, this casserole may be served as a luncheon dish.

Cauliflower with New Peas. Combine 7 lb. freshly cooked cauliflower with 5 lb. cooked frozen peas. Season with melted butter or margarine.

Cauliflower with Cheese Sauce. Pour 2–3 qt. Cheese Sauce (p. 385) over 12 lb. (E.P.) cooked fresh cauliflower.

CORN

Corn Pudding. Use 9 lb. uncooked frozen corn or 1 No. 10 can cream style corn, 3 qt. milk, 6 oz. melted butter or margarine, 2 T. salt, and 24 egg yolks, beaten. Mix and fold in 24 beaten egg whites. Pour into baking pan and place in pan of hot water. Bake approximately 45 min. at 325° F.

Corn in Cream. Add 1¼ qt. light cream, 6 oz. butter or margarine, 2 T. salt, and 1 T. white pepper to 10 lb. frozen whole-grain corn, cooked. Bring just to boiling point and serve immediately.

Scalloped Corn. Add 1 qt. cracker crumbs, salt and pepper to 8 oz. melted butter or bacon fat. Mix 1 qt. whole milk with 4½ qt. cream-style corn. Place alternate layers of buttered crumbs and corn mixture in greased baking pan. Bake approximately 45 min. at 325° F.

Corn and Tomato Casserole. Add to 1 No. 10 can of whole-kernel corn 1 gal. chopped fresh tomato, 1½ c. chopped green pepper, 2 T. salt, and ½ t. pepper. Place in greased baking pan, cover with 4 c. crushed crisp cereal, 3 c. grated sharp cheese, and 8 oz. butter or margarine.

Corn O'Brien. Drain 2 No. 10 cans whole grain corn. Add 1 lb. chopped bacon, ¾ lb. chopped green pepper, and ¾ lb. chopped onion that have been sautéed until lightly browned. Just before serving, add 3 oz. chopped pimiento, salt, and pepper.

EGGPLANT

Creole Eggplant. Melt 1 lb. fat, add 1 lb. chopped onion, 8 oz. coarsely chopped green pepper, and 1 lb. coarsely chopped celery. Cook until tender. Add 2 qt. tomatoes, 5 lb. diced eggplant, 3 T. salt, 1 t. pepper, and 1 T. sugar. Pour into baking pan. Cover with buttered crumbs. Bake until eggplant is tender.

MUSHROOMS

Sautéed Mushrooms. Clean thoroughly. Peel all but tender young caps. Sauté sliced or whole small mushrooms in butter or margarine. Allow 2 oz. butter for 1 lb. mushrooms.

ONIONS

Baked Onions. Peel 50 4-oz. onions and steam until tender. Sprinkle with salt and buttered bread crumbs. Pour 1 qt. water, broth, or milk over onions. Bake 20–30 min. at 400° F. or until browned.

Creamed Pearl Onions. Cook 12½ lb. tiny unpeeled white onions in boiling salted water until tender, drain, then peel. Add 2 qt. Medium White Sauce (p. 385) to which 4 oz. additional butter or margarine has been added. Garnish with paprika.

Stuffed Baked Onions. Scoop out center of 50 large onions. Fill with mixture of 1½ qt. Medium White Sauce (p. 385), 8 oz. butter or margarine, 6 beaten egg yolks, and onion centers cooked and chopped. 12 oz. chopped toasted almonds may be added. Cover tops of onions with buttered crumbs.

Onion Casserole. Combine 10 lb. cooked tiny onions, 10 oz. chopped walnuts, 1 c. pimiento strips, and 8 10½-oz. cans cream of mushroom soup. Cover with 1½ c. grated cheese. Bake approximately 30 min. at 400° F.

PARSNIPS

Browned Parsnips. Place 10 lb. cooked parsnips, cut lengthwise into uniform pieces, in baking pan. Sprinkle with 1½ T. salt and 4 oz. sugar. Pour 8 oz. melted butter or margarine over top. Bake at 425° F. until browned.

PEAS

New Peas with Mushrooms. Add 2 lb. fresh mushrooms, sliced, sautéed in 8 oz. butter or margarine, to 10 lb. cooked frozen peas.

Creamed New Potatoes and Peas. Combine 7 lb. freshly cooked new potatoes and 5 lb. cooked frozen peas with 3 qt. Medium White Sauce (p. 385).

Green Peas and Sliced New Turnips. Combine 2 40-oz. packages frozen peas, cooked, with 3 lb. new turnips, sliced and cooked. Add 8 oz. melted butter or margarine and salt to taste.

Green Peas with Pearl Onions. Combine 3 40-oz. packages frozen peas, cooked, with 3 lb. pearl onions, cooked. Add 8 oz. butter or margarine or 2–3 qt. Medium White Sauce (p. 385) to which 4 oz. extra butter or margarine has been added.

SPINACH

Wilted Spinach or Lettuce. To 10 lb. chopped spinach or letture, or a combination of the two, add 2–2½ qt. Vegetable Sauce (p. 381) just before serving.

SQUASH

Baked Acorn Squash. Cut 25 squash into halves, remove seeds, bake upside down in shallow pan with a little water, 20–25 min., or until just tender. Place hollow side up, add 8 oz. butter or margarine, 1½ T. salt, 12 oz. brown sugar, and reheat until sugar is melted. For a luncheon dish, place a 4-oz. sausage pattie or 2 link sausages, partially cooked, in each squash half, and continue baking. Cavity may also be filled with No. 12 dipper of a mixture of 5 qt. steamed rice, 4 lb. chopped cooked meat, 4 oz. sautéed minced onion, moistened with meat stock.

Mashed Butternut Squash. Cook 15 lb. peeled butternut squash until tender. Mash and add 1½ qt. hot milk, 8 oz. butter or margarine, 2 T. salt, and 8 oz. brown sugar. Whip until light. May be garnished with toasted slivered almonds.

Broiled Zucchini Squash. Remove ends of squash and cut in halves lengthwise. Simmer in boiling salted water, or steam until almost tender. Drain and arrange in a baking pan. Cover with melted butter or salad oil. Sprinkle with garlic salt, white pepper, grated Parmesan cheese, and a little oregano. Broil or bake in hot oven until lightly browned.

Zucchini Italian. Cook 1½ lb. sliced onions in 1 c. hot salad oil until tender but not brown. Add 5 lb. raw tomatoes that have been peeled, sliced, and cooked about 3 min. Add 12 lb. sliced zucchini, 2½ T. salt, 4 t. pepper. Cook slowly about 20 min., adding small amount of water if necessary. Add 1 bay leaf if desired.

SWEET POTATOES

Baked Sweet Potatoes. Select small even-sized sweet potatoes. Scrub and bake 40–45 min., or until done, at 425° F.

TURNIPS

Mashed White Turnips. Cook 15 lb. turnips, drain, and mash as potatoes. Season with 8 oz. butter or margarine, 1 T. salt, ½ t. pepper, and 1 c. hot milk or cream.

TOMATOES

Breaded Tomatoes. Add 1 lb. cubed bread, 8 oz. butter or margarine, and ¾ c. sugar to 2 No. 10 cans tomatoes. Bake approximately 30 min. at 350° F.

Creole Tomatoes. Drain 2 No. 10 cans tomatoes. To the juice add 1 lb. celery, 4 oz. onion, and 8 oz. green pepper, coarsely chopped. Cook about 15 min. Add the tomatoes, 2 T. salt, and ¾ t. pepper and place in greased baking pan. Cover with 2 qt. toasted bread cubes and bake about 30 min. at 350° F.

PART THREE
MENU
PLANNING

MENU PLANNING

Principles of Menu Planning

A carefully planned menu is the initial step toward a successful meal. It should provide food for adequate nutrition, tempt the appetite, and result in satisfaction for the guest. For the food service, the menu will predetermine the work to be done and largely control the resulting profit or loss. So important is the menu that, without it, there will be no successful food service.

Factors basic to menu planning may therefore be divided into two areas: those relating to the guest, and those to the food service management. The first includes age, sex, and occupation of the group, their nutritional needs and food preferences. The second deals with the type of food service, number to be served, equipment available, number and experience of employees, distribution of work, availability and seasonability of foods, and the food budget.

Meals outside of the home are eaten in such widely diversified places as the school lunchroom, university cafeterias and residence halls, hospitals, homes for children and adults, summer camps, industrial cafeterias, and many types of restaurants. Each of these services is planned to meet the needs of a particular group of customers. To insure that a menu will meet the demands of the customer, careful consideration must be given to each of the following factors.

1. *Age, Sex, and Occupation of Group to be Served.* The menu planner must consider the age, sex, occupation, nutritional needs, food habits, and preferences of the individual members of the group.

In a situation in which no choice of food is offered, as in homes for children and in nursing and retirement homes, meals must be planned to meet the complete nutritional needs of members of the group and also offer enough variety to minimize monotony and meet, in so far as possible, their food preferences.

Wherever a multiple choice of foods is offered, care must be taken to provide foods from which the individual patron may choose a well-balanced meal. The choice also must include enough variety to make it possible for him to select a meal that he will enjoy at a price he wishes to pay.

2. *Climate and Season.* The factor of climate and season is important in the choice of foods. Cool, crisp, fresh foods are often more appealing in hot weather, but at least one hot food should be included in each summer menu. In cold weather, the heavier foods high in caloric value may be used. A festive touch may be added on holidays and other special occasions by including foods not served regularly, and by adding unusual garnishes and special decorations.

3. *Flavor and Appearance of the Food.* Flavor combinations should receive special consideration. A balance should be maintained between tart and sweet, mild and highly flavored, light and heavy foods. Certain flavors seem to belong together, and if carefully selected will complement each other. Foods of the same or similar flavor, such as tomato soup and tomato salad, should not be repeated in one menu. A definite contrast in flavor between the foods of different courses is desirable.

Acid foods, such as grapefruit, stimulate the appetite and digestion. They are used effectively as a first course or with a bland entrée. Sweet foods are satiating and should be used sparingly. They are served to best advantage as dessert.

Foods selected for a menu should be of harmonious colors that present an inviting appearance on the plate, the hospital tray, or cafeteria counter. Just as uninteresting, colorless meals are to be avoided, so should those offering foods that clash in color, such as beets and carrots. When planning menus for a cafeteria or a buffet meal, foods that are to be displayed together, such as vegetables, salads, or desserts, should offer a pleasing color contrast.

Contrast in shape and form of different foods appearing on a plate likewise lends interest to the meal. Variety in preparation makes it possible to present food shaped in varied forms and sizes. Care should be taken to avoid too many mixed foods of similar shape at the same meal, such as beef stew, mixed vegetables, tossed green salad, and fruit cup. Indiscriminate use of the dippers when serving may cause all the food to assume the shape of tennis balls. A suitable sauce or garnish may be used effectively to give an appearance of unity to the plate.

There should be balance between soft and solid foods. A soft entrée calls for a crisp vegetable or salad. A mashed or creamed vegetable may be served more successfully with a solid meat than with a casserole dish. Two foods prepared in the same manner, such as creamed, buttered, fried, or mashed, should not be served together.

4. *Variety.* Variety is introduced not only in the kind of food, but also in the method of preparation, combinations, textures, and garnishes. With the exception of staples, the same food should not be served too often or repeated on the same day of the week. If the same food must be served often, a change in the method of preparation and the accompanying foods will give desired variety.

The menu planner in considering the needs and wishes of the guest, must be aware also of the problems of management that affect the food offerings. These factors include:

1. *Type of Food Service.* The menu pattern will be influenced by the type of food service. The simple cafeteria meal planned for the child eating in a school lunchroom will be different from the menu offered in a restaurant catering to business executives.

2. *Number to Be Served.* Besides affecting the variety of food that can be included in the menu, the number to be served also influences the method of preparing the food. For example, it would be difficult, under usual institutional conditions, to prepare grilled tomatoes or stuffed baked potatoes for a large group.

3. *The Food Budget.* The amount of income allotted for raw food cost and labor is a determining factor in the type of menu that can be planned and served. The menu planner should not only know how much money is available for food and labor, but should check this amount against the actual cost of the menu as served.

4. *Available Equipment.* To prepare suitable meals with the available equipment in a given length of time presents one of the major problems of those responsible for planning menus. Special attention needs to be given to oven capacity, refrigerator facilities, number and size of steam-jacketed kettles and steamers, and availability and capacity of mixers. Certain combinations of menu items often must be avoided because of lack of pans or dishes.

5. *Number and Experience of Employees.* The man hours of labor available and the efficiency and skill of employees are important to the successful preparation of any meal. When there is a lack of experienced workers, the menu items must be limited to simple foods, easily prepared.

6. *Distribution of Work.* The distribution of work among the various areas of preparation is of prime importance in meeting a time schedule and in maintaining the morale of the workers. In determining a day's work load, the menu planner needs to consider not only one day's menu but any prepreparation necessary for meals for the following day or for several days. Food prepared by the salad and bakery departments are

often of the type that require long-time preparation and need to be carefully scheduled to equalize the load. On days when the work load is light, foods may be prepared and stored in the freezer for future use.

The wise planner will make it possible to spread the employee's work load so that a limited number of foods requiring time-consuming preparation may be included. To add interest to the menu, foods such as stuffed baked potato, individual salads, fresh grapefruit sections, fresh fruit plates, homemade noodles, and tarts may be included in a menu if combined with other food items that require minimum preparation. The wide variety of ready-to-cook frozen foods, preprepared vegetables, and other convenience foods now makes possible a less restricted menu than can be offered when all food preparation is done in the kitchen. Discrimination in the selection and use of many of the prepared foods is needed to maintain high food standards and to preserve the individuality of the food service.

Some foods, including fresh and frozen vegetables, mashed potatoes, hot breads, and certain meats and fish, require last-minute cooking to assure products of high quality. To avoid confusion and delayed meal service, the menu should be so planned that there is a balance between items that may be prepared early and those that must be cooked just prior to serving.

7. *Availability and Seasonability of Foods.* Availability of foods in the local markets will exert a limited influence on the menu items. Although most foods are now available in fresh or frozen form in all sections of the country, fresh foods produced locally are often of better quality and less expensive during the growing season than are those shipped from distant markets.

8. *Cooked Foods on Hand.* Unused cooked foods are more often used to effect changes in a menu than as the basis of the original menu. However, the successful use of foods on hand requires careful thought and imagination to incorporate them in such a way that they will be acceptable.

Some foods may be offered in their original form as a choice on a selective menu. Others may be incorporated into combinations such as hash, meat roll, barbecued sandwiches, and croquettes. These dishes are often better made from cooked foods than from raw. Cooked vegetables, which should be reused sparingly, may be included in salads and casserole dishes. If suitable, they may be used in soup, or ground and combined with meat loaf or other luncheon entrées. Fresh fruits may be used in fruit cup, gelatins, or mixed salads, and stewed fruits may be combined in an appetizing compote. Cake and bread crumbs often are utilized in puddings, cakes and cookies, and for breading. However used, the food product must be prepared in such a way that it is as acceptable in the combined form as in its original state.

9. *Recipes.* Many a well-planned menu has been a failure because sufficient thought was not given to the selection of recipes. Cooks should be provided with standardized recipes, so that there will be no questions as to the yield or quality of the finished product. If deviations from the original recipes are necessary, great care should be exercised in making substitutions that may affect both quality and yield.

Menu-Planning Procedures

THE MENU PLANNER

The effectiveness of menu planning is largely influenced by the attitudes and ability of the planner, who should recognize that his task is an important one requiring imagination, creative ability, and a deep interest in food. It is important that the menu maker be free of prejudices and food dislikes. Menu planning should not be regarded as a routine duty, but as an opportunity to work through the medium of food to present a 3-dimensional picture of food that is attractive, nutritionally sound, and satisfying to the taste.

THE MENU-PLANNING CENTER

If at all possible, the menu should be planned during uninterrupted time in a place away from noise and confusion, and at a desk or table large enough to accommodate menu-planning materials. These include:
1. Menu forms as dictated by type and needs of food service.
2. Standardized recipe file.
3. Cook books, for large and small quantity cookery.
4. Periodicals, institutional and household.
5. Idea file of pictures and other material clipped from magazines.
6. Menu suggestion lists, as shown on pp. 455–467.
7. File of previous menus.

CYCLE MENUS

The trend in institutional meal planning is toward the construction and use of cycle or rotating menus. Such a set of menus is planned well in advance of the time it is to be used. Although many factors influence the length of the cycle, many institutions find a cycle of 3 to 5 weeks satisfactory. To ensure serving of foods that are appropriate to the season, many food services have a slightly different cycle for each of the 4 seasons.

Thoughtfully planned menus may be rotated successfully and have many advantages over short-time planning. Such a procedure results in keeping repetition of foods at a minimum and tends to aid in the control of food and labor costs. It further facilitates food purchasing, reduces waste, and provides for the effective use of employees' time. Most important, rotating menus are time-saving for the dietitian or food service manager, as their use greatly reduces the time spent in menu planning and food ordering. Carefully planned menus offer variety and interest in meals and bring greater satisfaction to patrons or guests. Interest may be added to cycle menus by varying the cookery methods of frequently recurring foods.

STEPS IN MENU PLANNING

Successful menus are planned systematically and should follow a definite pattern, about in the following order:

1. *Meat or Other Entrée.* First, determine the entrées for the entire time for which the menus are being planned, whether for a 5- or a 1-week cycle. Many managers who plan menus weekly like to schedule the entrées for a longer period, 4 or more weeks. When this has been completed, plan the remainder of each meal around the meat or main dish. In a multiple-choice menu, the entrées may consist of a roast or other "solid" meat, meat extender, poultry, fish, and a meatless entrée. Where no choice is offered, the meat or main dish needs to be varied from day to day. Variety may be obtained through the use of different kinds of meat, as well as different cuts and forms, such as roasts, cutlets, chops, ground and cubed meat. Beef, veal, pork, lamb, poultry, fish, and variety meats may be prepared and served in many interesting ways to offer a wide variety in appearance and flavor.

2. *Vegetables.* Vegetables appropriate to serve with the planned entrées should be considered next. Although there are a few widely accepted staple vegetables that necessarily must be repeated often, variety may be obtained through varied methods of preparation. Maximum use should be made of fresh vegetables when in season.

3. *Salads.* The choice of salads is of great importance in adding color, texture, flavor, and interest to the menu. There should be a well-balanced distribution of fruit, vegetable, and gelatin salads. Combinations are almost unlimited, and care should be taken to serve a dressing and a garnish that will complement the salad ingredients. On a cafeteria menu,

certain basic salads are usually offered daily. These might include head lettuce, combination vegetable salad, relishes, and cottage cheese.

4. *Bread.* A standard assortment of breads is usually offered, and one or more hot breads. Available oven space may be a limiting factor in offering a choice of hot breads.

5. *Desserts.* Dessert is the last item of the dinner and luncheon menu to be planned. The type of dessert offered depends on the rest of the meal. Where no choice is offered, a light dessert should be served with a heavy main course and a rich dessert with a light main course. When a choice is to be offered, it is customary to plan a two-crust pie, soft pie, cake, pudding, and gelatin dessert. In addition, ice creams and fruits are usually offered daily.

The menu is then completed by adding beverages, first course, if one is to be served, and breakfast items. Variety in the breakfast menu may be introduced through a choice of entrées, hot breads, fruits, and fruit juices.

CHECKING THE MENU

After the menu has been planned, it should be carefully checked to see if it has met the established criteria. Menus should also be checked for repetition by reviewing each day's meals and then comparing them with the previous and following day's menus. Menus should be compared with the previous menu cycle to avoid serving food items on the same day each week. The completed menu should, if possible, have a predominance of familiar and well-accepted menu items, with the introduction of new and less well-liked foods spaced throughout the menu period. In nonselective menus particularly, it is important that the less popular foods be accompanied by foods that are well liked by the majority of the customers.

RECORDING THE MENU

The recording of menus on a planning sheet is essential. The menu form to be used by office and kitchen personnel should include the listing of sauces, gravies, and accompaniments, as well as specific directions for preparation and service. The menu as presented to the customer will be in a different form from that designed for the preparation and service areas. In preparing the customer's menu, follow these two widely accepted rules: (1) list food items in the order of service; (2) capitalize all words except prepositions and conjunctions.

In many cases, the menu card is the customer's or patient's preview of the food and service he can expect. This emphasizes the importance of the appearance and wording of the menu. Suggestions for writing a menu card are:

1. List the main dish of each course across the center of the sheet. Write one accompaniment on the line below, on the right hand or in the center. If there are two accompaniments, place one at the right and one at the left on the line below.

Cream of Mushroom Soup
Melba Toast

Cream of Mushroom Soup
Celery Sticks　　　　Melba Toast

2. If more accompaniments are served, balance on sheet.

Breaded Veal Cutlet
Parsley Creamed Potatoes　　　Buttered Asparagus
Tossed Vegetable Salad
Butterhorn Rolls　　　Raspberry Jelly
Mocha Almond Frozen Pie
Coffee

3. Write beverage at the bottom of the menu or with the course with which it is to be served.

4. Do not include on the written menu such accompaniments as cream and sugar, salt and pepper, and condiments, such as mustard, catsup, and vinegar.

5. Use wording that is as descriptive as possible. Describe ham as Roast Sugar Cured Ham, Hawaiian style; or use terms to indicate the method of preparation, such as candied or honey-glazed. The method of preparation or some descriptive term always should be used for each item on the written menu.

POINTS TO REMEMBER IN MENU PLANNING

1. Leave nothing to chance. Be specific when recording menus. For example, pork chops should be shown as barbecued, stuffed, breaded, or whatever method of preparation is desired.

2. Avoid too many foods with accompaniments, sauces, and garnishes. This will increase the work load and may complicate the service.

3. Watch for "hidden" methods of preparation for different food items, as the name may not always be descriptive of the method. For example,

breaded pork chops, ham croquettes, cheese balls, browned potatoes, French fried onion rings are all fried foods, but only one is so indicated by name.

4. Avoid food clichés. Food combinations such as ham and pineapple, pork and apples, are highly acceptable, but should not always be served together. New combinations add interest to the menu.

5. Watch for repetition as menus are being developed. Strive for variety through the use of good basic standardized recipes and different methods of presentation, garnishes, and sauces. The menu maker should be aware of ingredients used in all recipes to avoid repetition of any one food. Sunshine salad, vegetable soup, braised liver, vegetable cheese pie, buttered carrot strips, frozen mixed vegetables all contain carrots, although "carrots" appear in the name of only one menu item.

6. Check completed menu carefully for all factors basic to successful menu planning.

The responsibility of the menu planner does not end with the writing of the menu. The task is completed only when the food has been prepared and served, the reaction of the consumer noted, and the relationship of raw food and labor costs to the selling price recorded.

Menus for School Lunches

The school lunch program has expanded rapidly since the National School Lunch Act was passed by Congress in 1946, and is now an integral part of the total educational program of elementary and secondary schools. The objective of the school lunch program is to serve nutritionally adequate, attractive, and moderately priced lunches. The nutritional goal is to furnish at least one third of the Recommended Daily Dietary Allowances of the National Research Council for children of various age groups.

TYPE A LUNCHES

The Type A lunch requirements provide the framework for nutritionally adequate school lunches. The kinds and amounts of foods listed in the Type A pattern are based on the Recommended Daily Dietary Allowances for 9–12 year old boys and girls.

As specified in the National School Lunch Regulations, a Type A lunch shall contain as a minimum:

1. *Fluid Whole Milk.* One-half pint of fluid whole milk as a beverage.
2. *Protein-Rich Foods.* Two ounces (edible portion as served) of lean

meat, poultry, or fish; or two ounces of cheese; or one egg, ½ cup of cooked dry beans or dry peas; or four tablespoons of peanut butter; or an equivalent of any combination of the above-listed foods. To be counted in meeting this requirement, these foods must be served in a main dish or in a main dish and one other menu item.

3. *Vegetables and Fruits.* Three-fourths cup serving consisting of two or more vegetables or fruits or both. A serving (¼ cup or more) of full-strength vegetable or fruit juice may be counted to meet not more than ¼ cup of this requirement.

4. *Bread.* One slice of whole-grain or enriched bread; or a serving of other bread such as cornbread, biscuits, rolls, muffins, made of whole-grain or enriched meal or flour.

5. *Butter or Fortified Margarine.* Two teaspoons of butter or fortified margarine.

Lesser quantities of the protein-rich foods, the vegetables and fruits, and butter or margarine may be served to children in the elementary grades, provided that such adjustments are based on the lesser food needs of younger children.

To help assure that all Type A lunches meet the nutritional goal, it is recommended that lunches include:

1. A vitamin C food each day.
2. A vitamin A food twice a week.
3. Several foods for iron each day and larger portions of some of these when possible.

In addition to meeting the nutritive requirements, the school lunch should provide satisfaction and pleasure to the pupil and help in the development of good eating habits. Planning menus that meet the nutritive requirements and are attractive, appetizing, and palatable at a price that pupils can afford to pay presents a challenge to the ability of those responsible for this function of the program.

The major factors to be considered by those planning school lunch menus include: variety in texture, color, flavor, and methods of preparation; use of foods in season; use of commodities distributed to lunchrooms operating under the National School Lunch Program; number, ability, and experience of personnel; amount and adequacy of equipment and space; time available for food preparation; food habits of the group to be served; nutritional requirements of the students; and amount of money available.

The cycle menu has been used to some extent in school cafeterias. However, in schools serving a Type A lunch the menu must be flexible enough to incorporate government purchased foods that are available to participating schools.

Some schools now offer in addition to a plate lunch a soup and sandwich meal that meets requirements for the Type A lunch; others are offering a modified selective Type A menu and some à la carte in the junior and senior high schools.

Suggested menu items for either a Type A meal or à la carte menu are given below. If separate items are offered, one or more choices for the day may be made from each of the following categories:

Soups. Cream of tomato, cream of potato, corn chowder, split pea, vegetable beef, beef noodle, bean, chicken and rice, chicken and noodle, frankfurter-bean.

Hot Dishes. Turkey and dressing, turkey and noodles, turkey à la king, oven-fried chicken, barbecued chicken, chicken pie, meat loaf, meat balls or patties, creole spaghetti, Spanish rice with meat, lasagna, creamed hamburger, chili con carne, meat pie, shepherd's pie, beef stew, pork and noodle casserole, creamed chipped beef, braised liver, chop suey, wieners and sauerkraut, scalloped potatoes and ham, lima beans with ham, ham and potato omelet, scrambled eggs with ham or bacon, baked beans, creamed salmon, salmon loaf, baked fish, fish sticks, fish fillets, tuna and noodles, macaroni and cheese, cheese and rice casserole, grilled cheese sandwich, hamburgers in buns, cheeseburgers, frankfurters in buns, hot meat sandwich, pizza, barbecued beef, pork or turkey sandwiches, Sloppy Joes.

Vegetables. Peas; carrots; green and wax beans; beets; spinach; tomatoes; cabbage; broccoli; asparagus; corn; squash; potatoes; sweet potatoes. Most vegetables may be creamed, buttered, or scalloped to offer variety.

Salads:
1. *Fruit Salads.* Peach, pear, pineapple, orange, and apple; apple, pineapple, and marshmallow; Waldorf; stuffed prune, apple, and banana; banana and nut; apple, grape, and banana; raisin and carrot; cranberry relish; combination; grapefruit.
2. *Vegetable salads or relishes.* Sliced tomato; head or leaf lettuce; celery stuffed with cheese or peanut butter; vegetable combination; carrot and celery; cole slaw; cabbage and pineappple; asparagus; apple, cabbage, and raisin; chopped lettuce and hard-cooked eggs; pickled beet; spiced pear or peach; carrot, celery, cauliflower, and turnip strips.
3. *Hearty Salads.* Kidney bean; potato; cottage cheese; deviled eggs; salmon; tuna.
4. *Gelatin salads.* Perfection; jellied Waldorf; pineapple and carrot; jellied fruit; jellied vegetable.

Sandwiches. Cold meat; ground meat moistened with salad dressing and mixed sweet pickle relish; egg salad; cottage cheese and nut; cheese; lettuce and tomato; nut bread; chicken salad; peanut butter and raisin; peanut butter and honey; peanut butter and cheese; raisin and date; date and nut; bacon and tomato; submarines.

Suggested School Lunch Menus (Plate Lunches)

1	2	3	4	5	6	7	8
Beef Stew with Vegetables Raw Spinach and Lettuce Salad Hot Biscuit, Butter Cinnamon Applesauce Milk	Pizza Buttered Green Beans Cole Slaw Hot Rolls, Butter Canned Peach Milk	Orange Juice Hot Turkey Sandwich Mashed Potatoes Lettuce-Egg Salad Jellied Fruit Milk	Pork and Noodle Casserole Buttered Spinach Cabbage Pineapple Salad Bread, Butter Peanut Butter Cookie Milk	Tomato Soup Grilled Cheese Sandwich Crisp Carrot Strips Banana Cake Milk	Steamed Frankfurter Scalloped Potatoes Head Lettuce Wedges Bread, Butter Orange (cut) Milk	Macaroni and Cheese Buttered Broccoli Deviled Egg Cinnamon Roll, Butter Cherry Cobbler Milk	Chili-Crackers Celery Sticks Corn Bread, Butter Canned Pear Milk

1	2	3	4	5	6	7	8
Meat Loaf Creamed Potatoes Raw Vegetable Relishes Rolls, Butter Cake with Pineapple Topping Milk	Barbecued Chicken Steamed Rice Buttered Green Beans Apple, Celery, Nut Salad Rolls, Butter Coconut Cream Pudding Milk	Hamburger in Bun Scalloped Corn Lettuce Wedge Ice Cream Milk	Chop Suey with Chow Mein Noodles Sliced Tomatoes Kolaches, Butter Fruit Cup Milk	Baked Fish Fillet Buttered Peas Molded Carrot-Pineapple Salad Corn Meal Rolls, Butter Icebox Cookie Milk	Meat Balls and Spaghetti Combination Green Vegetable Salad Rolls, Butter Apple Crisp Milk	Creamed Beef Baked Potato Peach with Cottage Cheese Salad Lettuce Sandwiches Gingerbread with Lemon Sauce Milk	Vegetable-Beef Soup Peanut Butter-Honey or Peanut and Cheese Sandwich Raw Vegetable Relishes Chocolate Pudding Milk

Desserts:

1. *Puddings.* Tapioca; rice; custard; bread; apple crisp; brown Betty; Norwegian prune; chocolate cream; lemon snow; lemon cake; vanilla cream; vanilla cream with fruit; chocolate fudge; date; butterscotch.

2. *Fruit.* Fresh, canned, or dried fruit; fruit cup; orange-banana-coconut combination; jellied fruit cup; fruit whips; baked apple.

3. *Gelatin.* Fruit gelatin; fruit whip; Bavarian cream.

4. *Cakes.* Plain with fruit sauce; cherry, applesauce, prune, or banana; fudge; chocolate cup; upside-down fruit; cottage pudding; Washington pie; jelly roll; gingerbread.

5. *Cookies.* Oatmeal; ginger; sugar; butterscotch drop; filled; icebox; peanut butter; chocolate chip; brownies; prune; fruit bars.

6. *Pastry.* Fresh, frozen, canned or dried fruit cobbler or pie; cream puffs; fruit turnovers or dumplings.

7. *Ice cream.*

Beverages. Chocolate and plain milk; malted milk; cocoa; vegetable juices; fruit juices.

Menus for University Residence Halls and Cafeterias

Meals for college and university students may be provided in individual residence halls, large residence hall food centers, university cafeterias, student unions, or smaller living groups.

RESIDENCE HALLS

The daily menu in a college or university residence hall must be adequate to meet the nutritional needs of the residents. The number to be served is fairly constant, so amounts may be carefully planned, resulting in little or no waste. Although some residence halls still serve a "fixed" or complete meal three times a day, others are finding the use of selective menus popular and advantageous. In this case, the selective menus are simplified cafeteria menus, and may offer a choice of two items in each category, or the choice may be limited to certain menu items only. For example, when a well-accepted entrée is provided, no choice may be needed, or students may select from two entrées and from three or four salads. Certain salad or dessert items may be offered each day.

There is little difference in menus planned for men and women except in the size of servings. In many universities meals are served to both men and women in a central food service. Some selection of menu items and adjustment in size of servings enables the same menu to be served to both men and women students.

Suggested Menu Outline* for a Residence Hall Serving 3 Meals a Day

Breakfast	Lunch		Dinner
	I or II		
Fruit	Main Dish	Soup	Main meat dish
Cereal, Hot	Vegetable	Salad and/or	Potato or other
and/or cold	Salad or relish	sandwich	starchy vegetable
Protein Dish	Bread, butter	Dessert	Vegetable
Sweet Roll or	Fruit or other	Milk, tea, or	Bread, butter
hot bread	light dessert	coffee	Salad, ice, or
Toast, Jelly	Coffee or Tea		relishes
Coffee, cocoa,			Dessert
or milk			Coffee, milk, or tea

Daily Recommended Food Allowances for College Students

1 citrus fruit
2 vegetables in addition to potatoes, 1 of which should be green or yellow and
   1 raw
1 pint or more milk per person, in addition to that used in cooking
Fresh fruit
3 whole grain or enriched cereals, including bread
2 protein foods;
   1 meat dish
   1 dish including eggs, cheese, beans, or meat extender
1 T. or more butter or fortified margarine
1 egg, or 4 weekly in addition to those used in cooking
Frequently 1 glandular organ, such as liver, heart, tongue, or sweetbreads

* For a selective menu, a suggested pattern for lunch would be soup, juice, or vegetable; sandwich or hearty salad; a hot main dish; choice of 2 or more salads; choice of 2 or more desserts. For dinner, two main dishes might be offered except where the popularity of the item does not warrant offering an alternate; a potato or other starchy vegetable; 2 or more vegetables; 2 or more salads; 2 or more desserts. Certain standard menu items may be offered every day, as cottage cheese, peanut butter, tossed vegetable or head lettuce salad, fresh or canned fruit, and ice cream. An assortment of breads and beverages would also be offered daily.

Selective Menus for a College or University Residence Hall (*Continued*)

BREAKFAST

Monday	Tuesday	Wednesday	Thursday	Friday	Saturday	Sunday
Assorted Fruits Hot or Cold Cereal Bacon Slices Scrambled Eggs Toast—Jelly Sweet Rolls Coffee, Cocoa, Milk	Assorted Fruits Hot or Cold Cereal Fried Scrapple Sirup Toast—Jelly Coffee, Cocoa, Milk	Assorted Fruits Hot or Cold Cereal Hard & Soft Cooked Eggs Toast—Jelly Coffee Cake Coffee, Cocoa, Milk	Assorted Fruits Hot or Cold Cereal Poached Eggs Toast—Jelly Sweet Rolls Coffee, Cocoa, Milk	Assorted Fruits Hot or Cold Cereal Pancakes Sirup Link Sausages Toast—Jelly Coffee, Cocoa, Milk	Assorted Fruits Hot or Cold Cereal Bacon Fried Eggs Toast—Jelly Bishop's Bread Coffee, Cocoa, Milk	Assorted Fruits Hot or Cold Cereal Toast—Jelly Sweet Rolls Coffee, Cocoa, Milk

LUNCH

Monday	Tuesday	Wednesday	Thursday	Friday	Saturday	Sunday
Tomato Juice Macaroni & Cheese or Hamburger—Bun Buttered Limas Relish Plate or Pineapple—Banana—Orange Salad Brownies Beverages	Cream of Mushroom Soup Meat Pie or Submarine Sandwich—Potato Chips Head Lettuce Salad Cucumbers in Sour Cream Peach Crisp Beverages	Pepper Pot Soup Turkey Tetrazinni or Chef's Salad Buttered Green Beans Citrus Fruit Salad Oatmeal Cookies Beverages	Vegetable Beef Soup Creamed Tuna on Biscuit or Reuben Sandwich Carrifruit Salad or Pear Salad Gingerbread Beverages	Cream of Tomato Soup Chow Mein or Egg Salad Sandwich Head Lettuce Salad or Fruit Gelatin Salad Chocolate Cream Pudding Beverages	Bean Soup Pizza or Fresh Fruit Plate Fresh Spinach Salad or Cottage Cheese Butterscotch Drop Cookies Beverages	Chilled Fruit Juice Roast Pork Loin Mashed Potatoes—Gravy French Green Beans Amandine or Browned Parsnips Applesauce Mold Salad or Fresh Fruit Salad Frozen Filled Angel Food Cake Beverages

Selective Menus for a College or University Residence Hall (Continued)

DINNER

Monday	Tuesday	Wednesday	Thursday	Friday	Saturday	Sunday
Roast Beef	Breaded Veal	Swiss Steak or	Fried Chicken	Barbecued Ribs	Salisbury Steak—	
Browned Pota-	Cutlets or	Ham Patty on	Whipped Pota-	or French Fried	Mushroom Sauce	
toes, Gravy	Braised Liver	Pineapple Slice	toes, Gravy	Shrimp	French Fries	
Cauliflower—	Creamed	Baked Potato	Buttered	Parsley Buttered	Buttered Carrots	
Cheese Sauce	Potatoes	Buttered Broccoli	Asparagus or	Potatoes	or Brussels Sprouts	
or Green Beans	Breaded Toma-	Buttered Whole	Buttered Mixed	Buttered Peas	Sliced Tomato Salad	
Southern Style	toes or	Kernel Corn	Vegetables	Creamy Cole	or Head Lettuce	
Tossed Green	Buttered Peas	Head Lettuce	Molded Cran-	Slaw or Salad	Salad	
Salad or	Stuffed Celery	Salad or	berry Salad or	Greens with	Fruit Cup	
Fruit Salad	or Spicy	Beet Pickles	Tossed Green	Grapefruit	Beverages	
Pumpkin Pie	Apricot Mold	Vienna Bread	Salad	Hard Rolls		
Dinner Rolls	Fan Tan Rolls	Apple Dumpling	Cloverleaf Rolls	Pineapple–		
Beverages	Strawberry Sun-	Beverages	Cheese Cake	Cashew Cake		
	dae or		Beverages	Beverages		
	Coconut Cake					
	Beverages					

Fruit and ice cream offered daily in addition to desserts listed.

STUDENT UNION OR CAFETERIA

Characteristic of menus planned for a university cafeteria or student union is simplicity in offerings, with emphasis on pleasing combinations and well-prepared food. Menus that meet nutritional needs, offer variety, and can be sold at a moderate cost must be planned for students, faculty, and off-campus guests. The uncertainty of numbers and often unexpectedly small volume of business creates a problem of excess prepared food and of food cost control.

The use of a cycle menu is of value in some instances. However, the need for using leftovers and the desirability of including seasonable foods available on the market lead some directors to plan for periods as brief as one week, while others prefer a five-week cycle.

The menu patterns for lunch and dinner in a university cafeteria are so similar that the suggested menus planned for this type of operation (pp. 444–445) may be used for either lunch or for dinner for a two-week period.

The breakfast menu should offer some choice in food items each day, although there is less need for variety from day to day than is desirable for lunch and dinner. Breakfast should include one or more citrus juices and one other juice; fresh fruits in season; cooked or ready-to-eat prepared cereals; breakfast hot breads and toast; eggs and bacon, ham, or sausage; jam and jelly; and a choice of beverages.

In addition to the items listed on Suggested Luncheon and Dinner Menus for a University Cafeteria (pp. 444–445), certain other items are available daily.

These include:

Entrées: The four entrées include one meat and three others. These may be a meat extender, a meatless entrée, poultry, or fish. This variety may be increased or decreased to fit the demands of the food service.

Vegetables: Mashed potatoes.

Salads: Cottage cheese, head lettuce, tossed fresh vegetable salad with assorted dressings, carrot and celery sticks.

Breads: Whole wheat bread, white bread, and a hot bread.

Desserts: Baked custard, fresh fruit in season, fruit juices, and a variety of ice creams.

Beverages: Coffee, tea, hot and iced, cocoa, milk, whole, nonfat and cultured buttermilk.

Suggested Luncheon and Dinner Menus for a University Cafeteria

Pattern	Monday	Tuesday	Wednesday	Thursday	Friday	Saturday	Sunday
Soup	Vegetable	Barley	Pepper Pot	Mushroom	Bean	Tomato Bouillon	French Onion
Entrées	Swiss Steak Creamed Chipped Beef on Corn Bread Baked Haddock Chinese Omelet	Roast Pork Turkey Loaf Salmon Croquettes Macaroni and Cheese	Pot Roast Beef Chicken à la Maryland Salmon Loaf Egg Cutlet	Deviled Pork Chop Meat Loaf Chicken Turnover—Mushroom Sauce Russian Salad Bowl	Roast Leg of Lamb Creamed Ham & Celery on Hot Biscuit Fried Whiting Fish Corn Fritters	Country Fried Steak Sweetbread Cutlets Pizza Cheese Soufflé—Shrimp Sauce	Baked Ham with Honey Glaze Fried Chicken Baked Fillet of Sole Beef Stew with Dumplings
Vegetables Mashed potatoes available daily	Baked Potatoes Chilled Tomatoes Broccoli au Gratin Corn on the Cob	Scalloped Sweet Potatoes—Apples Buttered Wax Beans Buttered Asparagus Julienne Carrots	French Baked New Potatoes Cauliflower—Cheese Sauce Buttered Mixed Vegetables Scalloped Tomatoes and Celery	Sautéed Green Tomatoes New Corn in Cream Buttered Spinach with Lemon Mashed Summer Squash	Parsley Buttered Potatoes Baked Tomatoes Braised Celery Buttered Green Peas	French Fried Potatoes Wilted Greens Buttered Zucchini Squash Creole Corn	Baked Sweet Potato Buttered Peas, Rice, Mushrooms Creamed Onions Buttered Baby Limas
Salads	Spicy Apricot Mold Grapefruit—Orange—Red Apple Section Cabbage—Cucumber—Tomato—Green Pepper Beet Relish	Perfection Stuffed Tomato Waldorf Deviled Egg	Lime Gelatin—Spiced Grape Celery Cucumber and Onion Sour Cream Shredded Carrot—Pineapple Mixed Fruit	Molded Pineapple—Cottage Cheese Tomato—Avocado Sections Banana Slice—Cubed Pineapple—Orange Sections Cabbage—Green Pepper—Pimiento	Jellied Beet Cantaloupe—Honeydew Wedge—Grape Vegetable Nut Stuffed Celery—Cheese	Cabbage Parfait Salad Banana Nut Sliced Tomatoes Carrifruit	Raspberry Ring Mold Fresh Fruit Bowl Sliced Orange—Onion Ring Green Bean—Pimiento
Hot Bread	Blueberry Muffins	Dinner Rolls	Kolaches	Bishop's Bread	Corn Bread	All Bran Muffins	Vienna Bread
Desserts	Green Apple Pie Lemon Pie Applesauce Cake English Toffee	Raisin Pie Coconut Cream Pie Lemon Sponge Cake Cherry Crisp	Apricot Pie Strawberry Glazed Cream Pie Angel Food Cake Apple Brown Betty	Cherry Pie Pumpkin Pie Fruit Upside-Down Cake Caramel Custard	Blueberry Pie Frozen Lemon Pie Burnt Sugar Cake Blue Plum Cobbler	Apple Pie—Cheese Crust Date Cream Pie German Chocolate Cake Peach Crisp	Fresh Rhubarb Pie Pecan Pie Lady Baltimore Cake Strawberry Shortcake

Pattern	Monday	Tuesday	Wednesday	Thursday	Friday	Saturday	Sunday
Soup	Cream of Potato	Creole	Tomato	Clam Chowder	Split Pea	Vegetable Beef	Cream of Tomato
Entrées	Breaded Pork Cutlet Corned Beef—Horseradish Sauce Grilled Cheese Sandwich	Roast Veal Ham Loaf Baked Halibut Baked Beans	Chicken Tahitian Braised Liver Beef Stroganoff Cheeseburger Pie	Grilled Ham Slices Spaghetti and Meat Balls Scalloped Chicken Fruit Plate with Cottage Cheese	Veal Chops in Sour Cream Beef Pot Pie Fried Shrimp Cheese Balls with Pineapple	Barbecued Spareribs Baked Meat Croquettes Chicken Fricassée Tuna Salad	Roast Turkey Mock Drumsticks Hungarian Goulash Steamed Salmon Lemon Butter
Meat Roll							
Vegetables Mashed potatoes available daily	Fried Hominy New Peas in Cream Buttered New Cabbage Spanish Green Beans	Green Rice Scalloped Tomatoes Buttered Brussels Sprouts Sautéed New Carrots	Scalloped Corn with Bacon New Potatoes with Peas Buttered Broccoli French Fried Eggplant Succotash with Green Beans	Creamed Potatoes Fresh Spinach with Bacon Corn on the Cob Harvard Beets	New Potatoes in Jackets Grilled Tomatoes Green Peas with Mushrooms Hot Slaw with Poppy Seed	Lattice Potatoes Buttered Green Beans with Celery Baked Onions with Cheese Buttered Summer Squash	Browned New Potatoes Buttered Fresh Asparagus Succotash Buttered Apples
Salads	Molded Grapefruit Cranberry Relish Prune—Apricot Tomato—Cucumber	Frosted Cherry Mold Cabbage Relish Asparagus—Pimiento Green Applesauce	Frozen Fruit Avocado—Orange Sections Cabbage—Pepper Slaw Stuffed Peach	Autumn Mold Pineapple—Cream Cheese—Date Melon Slice—Bing Cherry Tomato—Shrimp	Apple—Grapefruit Mold Green Pepper—Cottage Cheese Orange—Endive Fresh Pineapple—Strawberry	Molded Pineapple—Cucumber Fruit Salad Bowl Raw Spinach—Egg Spiced Apple	Under the Sea Salad Avocado—Grapefruit Stuffed Prune Peaches—Banana—Grape
Hot Bread	Whole Wheat Rolls	Boston Brown Bread	Cinnamon Rolls	Raised Muffins	Butterhorn Rolls	Honey Cornflake Muffins	Butter slices
Desserts	Fresh Peach Pie Custard Pie Chocolate Angel Food Tapioca Cream	Strawberry Pie Butterscotch Pie Jelly Roll Orange Cream Puff	Dutch Apple Pie Eggnog Pie Pineapple—Cashew Cake Apricot Whip	Gooseberry Pie Banana Cream Pie Fudge Cake Fruit-Cup—Cookies	Plum Pie Chocolate Cream Pie Lazy Daisy Cake Date Pudding	Cherry Pie—Lattice Crust Lemon Chiffon Pie Chocolate Cup Cake Vanilla Cream Pudding	Boysenberry Pie Mocha Almond Frozen Pie Marble Cake Apple Dumplings

445

Menus for Hospitals

The basis for successful operation of a hospital dietary department is the production and service of high-quality foods that not only meet the nutritional requirements of patients and personnel but that are provided at a cost within budgetary allowance. Although often more complex, the principles of meal planning in a hospital are the same as in other types of institutions. For one service period foods must be provided for many kinds of diets. These may range from liquid, ground, soft, or regular to bland, low sodium, fat restricted, with a wide range in caloric requirements. Often foods must be available 24 hours a day.

When developing a hospital meal pattern, the first step is to plan a regular or normal diet that will supply all food essentials necessary for good nutrition. This pattern then becomes the foundation for most diets required for therapeutic purposes and is the core of all meal planning in a hospital of any type or size. Patients requiring other than a normal diet will receive various modifications of the regular diet to fit their particular needs. A Guide for Planning Normal Diets with Modifications is given.

Hospital menus may be nonselective, which gives the patient no choice and does not allow for individual food likes or dislikes; or selective, in which the patient may select from two or more menu items. The cycle menu may be either selective or nonselective.

The selective menu adds much to the satisfaction of patients and also helps to prevent waste. Choices that appeal to various patients usually can be made available with little extra work, if careful planning is used in pairing items on the menu. The main items on the selective menu are the same as the general menu. Some items, as the choice of dinner meat and vegetables, may be the same as foods prepared for one of the modified diets or for the cafeteria. Other choices may be soup or fruit juice, or fruit or ice cream in place of a prepared dessert. On the supper menu, choices of light or heavy items may do much to promote patient satiety.

Food for hospital personnel usually is served cafeteria style. The menu may be a modification of the patient menu, with a few additions to offer a wider selection than is desirable for the patients.

In planning a normal or regular diet, meals should be planned for each day as a unit; that is, for breakfast, dinner, and supper. Each day's menu then may be checked to be sure that all essential foods have been included. A suggested 3 meal-a-day menu pattern for a normal diet follows:

Breakfast	Dinner	Supper or Lunch
Fruit or juice	Soup (optional)	Cream soup or
Cereal with milk	Meat, poultry or fish	Main dish (made with
Egg	Potato or alternate starchy	meat, fish, poultry,
Bread or toast	vegetable	egg, or cheese)
Butter or margarine	Green or yellow vegetable	Vegetable or salad
Beverage	Salad: fruit or vegetable	Bread with butter or
	Bread with butter or	margarine
	margarine	Fruit or other simple
	Dessert	dessert
	Beverage	Beverage

Many hospitals now find it advantageous to use a 5-meal plan. Patients like eating smaller meals and more often. Doctors say it is better for the patient, and dietitians claim the cost of food and labor are somewhat reduced because all food requiring skilled cooks can be prepared during one work shift. An outline menu pattern for the 5-meal plan follows:

7 A.M. Coffee, with toast or sweet roll.
10 A.M. Breakfast: Fruit or juice, cereal with milk, egg or other entrée, toast, coffee, milk, or both.
1 P.M. Soup, crackers. Cheese, fruit or juice, and melba toast.
4 P.M. Dinner: Fruit juice, meat, potato and other vegetable, dessert, coffee, or milk.
8 P.M. Sandwich, milk, custard, or ice cream.

Menus for Homes for Children and Extended Care Facilities

Characteristic factors involved in menu planning for institutional homes caring for children or older adults are somewhat similar. With few exceptions, all 3 meals are eaten in the same place every day throughout the year. Under such conditions, the nutritional needs of the individuals being served must be met in the daily food provided for them. Although meals are served to many senior citizens today in nursing or retirement homes whose budgetary allowances are quite liberal, many institutions for older people must serve meals at a per capita cost at or below that termed the irreducible minimum. Careful thought must be given to menu planning to incorporate variety and interest into the menu in order to prevent the low-cost foods commonly used from falling into a monotonous pattern. Those who plan meals for children living away from home must consider much more than merely meeting their nutritional requirements. The atmosphere in which food is prepared, served, and eaten, if a pleasant one, is highly important in developing good food habits and attitudes toward food needed for growth and good health. Every meal should be a satisfactory and pleasant experience.

The basic principles of menu planning should be followed (p. 427) but when planning specifically for children, unfamiliar foods should be used sparingly to avoid rejection. The age of the children, who eat three meals a day in one place, must be given careful consideration. The same foods may be served children of all ages but the size of the portion of each food accepted by the child varies with age. It is important also to consider individual differences in activity, sex, body build, and other physical and temperamental characteristics when determining the amount of food a child needs and will eat. Teen age boys, for example, need much more food energy and more of every nutrient except iron and vitamin D than girls of the same age.

Those persons planning meals for older adults should be aware of the problems peculiar to this age group. Their fixed habits and food preferences developed through many years may influence but should not determine entirely the meals planned for them. Healthy adults regardless of age need a well-balanced diet, and in planning the day's food the basic pattern for the normal diet should be followed. Individual problems of the group members, such as difficulty in chewing solid food and special diet requirements, must also be of major concern. The amount of food required is the only difference between the food needs of this age group and that of a child or young adult. The same nutrients are needed but in smaller amounts, especially starches, sweets, and fats.

Menus for Summer Camps

The rapid increase in the numbers of children and adults in attendance in organized summer camps has been paralleled, in most situations, by an equally rapid expansion in the educational plans of camp directors and leaders. An important phase of the expanding program of organized summer camps is the provision of adequate dietary departments. Few staffs of well-organized camps are considered complete without the inclusion of an experienced dietitian. The problems met by a camp dietitian are often accentuated by lack of adequate mechanical equipment, limited market facilities for fresh foods, and inexperienced helpers usually employed. These inconveniences are compensated for in part by satisfactions which come from feeding hungry, happy children.

Menus planned for a camp should be simple and based on the nutritional needs of the growing children, the climate, the children's acceptance of foods, and any religious restrictions of certain foods. Consideration should also be given the equipment available for food preparation, type and skill of kitchen employees, and the time required for preparation. Convenience foods in the form of recipe ingredients and complete menu items should be considered in planning menus for summer camps. Dehydrated foods, mixes, and frozen foods, if freezer space is available, will be helpful especially with inexperienced cooks. Paper service may help solve the dishwashing problem often present in camps.

The amount of food to be prepared is usually larger in proportion to the number served than is usual for most other types of services. Portions are larger, and there is usually a demand for "seconds."

Meal patterns suggested for a camp are as follows:

Breakfast	Lunch[1]	Dinner
Fruit juice or fresh fruit when available	High-protein dish (or soup and sandwiches)	Meat or meat extender
Cereal, hot or cold	Hot vegetable, creamed or buttered	Potatoes
Bread (type depending on the equipment)	Salad or relish	Hot vegetable
Milk or hot cocoa	Simple dessert, such as pudding	Salad or relishes
	Milk	Dessert
		Milk

[1] See suggested menus for school lunchrooms and residence halls, pp. 438–442.

Before making an order list of foods, determine fresh food supplies available at local markets; then plan all menus to be served each group. Amounts of foods to be ordered may be determined by consulting the proper tables (pp. 4–14). Since the group membership may change every week or 10 days, menus found suitable for one group may be repeated with necessary variations.

Menus for Industrial Restaurants

Menu planning for an industrial cafeteria or restaurant has much in common with menu planning for other cafeterias. Consideration must be given to the basic rules of successful meal planning and food combination as well as the specific requirements of the industrial establishment being served. As in any other food service, labor is one of the largest items of expense and one of the most difficult to control. The use of preportioned foods such as catsup, jelly, and butter, of portion-ready entrées such as chicken legs and prefabricated meat cuts, of ready-to-cook foods such as French fried potatoes, and of other built-in labor-saving devices is of major importance in effecting economies of time and cost.

The use of rotating menus has proved valuable in reducing the time spent in planning and as an aid in the equitable distribution of labor and food. Four (1-week) menus comprise a cycle suitable for the 5-day week of industry. This cycle is repeated 3 or 4 times, and then a new cycle is begun. Cycles should correspond with the seasons of the year, with appropriate adjustments being made for holidays and vacations. Breads, sandwiches, salads, desserts and beverages are planned on a separate menu. A 4-week winter menu cycle (pp. 451–454) which has been successfully used in one large industrial cafeteria follows.

Industrial Cafeteria Weekly Winter Menu Cycle: Menu 1

Item	Monday	Tuesday	Wednesday	Thursday	Friday
Soup	Chicken Gumbo	Scotch Broth with Barley	Yellow Split Pea	Turkey Noodle	Clam Chowder
Entrée 1	Creamed Chipped Beef on Toast	Boston Baked Beans —Brown Bread	Baked Eggs and Noodles	French Fried Cauliflower Rarebit Sauce	Macaroni and Cheese Loaf Tomato Sauce
Entrée 2	Salisbury Steak with Brown Sauce	American Chop Suey on Steamed Rice	Barbecued Beef on Bun Plate Potato Chips	Baked Ham Loaf Glazed Pineapple Ring	Deep-sea Scallops Tartar Sauce Cole Slaw
Entrée 3	Roast Leg of Lamb Mint Jelly	Country Smoked Loin of Pork— Sauerkraut	Roast Turkey Dressing Cranberry Sauce Gravy	Potted Swiss Steak with Vegetables	Baked Stuffed Pork Chops—Gravy
Hot sandwich	Roast Pork with Gravy	Roast Veal	Baked Ham	Roast Beef	Corned Beef
Potatoes	Mashed Potatoes	Scalloped Potatoes	Mashed Potatoes	Mashed Potatoes	Parsley Potatoes
Vegetables	Cauliflower Polonaise French Green Beans with Bacon	Julienne Beets Baked Squash	Buttered Frozen Peas with Mushrooms Cream-style corn	Stewed Tomatoes Buttered Lima Beans	Carrots Lyonnaise Buttered Brussels Sprouts

Industrial Cafeteria Weekly Winter Menu Cycle: Menu 2

Item	Monday	Tuesday	Wednesday	Thursday	Friday
Soup	Potato and Leek	Navy Bean	Vegetable	Beef Broth with Barley	Mushroom
Entrée 1	Cheese Soufflé Mushroom Sauce	Smoked Link Sausage	Chili Con Carne on Spaghetti	Apple Fritters—Maple Sirup	Scrambled Eggs on Toast
Entrée 2	Braised Beef Stew with Dumpling	Potato Pancakes—Applesauce	Turkey Pot Pie	Spaghetti with Meat Sauce, French Bread	Baked Haddock Fillet Tartar Sauce
Entrée 3	Baked Ham with Raisin Sauce	Yankee Pot Roast of Beef—Noodles	Braised Liver with Bacon	Quarter Fried Chicken with Baked Rice	Country-fried Steak Cream Gravy
Hot sandwich	Hot Turkey	Roast Lamb	Corned Beef	Roast Pork with Gravy	Roast Beef
Potatoes	Lyonnaise Potatoes	Paprika Potatoes	Au Gratin Potatoes	Mashed Potatoes	Mashed Potatoes
Vegetables	Baked Acorn Squash Spinach Soufflé	Whole Kernel Corn O'Brien Hot Slaw	French Fried Eggplant Harvard Beets	Buttered Broccoli Spears Mixed Vegetables	Buttered Peas Savory Carrots

452

Industrial Cafeteria Weekly Winter Menu Cycle: Menu 3

Item	Monday	Tuesday	Wednesday	Thursday	Friday
Soup	Homemade Chicken	Minestrone	Philadelphia Pepper Pot with Spatzels	Green Split Pea	Tomato with Barley
Entrée 1	Oven Baked French Toast with Maple Sirup Link Sausage	Baked Corn Pudding	Mostaccioli—Meat Sauce French Bread	Vegetable Chop Suey Steamed Rice	Scalloped Macaroni and Cheese
Entrée 2	Veal Ragout with Spaghetti	Stuffed Bacon Wrapped Frankfurter on Bun Potato Chips Sliced Tomato	Pork Patties Baked Acorn Squash Applesauce	Baked Meat Loaf—Mushroom Sauce	Salmon Patties with Egg Sauce
Entrée 3	Pepper Steak	Roast Veal Dressing	Braised Short Ribs of Beef with Vegetable Sauce	Roast Loin of Pork Stewed Apples	Roast Round of Beef Natural Gravy
Hot sandwich	Roast Pork with Gravy	Brisket of Corned Beef	Roast Lamb	Hot Turkey	Baked Ham
Potatoes	O'Brien Potatoes	Parsley Potatoes	Mashed Potatoes	Browned Potatoes	Rissolè Potatoes
Vegetables	Frozen Baby Lima Beans Zucchini Squash	Fresh Cabbage Glazed Carrots	Acorn Squash Buttered Peas	Mashed Rutabagas Hot Spiced Beets	Cauliflower Polonaise Creole Green Beans

453

Industrial Cafeteria Weekly Winter Menu Cycle: Menu 4

Item	Monday	Tuesday	Wednesday	Thursday	Friday
Soup	Lima Bean	Vegetable	Chicken Broth with Rice	Beef Broth with Barley	Clam Chowder
Entrée 1	Ravioli with Meat Sauce and Italian Cheese	Baked Corned Beef Hash	Baked Lima Beans with Salt Pork	Eggs à la King on Crisp Chinese Noodles	Scalloped Tuna and Peas
Entrée 2	Hamburger on a Bun Plate Potato Chips Cole Slaw	Turkey and Vegetable Fricassée Corn Bread	Stuffed Cabbage Rolls, Creole Style	Braised Lamb Stew with Vegetables	Halibut Steak—Lemon Butter
Entrée 3	Roast Leg of Veal Baked Peach	Fried Pork Chops Applesauce	Boiled Beef, Horse-radish Sauce	Pot Roast of Beef Brown Gravy	Baked Ham Loaf, Mustard Sauce
Hot sandwich	Corned Beef	Roast Beef	Baked Ham	Smoked Pork Butt	Hot Turkey
Potatoes	Cottage Potatoes	Mashed Potatoes	Parsley Potatoes	Hash-browned Potatoes	French Fried Potatoes
Vegetables	French Fried Eggplant Frozen Mixed Vegetables	Buttered Peas Braised Red Cabbage	Glazed Carrots Onions in Cream Sauce	Wilted Spinach Cream-style Corn	Stewed Tomatoes Mashed Squash

454

Menu-Planning Suggestions

ENTRÉES

MEAT

Beef

Beef à la Mode
Corned Beef
Roast Round
Pot Roast
Chuck Roast
Standing Rib Roast
Rolled Rib Roast
Corned Beef and
  Cabbage
Braised Brisket
Broiled Steak
  T-Bone
  Sirloin
  Filet Mignon
  Club
Cubed Steak
Country Fried Steak
Spanish Steak
Swiss Steak
Beef Stroganoff
Yankee Pot Roast
Mock Drumsticks
Barbecued Kabobs
Barbecued Short
  Ribs
Braised Short Ribs
Salisbury Steak
Beef Pot Pie
Beef Stew with
  Vegetables
Beef Stew with
  Dumplings
Hungarian Goulash
Chop Suey
Meat Loaf
Swedish Meat Balls
Spanish Meat Balls
Meat Balls and Spa-
  ghetti

Veal

Roast Leg of Veal
Roast Veal Shoulder

Baked Veal Chops
Veal Chops in Sour
  Cream
Breaded Veal Cutlets
Veal Birds
Veal Fricassee with
  Poppyseed
  Noodles
Veal Stew with
  Vegetables
Veal à la King
Veal Patties
Veal Paprika with
  Rice
Curried Veal with
  Rice

Lamb

Roast Leg of Lamb
Roast Lamb
  Shoulder
Broiled Lamb Chops
Lamb Stew
Braised Lamb
  Riblets
Barbecued Lamb
  Shanks
Lamb Patties
Curried Lamb with
  Rice
Lamb Fricassee with
  Noodles

Pork (Fresh)

Baked Fresh Ham
Roast Pork Loin
Roast Pork Shoulder
Roast Pork with
  Dressing
Baked Pork Chops
Breaded Pork Chops
Deviled Pork Chops

Barbecued Pork
  Chops
Stuffed Pork Chops
Breaded Pork Cutlets
Barbecued Spareribs
Sweet-Sour Spareribs
Spareribs with
  Dressing
Pork Birds
Sweet-Sour Pork

Pork (Cured)

Baked Ham
Baked Ham Slices
  with Pineapple
  Rings
  with Orange Sauce
Grilled Ham Slices
Baked Canadian
  Bacon
Ham Loaf
Ham Patties
Glazed Ham Balls
Smoked Pork Chops

*Miscellaneous or
Variety Meats*

Baked Heart with
  Dressing
Braised Tongue
Smoked Tongue
Liver and Bacon
Braised Liver and
  Onions
Grilled Liver and
  Onions
Liver with Spanish
  Sauce
Sweetbread Cutlets
Weiners and Sauer-
  kraut
Cheese Stuffed
  Wieners

Menu-Planning Suggestions

ENTRÉES

Barbecued Wieners

MEAT EXTENDERS

Baked Hash
Corned Beef Hash
Stuffed Peppers
Beef Roll
Spaghetti with Meat
 Sauce
Creole Spaghetti
Cheeseburger Pie
Beef and Pork Cas-
 serole
Spanish Rice
Creamed Beef
Creamed Chipped
 Beef
Chipped Beef and
 Noodles
Veal Croquettes
Meat Turnovers
Veal Soufflé
Creamed Ham
Ham à la King
Ham Croquettes
Ham Soufflé
Ham Timbales
Ham and Egg
 Scallop
Creamed Ham on
 Spoon Bread or
 Biscuits
Ham Biscuit Roll
Ham Turnover with
 Cheese Sauce
Ham and Sweet-
 bread Casserole
Sausage Rolls
Sausage Cakes
Fried Scrapple
Bacon and Potato
 Omelet
Pork and Noodle
 Casserole

Baked Lima Beans
Boiled Lima Beans
 with Ham
Baked Lima Beans
 with Sausage
Baked Navy Beans
Chili Con Carne
Chili Spaghetti
Ranch Style Beans
Baked Eggs and
 Bacon Rings
Pizza
Lasagne

Poultry

Roast Turkey
Baked Turkey Roll
Turkey Divan
Turkey-Noodle Cas-
 serole
Baked Chicken
Broiled Chicken
Fried Chicken
Barbecued Chicken
Chicken Tahitian
Breast of Chicken
 with Ham Slice
Chicken à la Mary-
 land
Fricassee of Chicken
Chicken with Dum-
 plings
Chicken with
 Noodles
Chicken Pie
Chicken or Turkey
 Loaf
Chicken Soufflé
Chicken or Turkey
 Tetrazzini
Chicken or Turkey
 Turnovers
Chicken and Rice
 Casserole
Chicken à la King

Hot Chicken Salad
Singapore Curry
Creamed Chicken,
 on Biscuit
 in Patty Shell
 in Toast Cups
 on Chow Mein
 Noodles
 on Spoon Bread
Chicken Croquettes
Chicken Cutlets
Scalloped Chicken
Chicken Timbales
Chicken Chow Mein
Chicken Biscuit Roll
 with Mushroom
 Sauce

FISH

Fresh and Frozen Fish

Fried Salmon Steaks
Poached Salmon
Baked Halibut Steak
Poached Halibut
Fried Halibut Steak
Fried or Baked Fil-
 lets of Haddock,
 Perch, Sole,
 Whitefish, Catfish
Fried Whole Fish
 Whiting
 Smelts
 Trout
French Fried Shrimp
Creole Shrimp with
 Rice
French Fried
 Scallops
Fried Clams
Fried Oysters
Scalloped Oysters
Deviled Crab
Broiled Lobster

Menu-Planning Suggestions

ENTRÉES

Canned Fish

Salmon Loaf
Salmon Croquettes
Creamed Salmon on
 Biscuit
Salmon Biscuit Roll
 with Creamed
 Peas
Scalloped Salmon
Salmon and Potato
 Chip Casserole
Casserole of Tuna
 and Rice
Tuna Croquettes
Creamed Tuna on
 Toast or Biscuits
Tuna Soufflé
Scalloped Tuna
Tuna Biscuit Roll
 with Cheese Sauce
Tuna–Cashew Cas-
 serole
Tuna and Noodles
Tuna and Potato
 Chip Casserole

MEATLESS ENTREES

Cheese Rarebit
Cheese Balls on Pine-
 apple Slice
Cheese Croquettes
Cheese Soufflé with
 Shrimp Sauce
Cheese Fondue
Macaroni and Cheese
Rice Croquettes with
 Cheese Sauce
Chinese Omelet
Rice with Mushroom
 and Almond Sauce
Fried Mush
Baked Eggs with
 Cheese
Curried Eggs

Creamed Eggs
Eggs à la Goldenrod
Egg Cutlets
Noodle Casserole
Hot Stuffed Eggs
Eggs à la King
Scalloped Eggs and
 Cheese
Scrambled Eggs
Omelet
Potato Omelet
Spanish Omelet
Vegetable Timbales
Cheese Puff
Spoon Bread
Corn Rarebit
Scalloped Corn
Hot Potato Salad
Creamed Asparagus
 on Toast
French Toast
Fritters, Sirup
Corn Fritters
Fruit Fritters

SANDWICHES

Baked Ham
Ham and Cheese
Ham Salad
Bacon and Tomato
Bacon and Tomato
 on Bun with
 Cheese Sauce
Hamburgers on Buns
Barbecued Ham-
 burgers
Wieners with Meat
 Sauce on Bun
Oven Picnic Buns
Hot Roast Beef
Hot Roast Pork
Barbecued Ham,
 Pork, or Beef

Western Sandwich
Toasted Chipped
 Beef and Cheese
Reuben
Submarine
Hot Turkey
Chicken Salad
Sliced Turkey
Hot Tuna Bun
Tuna Salad, Plain or
 Grilled
Grilled Cheese
Egg Salad
Peanut
Runzas

MAIN DISH SALADS

Chef's Salad Bowl
Chicken and Bacon
 Salad
Baked Ham with
 Potato Salad
Russian Salad Bowl
Chicken or Turkey
 Salad
Chicken Salad in
 Raspberry Mold
Crab Salad
Lobster Salad
Shrimp Salad
Tuna Salad
Salmon Salad
Cold Salmon with
 Potato Salad
Fruit Plates
Cottage Cheese
 Salad
Deviled Eggs
Macaroni Salad
Brown Bean Salad
Stuffed Tomato
 Salad

Menu-Planning Suggestions

VEGETABLES

POTATO OR SUBSTITUTE

Potatoes, Irish

Au Gratin
Baked
Browned
Buttered New
Chips
Creamed
Croquettes
Duchess
Fried
French Fried
Lyonnaise
Mashed
O'Brien
Potato Cakes
Potato Pancakes
Potato Salad, hot or cold
Rissolè
Scalloped
Stuffed Baked

Potatoes, Sweet

Baked
Candied or Glazed
Croquettes
Mashed with Apples

Pasta

Macaroni and Cheese
Macaroni Salad
Buttered Noodles
Poppyseed Noodles
Buttered Rice
Curried Rice
Fried Rice with Almonds
Green Rice
Rice Croquettes

Other Starchy Vegetables

Corn
Buttered
In Cream
On Cob
Corn and Tomato
Corn Pudding
O'Brien
Scalloped
With Celery and Bacon
Succotash
Lima Beans
Buttered
In Cream
With Bacon
With Mushrooms
With Almonds
Parsnips
Buttered
Browned
Glazed
Squash
Baked Acorn
Baked Hubbard
Mashed Butternut
Mashed Hubbard

GREEN VEGETABLES

Asparagus
Buttered or Creamed
With Cheese or Hollandaise Sauce
Beans, Green
Buttered
Creole
With Almonds or Mushrooms

Southern Style
Broccoli
Almond Buttered
Buttered
With Cheese Sauce, Lemon Butter
Hollandaise Sauce
Crumb Butter
Brussels Sprouts, Buttered
Cabbage
Au Gratin
Buttered or Creamed
Creole
Fried
Hot Slaw
Celery
Buttered or Creamed
Creamed Almond
Peas
Buttered or in Cream
With Carrots, Cauliflower, or Onions
With Mushrooms or Almonds
Spinach
Buttered
Wilted
With Egg or Bacon
With New Beets

OTHER VEGETABLES

Beets
Buttered
Harvard

VEGETABLES

Julienne
In Sour Cream
With Orange
    Sauce
Hot Spiced
Pickled
Carrots
    Buttered or
      Creamed
    Candied
    Glazed
    Lyonnaise
    Mint Glazed
    Savory
    With Celery
    With Peas
    Parsley Buttered
    Sweet–Sour
Cauliflower
    Buttered
    Creamed
    French Fried
    With Almond
      Butter
    With Cheese
      Sauce
    With Peas

Eggplant
    Creole
    Fried or French
      Fried
    Scalloped
Mushrooms
    Broiled
    Sautéed
Onions
    Au Gratin
    Baked
    Buttered
    Creamed
    French Fried

Stuffed
    With Spanish
      Sauce
Rutabagas
    Buttered
    Mashed
Squash, Summer
    Buttered
    Creole
Tomatoes
    Baked
    Breaded
    Broiled Tomato
      Slices
    Creole
    Scalloped
    Stewed
    Stuffed
Turnips
    Buttered
    In Cream
    Mashed
    With New Peas

FRUITS SERVED AS VEGETABLES

Apples
    Buttered
    Fried
    Hot Baked
Bananas
    Baked
    French Fried
Grapefruit
    Broiled
Peaches
    Broiled
Pineapple Ring
    Broiled
    Sautéed
    Glazed

Menu-Planning Suggestions

SALADS AND RELISHES

FRUIT SALADS

Apple and Celery
Apple and Carrot
Apple and Cabbage
Banana
Carrifruit
Cranberry Relish
Cranberry Sauce
Frozen Fruit
Grapefruit–Orange
Melon Ball–Orange
Mixed Fruit
Peach Half
Pear–Orange
Pineapple
Spiced Apple
Waldorf
(See p. 341 for additional suggestions)

VEGETABLE SALADS

Beet Pickles
Beet Relish
Brown Bean
Cabbage Relish
Cabbage
Cabbage–Carrot
Cabbage–Marshmallow
Cabbage–Pineapple
Carrot–Raisin
Celery Cabbage
Cole Slaw
Creamy Cole Slaw
Cucumber–Onion in
Sour Cream
Hawaiian Tossed
Head Lettuce
Potato
Red Cabbage
Salad Greens with
Grapefruit
Stuffed Tomato

Tossed Green
Tomato
Tomato–Cucumber
Triple Bean

GELATIN SALADS

Applesauce Mold
Arabian Peach
Autumn
Beet
Bing Cherry
Cabbage Parfait
Cranberry Ring Mold
Frosted Cherry
Frosted Lime
Ginger ale Fruit
Jellied Citrus
Jellied Vegetable
Jellied Waldorf
Molded Grapefruit
Molded Pear
Perfection
Molded Pineapple–
Cheese
Molded Pineapple–
Cucumber
Molded Pineapple–
Relish
Molded Pineapple–
Rhubarb
Raspberry Ring Mold
Ribbon Mold
Spicy Apricot
Sunshine
Swedish Green Top
Tomato Aspic
Under-the-Sea

SHERBETS AS SALAD

Cranberry
Lemon
Lime

Mint
Orange
Pineapple
Raspberry
Tomato

RELISHES

Burr Gherkins
Carrot Curls
Carrot Sticks
Cauliflowerets
Celery Curls
Celery Fans
Celery Hearts
Celery Rings
Cherry Tomatoes
Cucumber Slices
Cucumber Wedges
Green Pepper Rings
Olives
Green
Ripe
Stuffed
Onion Rings
Radish Accordions
Radish Roses
Spiced Crabapples
Spiced Peaches
Spiced Pears
Stuffed Celery
Tomato Slices
Tomato Wedges
Watermelon Pickles

Menu-Planning Suggestions

DESSERTS

CAKES AND COOKIES

Cakes

Angel Food, Plain, Chocolate, and Filled
Applesauce
Banana
Boston Cream
Burnt Sugar
Chiffon
Chocolate and Jelly Roll
Coconut
Cup Cakes
Fruit Upside Down
Fudge
German Sweet Chocolate
Gingerbread
Lazy Daisy
Marble
Pineapple Cashew
Poppy Seed
Praline Gingerbread
Prune
Spice
White

Cookies

Brownies
Butter Tea
Butterscotch Pecan
Butterscotch Squares
Chocolate Chip
Coconut Macaroons
Coconut Pecan Bars
Date Bars
Oatmeal
Fudge Balls
Ginger
Marshmallow Squares
Oatmeal–Date Bars
Peanut Butter

Sandies
Sugar Cookies

PIES AND PASTRIES

One-Crust Pies

Apricot Cream
Banana Cream
Butterscotch
Chiffon
Chocolate Cream
Chocolate Sundae
Coconut Cream
Coconut Custard
Custard
Date Cream
Dutch Apple
Frozen Lemon
Frozen Mocha Almond
Fruit Glazed Cream
Ice Cream Pie
Lemon
Pecan
Pineapple Cream
Praline Pumpkin
Pumpkin
Sour Cream Raisin
Rhubarb Custard

Two-Crust Pies

Apple
Apricot
Blackberry
Blueberry
Boysenberry
Cherry
Gooseberry
Mincemeat
Peach
Pineapple
Plum or Prune
Raisin
Rhubarb
Strawberry

FROZEN DESSERTS

Ice Creams

Apricot
Banana
Butter Brickle
Caramel
Chip Chocolate
Chocolate
Coffee
Lemon Custard
Macaroon
Peach
Peanut Brittle
Pecan
Peppermint Stick
Pineapple
Pistachio
Raspberry
Strawberry
Toffee
Tutti Frutti
Parfaits

Sherbets

Apricot
Cherry
Cranberry
Green Gage Plum
Lemon
Lime
Orange
Mint
Pineapple
Plum
Raspberry
Rhubarb
Watermelon

PUDDINGS

Apple Crisp
Apple Dumplings
Apple Brown Betty
Apricot Whip
Baked Custard
Banana Cream

Menu-Planning Suggestions

DESSERTS

Bavarian Cream
Bread Pudding
Butterscotch
  Pudding
Caramel Custard
Caramel Tapioca
Cheese Cake
Cherry Crisp
Chocolate Cream
Coconut Cream
Cottage Pudding
Cream Puffs
Date Cream
Date Pudding
Date Roll
Éclairs
English Toffee
  Dessert
Floating Island
Fruit Cobblers
Fruit Gelatin
Fudge Pudding
Lemon Cake
  Pudding
Lemon Snow
Meringue Shells
Peach Crisp
Peach Melba
Pineapple Cream
Pineapple Refrig-
  erator Dessert
Royal Rice Pudding
Rice Custard
Shortcake
Steamed Pudding
Tapioca Cream
Vanilla Cream

Pears
Rhubarb
Fresh Pineapple
  with Lemon
  Sherbet
Fruit Compote
Canned or Frozen
  Apricots
  Berries
  Cherries
  Figs
  Fruit Cup
  Peaches
  Pears
  Pineapple
  Plums or Prunes
  Rhubarb

MISCELLANEOUS
DESSERTS

Cheese, assorted
  with Crackers
  & Fruit
Fruit
  Baked or Stewed
    Apples

Menu-Planning Suggestions

SOUPS

CREAM SOUPS

Asparagus
Celery
Cheese
Chicken
Corn Chowder
Mushroom
Oyster Stew
Pea
Potato
Potato Chowder
Spinach
Tomato
Vegetable Chowder

STOCK SOUPS

Barley
Navy Bean
Beef Noodle
Beef Bouillon
Chicken Bouillon
Chicken and Noodle
Chicken with
    Spatzels
Chicken Gumbo
Chicken Mushroom
Clam Chowder
Consommé
Creole
French Onion
Julienne
Jellied Consommé
Lentil
Minestrone
Pepper Pot
Rice
Spanish Bean
Split Pea
Tomato Bouillon
Tomato–Rice
Vegetable–Beef

Menu-Planning Suggestions

GARNISHES

YELLOW-ORANGE

Cheese and Eggs

Balls, Grated, Strips
Rosettes
Egg, Hard-cooked
 or Sections
Deviled Egg Halves
Riced Egg Yolk

Fruit

Apricot Halves,
 Sections
Cantaloupe Balls
Lemon Sections,
 Slices
Orange Sections,
 Slices
Peach Slices
Peach Halves with
 Jelly
Spiced Peaches
Persimmons
Tangerines

Sweets

Apricot Preserves
Orange Marmalade
Peach Conserve
Peanut Brittle,
 Crushed
Sugar, Yellow or
 Orange

Vegetables

Carrots, Rings,
 Shredded, Strips

Miscellaneous

Butter Balls
Coconut, Tinted
Gelatin Cubes
Mayonnaise

RED

Fruit

Cherries
Cinnamon Apples
Cranberries
Plums
Pomegranate Seeds
Red Raspberries
Maraschino Cherries
Strawberries
Watermelon Cubes,
 Balls

Sweets

Red Jelly
 Apple, Cherry,
 Currant, Logan-
 berry, Raspberry
Cranberry Glacé,
 Jelly
Gelatin Cubes
Red Sugar
Beets, Pickled,
 Julienne
Beet Relish
Red Cabbage
Peppers, Red, Rings,
 Strips, Shredded
Pimiento, Chopped,
 Strips
Radishes, Red,
 Sliced, Roses
Stuffed Olives,
 Sliced
Tomato, Aspic, Cat-
 sup, Chili Sauce,
 Cups, Sections,
 Slices, Broiled

Miscellaneous

Paprika
Tinted Coconut

Cinnamon Drops
 "Red Hots"

GREEN

Fruit

Avocado
Cherries
Frosted Grapes
Green Plums
Honeydew Melon
Lime Wedges

Sweets

Citron
Green Sugar
Gelatin Cubes
Mint Jelly
Mint Pineapple
Mints

Vegetables

Endive
Green Pepper,
 Strips, Chopped
Green Onions
Lettuce Cups
Lettuce, Shredded
Mint Leaves
Olives
Parsley, Sprig,
 Chopped
Pickles
 Burr Gherkins
 Strips, Fans, Rings
Spinach Leaves

Miscellaneous

Coconut, Tinted
Mayonnaise, Tinted
Pistachios

Menu-Planning Suggestions

GARNISHES

WHITE

Fruit

Apple Rings
Apple Balls
Grapefruit Sections
Gingered Apple
White Raisins
Pear Balls
Pear Sections

Vegetables

Cauliflowerets
Celery Cabbage
Celery Curls, Hearts,
  Strips
Cucumber Rings,
  Strips, Wedges,
  Cups
Mashed Potato
  Rosettes
Onion Rings
Onions, Pickled
Radishes, White

Miscellaneous

Cream Cheese
  Frosting
Sliced Hard-cooked
  Egg White
Shredded Coconut
Marshmallows
Almonds
Mints
Whipped Cream
Powdered Sugar

BROWN-TAN

Breads

Crustades
Croutons
Cheese Straws
Fritters, Tiny
Noodle Rings

Toast, Cubes, Points,
  Strips, Rings

Miscellaneous

Cinnamon
Dates
French Fried Cauli-
  flower
French Fried Onions
Mushrooms
Nutmeats
Nut-covered Cheese
  Balls
Potato Chips
Rosettes
Toasted Coconut

BLACK

Caviar
Chocolate-covered
  Mints
Chocolate Sprill
Chocolate, Shredded
Chocolate Sauce
Olives, Ripe
Prunes
Prunes, Spiced
Pickled Walnuts
Raisins, Currants
Truffles

Menu-Planning Suggestions

UTILIZATION OF EXCESS PREPARED FOODS

Bread and Crackers

Bread Crumbs, for
crumbing Cutlets,
Croquettes, and
other fried food;
thickening
steamed and
other puddings
Canapés
Cinnamon Toast
Croutons, as soup
accompaniment
Desserts, Bread Pud-
ding, Brown Betty
French Toast
Hot Dishes, Cheese
Fondue, Scalloped
Macaroni, Soufflé,
Stuffing for Meat,
Poultry or Fish
Melba Toast
Toast Points, as gar-
nish

Cereals

Chinese Omelet
Fried or French
Fried Corn Meal
Mush or Hominy
Grits
Meat Balls with
Cooked Cereal as
an Extender
Rice and Tuna
Rice Croquettes
Rice Custard
Soup with Rice, Spa-
ghetti, or Noodles

Cakes and Cookies

Baked Fruit Pudding
Cottage Pudding
Crumbs to coat balls
of ice cream
Crumb Cookies

Icebox Cake
Spice Crumb Cake

Eggs

Boiled or Poached,
add to Cream
Sauce, Mayon-
naise, or French
Dressing, as a gar-
nish for Vegeta-
bles, Egg Cutlets,
in Salad
Scrambled, Potato
Salad, Sandwich
Spread
Egg Whites, raw,
Angel Food Cake,
Bavarians, Fluffy
or Boiled Dressing,
Macaroons, Me-
ringue, Prune
Whip, White
Sheet, or Layer
Cake
Egg Yolks, raw,
Cooked Salad
Dressing, Custard
Sauce, Filling or
Pudding, Duchess
Potatoes, Hollan-
daise Sauce, Hot
Cake Batter,
Scrambled Eggs,
Strawberry Bava-
rian Cream Pie,
Yellow Angel
Food Cake

Fish

Creamed, à la King
or Scalloped
Fish Cakes or Cro-
quettes
Salad

Sandwich Spread

Fruit

Applesauce Cake
Apricot or Berry
Muffins
Frozen Fruit Salad
Fruit Slaw
Fruit Tarts
Jellied Fruit Cup or
Salad
Jelly or Jam
Mixed Fruit Salad or
Fruit Cup
Prune or Apricot
Filling for Rolls
or Cookies
Sauce for Cottage
Pudding

Meat

Apple stuffed with
Sausage
Bacon in Sauce for
Vegetable
Baked Beef Hash
Boiled Lima Beans
with Ham
Chili con Carne
Chop Suey
Creamed Ham or
Meat on Toast
Creamed Ham in
Timbale Cases
Creole Spaghetti
Ham or Bacon
Omelet
Hot Tamale Pie
Meat Croquettes
Meat Roll or Meat
Pie
Meat Turnovers
Salad
Sandwiches

Menu-Planning Suggestions

UTILIZATION OF EXCESS PREPARED FOODS

Scalloped Potatoes
  with Ham
Scrapple
Stuffed Peppers

Milk and Cream, Sour

Biscuit Brown Bread
Butterscotch Cookies
Fudge Cake
Griddle Cakes
Salad Dressing
Sour Cream Pie
Spice Coffee Cake
Veal Chops in Sour
  Cream

Poultry

Chicken and Rice
  Casserole
Chicken Timbales
Creamed Chicken in
  Patty Cases
Chicken à la King
Croquettes
Cutlets
Jellied Chicken Loaf
Pot Pie
Salad
Sandwiches
Soufflé
Soup
Turnovers

Vegetables

Combination—Car-
  rots and Peas,
  Corn and Beans,
  Corn and Toma-
  toes, Peas and
  Celery
Fritters
Potatoes—Duchess,
  Hashed-brown,
  Lyonnaise, Cakes,

Omelet, Salad
  (hot and cold)
Salad in combination
  (when suitable)
Soup
Vegetable Pie
Vegetable Timbales

Menu Terms

à la (ah lah), *Fr.* To the, with, in the mode or fashion of, or in, as in *à la Crême,* with cream; *à la Newburg,* Newburg fashion; *à la Moutarde,* in mustard.

à la carte, *Fr.* On the menu, but not part of a complete meal, usually prepared as ordered.

à la king, *Fr.* Served in cream sauce containing green pepper, pimiento, and mushrooms.

à la mode, *Fr.* in style. When applied to desserts, means with ice cream. *Beef à la mode,* a well-larded piece of beef cooked slowly in water with vegetables, similar to braised beef.

à la Newburg. Creamed dish with egg yolks added, originally flavored with lime or sherry. Most often applied to lobster, but may be used with other foods.

allemande (al-mângd), *Fr.* German; a smooth yellow sauce consisting of white sauce with the addition of butter, egg yolk, catsup, etc.

amandine. Served with almonds.

anglaise (ng-glayz), *Fr.* English; *À la anglaise,* in English style.

antipasti (än-tēē-päs-tēē), *It.* Appetizer; a course consisting of relishes.

au gratin (o grat-ang), *Fr.,* made with crumbs, scalloped. Often refers to dishes made with a cheese sauce.

au jus (o zhüs), *Fr.,* meat served in its natural juices or gravy.

Bardé (bar-day), *Fr.* Larded. Covered with salt pork or with slices of bacon. *Un poulet Bardé de Lard,* a pullet larded with bacon.

bar-le-Duc (bar-luh-dük), *Fr.* A preserve originally made of selected whole white currants seeded by hand with the aid of knitting needles. Now gooseberries, strawberries, etc., may be used. It frequently forms a part of the cheese course.

Bavarian Cream. A gelatin dish into which whipped cream is folded as it begins to stiffen.

Bavarois (bav-ar-wâz), *Fr.* Bavarian.

Béchamel (bay-sham-ayl), *Fr.* Refers to a sauce supposed to have originated with the Marquis de Béchamel, maître d'hôtel of Louis XIV. A cream sauce made of chicken stock, cream, or milk, and usually seasoned with onion. Sometimes applied to all sauces having a white sauce foundation.

beef à la mode (bēf ah lah mōd), *Fr.* A well-larded piece of beef cooked slowly in water with vegetables, similar to braised beef.

bellevue (bel-vü), *Fr.* A pleasing sight; in aspic. *À la bellevue,* a food enclosed in aspic through which it can be plainly seen.

Bénédictine (bay-nay-dik-tang), *Fr.* A liqueur made principally at the Abbey of Fécamp in Europe. *Eggs à la Bénédictine,* poached eggs served on broiled ham placed on split toasted muffins and garnished with Hollandaise sauce.

beurre (buhr), *Fr.* Butter. *Au beurre noir,* with butter sauce browned in a pan; *Beurre Fondue,* melted butter.

beurré (buhr-ay), *Fr.* Buttered.

biscotte (bis-kot), *Fr.* Rusk, biscuit.

bisque (bisk), *Fr.* A thick soup usually made from fish or shellfish. Also a frozen dessert. Sometimes defined as ice cream to which finely chopped nuts are added.

blanquette (blâng-ket), *Fr.* A white stew usually made with veal. A cheese similar to Roquefort.

bleu (bluh), *Fr.* Blue. *Au bleu,* plain boiled; Used with reference to fresh-water fish.

boeuf (buhf), *Fr.* Beef. *Boeuf à la lardinière,* "braised beef with vegetables; boeuf kôti, roast beef.

bombe (bongh), *Fr.* Also called *bombe glacée.* A frozen dessert made of a combination of two or more frozen mixtures packed in a round or melon-shaped mold.

bonne femme (bong fam), *Fr.* Good wife; in simple home style. Applied to soups, stews, etc.

bordelaise (bord-lez), *Fr.* Of Bordeaux. *Sauce bordelaise,* a sauce with Bordeaux wine as its foundation, with various seasonings added.

borsch or **bortsch** (bōrsh), *Rus.* A Russian or Polish soup made with beets. Often sour cream or citric acid is added to give an acid taste.

bouillabaisse (bool-yab-ays), *Fr.* A national soup of France. The word comes from the verbs *bouiller,* to boil, and *abaisser,* to go down. A highly seasoned fish soup made especially at Marseilles. Served in plates with dry toast.

bourgeoise (boor-zhwâz), *Fr.* Middle-class, family-style. *À la bourgeoise* usually means served with vegetables.

brioche (bre-yosh), *Fr.* A slightly sweetened rich bread of French origin.

broche (brosh), *Fr.* Skewer, spit for roasting. *À la broche,* cooked on a skewer.

café (kaf-ay), *Fr.* Coffee; coffee house; restaurant. *Café au lait,* coffee with hot milk; *Café noir,* black coffee, after-dinner coffee.

canapé (kan-ap-ay), *Fr.* Originally couch, sofa, or divan; now an appetizer served either hot or cold. Usually fried or toasted bread spread with or supporting a wide variety of highly seasoned foods. Generally used as the first course of a meal as an hors d'oeuvre and eaten with the fingers, unless accompanied by a sauce or otherwise made impossible to eat this way. Often served on a doily.

carte (kart), *Fr.* Card; bill of fare. *À la carte,* according to the bill of fare; *carte au Jour,* bill of fare or menu for the day.

Chantilly (shâng-tē-yē), *Fr.* Name originally given to savoy cakes, which were scooped out, filled with preserved fruit, and garnished with whipped cream; now applies to anything served with sweetened and flavored whipped cream. *Chantilly cream,* sweetened and flavored whipped cream.

Chartreuse (shar-truhz), *Fr.* Having a hidden filling or stuffing, as meat molded in rice or molded aspic filled with vegetables, meat, or fruit filling in the center; also famous liqueur.

chaud (shô), *Fr.* Hot.

chemise (sh-mēz), *Fr.* Shirt. *En chemise,* with their skins on; generally applied to potatoes.

chiffonade (shēr-fōn-ăd), *Fr.* Rags; minced or shredded vegetables or meat sprinkled over soups or salads.

cloche (klosh), *Fr.* Bell, dish cover. *Sous cloche,* under cover.

confit or **confiture** (kong-fee), *Fr.* Preserves or jam made from fruit.

Consommé (kon-so-may), *Fr.* A clear soup usually made from 2 or 3 kinds of meat.

creole (krē'ōl), *Fr.* Relating or peculiar to the Creoles, made with tomatoes, peppers, onions, and other seasonings. Applies to soups, garnishes, sauces, etc. so prepared.

crépe suzette (krayp), *Fr.* The product is small, very thin and crisp pancake served for tea or as dessert.

croissant (krwâ-sâng), *Fr.* Crescent. Applied to rolls and confectionery of crescent shape.

curry (kŭr'ĭ). Highly spiced condiment from India, a stew seasoned with curry.

déjeuner (day-zhuh-nay), *Fr.* Breakfast, lunch.

de jour, *Fr.* Ready to serve.

de la maison, (de-lah-mā-zōn'), *Fr.* Specialty of the house.

demi-tasse (dŭh-mee-tâss), *Fr.* Half-cup; after-dinner coffee served in small cups.

dîner (de-nay), *Fr.* Dinner; to dine.

duglère (doog-lâr), *Fr.* After French restaurateur who popularized tomatoes. Signifies the use of tomatoes.

écarlate (ay-kar-lat), *Fr.* Scarlet; a red sauce containing lobster roe, red tongue, etc.

entrecote (ângtr'kôt), *Fr.* Between ribs; a steak cut from between the ribs. Supposed to be second in quality only to the fillet or tenderloin.

entrée (âng-tray) *Fr.* The main course of a meal; formerly, and still in some countries, a dish served before the roast or between the main courses, as between the fish and the meat.

espagnole (ays-pah-nyol), *Fr.* Spanish; brown sauce.

fanchonette (fâng-sho-net), *Fr.* Small pie or tart covered with a meringue.

farci (far-see), *Fr.* Stuffed.

fermière (fayr-myayr), *Fr.* Farmer's wife; in plain country style.

foie gras (fwâ gra), *Fr.* Fat liver. Applied especially to the liver of fat geese. *Foie gras au naturel,* plain cooked, whole foie gras; *Paté de foie gras,* cooked livers seasoned with truffles, wine, and aromatics; most popular form of foie gras.

fondue (fong-dü), *Fr.* Melted or blended.

Franconia. Ancient German duchy; in the culinary sense, browned. Franconia potatoes, whole potatoes browned with the roast.

frappé (frap-pay), *Fr.* Beaten and iced. Applied to a water ice frozen to a mush while stirring; usually drunk rather than eaten with a spoon or fork.

glacé (glah-say), *Fr.* Iced, frozen, glassy, glazed, frosted, candied, crystallized. *Glacé fruit,* fruit dipped in a hot sirup which has been cooked to a hard-crack stage.

gumbo. Okra; a rich, thick Creole soup containing okra.

haché (hah-shay), *Fr.* Minced, chopped.

hors d'oeuvre (or-duh-vr'), *Fr.* Side dish or relish served at the beginning of a meal. Used for luncheons, but not for dinners in France.

Italienne (e-tal-yang), *Fr.* Italian style.

Jardinière (zhar-de-nyayr), *Fr.* The gardener's wife; a dish of mixed vegetables.

julienne (zhü-lyayn), *Fr.* Vegetables cut into fine strips or shreds. Named from the famous chef, Jean Julienne, who invented clear vegetable soup with the vegetables cut into match-like strips.

jus (zhüs), *Fr.* Juice or gravy. *Au jus,* meat served in its natural juices or gravy.

kippered. Scotch term originally applied to salmon; now a method of preserving fish, especially herring and salmon. The fish are split, then lightly salted and smoked.

kosher (kō'shĕr). Jewish term. *Kosher meat*, meat from a strictly healthy animal that has been slaughtered and prepared in accordance with the Jewish requirements.

Kuchen (kōō-ckhen), *Ger.* Cake, not necessarily sweet.

Laitue (lay-tü), *Fr.* Lettuce.

Lebkuchen (lāp'kōō-ckhen), *Ger.* Famous German cake, sweet cakes or honey cakes.

limpa. Swedish rye bread.

lox. Smoked salmon.

lyonnaise (lyo-nayz), *Fr.* From Lyons; seasoned with onions and parsley, as *Lyonnaise potatoes.*

macédoine (mah-say-dooan), *Fr.* Mixture or medley; usually applied to cut vegetables, but also to fruit.

maître d'hôtel (maytr' dotayl), *Fr.* Steward. In the culinary sense, implies the use of minced parsley. *Maître d'hôtel sauce* (parsley butter), a well-seasoned mixture of creamed butter, chopped parsley, and lemon juice. Served on broiled meats, broiled or boiled fish, and on some vegetables, as potatoes.

marinade (mar-e-nad), *Fr.* French dressing in which foods, as cooked vegetables and meats, are allowed to stand to render them more palatable. Also used with uncooked meat to soften tough fibers and to keep meat fresh, in which case it may be no more than a brine or pickle solution.

marinate. To treat with a marinade.

milanaise (me-lan-ayz), *Fr.* From Milan. Implies the use of macaroni and Parmesan cheese with a suitable sauce, often Béchamel.

Minestrone (mēē-nāys-trō'ne), *It.* Famous Italian thick vegetable soup.

Mulligatawny. Derived from two East Indian words signifying pepper water. A highly seasoned, thick soup characterized chiefly by curry powder. Meats, vegetables, mango chutney, coconut flesh, rice, cayenne, etc., may be added to taste.

Napoleans. Puff pastry kept together in layers with a custard filling, cut into portion size rectangles, and iced.

Neapolitan. (Also **Harlequin** and **Panachée**). Molded dessert of 2 to 4 kinds of ice cream or water ice arranged lengthwise in layers. The mixture is sliced across for serving. Also applied to a gelatin dish arranged in layers of different colors.

Nesselrode pudding. Frozen dessert with a custard foundation to which chestnut purée, fruit, and cream have been added. Has been termed the most perfect of frozen puddings.

Newburg. Creamed dish with egg yolks added, originally flavored with lime or sherry. Most often applied to lobster, but may be used with other foods.

noisette (nooâ-zet), *Fr.* Literally hazelnut; nut-brown color. May imply nut-shaped. A small piece of lean meat. Generally a chop minus the bone (fillet). Potatoes Noisette, "potatoes cut into the shape and size of hazel-nuts and browned in fat."

normande (nor-mând), *Fr.* From Normandy. *À la Normande*, a delicate, smooth mixture often containing whipped cream.

pané (pan-ay), *Fr.* Covered with bread crumbs or breaded.

parfait (par-fay), *Fr.* Perfect; a mixture containing egg and sirup which is frozen without stirring. May be molded, but is more commonly served in parfait glasses.

parmentière (par-mang-tyayr), *Fr.* Potato. Named after Baron Augustine Parmentier, who introduced potatoes to France and originated many methods of preparing them. À la parmentière, with or of potatoes.

pastrami (pa-strä'mi), *Hung.* Boneless beef cured with spices and smoked.

pâte (pât), *Fr.* Paste, dough.

pâté (pâ-tay), *Fr.* Pie, patty, pastry. Also a meat preparation packed in earthenware jars and small tins, prepared largely in Germany and France, so called because it was sold in pies or *pâté* form. *Pâté de foie gras,* paste of fat livers.

persillade (payr-se-yad), *Fr.* Served with or containing parsley.

petit pois (puh-tee pooâ), *Fr.* A fine grade of very small peas with a delicate flavor but of low food value.

petits fours (puh-tee fŏŏr), *Fr.* Small fancy cakes.

piquant (pe-kâng), *Fr.* Sharp, highly seasoned. Applied to sauces, etc: *Sauce piquante,* "a highly seasoned brown sauce containing lemon juice or vinegar, capers, pickles, etc."

plank (plänk). Hardwood board used for cooking and serving broiled meat or fish. Thought to improve the flavor of foods so cooked. *Plánked steak,* a broiled steak served on a plank attractively garnished with a border of suitable vegetables or fruits.

plat (plah), *Fr.* Dish. *Plat au jour,* food of the day, as featured on the menu.

Polenta (po-lĕn'ta), *It.* Popular Italian dish originally of chestnut meal, but now often made with farina or corn meal. Cheese is usually added before serving.

polonaise (po-lo-nay), *Fr.* Polish. Dishes prepared with bread crumbs, chopped eggs, brown butter, and chopped parsley.

pomme de terre (pom de tare), *Fr.* Apple of the earth potato. *Pommes de terre à la Lyonnaise,* Lyonnaise potatoes.

purée (pü-ray), *Fr.* Foods rubbed through a sieve; also a nutritious vegetable soup in which milk or cream is seldom used.

ragout (rag-oo), *Fr.* Stew; originally something to restore the taste and tempt the appetite. Generally a thick, well-seasoned stew containing meat.

ramekin (rãm'e-kĭn). Small, individual baking dish or a pastry shell; also a cheese cake.

ravigote (rav-e-got), *Fr.* Sauce seasoned with tarragon vinegar, chives, shallots, etc.

ravioli (rä'vē-ō'lē), *It.* Little shapes of Italian or noodle paste rolled thin, one half spread with a filling of minced meat or vegetables and moistened with a sauce if necessary, then folded over and poached in stock.

rémoulade (ray-moo-lad), *Fr.* Pungent sauce made of hard-cooked eggs, mustard, oil, vinegar, and seasonings. Served with cold dishes.

rissoler (re-so-lay), *Fr.* To roast until golden brown; to brown. *Rissolé,* browned.

rouelle (roo-ayl), *Fr.* Round slice or fillet.

roulade (roo-lad), *Fr.* Roll; rolled meat.

roux (roo), *Fr.* Browned flour and fat used for thickening sauces, stews, etc.

Sabayon *Fr.* Custard sauce with wine added.

scallion. Any onion which has not developed a bulb.

Schaumtorte (schoum tor'te), *Ger.* Foam cake; layers of meringue and crushed fruit.

shallot. Onion having a stronger but more mellow flavor than the common variety.

sorbet (sor-bay), *Fr.* Sherbet made of several kinds of fruits.

soubise (soo-bēz), *Fr.* White sauce containing onion and sometimes parsley.

Springerle (spring'er-le), *Ger.* A popular Christmas cake or cookie. The dough is rolled into a sheet and pressed with a springerle mold before baking.

table d'hôte (tabl' dôt), *Fr.* Table of the host or innkeeper. *Service table d'hôte,* a meal planned by the establishment at a set price, permitting a wide choice of foods.

terrine (tay-reen), *Fr.* Tureen, an earthenware pot resembling a casserole. *Chicken en terrine,* chicken cooked and served in a tureen.

torte (tôr'te), *Ger.* Rich cake made from crumbs, eggs, nuts, etc.

tortilla (tô-tē'ya), *Sp.* A round thin "bread" made of corn meal.

tortoni (tôr-tōn'ēē), *It.* Originally *tortonois,* meaning from the Italian city Tortona. *Biscuit tortoni,* a frozen mixture containing dried, ground macaroons and chopped, blanched almonds.

tournedos (toor-nāy-dōz), *Sp.* Small round fillets of beef.

truffles (trŭf'ls). A species of fungi similar to mushrooms, found chiefly in France. They are black and grow in clusters under oak trees, several inches below the surface of the ground. They are rooted out by pigs trained for the purpose. Used chiefly for garnishing and flavor.

velouté (vu-loo-tay), *Fr.* Velvety; a rich white sauce usually made of chicken or veal broth. Considered the principal white sauce just as *Espagnole* is the chief brown sauce, although some confusion exists in the use of the terms.

volaille (vo-lah-yuh), *Fr.* Poultry.

vol-au-vent (vol-o-vang), *Fr.* Flying at the mercy of the wind; large patties of puff paste made without a mold and filled with meat, preserves, etc.

Wienerschnitzel (vē'nēr shnit's'l), *Ger.* An entrée made of thin veal steak (cutlets) breaded and fried slowly in butter.

Yorkshire pudding. English dish, usually served with roast beef, consisting of a popover-like mixture which may be baked with the meat or separately with some of the drippings.

Zwieback or **Zwiebach** (tsvē'bäk), *Ger.* Twice-baked bread, crisp and slightly sweet. Now used largely as a food for very young children.

PART FOUR
SPECIAL MEAL SERVICE

SPECIAL MEALS

Meals for special occasions may call for the organization of a special temporary service staff. Procedures will differ in many ways from those established for the usual routine of daily food service. To many the organization and administration of these unusual meals is a task to be dreaded and, if possible, to be avoided. This attitude is often common among persons without institutional training, although it is not infrequently found among trained directors who are completely preoccupied with their daily tasks.

When a meal is to be served outside of the routine daily schedule, a temporary organization is often set up for the unusual task. The cooks who will prepare the meal may be experienced in large-quantity food preparation, but waiters and waitresses may be untrained.

The major responsibilities of the manager or food service director in charge of a special meal are as follows:

1. Confer with representatives of the organization to be served to determine such details as the type of group and number to be served, the service desired, price to be paid, and time and place of service.

2. Plan menu with the organization representative.

3. Determine quantity, quality, and estimated cost of food to be served.

4. Place food order.

5. Check dishes and equipment on hand. Make arrangements for obtaining additional items needed.

6. Set up temporary organization.
   (a) Assign cooks, regular or special, to prepare food.
   (b) Assign cooks and other personnel to the serving counter from which the plates will be filled.
   (c) Assign and instruct waiters or waitresses for dining room service.

7. Make detailed work schedule for each group of workers, if inexperienced.

8. Supervise the preparation and service of food.

9. Supervise the dishwashing and cleanup of preparation and service areas.

10. Write a detailed report including information concerning numbers served, income and expenses, and useful comments for service of similar meals in the future.

Suggestions for the organization and administration of a typical simple meal for 150 people, such as might be prepared and served in various types of food services, are offered here as an aid for those inexperienced in the service of meals for special occasions. Most schools have kitchens in their student centers, residence halls, or lunchroom in which special meals may be prepared by the regular cooks. Many communities and church centers also have well-planned and adequately equipped facilities for preparing and serving special meals. The plan presented here can be adjusted to other situations to meet changes in the menu, the number served, and equipment and labor available.

Planning the Meal

It is desirable that the person acting as manager for the special meal confer with an authorized representative of the group to be served. Such a conference provides information as to the menu to be planned, the estimated or guaranteed number to be served, the price to be charged for the meal, the type of service, the date, time, and place the meal is to be served. It is well also to discuss program arrangements and responsibility for table decorations.

Duplicate copies of the menu plans should be signed and kept by the group's representative and the food director. This confirms the agreement and may prevent a misunderstanding of details and avoid last minute changes. Menu plans may be recorded on a blank, such as that shown on p. 479.

After the menu has been planned, the next step is to determine the kind and amount of food to be purchased. A list of foods and amounts needed for the suggested menu is given on p. 480.

A carefully planned work schedule is important to the success of any special meal. The number of workers and time required for preparation will depend largely on equipment available and the experience of the workers. The work schedule on pp. 482–483 is offered only as a guide. In this plan for a Father and Son Dinner, to be served in a school lunchroom, the detailed schedule assumes that the kitchen used for the preparation of the meal is equipped with an electric mixer with attachments, adequate oven and refrigerator space, and a mechanical dishwasher. The cooks are experienced in quantity food preparation; the waiters and waitresses are students. If there is less equipment and the cooks are inexperienced, an adjustment in work schedules will need to be made.

A list including the amount and kind of linen, dishes, silver, glassware, and serving utensils required should be made by the manager and arrangements made for assembling these, at least one day before they are to be used. Such a list is shown on p. 481.

Central High School

		Menu
Date to be served	*Nov. 10*	
Dining room	*North*	*Hot Spiced Tomato Juice*
Time	*6:15 P.M.*	*Cheese Crackers*
Organization	*Father and Son*	*Honey-glazed Baked Ham*
Plates estimated	*150*	*Potatoes au Gratin*
Plates guaranteed	*145*	*French Style Green Beans with Almonds*
Price per plate	*$1.50*	*Ginger Ale Fruit Salad—Chantilly Dressing*
Number served		*Dinner Rolls—Butter*
Amount paid		*Pumpkin Pie—Whipped Cream*
Cash		*Coffee, Milk*
Charge		
Comments		
Representative of Organization		*George Johnson*
Food Director		*Helen Smith*

Food to Be Purchased[1]

Menu Item	Food	Quantity
Spiced Tomato Juice—Cheese Crackers	Tomato juice	10 46-oz. cans
	Onions	1½ lb.
	Consommé	5 46-oz. cans
	Cheese crackers	6 pkgs.
Honey-glazed Baked Ham	Ham, cured, ready-to-eat boned, sliced and tied	50–55 lb.
	Honey	1 qt.
	Orange juice, frozen	2 6-oz. cans
Potatoes au Gratin	Potatoes	45–50 lb.
	Cheese, Cheddar	6 lb.
Green Beans with Almonds	Frozen green beans, French cut	12 2½-lb. pkg.
	Almonds, slivered	1 lb.
Ginger Ale Fruit Salad	Gelatin, lemon-flavored	3 24-oz. pkg.
	Ginger ale	6 qt.
	Grapes	3 lb.
	Apples	4 lb.
	Celery	3 bunches
	Pineapple chunks	3 No. 10 cans
	Lemon juice, frozen	1 6-oz. can
	Lettuce, head	1 doz.
	Mayonnaise	2 qt.
Rolls, Dinner	Yeast, compressed	9 oz.
Pumpkin Pie	Pumpkin	9 No. 2½ cans
	Eggs	5 doz. (for pie and rolls)
	Milk	12–15 gal. (for cooking and serving)
	Shortening	6 lb. (rolls and pastry)
Cream	Cream, whipping	3 qt. (for pie and salad dressing)
	Cream, half-and-half	2 qt.
Coffee	Coffee, regular grind	2–3 lb.
Butter	Butter or margarine	7 lb. cooking and serving
Sugar	Sugar, granulated	10 lb. cooking and serving
	Sugar, brown	3 lb.
	Sugar, powdered	1 lb.

[1] Flour, condiments, and spices in stock. Based on menu to serve 150 (p. 479).

Dish List for Father and Son Dinner

Item	Number
CHINA:	
Service plates (6 in.)	150
Dinner plates (9 in.)	160
Salad plates (6 in.)	150
Dessert plates	150
Cups	100
Saucers	100
GLASSWARE:	
Glasses for water and milk	250
Sugar bowls	20
Creamers	20
Salts and peppers	20
Water pitchers	12
Punch cups	150
LINEN:	
Place mats	150
Napkins	175
SILVERWARE:	
Knives	150
Forks	300
Teaspoons	175
Extra silver or trays	10 each
MISCELLANEOUS:	
Turner for meat service	3
Solid serving spoons	3
Slotted serving spoons	3
Hot pan holders	6
Dish towels	1 doz.
Roll baskets or plates	15
Coffee servers	6

The plans for organization that have been presented have presupposed some one person to be in charge, with others working under her direction, either as students or employees. Such is not the case with many special meals that are prepared and served by community and church organizations. These meals are a responsibility which many women, active in church and community life, are asked to assume. Often these women, who are efficient organizers in their own homes, are at a loss to know how best to proceed in the preparation and planning of food for a large group. Detailed plans previously presented as necessary for the efficient management of a special meal (p. 477) may be modified

Suggested Work Schedule for Cooks and Waitresses

Time	Cook I	Cook II	Waitresses 1–2–3	Waitresses 4–5–6	Waitresses 7–8–9	Waitresses 10–11–12
10:00	Make and roll out pastry for pies	Make salad and prepare lettuce for salads				
11:00		Refrigerate				
11:45	Make pie filling Bake pies	Prepare pans for rolls				
12:30		Make roll dough				
1:00	Eat lunch	Eat lunch				
1:30	Pare and cook potatoes	Assist Cook I with potatoes				
2:30		Count dishes and silver and instruct waitresses				Set tables
3:00	Cube potatoes Make cheese sauce				Set tables	
3:45	Place hams in pans. Place in oven Combine tomato juice ingredients Assist Cook II shape rolls	Shape rolls				
4:30		Heat water for coffee and beans				

Time	Cook	Cook / Head	Waitress	Waitress	Waitress	Waitress
4:45	Remove hams from oven Glaze and return to oven	Instruct and assist waitresses in cutting butter and salads	Cut butter	Cut butter	Cut salads	Cut salads
5:15	Combine potatoes and cheese sauce	Make salad dressing	Place salad and butter on salad plates	Place salad and butter on salad plates	Arrange lettuce cups and place on salad plates	
5:30	Remove hams from oven	Cook beans				
5:40	Bake rolls Bake potatoes au Gratin	Make coffee Assist waitresses in setting up serving counter	Set up serving counter Place salads on table	Place crackers on serving plate Place salads on table	Fill water glasses with ice and water Place salads on table	
6:00	Prepare hams for service on counter	Heat tomato juice				
6:10	Remove rolls from oven Remove potatoes from oven	Season beans, add almonds	Place rolls on plate and on table	Place rolls on plate and on table	Duties same as for waitresses 4-5-6	
6:15	Remain in kitchen during serving period Assist in placing pie on plates	Pour tomato juice Serve plates from counter Remove food from counter Place pie on plates	Pour tomato juice Serve plates from counter Fill pitchers with coffee Stack dishes Place whipped cream on pie	Place tomato juice after guests are seated Remove first course Place plates on table Serve coffee and milk Clear plates from table Serve dessert		
7:00	Clean counter and stack dishes	Put away food	Stack dishes	Clear tables of all food and dishes		
7:15	Eat	Eat	Eat	Eat		

A helper for the cooks will report at 4 P.M. to assist cooks, wash pots and pans, and remain to wash dishes.

to fit the needs of a group of adult women. This group may be familiar with time requirements for food preparation but who have had little experience in the managerial aspects of large quantity meal preparation, including the division of labor and the delegation of various responsibilities. A necessary initial step in such planning is the assignment of definite tasks to committees. A suggested plan for such a group follows:

DUTIES AND PROCEDURE OF COMMITTEES

Planning Committee:
1. Plan menu.
2. List foods to be purchased.
3. Plan amounts of food to be purchased.
4. Select and assemble recipes.
5. Appoint the following committees: Preparation, Serving, Clean-up.
6. Furnish copies of menu and amount to be prepared and served to above-named committee.

Preparation Committee (Number Determined by Menu and Amounts to Be Prepared):
1. Study menu and recipes.
2. Make a preparation work schedule.
3. Prepare food according to the work plan.

Serving Committee:
1. Make lists of, and have available when needed, necessary dishes, silver, linen and other table appointments.
2. Arrange tables.
3. Lay covers and decorate tables.
4. Serve food on plates.
5. Serve food to guests in dining room.

Clean-up Committee:
1. Provide space for soiled dishes.
2. Scrape and stack soiled dishes and cooking utensils. Wash.

Serving the Meal

PREPARATION OF THE DINING ROOM

All personnel assisting with the food service should be given definite instructions. A mimeographed sheet of detailed procedures and instructions should be given to everyone new on a job.

The first step toward the service of a meal is the preparation of the room. It should be thoroughly cleaned, lighted, and ventilated; and the temperature should be regulated, if possible. The tables and chairs must be placed so there will be adequate space for serving after the guests are seated. Serving stands, conveniently placed, make service faster. Such provision is especially important when the distance to the kitchen is great.

ARRANGEMENT OF THE TABLE

In order that the food may be served properly, great care must be taken to follow certain accepted rules for table setting. The physical setup, help available, or other conditions may demand some deviation from the rules given. However, there is often more than one right way.

1. *Tablecloth.* Lay the tablecloth, unfolding it carefully on the table to avoid creases. Place the cloth upon the table so that the center lengthwise fold comes exactly in the middle of the table and the four corners are an equal distance from the floor. The cloth should extend over the table top at least a quarter of a yard at each end. The tablecloth should be ironed with one lengthwise fold down the center, the cloth opened up, and each side folded to the center crease, to make 3 lengthwise creases. Because of its length, institutional linen is usually folded crosswise to facilitate handling and storage. For some types of meals served to large groups, plastic and paper cloths are entirely acceptable. The use of these practical covers often would be limited to informal meals where labor and overall costs must be kept at a minimum. Tablecloths made of these materials are available in interesting and colorful designs and their use is gaining favor with guests and management.

2. *Place Mats.* Place mats make an attractive table setting when the finish of the table top permits. They are often used in institutions where no linen is available. Rectangular place mats may be sufficiently large that a single one will provide protection for the entire cover. If the mats are small, however, it is necessary to have enough paper doilies, of assorted sizes, to put under glasses, cups and saucers, bread and butter plates, and dishes containing food. In many institutions polished wood, lacquered, glass, or attractive composition table tops are used so the cover may be laid without cloth. They, too, often are used in institution food service and like tablecloths are made in various fabrics, including plastic and paper. Whatever the material, place mats should be chosen for the attractiveness of their design, color and the way in which they enhance other table appointments. Paper napkins also vary widely in quality, color, and design and now are acceptable for use on many occasions.

3. *The Cover.* The plate, silver, glasses, and napkin to be used by each person are called a "cover." Consider 20 in. of table space as the smallest permissible allowance for each cover; 25 or 30 in. is better. Arrange covers as symmetrically as possible. Place all silver and dishes required for one cover as close together as possible without crowding.

Fig. 15. Cover for a simple meal. (1) Bread and butter plate; (2) water glass; (3) napkin; (4) salad fork; (5) dinner fork; (6) knife; (7) tea spoon.

4. *Silver.* Place the silver about 1 in. from, and at right angles to, the edge of the table. If the table is round, only the outside pieces can be thus arranged. Place knives, forks, and spoons in the order of their use, those first used on the outside with the possible exception of the dinner knife and fork which may be placed immediately to the right and left of the plate, thus marking its position. Some prefer to place the salad or dessert fork next to the plate as the menu dictates. The trend is away from the use of salad forks when salad is not served as a separate course.

Place the knives at the right of the plate, with the cutting edge turned inward. If the menu requires no knife, omit it from the cover. Place the spoons, bowls up, at the right of the knives. Place the forks, tines up, at the left of the plate. Oyster and cocktail forks are exceptions to this rule; place these at the extreme right of the cover beyond the spoons.

The fork may be substituted for the knife at a luncheon where no knife is needed. Place it on the right side of the plate with the spoon beside it, if one is used. If more than one spoon is needed, the balance is better if the fork is placed to the left of the plate. With two forks and a spoon it may be better to place the forks in the usual position.

Lay the butter spreader across the upper right hand side of the bread and butter plate, with the cutting edge turned toward the center of the plate. It may be placed straight across the top of the plate or with the handle at a convenient angle. The butter spreader is sometimes placed with the other knives at the right of the plate beyond the spoons. This practice is followed chiefly in public places.

Fig. 16. The salad is placed at the left of the fork when salad and beverage are both served with the main course. If space does not permit, place salad plate at tip of fork and bread and butter plate above the dinner plate. (1) Bread and butter plate; (2) sherbet dish; (3) water glass; (4) salad plate; (5) dinner plate; (6) cup and saucer.

Do not place the dessert silver on the table when the cover is laid, except when the amount of silver required for the entire meal is small. Never lay covers with more than 3 forks or a total of 6 pieces of silver. If a dinner is sufficiently elaborate to require too much silver to be put on at one time, quietly place from a tray the silver needed for the later courses just before the course is served.

5. *Napkin.* Place the napkin at the left of the forks. It may be placed between the knife and fork if space is limited.

6. *Glass.* Place the glass at the tip of the knife or slightly to the right. Goblets and footed tumblers are often preferred for luncheon or dinner and should be used at a formal dinner.

7. *Bread and Butter Plate.* Place the bread and butter plate at the tip of the fork or slightly to the left.

8. *Salt and Pepper.* Salt and pepper shakers should be provided for each 6 covers. They should be placed parallel with the edge of the table

and in line with sugar bowls and creamers. Salt shakers are placed to the right.

9. *Nut or Candy Dishes.* Place individual nut or candy dishes directly at top of the cover. Larger dishes for nuts or bonbons are placed symmetrically upon the table, usually allowing 1 dish for each six or eight guests.

10. *Chairs.* Place the chairs so that the front edge of each touches or is just below the edge of the tablecloth. The chair should be so placed with relation to the table that it need not be moved when the guest is seated.

11. *Decorations.* Some attractive decorations should be provided for the center of the table. It should be low so the view across the table will not be obstructed. The decoration usually varies in elaborateness with the formality of the meal. Cut flowers should harmonize in color with the menu, the appointments of the table, and the room. The decorations on the table should, if possible, be in charge of someone not connected with the food service.

The use of candles in the daytime is permissible only when the lighting is inadequate or the day is dark. When used they should be the sole source of light. Do not mix candlelight and daylight or candlelight and electric light. Candles often form part of the decorations. Tall ones in low holders should be high enough so that the flame is not on a level with the eyes of the guests.

Place cards usually are placed on the napkin or above the cover. Menu cards, or booklets containing the menu and program, are commonly used at banquets. Infrequently the placing of cards is left to the food director.

SEATING ARRANGEMENT

It is difficult to lay down arbitrary rules for the seating of guests, since the matter is governed largely by the number and by the degree of formality of the meal. The guest of honor, if a woman, usually is seated at the right of the host; if a man, at the right of the hostess. The woman next in rank is seated at the left of the host. At a women's luncheon, the guest of honor sits at the right of her hostess. At banquets and public dinners, a woman is seated at the right of her partner.

TABLE SERVICE

1. Waitresses should report to the supervisor to receive final instructions at least 15 min. before the time set for serving the banquet.

2. If the salad is to be on the table when the guests arrive, it should be placed there by the waitresses not more than 15 min. before serving

time. It should be placed at the left of the fork. If space does not permit this arrangement, place salad plate at tip of fork and the bread and butter plate if used, directly above the dinner plate between the water glass and the salad plate.

3. Place creamers at right of sugar bowls.

4. Place relishes on the table, if desired.

5. For small dinners, the first course may be placed on the table before dinner is announced. For large banquets, however, it is best to wait until the guests are seated. Soups or hot canapés are always served after the guests are seated. To simplify service and to create an atmosphere of cordial hospitality, a first course of fruit or vegetable juices and accompaniments may be served as the guests arrive in the reception area.

6. Place butter on the right side of the bread and butter plate. If no bread and butter plate is used and the salad is to be on the table when the guests arrive, place the butter on the side of the salad plate. This is often necessary where dishes and table space are limited.

7. Place glasses filled with ice and water just before guests are seated.

8. When the guests are seated, waiters or waitresses line up in the kitchen for trays containing the first course. Two persons work together, one carrying the tray and the other placing the food. Place the cocktail glasses, soup dishes, or canapé plates on the service plates, which are already on the table.

9. Place and remove all dishes from the left with the left hand, except those containing beverages, which are placed and removed from the right with the right hand.

10. Serve the head table first, progressing from there to the right. It is preferable to have the head table the one farthest from the kitchen entrance.

11. When the guests have finished the first course, waitresses remove the dishes. Follow the same order in removing dishes as in serving.

12. For serving the main course, plates may be brought to the dining room on plate carriers or large trays holding several plates and set on tray stands. Each waitress serves the plates to a specified group of guests.

An alternate method is often used in serving large groups. A tray of filled plates is brought from the kitchen to a particular station in the dining room, where waitresses serve the plates. Waitresses remain at their stations during the serving period.

13. Place the plate 1 in. from the edge of the table with the meat next to the guest.

14. As soon as a table has been served with dinner plates and salad,

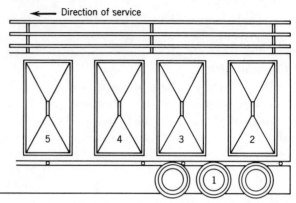

Fig. 17. Food arranged on a hot counter in the order it is to be placed on the plate facilitates service. (1) Plates; (2) meat; (3) potatoes; (4) vegetable; (5) garnish.

specially appointed waitresses should follow immediately with rolls and coffee.

15. At a large banquet, when serving a sherbet with the dinner course, carry it in on trays and place directly above the plate. Two waitresses work together as for first course.

16. Serve rolls at least twice. Offer them from the left at a convenient height and distance. Plates or baskets of rolls may be placed on the table to be passed by the guests.

17. Place the coffee at the right of the spoons with the handles of the cups toward the right.

18. Refill water glasses as necessary. If the tables are crowded, it may be necessary to remove the glasses from the table to fill them. Handle the glass near the base.

19. At the end of the course, remove all dishes and food belonging to that course. Remove dishes from left of the guest.

20. The silver for the dessert may or may not be placed on the table when the table is set. If passed later, take in on a tray and place at the right of the cover.

21. Serve desserts 2 at a time and in the same order that the plates were served. When pie is served, place with point toward the guest.

22. Coffee is served by waitresses who served it with the dinner course.

23. If possible, the table should be cleared except for decorations before the program begins.

24. The handling of dishes should cease before the program begins. The rattling of dishes has ruined many banquets and is an unnecessary offense to the guest.

SERVERS

Waitresses may wear black or dark dresses with small white aprons or light wash dresses; however, uniforms are usually preferable. Shoes with low, or medium-low, rubber heels should be worn. Waiters should wear dark trousers, white shirts, dark ties, and white coats. Waiters or waitresses should observe the following points:

1. Be immaculately clean in person and dress.
2. Report promptly on duty at scheduled time.
3. Be quick to see errors in table setting or service and to give help in case of accidents.
4. Appear pleasant and courteous at all times.
5. Step lightly, move quickly, but do not show a flurried manner.
6. Close doors without noise. Handle dishes and silver quietly.
7. Do not converse unless it is absolutely necessary.
8. Be as inconspicuous as possible.

KITCHEN ORGANIZATION

Food should be served from hot counters if these are available. If there are no hot counters, the utensils containing food should be placed in hot water to keep food hot. Some provision must be made also for keeping plates and cups hot. For serving 50 plates or less, the plan should provide that 1 person serve meat, vegetables, 1 potatoes, and so on. Such an arrangement for serving may be termed a "setup." For 60 to 100 persons, 2 setups should be provided in order to hasten service. For more than 100 persons it is well to provide additional setups.

It usually is convenient to have the food placed on the hot counter in the following order: meat, potatoes, vegetables, and sauces. Butter, garnish, and relishes are placed on an adjoining table.

The supervisor should demonstrate the size of portions to be given and their arrangement on the plate by serving the first plate and calling attention to the points to be considered.

There should be a checker at the end of the line to remove with a damp cloth any food spots from the plate, to check the plate for completeness, arrangement, and uniformity of servings.

PORTIONS

The importance of standardized serving can hardly be overestimated, for on this may depend the enjoyment of the guests and the financial success or failure of a meal.

There are various ways in which standard portions may be obtained.

Perhaps the first way is by specifying the size or weight of units comprising the purchase if these are to serve as individual portions. Meats such as veal cutlets, chops, or steaks may be ordered 3, 4 or 5 to the pound, as desired, thus providing for standardized service.

Many foods cannot be brought under this plan because they are mixtures or combinations of various foods, or are served in a form quite different from that in which they are purchased. Meat balls, croquettes, mashed potatoes, pudding, cakes, and pies all illustrate this point. Several different methods are followed to obtain standardized individual portions in foods belonging to this group:

1. Portions may be determined by weight during the process of preparation, as is sometimes done in the making of chicken pie.

2. Portions may be determined by the use of dippers of standardized size (p. 32). This method is commonly used in the preparation of such foods as meat balls and sandwich ingredients. Dippers also are used for serving puddings and salads.

3. Foods that take the form of the container in which they are prepared, such as gelatin salads, desserts, cakes, pies, and meat loaf, are prepared in pans of uniform size, and the prepared product is cut into uniform portions.

To obtain standardized portions by any of these methods, it is essential that the recipe used be standardized.

Menus for Special Meals

SPECIAL DINNER MENUS

The Selective Menu Planner (pp. 493–499) is designed as a guide for those responsible for planning dinners for special occasions. Food combinations suggested here may be suitable for community meals, special occasions in residence halls, school banquets or holiday meals, or wherever a special meal for a group is being planned.

Seven entrée groups are included in the Menu Planner. Salads, vegetables, breads, and desserts suitable to serve with entrées listed in that group are suggested. To use this guide, first decide on the entrée, then select any vegetable, salad, bread, and dessert given in that group. For example: with roast leg of veal and dressing, you may use Blue Lake green beans, mint-glazed carrots, or any of the other vegetables in that column; then make a choice of salad, rolls, and dessert from those listed in the adjoining columns. Any combination of items within a group, with minor adjustments, is designed to make a well-balanced dinner menu.

Selective Menu Planner

Roast				
Entrée Group 1	*Vegetable*	*Salad*	*Bread*	*Dessert*
1. Roast Top Round of Beef O'Brien Potatoes Brown Gravy	Mint-glazed Whole Carrots	Celery Hearts Radishes, Olives	Raised Muffins	Chocolate Mint Parfait- Sandies
2. Roast Leg of Veal Dressing Mushroom Sauce	Butternut Squash	Mixed Salad Greens with Parisian Dressing	Sesame Twists	Cheese Apple Crisp
3. Standing Rib Roast Parsley Buttered New Potatoes	Blue Lake Green Beans	Bing Cherry Mold— Chantilly Dressing	Cornflake Muffins	Walnut Chiffon Cake —Praline Topping
4. Roast Sirloin of Beef au Jus Yorkshire Pudding	Asparagus Polonaise	Melon Boats Fresh Fruits Thick French Dressing	Orange Rolls	Cream Puffs
5. Beef Rump Roast Small Corn Fritters	Zucchini Italian	Hearts of Romaine with Anchovy French Dressing	Whole Wheat Twin Rolls	Date Torte— Whipped Cream
6. German Pot Roast Egg Noodles in Casserole Gravy	French Fried Onion Rings	Grapefruit Sections— Avocado Strips Poppyseed Dressing	Cloverleaf Rolls	Lemon Sherbet with Fresh Strawberries Butter Tea Cookie

493

Selective Menu Planner (Continued)

Broiled Steak Entrée Group II	Vegetable	Salad	Bread	Dessert
1. Broiled Center Cut Lamb Chop Creamed New Potato Chutney	Buttered Frozen Peas with Mushrooms	Pineapple, Melon and Orange Celery Seed Fruit Dressing	Fig Coffee Ring	Chocolate Chiffon Pie
2. Broiled T-Bone Steak Corn Pudding Parsley	Baked Stuffed Tomato	Spicy Apricot Mold	Hard Rolls	Pineapple-Cashew Cake
3. Broiled Sirloin Strip Steak French Fried Potatoes	Green Beans Amandine	Fresh Fruit Wedges Pistachio Garnish	Butterhorn Rolls	English Toffee Dessert
4. Filet Mignon Baked Potato with Sour Cream	Cauliflower— Whipped Lemon Butter and Paprika	Crisp Green Salad Bowl Roquefort Dressing	Cranberry Nut Muffins	Peach Melba
5. Porterhouse Steak Stuffed Baked Potato Green Corn Relish	Fresh Julienne Beets	Head Lettuce with Avocado and Grape- fruit Sections— Piquante Dressing	Hot Cheese Biscuits Jelly	Frozen Mocha Almond Pie

494

Selective Menu Planner (*Continued*)

Fresh Pork Entrée Group III	Vegetable	Salad	Bread	Dessert
1. Stuffed Pork Chops Broiled Fresh Pineapple Slice with Chutney	Cauliflower Cheese Sauce Pimiento Strip	Grapefruit and Orange Sections on Curly Endive French Dressing	Cornbread	Chocolate Sundae Pie
2. Roast Loin of Pork Sage Dressing	Broccoli Drawn Butter	Cranberry Ring Mold	Butterhorn Rolls	Meringue Shells Ice Cream and Fresh Strawberries
3. Barbecued Pork Chops Baked Rice	Buttered Green Peas	Guacamole and Tomato	All-Bran Muffins	Lemon Cake Pudding
4. Breaded Pork Tenderloin Sweet Potato and Apple	Frozen Asparagus Tips	Bibb Lettuce Chiffonade Dressing	Crown Rolls	Fruit Sherbet— Fudge Balls
5. Baked Pork Chops Scalloped Potato	French Green Beans	Stuffed Prune on Peach Half	Cinnamon Knots	Frozen Filled Angel Food Cake

Selective Menu Planner (*Continued*)

Cured Ham Entrée Group IV	Vegetable	Salad	Bread	Dessert
1. Baked Ham Slice Mustard Sauce	Mashed Sweet Potato	Waldorf on Pineapple Slice	Oatmeal Muffin	Rainbow Ice Cream Balls
2. Broiled Ham Slice Cranberry Relish	Creamed New Potatoes	Ginger Ale Fruit	Poppyseed Twin Rolls	German Sweet Chocolate Cake
3. Glazed Baked Ham Currant Jelly	Buttered Whole Kernel Corn— Green Pepper Ring	Combination Fresh Julienne Vegetables	Parkerhouse Rolls	Strawberry Shortcake
4. Baked Chicken Breast on Ham Slice Glazed Apple Ring	Green Lima Beans in Cream	Melon—Fresh Pineapple— Cherry	Pecan Rolls	Chilled Fresh Fruit Cup with Lime Sherbet Tea Cookie
5. Ham Loaf Horseradish Sauce	Southern Style Green Beans	Head Lettuce Roquefort Dressing	Pan Rolls	Fresh Peach Cobbler— Hard Sauce

496

Selective Menu Planner (Continued)

Poultry Entrée Group V	Vegetable	Salad	Bread	Dessert
1. Fricassée of Chicken Noodle Casserole	Fresh Green Beans with Dill Sauce	Head Lettuce with Florida Fruits— Mint Leaf	Hot Biscuits Honey	Pink-Frosted Ribbon Layer Cake
2. Roast Tom Turkey Dressing Giblet Gravy Orange-Cranberry Relish	Glazed Carrots	Creamy Cole Slaw Green Pepper Ring	Parkerhouse Rolls	Brownie à la Mode
3. Barbecued Chicken Wild Rice Casserole Parsley	Fresh Frozen Peas with Sautéed Mushrooms	Peach Apple Salad Pecan Garnish	Prune-Date Coffeé Ring	Strawberry Pie
4. Country Fried Chicken Cream Gravy Mashed Potatoes Spiced Apricot	Buttered Fresh Corn	Sliced Cucumbers in Sour Cream Watercress Garnish	Bran Rolls	Lemon Sherbet— Melba Sauce
5. Chicken Tahitian Fried Rice with Almonds	Chive Baked Tomato	Mixed Salad Greens Chiffonade Dressing	Dinner Rolls	Praline Pumpkin Pie

Selective Menu Planner (*Continued*)

Fish *Entrées Group VI*	*Vegetable*	*Salad*	*Bread*	*Dessert*

1. Baked Salmon Steak
   Tartar Sauce
   Parsley New Potatoes
	Buttered Julienne
	Beets
		Stuffed Apricot
		Sliced Orange
		and Glazed Prune
			Cornmeal
			Muffin
				Date Torte
				Whipped Cream
				Cherry Glazed
				Cheese Cake

2. Broiled Fillet of White
   Fish and Mushrooms
   Lemon Butter
   Corn on Cob
	Sliced Buttered
	Zucchini
	Grated Italian
	Cheese
		Cucumber Soufflé	Hard Rolls	Apple Dumpling
				Nutmeg Sauce

3. Poached Halibut
   Amandine Sauce
   Green Rice
	Broiled Fresh
	Tomato
		Assorted Relishes	Tea Biscuits	Lemon Chiffon Pie

4. Baked Stuffed Fillet
   of Sole
   Cucumber Sauce—
   Pimiento
   Baked Idaho Potato
   in Foil
	Fresh Green Peas—
	Drawn Butter
		Tossed Fresh Salad Bowl
		Roquefort Dressing
			Braids	Chilled Melon
				Lime Wedge

5. Deviled Crab	Broccoli Polonaise	Pear on Orange Slice with Lime Gelatin and Cherry Garnish	All-Bran Rolls	Vanilla Ice Cream Hot Mincemeat Sauce

498

Selective Menu Planner (Continued)

Braised Steak Entrée Group VII	*Vegetable*	*Salad*	*Bread*	*Dessert*
1. Cubed Steak Swiss Style Oven Browned Potato Radish Rose	Brussels Sprouts Brown Butter Sauce	Melon and Grape-fruit Salad Honey Lime Dressing	Blueberry Muffin	Apple Pie with Streusel Topping
2. Country Fried Steak Mushroom Gravy Stuffed Baked Potato	Fresh Garden Spinach	Green Salad Bowl with Avocado Mexican French Dressing	Sesame Seed Bread	Peppermint Mousse
3. Baked Veal Cutlets in Sour Cream Glazed Sweet Potato	Jumbo Asparagus Spears Hollandaise	Stuffed Peach and Strawberry French Dressing	Orange Rolls	Pineapple Refrigerator Dessert
4. Veal Birds Mashed Potatoes Mushroom Gravy	Buttered New Beets and Greens	Cheese-Stuffed Celery	Parkerhouse Rolls	Red Cherry Tarts
5. Mock Drumsticks Lyonnaise Potato	Baby Lima Beans and Carrots Julienne	Molded Spiced Fruit	Hot Biscuits Jelly	Washington Cream Pie
6. Breaded Veal Steak Parsleyed New Potato Spiced Crabapple	Whole Kernel Corn O'Brien	Head Lettuce Thousand Island Dressing	Cinnamon Twists	Hot Chocolate Sundae

Special Luncheon Menus

(1)

Orange Soup

Turkey Tetrazinni   Buttered Broccoli Spears
Fresh Fruit Salad
Raised Muffins
Frozen Mocha Almond Pie
Coffee

(2)

Broiled Lamb Chops   Green Rice
Cauliflower with Cheese Sauce
Frozen Fruit Salad—Celery Seed Dressing
Tea Biscuit
German Sweet Chocolate Cake
Coffee

(3)

French Onion Soup   Toasted Crackers
Cheese Soufflé with Mushroom Sauce
Buttered Italian Green Beans   Green Salad Bowl
Hot French Garlic Bread
Lemon Sherbet with Frosted Raspberries
Coffee

(4)

Hot Consommé   Bread Sticks
Deviled Crab   Broiled Tomatoes
Buttered Asparagus Tips with Sesame Seed
Relish Plate
Twin Rolls
English Toffee Dessert
Coffee

(5)

Hot Spiced Tomato Juice   Cheese Balls
Chicken Salad in Raspberry Mold
Buttered Lima Beans   Stuffed Celery
Honey Cornflake Muffins
Filled Angel Food Cake
Coffee

Buffet Service

Buffet suppers and luncheons are increasing in popularity as a means of serving relatively large groups of people. They may be formal or informal with an atmosphere of friendliness, which extends their appeal to people in every age and occupation group. The menu may be simple or elaborate. In general the buffet meal is limited to two courses, but an assortment of hors d'oeuvres and a refreshing beverage may be served to the guests before they go to the buffet.

The success of a buffet meal depends not only on the quality of food but on the attractiveness of the buffet table. Interesting colors may be introduced in the table covering, the serving dishes, the food, or the decorations. A bowl of fruit, gourds, and nuts may replace the more usual floral decorations in the buffet service. Consideration must be given contrasts in colors, shapes, and sizes in the food and to the combining of food flavors. It is important to limit the kinds of hot foods to those that can be prepared and served easily.

ARRANGEMENT AND SERVICE

Food in a buffet service is arranged in the order in which it usually is served: Meats or other entrées, potatoes, vegetables, or salads, and relishes. If more than one kind of cold meat or cheese is included in the menu, a pleasing grouping of the various kinds of food of this type is usually made on one platter (Fig. 18a).

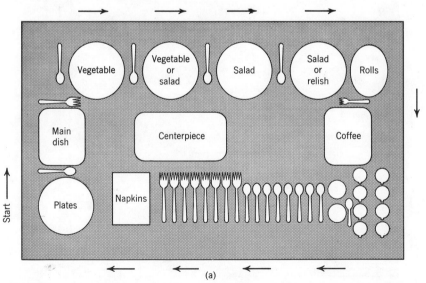

Fig. 18. (a) Table arrangement for buffet service, single line. (b) (*on following page*) Table arrangement for buffet service, double line. Coffee served at tables.

For large groups, a double line will speed service (Fig. 18b). More space and duplicate serving dishes would be required.

Desserts may be placed on a table other than the one containing the main course, from which the guest will later serve himself. Usually if the guests are seated, the dishes from the first course will be removed and the dessert served.

The type of service depends largely on the equipment available. If ample table space is provided places may be set with covers, rolls, and water, and provision may be made for the beverage to be served by a waiter. In this case, the guests need only to pass before a buffet table and select the foods desired. Hot foods at the buffet may be served by a hostess, by a waiter or waitress, or the guest may serve himself. When

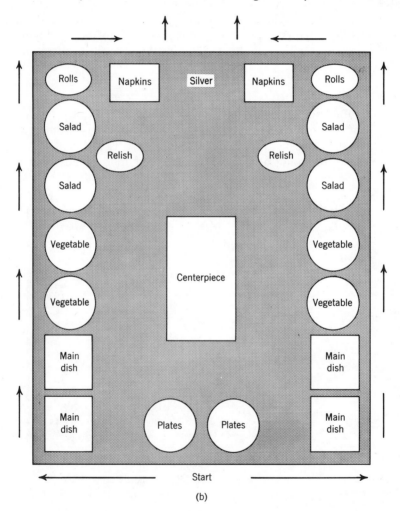

(b)

his plate is filled he takes his place at one of the covers prepared. If table room for all is not available, each guest may be given an individual tray on which to place silver, napkin, water, glass, and the plate containing the assembled food. Hot beverages and rolls are then commonly served by a waitress.

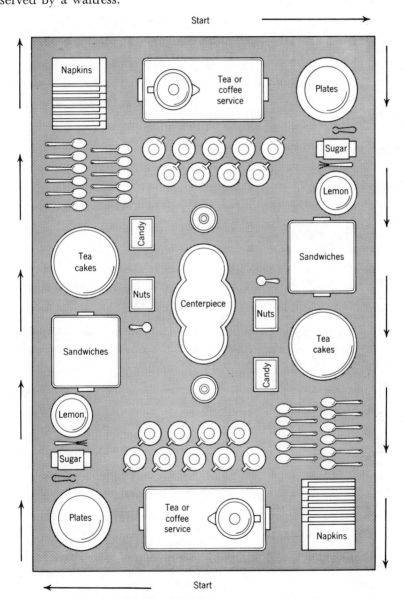

Fig. 19. Tea-table arrangement.

FOOD FOR BUFFETS

A greater variety of food generally is included in a buffet menu than can be offered at table d'hote meals, although the extent of the variety will depend on preparation time and space on the buffet table, among other factors. The menu may be built around one main dish, with one or two vegetables, a salad, relishes, hot bread, dessert, and beverage. The menu may consist of a more elaborate offering of main dishes, as sliced cold meats, a chicken or fish casserole, and a hot meat, with accompanying vegetables, a variety of salads and relishes, bread, and dessert. An assortment of breads is often used to add interest and variety to the buffet table. Dessert for a buffet meal should highlight the meal and should be appropriate to the type of service that will be used for the dessert.

In planning a menu for a buffet, certain precautions should be observed:

1. Keep the service as simple as possible, i.e., avoid foods difficult to serve or that are soft or "soupy" on the plate. Foods that require extra utensils, as bread-and-butter spreaders, salad or cocktail forks should be avoided. If the guests will be eating from a tray, plan a main dish that can be cut with a fork.

2. Include a few attractively decorated foods, assorted salads, and an assortment of relishes. Attractive garnishing is important.

3. Plan hot foods that can easily be kept hot. Large or individual casseroles, chafing dishes, shells for deviled fish and similar foods, or heated trays are essential if hot food is to be served.

4. Plan the arrangement of the table at the same time the menu is planned to be sure of adequate table space and suitable serving dishes.

Suggested Foods for Buffet Menus

Main Dishes

Shrimp Creole
Scalloped Salmon
Deviled Crab
Scalloped Oysters
Tuna–Cashew Casserole
Chicken Loaf
Chicken–Almond Casserole
Scalloped Chicken
Hot Chicken Salad
Chicken or Turkey à la King
Chicken Pie
Chicken Tahitian
Turkey Tetrazinni
Turkey Divan

Barbecued Beef Brisket
Veal Birds en Casserole
Beef Stroganoff with Noodles
Curried Veal with Rice
Swedish Meat Balls
Sweet and Sour Pork
Ham Loaf
Ham Patties with Pineapple Ring
Creamed Ham and Mushrooms
Creamed Sweetbreads and Mushrooms
Sliced Ham and Turkey
Tomato Stuffed with Crab or Shrimp
 Salad
Singapore Curry (p. 279, 507)

Vegetables

Scalloped Potatoes
Potatoes au Gratin
Sweet Potatoes and Apples
Green Rice
Scalloped Corn
French Fried Onions
Spinach Soufflé

Baby Limas in Butter
Green Beans, Almond Butter
Shredded New Harvard Beets
Buttered Peas, Rice, and Mushrooms
Broiled or Baked Tomatoes
Creole Eggplant
Zucchini Italian

Salads and Relishes

Stuffed Tomato Salad
Potato Salad
Frozen Fruit Salad
Orange and Grapefruit Sections
Stuffed Cinnamon Apple Salad
Fruit Combinations

Molded Fruit Gelatins
Avocado Ring with Fresh Fruit
Cranberry Relish
Spiced Peaches
Assorted Relishes

Salad Bowls

Julienne Vegetables
Creamy Cole Slaw
Salad Greens with Grapefruit

Tossed Green Salad
Hawaiian Tossed Salad
Celery Curls and Carrots

Desserts

Filled Angel Food Cake
German Sweet Chocolate Cake
Lemon or other Chiffon Pie
Pecan Pie
Ice Cream Pie
Meringue Shells with Ice Cream
  or Fruit Filling

Strawberry Shortcake
Peach Melba
Orange Cream Puffs with Chocolate
  Filling
Assorted Fresh Fruits
Assorted Cheese and Crackers

Buffet Menus

(1)

Hot Chicken Salad
Buttered Broccoli
Grapefruit-Orange Salad   Cranberry Mold
Celery—Carrot Strips—Olives
Cloverleaf Rolls
Frozen Filled Angel Food Cake
Coffee

(2)

Pork Cutlets with Mushroom Sauce en Casserole
Buttered Cauliflower with Peas   French Baked Potatoes
Stuffed Tomato Salad   Frozen Fruit Salad
Celery Curls—Olives—Watermelon Pickles
Garlic Bread
Blueberry-glazed Cream Pie
Coffee

(3)

Veal Paprika with Poppyseed Noodles
Glazed Carrots
Jellied Waldorf Salad   Julienne Vegetable Salad Bowl
Whole Wheat Rolls   Jelly
Praline Pumpkin Pie
Coffee

(4)

Ham and Sweetbread Casserole
Buttered Asparagus Spears   Broiled Fresh Pineapple Slice
Pear Salad with Prune Garnish
Carrot Strips, Radishes, Olives, and Pickles
Assorted Hot Breads
Strawberry Tarts
Coffee

(5)

Chicken Tahitian
Broiled Tomatoes   Green Rice
Sliced Cucumbers in Sour Cream   Spicy Apricot Mold
Orange Coffee Ring
Peppermint Ice Cream Pie—Hot Chocolate Sauce
Coffee

(6)

Sliced Turkey Roll
Ham Loaf—Horseradish Sauce   Deviled Crab
Green Beans with Herb Butter
Potato Salad   Creamy Cole Slaw   Fresh Fruit Plate
Celery—Radishes—Green Pepper Rings
Crown Rolls
Almond Blitz Torte
Coffee

(7)

Singapore Curry (p. 279, 507)
Fresh Raspberry Parfait   Sandies
Tea

FOREIGN BUFFETS

Interest in international foods has increased as indicated by the many books dealing with food habits and the choice recipes available from various countries. Buffet meals featuring foods from foreign countries afford a ready means of introducing variety and interest into meals that might tend to become routine. Buffet menus typical of China, Hungary, and Sweden are given in the following pages. Also included are recipes necessary for the successful preparation of the meal. Recipes are not given for foods often used on American menus, or for foods ordinarily purchased ready to serve.

CHINESE BUFFET SUPPERS

Americans find Chinese dishes enjoyable and unlike those of any other nation except possibly Japan. Food items desired by a Chinese cook might include: Litchi nuts, mushrooms, dry lotus seeds, bamboo shoots, lotus roots, bean sprouts, shark fins, very fine noodles, rice, millet, rice flour, ginger root, bean meal, shell fish and other fish, chicken, pork, chestnuts, almonds, and walnuts. Preserved eggs, condiments and preserved fruits and ginger are frequently used. Chinese sauce or soya sometimes take the place of salt in Chinese cookery. Peanut oil is used for frying.

Tea is the popular beverage and is served without cream or sugar in small covered cups without handles. A party menu usually contains several meat dishes—including chicken, fish, goose, pork, lobster, crab, or shrimp. Each dish is said to be 1 course. Tea may be served with each course. Almond meal cookies and fruits are common desserts.

SINGAPORE CURRY (50 SERVINGS)

Singapore Curry, an unusual combination of foods, is popular not only in the Far East where it originated but has been well accepted by those persons interested in "something different." Basically, this is a curried meat served over rice with a variety of accompaniments.

For the curried meat, a good combination is chicken and fresh pork. However, other meat, such as lamb or veal, may be used. For a generous serving, allow about ½ lb. meat per person. Brown the meat and simmer in meat or chicken broth. When done, dice meat and add to a sauce make from 5 quarts broth, 1 lb. 4 oz. flour, and 1 lb. fat. When thick, season with salt, pepper, and curry powder to taste. Add diced meat and stir gently. Let set to blend flavors. Taste and add more seasoning as the meat takes up the curry flavor. It should be quite yellow in color and have a distinct curry flavor. Serve with accompaniments:

5 lb. rice cooked (p. 309)
50 servings French fried onion rings
10 lb. tomatoes, sliced
15 lb. bananas, sliced or diced

2 No. 10 cans pineapple chunks
2 lb. coconut
1 lb. salted peanuts
2 1-lb. jars chutney

Arrange on buffet table in the following order: rice, curried meat, French fried onions, sliced tomatoes, sliced bananas, pineapple chunks; shredded coconut, salted peanuts and chutney. Each guest serves rice in the center of his plate, dips curried meat over the rice, then adds accompaniments. A well-served plate will be nicely rounded and self-garnished. Only a dessert need be added to make a complete meal. Fruit, melons, sherbet, or sundaes are especially good for dessert. Hot tea should be served.

HUNGARIAN BUFFET SUPPERS

Knowledge of Hungarian cookery is for many people restricted to the more or less enthusiastic acceptance of Hungarian goulash, a dish said to be "the savory ancestor of all stews."

The vegetables in common use are similar to those in the American dietary and include beets, red and white cabbage, sauerkraut, carrots, cauliflower, kale, kohlrabi, peppers, and lettuce. The popular fruits include apples, apricots, cherries, melons, peaches, pears, and bananas. The large rôle of cereals in the diet is shown by the appearance of noodles and bread dumplings in many menus along with rye breads and fancy rolls.

Cheese is used freely in cooked dishes and in its natural state, and on the other hand butter is used sparingly and then unsalted. Sour cream is widely used both as a garnish and as an ingredient in cooking. Its use with paprika is regarded by many as the characterizing feature of a Hungarian dish, so popular are both with these people. Paprika, although popular, is only one of the numerous condiments used, as the Hungarians are fond of spicy foods.

SWEDISH BUFFET SUPPERS

Sweden is famous for its Smörgåsbord, or hors d' oeuvres, which is an ancient tradition and an important accompaniment to all Swedish dinners. The hors d'oeuvres for a family of moderate means are grouped in the center of a long table laid with a spotless white linen tablecloth, plates, and silver. The guests are seated at the table and the hors d'oeuvres are passed and eaten just before a regular meal of two or more courses is served. A maid removes the dishes from the first course. Typical food for the family hors d'oeuvres might include: Meats—cold spiced tongue, smoked venison, smoked salmon (sliced), fish in aspic jelly, anchovies, herring served in two ways, large shrimps with Thousand Island dressing, parsley, and dried beef; vegetables—radishes, sliced tomatoes, salads (two or more kinds), and a scalloped dish; bread—rye bread, white bread baked in ornamental shapes; cheese—served in a big piece on a cheese plate with a cheese knife.

Hors d'oeuvres for a family, or for a hotel, might be arranged on a separate table as for a buffet supper. Each guest would help himself and then take his place at the dining table.

The service by waitresses or waiters would be much the same as for the less elaborate meal described above. The food would be of greater variety, including 20 to 125 articles—Rye Krisp, butter curls, 6 or 7 kinds of cheese, very small Swedish meat balls fried in deep fat, a hot scalloped dish of fish or vegetable, pickled onions, pickled beets or cucumbers; vegetable salads—similar to our own, a bowl of mayonnaise; jellies and marmalades. A regular 3- or 4-course dinner is served after the hors d'oeuvres are eaten.

The use of colorful foods or decorations is an outstanding feature of the Swedish table. Candles are not used for decorations except for banquets. Flowers are always used and often two or more bouquets are placed on the table, if long.

A Swedish buffet supper suitable for service in this country is planned to include only the Smörgåsbord and the dessert, omitting what the Swedish diner would regard as the main part of the meal.

Suggested Menus for Foreign Buffets
Chinese Menu and Recipes
Chinese Chow

Boo Loo Gai (Pineapple Chicken)	Plain Boiled Rice
Hop Too Guy Ding (Almond Chicken)	Celery Hearts
*Egg Foo Yung (Omelet)	Kumquat and Ginger Preserves
**Chow Lon Fon (Fried Rice)	Soy Sauce
Fried Shrimp	Litchi Nuts

Fortune Cookies
Fruit: Fresh and Candied
Jasmine Tea

Pineapple Chicken (Boo Loo Gai)

Cut a young chicken as for fried chicken, season with soy sauce, salt, and sugar and let stand 1 hr. Drain, dredge with flour and brown in hot fat. Add a little hot water and simmer until tender. Add 1 small can of diced pineapple and 1 t. soy sauce. Thicken liquid with flour and serve as soon as flour is cooked. Garnish with parsley.

* Recipe on p. 305.   ** Recipe on p. 309.

Almond Chicken (Hop Too Guy Ding)

Fry 2 c. shredded onions, 2 c. shredded water chestnuts, and 2 c. shredded celery until slightly browned, then add chicken broth or white stock to cover, and cook until vegetables are tender. Add 1 young chicken that has been cut into cubes and cooked in peanut oil (or vegetable oil). Thicken liquid with a little cornstarch and water mixed. Add 1 T. soy sauce and place in a hot casserole. Add 1 c. toasted almonds just before serving.

Almond Cakes (Gum Loo)

1 c. flour	1 egg, beaten
¾ c. powdered sugar	3 T. vegetable oil
¼ c. almonds, chopped	

Mix dry ingredients. Add oil and then the beaten egg. Mold into small balls, brush with egg, garnish with a whole almond, and bake in a moderate oven.

Litchi nuts have a characteristic flavor and may be purchased dried or canned.

Hungarian Menu

Hungarian Buffet

Paprika Chicken with Spatzels
Stuffed Squash   Green Beans with Dill Sauce
Cucumber Salad—Sour Cream Dressing
Poppyseed Crescent Rolls   Sweet Butter
Cheese Cake   Fresh Fruit Compote
Coffee

Swedish Menus and Recipes

Swedish Smorgåsbord

Pickled Herring   Canapés
Pickled Beets   Celery Curls   Radish Roses
Deviled Eggs with Parsley Garnish   Sliced Tomatoes
Cucumbers in Sour Cream
Cottage Cheese   Assorted Cheese
Swedish Meat Balls   Potato Sausage
Cold Sliced Baked Ham
Parsley Buttered Potatoes or Potato Salad
Swedish Brown Beans or Green Beans with Mushrooms
Fruit Salad Mold   Swedish Green Top Salad
Cabbage Slaw
Swedish Salad Bowl
Rye Bread   Swedish Tea Ring
Cheese Pudding with Thickened Grape Juice
Lingenberry Tarts
Swedish Apple Cake   Assorted Cookies
Swedish Mints
Coffee

Bordstabbel Bakels (Lumberpile Cookies)

½ c. butter	1¼ c. flour
1 c. light brown sugar	½ t. soda
1 egg	¼ t. salt
½ t. vanilla	½ c. chopped nutmeats

Cream butter and sugar. Add well-beaten egg and vanilla. Add flour sifted with soda and salt, then nutmeats dredged in portion of flour. Mold dough. Let stand in refrigerator overnight. Cut into strips, 3 inches by 1 inch. Bake in a moderate oven. When done, cover with White Mountain Frosting and sprinkle with chopped almonds, caraway seed, or candies. Pile like lumber on serving plates.

Sandbakelser (Sand Tarts)

1 lb. butter	1 c. white sugar
pinch of salt	1 T. cream or milk
⅓ t. baking powder	2 eggs
5 c. flour (about)	3 T. almond extract

Cream butter and sugar. Add eggs. Blend well, add extract, then flour. Press into small "picture" tins or put through cookie press. Chopped almonds may be added to dough if "picture" tins are used. Turn out of tins at once after baking or they will stick.

Smörbakelser (Butter Cookies)

1 c. butter (sweet)
1 c. powdered sugar
2 c. flour

Mix and pat out in 2 10-inch baking tins. Bake in a moderate oven approximately 20–30 min. Cut as soon as removed from oven. This is the same as Scotch Shortbreads.

Svenska Kringlor (Swedish Kringle)

1 c. butter	3½ c. flour or enough to make
1¼ c. brown sugar	soft dough
½ c. milk	2 T. baking powder
2 eggs	1 T. cinnamon

Sift dry ingredients. Cream butter and sugar. Add egg yolks and flour and milk alternately. Fold in beaten whites. Bake as drop cookies.

Svenska Peppar Nötter (Swedish Peppernuts)

The oldest of all cakes we know today are the peppernuts. They were in popular use long before the 11th century.

4 eggs	1 t. cardamon (ground)
2 c. sugar	½ c. nuts
1 c. butter	½ c. raisins
1 t. cinnamon	4 c. flour (bread)
1 t. cloves	1 t. soda
1 t. pepper	2 T. hot water

Drop on cookie sheet and bake at 450° F.

Fattigman Bakels (Poorman's Crullers)

2 eggs
2 T. sugar
⅛ t. salt

f.g. cardamon
3 T. heavy sweet cream
1¾ c. flour (or less)

Beat eggs until light, add sugar, salt, spice, and continue beating. Add cream and enough flour to make a soft dough. Turn out on floured board, roll very thin. Cut into diamond shapes. Slash opposite ends. Pull end through slit, or cut in star shapes. Fry in deep fat. Drain on heavy paper. Dust with sugar.

Swedish Salad Bowl

1 can of pineapple (size 2½)
1 tart apple
lettuce

1 stalk celery
5 tomatoes
½ cucumber

Cut the pineapple and tomato into wedges, dice the apple and celery, cut the cucumber en julienne. Mix with pineapple dressing just before serving and add shredded lettuce leaves.

Pineapple Dressing

Mix 2 raw egg yolks with the juice drained from the can of pineapple, stir constantly, and cook over a low heat until thick. Cool, then add 1 mashed cold hard-cooked egg yolk that has been mixed with ¼ t. mustard and 3 T. of vinegar. Fold in 2 c. whipped cream.

Serve salad in a salad bowl. Yield approximately 10 servings.

Ost Kaka (Cheese Pudding)

2 gal. milk
2 c. flour
½ cake of cheese rennet
   (purchased from drug store)

6 eggs
1½ qt. cream, coffee
½ c. sugar

Heat the milk until lukewarm and stir into it the flour that has been smoothed to a paste. Add the cheese rennet that has been dissolved in 2 T. water. Stir well and let stand. As soon as the milk has set, stir gently to separate the curds and whey. Let stand a few minutes then pour off whey or use a strainer to remove curds. (The curds should be quite moist.) Place curds in 2 medium-sized casseroles and pour over them a custard mixture made from the eggs, cream, and sugar. Sprinkle nutmeg over the top. Bake and test as a plain custard. Serve warm with strawberry jam or grape juice thickened to the consistency of thick cream.

Köttbullar (Meat Balls)

1 lb. beef loin	3–4 egg yolks
8 oz. veal	3 T. onion, chopped
8 oz. pork	2 T. salt
½ c. bread crumbs, dry, ground	½ t. pepper
1 c. cream	⅛ t. allspice
½ c. soda water, dilute	1 c. butter

Pass the meat through a meat grinder three times or more if a coarse grinder is used. Add the bread crumbs, which have been soaked in the cream. Add soda water and egg yolks, mix well, and shape into small balls. Fry the onion in butter but do not brown; add the meat balls and fry, using a low heat. Fry in deep fat. Shake the pan occasionally to keep the balls in shape. Place balls in casserole and pour over them the fat in which they were cooked. Garnish with a border of fried onions.

Krokoner

¼ c. sugar	1 c. milk
1 c. butter	f.g. salt
4 t. baking powder	1 t. vanilla (or ½ t. vanilla and
flour to make a roll dough	½ t. almond)
1 egg	

Roll dough and cut into strips 5 inches long and 1½ inches wide. Bake over semicircular tins 12 inches long, so that cookies form a semicircle when baked. Ice with orange icing and decorate with tiny colored candies.

Brunches

Brunch, a cross between breakfast and lunch, is becoming increasingly popular as a way of entertaining. The meal may be served to guests seated at tables or it may be served from a buffet table.

The menu may be made up of foods normally served at breakfast or may resemble a luncheon menu, depending partly on the hour of service. The menu may be quite simple, consisting of fruits, hot breads, and coffee; or may be a more filling meal that will replace lunch.

Brunch usually starts with fruit or juice placed on the table just before the guests are seated or served to guests from a punch bowl before they go to the buffet table. The main dish may be bacon, ham, sausage, eggs in some form or may be a luncheon type entrée of chicken, turkey, or fish. Attractive trays of bite size fruits and an assortment of small squares of coffee cake, small sweet rolls, and other hot breads enhance a buffet table set for a brunch. A dessert may be served, if the meal is scheduled late in the morning, but it should be light.

Suggested Menus for a Buffet Brunch

(1)

Orange Juice
Canadian Bacon   Sausages   Scrambled Eggs
Blueberry Coffee Cake   Pecan Rolls
Small Banana Bread Sandwiches
Fruit Tray
Coffee

(2)

Tomato Juice
Grilled Ham   Small Egg Cutlets
Chicken Hash
Broiled Fresh Pineapple Slice
Coffee Cake   Small Orange Rolls   Glazed Donuts
Bowl of Fresh Strawberries—Powdered Sugar
Coffee

Suggestions for a Sit-Down Brunch

(1)

Hot Consommé
Ham Slice and Sliced Hard Cooked Eggs on Toasted English Muffins—
Cheese Sauce
Green Rice   Broiled Peach Half
Hot Rolls   Strawberry Jam
Fresh Fruit Cup   Pound Cake
Coffee

(2)

Honey Dew Melon
Creamed Chicken on Spoonbread
Buttered Broccoli   Pear Half with Cranberry Relish
Assorted Hot Breads
Strawberry Bavarian Cream
Coffee

Coffees, Teas, and Receptions

Coffees, teas, and receptions may vary widely in degree of formality or informality and may accommodate a few guests or a large number. The menu must be planned and plans made according to the type of event, the time of day, and the number to be served. Certain general rules apply to all of these events.

A table set for tea or coffee service depends upon its attractive appointments for its charm. The table covering, centerpiece, tea service, silver, and serving dishes should be the best available and the food colorful, dainty, and interestingly arranged. To prevent a crowded appearance there should be a limited amount of silver, china, napkins, and food on the tea table when the serving begins. A small serving table with extra china and silver near the tea table is a convenience. Replacements of small dishes and appointments are brought on trays from the kitchen. Cookies, sandwiches, and other foods should be arranged so they do not present a crowded appearance. It is best to use small serving plates and replace them frequently so there is an assortment of food at all times.

Tea and coffee may both be served. They are placed on either end of the table and served to guests, who then help themselves to the accompaniments. In warm weather an iced beverage may be served to replace one or both of the hot drinks. (See p. 503.)

Formal teas generally are used for entertaining large groups. The occasion may be a wedding anniversary, to introduce someone to a group, or to honor one or more individuals. The degree of formality will vary with the occasion and the desires of the hostess.

Foods served at a formal tea or reception are of the same type as those served at an informal tea, except that they are often more elaborately prepared and of greater variety.

A formal tea served in the place of supper is sometimes called a high tea. It is more elaborate than afternoon tea and is similar to a buffet supper.

Types of food served at a tea include:

BEVERAGES

Hot. Coffee and tea, Russian tea, cocoa, French chocolate, spiced cider, grape juice, or tea.

Iced. Tea or fruit punch (plain or with sherbet).

BREAD AND MISCELLANEOUS

Open-face Sandwiches. Assorted fancy shapes spread with desired filling and decorated.

Closed sandwiches. Assorted breads as nut, orange, banana, date, cheese, or plain with suitable filling. Rolled, ribbon, checkerboard pinwheel sandwiches.

Miscellaneous. Cheese wafers, cheese straws, party crackers, miniature cream puffs filled with cream cheese or chicken salad.

CAKES AND COOKIES

Petits fours, small cup cakes, macaroons, kisses, shortbread, chocolate or date bars, tiny cookies—rolled or dropped.

ICE CREAMS, SHERBETS, OR ICES

Any desired flavor—served in individual cups in which frozen or in sherbet glasses.

NUTS AND CANDIES

Salted, toasted, spiced, or crystallized nuts. Preserved ginger, candied orange or grapefruit peel, mints in pastel colors, and various flavors; chocolate mint patties, small hard candies, opera sticks, crystallized mint leaves. Turkish paste in various flavors, colors, and shapes, and stuffed or candied fruits.

MISCELLANEOUS ACCOMPANIMENTS

Cube or loaf sugar, plain or decorated.

Orange or lemon—cut into thin slices, sections, or fancy shapes and often garnished with whole cloves.

Informal Tea Menus

(1)

Cheese Pinwheel Sandwiches　　　　Nutbread Sandwiches
Fudge Balls　　　Miniature French Pastries
Pastel Mints
Hot Spiced Tea

(2)

Tiny Pink Iced Cream Puffs filled with Strawberry Whipped Cream
Sandies　　　　　　　　Tea Brownies
Salted Mixed Nuts
Tea　　　　　　　　　Coffee

(3)

Pecan Tea Time Tarts
Ribbon Sandwiches　　　Raspberry Thimble Cookies
Candied Orange Peel
Tea

(4)

Banana Bread Finger Sandwiches
Frosted Tea Cakes　　　Assorted Chocolate Spritz and
Butter Tea Cookies
Toasted Nuts
Jasmine Tea

(5)

Nut Bread Sandwiches   Two-Tone Cheese Sandwiches
Red Cherry Tartlets   Butterscotch Squares
Mints
Fruit Punch   Coffee

Formal Tea Menus

(1)

Small Cream Puffs filled with Chicken Salad
Assorted Open-face Sandwiches
Scotch Shortbread   Caramel Marshmallow Squares
Orange Sherbet Cups
Spiced Pecans   Mints
Tea   Coffee

(2)

Christmas Tea
White Meat of Turkey on   Glazed Shrimp Canapés
Midget Parkerhouse Rolls
Norwegian Christmas Bread Tea Sandwiches
Assorted Christmas Cookies from Foreign Lands
Fruit Cake Slices   Mints   Salted Nuts
Sparkling Cranberry Punch

(3)

Wedding Reception
Strawberry Ice Cream in Pastel Cups
Bride's Cake   Groom's Cake
Wedding Punch   Coffee

(4)

Wedding Breakfast
Creamed Chicken and Mushrooms in Timbale Cases
Spiced Peaches   Ripe Olives
Lemon Buttered Asparagus Tips
Assorted Hot Rolls
Raspberry Sherbet   Wedding Cake
Punch   Coffee

MORNING COFFEE

An informal get-together in the morning with coffee as the beverage is often called a Kaffee Klatch. The food served is usually more substantial and the variety more limited than is the tea menu. There is always an ample supply of hot fresh coffee served with one or more hot breads. These may include: pecan rolls, glazed marmalade rolls, doughnut holes, Bishop's bread, quick coffee cake, Kolaches, Danish pastry and toasted English muffins. Fresh fruit or juice may also be included on the menu. A fruit tray, with bite size pieces of fresh fruit arranged on on a silver or wooden tray, serves as an attractive centerpiece as well as an interesting addition to a coffee hour.

A 6-layer Ribbon Butter Cake is the only coffee accompaniment necessary for a simple and elegant afternoon Coffee Hour. Napoleans, Cheese Cake, Bismarcks, Danish pastry, and Crown Rolls also are popular Kaffee Klatsch items.

Morning Coffee Menus

(1)

Danish Pecan Coffee Cake
Assorted Cookies   Date Bread and Cream Cheese Sandwiches
Sprigs of Frosted Grapes
Coffee

(2)

Slivers of Virginia Ham on Hot Party Biscuit
Glazed Raised Doughnuts   Orange Bread Sandwiches
Fresh Fruit Kabobs
Coffee

(3)

Apricot-filled Kolaches   Sugared Doughnut Balls
Stuffed Dates
Coffee

INDEX

519